Esther Sansken 45+6

220

MACMILLAN CLASSICAL SERIES

EDITED BY B. L. ULLMAN . . . .

LATIN FOR AMERICANS
FIRST BOOK

Latin for Americans—Minerva, the Roman goddess of wisdom, stands behind the men who strike the hour in Herald Square, New York.

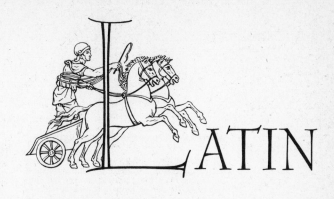

LATIN

FOR AMERICANS

By *B. L. ULLMAN* and *NORMAN E. HENRY*

FIRST BOOK

New York   THE MACMILLAN COMPANY   *1941*

LATIN FOR AMERICANS, FIRST BOOK, is based in part
on ELEMENTARY LATIN, published and copyrighted by
The Macmillan Company in its various editions in
1936, 1929, and 1923.

PREFACE

The title *Latin for Americans*, justifiable in earlier editions of this book though not used in them, is particularly appropriate to this edition. The comparisons between ancient and modern life in the "Glimpses of Roman Life" and in the reading selections, the allusions to important features of the American way of life, to good citizenship, and to democracy, the prominence of the English word studies, which occur in every lesson, the emphasis on correct grammatical usage in English, the many illustrations of American buildings which imitate the ancient models and of other American material, the quotation of Latin phrases used on American buildings and as American mottoes, all these and many other features carry out the idea in the title. It is firmly believed that the use of this book will help make better Americans.

In this edition greater importance has been given the reading selections not only by putting them first in each lesson but by lengthening and rewriting some of them rather extensively in order to repeat vocabulary, forms, and syntax even more frequently than previously. On the other hand, the exercises, consisting of detached sentences for translation from Latin into English and English into Latin, have been reduced in length. Some teachers may prefer to reduce them still further or omit them entirely. Though it is assumed that most teachers will begin each lesson with the reading selection, there is nothing to prevent starting with the grammar or the vocabulary, if this method of approach is preferred.

The review lessons have been increased from nine to thirteen and extensively revised. New types of drill have been added here and elsewhere in the book.

The "Glimpses of Roman Life" have been increased by four, dealing with advertisements, notices, and scribblings on Roman walls; social and economic conditions; Roman ways of making a living; and Roman citizenship. The fourteen "Glimpses," together with the illustrations and the reading selections, furnish a basis for study of Roman civilization. In addition, references are given for further study. The newly added questions for discussion suggest comparisons between ancient and modern life.

Some grammatical material, shown by investigation to be of little importance, has been eliminated. As in earlier editions, no knowledge of English grammar is assumed and basic English grammar in simple form is presented as needed.

It should be remembered that this book gives special attention to the verb; its importance for both Latin reading and English derivation is recognized by the introduction of many verbs in reading selections and vocabularies and by rapid development of verb forms. In this way reading power is attained more quickly.

The Latin and English Word Studies, covering such matters as prefixes, suffixes, loan words, phonetic changes, interesting derivations, Latin phrases, abbreviations, and quotations, have always been a particular feature of this series. They have been increased and enlarged in this edition. They are closely integrated with the reading selections and are not disjointed presentations of material which has little or no organic connection with the rest of the book. They are the more valuable because the vocabulary of the reading selections consists in large part of the words which are most important for English derivation. At the same time the words occur in the College Board Word List.

A supplement presents in simple form the chief changes occurring in words that passed from Latin to French, Spanish, and Italian. This enables pupils to make the greatest possible use of Latin in studying the Romance languages.

The illustrations, more numerous even than in earlier editions, are an essential part of the instructional material. Much time, effort, and thought have been devoted to the selection of a useful and attractive group of pictures. Among them will be found pictures of classical buildings in the Americas and elsewhere, Latin inscriptions on American buildings, and other material which shows the continuing influence of Roman civilization. The illustrations of postage stamps which have classical motifs should interest the many pupils who are enthusiastic stamp collectors.

Teachers are urged to secure copies of the Manual which accompanies this book, as it contains many useful suggestions.

The changes made in this edition make it all the more desirable for use in junior as well as senior high schools.

Acknowledgments

Grateful acknowledgment is made here for many excellent suggestions to Miss Claire C. Thursby of the University High School, Berkeley, California, Miss Ada Stewart of the Peoria, Illinois, High School, and Mrs. Viva G. Gault of the Porterville, California, High School.

CONTENTS

If elegancy still proceedeth and English pens maintain that stream [of new words] we have of late observed to flow from many, we shall within few years be fain to learn Latin to understand English.

—Sir Thomas Browne, 1646.

Modern life owes its highest ideals, directly or indirectly, to the inspiration of Greece; it owes its whole structure and existence to the creation of Rome.

—J. W. Mackail.

The Supreme Court of the United States at Washington sits in a Roman temple. The beautiful government buildings of our national capital are based on classical models. Watch for other examples and compare with the Roman buildings on pages 3, 4, 8, etc.

1.   WHAT LATIN WILL MEAN TO YOU

You and thousands of others are studying Latin. Yet you will never use Latin to ask for a milk shake or a postage stamp, and maybe you will not even read Latin books after you leave school although we hope you will. For Latin is not the language of any country today, nor has it been for hundreds of years. Surely Latin must have unusually great value in other ways or you would not be studying it. Let us try to explain.

Twenty-five hundred years ago Rome was one of many small towns in Italy. Its language, Latin, got its name from the district of Latium in which the town was situated. As the power of Rome spread, first over Italy and then over most of the civilized world of that day, its language came to be used everywhere. On the map on page 260 you can trace the growth of the great Roman Empire. You will note how it became a sort of United States of the Mediterranean World. Rome was at the same time **urbs et orbis,** *city and world*.

Not only did the people living in the Roman Empire acquire Roman culture, but in the course of centuries all Europe was affected by it. This European civilization was then carried to all parts of the world by the English, French, Spanish, Portuguese, and others. So all the world owes a debt to ancient Rome. One reason for studying Latin is to learn something about the Roman civilization in order to understand our own. How did an ancient Roman live, what did he think, how did he solve the problems that we too must face, how did he govern his vast empire, how did he find happiness? The answers to these and many other questions you will discover in your study of Latin, and you will find those answers very interesting. For the Romans were human

1

beings like ourselves. You will be fascinated by the stories of their lives. They were not perfect; you will learn that they had their faults and that there were bad Romans as well as good ones.

When we consider the influence of Rome, we do not wonder that Latin is an important subject of study in England, France, Germany, Italy, and all over Europe, as well as in North and South America and other parts of the world. In the United States more pupils are studying Latin than ever before; in our high schools there are more students of Latin than of any other foreign language. Latin is truly international and is a bond between nations.

The Romans, however, have handed down not only their ideas but also their language. The Romance languages are the various forms which the Roman (Latin) language has taken in the course of centuries in the various parts of the Roman Empire. They are Italian, French, Spanish, Portuguese, Rumanian, and even, to a large extent, English, since about sixty per cent of our English words are derived from Latin. French, Spanish, and Italian become very easy after a study of Latin (see p. 410). But the chief reason why you are going to study Latin is to get a better knowledge of English. Most of the more difficult words in English are from Latin or Greek. In a few weeks you will know the meaning of *impecunious*, *emigrate*, *mandate*, *predatory*, and many others. If you know them already, you will get to know them better. Soon you will know why a *submarine* is so called, what a *Pyrrhic* victory is, and the real meaning of such words as *neutrality* and *repatriate* —all words found in the daily newspapers. Your English spelling will improve.

The study of Latin will make English grammar much easier to understand. Then, again, there are Latin words, phrases, and mottoes used in English, such as *radius*, *per annum*, and *e pluribus unum*. Many abbreviations used in English are Latin, such as *i.e.* for *id est*.

Whatever line of work you will enter, you will find Latin useful. If you plan to be a doctor, you will learn that nearly all Class A medical schools require or recommend Latin—most of them four years of it. If you intend to be a lawyer, Latin will prove useful and necessary in many ways—as, for example, in understanding the many Latin phrases used in law, such as *habeas corpus*. Teachers of many subjects, such as English and history, should or must know Latin. The technical terms in science and other subjects, the terms which make those subjects difficult, are chiefly from the Latin or Greek and become easier when the root words out of which they grew are studied.

Latin is not an easy subject, but, if you study your lesson every day and are not afraid to ask your teacher to explain what you do not understand, you will discover that it is both delightful and useful.

2. **Exercise**

1. *How many events of Roman history can you think of?*
2. *What famous Romans do you remember?*
3. *What Roman gods can you recall?*
4. *What do you know about the city of Rome as it is today?*
5. *How many Latin words, phrases, legal terms, scientific terms, mottoes, proverbs, and abbreviations can you give?*

The ancient Roman Forum as a modern artist imagines it

The Temples of Caesar and Castor and part of the Basilica Julia (a courthouse) in the Forum as they once were

3. The Alphabet

Civilization owes more to the invention of writing than to anything else. It has truly been said that the pen is mightier than the sword—or, in more modern language, than a machine gun. The earliest forms of writing, invented before history began, told their stories by means of pictures. Such methods have lasted into modern times; the writing of the American Indians is an example. No less important than the invention of writing was that of the alphabet, which made it much easier to learn to read and write. The alphabet was invented by Semites in western Asia, but it was not perfect because it had no vowels (*a, e, i, o, u*). These were added by the Greeks when they got the alphabet from the Semitic Phoenicians. The Etruscans, northern neighbors of the Romans in Italy, learned it from the Greeks and taught it to the Romans. The Romans made some changes in the values and forms of the letters and passed them on to the modern world

4

along with the rest of their culture. Their alphabet is one of the great contributions of the Romans to our civilization. It is impossible to measure its influence. It is by far the best of existing alphabets and is one of the great international forces of our day. A few years ago Turkey abandoned the Arabic alphabet, a descendant of the early Semitic, in favor of the simpler and more widely used Latin letters. European nations do not understand one another's languages and have many a quarrel, but nearly all except Greece and Russia (which uses a modified form of the Greek alphabet) write out their thoughts in Latin letters. The Latin alphabet is a symbol of international coöperation.

Since Roman days the alphabet has changed little. The Romans used *i* for *i* and *j*. In the seventeenth century it became the custom in English to use a long form of *i* for *j*, and thus our *j* was formed. Similarly the Romans used only one character for *u* and *v*, but we have introduced the useful distinction between them, even in Latin. The original identity of the two is shown by another mod-

The three columns of the Temple of Castor today. These remains made it possible for an artist to draw the picture on the opposite page.

ABC's of more than 2600 years ago. An Etruscan wax tablet with the alphabet scratched on the rim. The letters run from right to left, as in the Semitic alphabet.

ern letter, *w*, which is a double *u* in name and a double *v* in form. The letters *j* and *w* are, therefore, not found in Latin words in this book.

The Romans made no distinction between capitals and small letters. Our small letters gradually developed out of capitals in late antiquity and the Middle Ages.

4. Pronunciation

The pronunciation of Latin is quite different from that of English, especially in the vowels (*a, e, i, o, u*), and resembles that of Italian, French, German, and other foreign languages. It is relatively very easy because it conforms to a few simple rules. There are no silent letters in Latin. For tables of sounds see 531–538.

5. Exercises in Pronunciation

I

Pronounce ā, Mārs, pār, ab, iam, dat, nār′rat, ma′lā, ē, mē, pēs, ex, sed, per, cer′tē, lē′ge, quī, hīc, vīs, in, quid, fit, di′gitī, mī′litis, nōn, prō, mōns, nox, post, mors, cō′gor, ro′gō, iūs,

6

cūr, lūx, nunc, cum, dux, iūs'tus, cur'rū, aes, quae, Aet'nae, aut, clau'sae, poe'nae.

II

Mi'cā, mi'cā, par'va stēl'la!
Mī'ror quae'nam sīs, tam bel'la,
Splen'dēns ē'minus in il'lō,
Al'ba ve'lut gem'ma, cae'lō.

III

Read the following translation of "America" which was made by George D. Kellogg:

Tē ca'nō, Pa'tria,   Tū'tor es ū'nicus,
Can'dida, lī'bera;   Ū'nus a'vum De'us!
  Tē re'feret   Lau'dō li'bēns.
Por'tus et ex'ulum   Pa'tria lū'ceat,
Et tu'mulus se'num;   Lī'bera ful'geat,
Lī'bera mon'tium   Vīs tu'a mū'niat,
  Vōx re'sonet.   Omni'potēns!

IV

The following are ancient Latin quotations, some of which you probably have seen:

Tomb inscription which Ti(berius) Quaestorius Secundus, a captain of army engineers, set up for himself and his good wife, Claudia Anthemis, who lived only twenty years, poor thing!

QVAESTORIVSTII·COL·SECVNDVS
PREF · FABR · ĪĪ · SIBI · ET
LAVDIAEANTHEMIDI·CONTVBERNAL
OPTIMAE · VIX · ANN · XX

1. **Vē′nī, vī′dī, vī′cī,** *I came, I saw, I conquered* (Caesar's famous dispatch to the senate after a victory).

2. **In hōc sig′nō vin′cēs,** *In this sign you will conquer* (motto of Constantine, the first Christian emperor).

3. **Nōn nō′vit vir′tūs calamitā′tī cē′dere,** *Courage knows not how to yield to disaster.*

4. **Iniūriā′rum reme′dium est oblī′viō,** *Forgetfulness is the cure for injuries.*

5. **Pos′sunt qui′a pos′se viden′tur,** *They can because they think they can.*

V

The two verses which follow were used by Roman children in some of their games:

1. **Ha′beat sca′biem quis′quis ad mē vē′nerit novis′simus,** *May he have the itch who comes to me last.*

2. **Rēx e′rit quī rēc′tē fa′ciet; quī nōn fa′ciet nōn e′rit,** *He will be king who does right; he who does not will not be king.*

The Forum of Augustus and Temple of Mars as an artist rebuilt it in imagination from the existing remains

London as it was under the Romans. Many traces of Roman London have been found under the modern city.

LESSON I

6. ĪNSULAE

Britannia[1] est īnsula. Eurōpa nōn est īnsula. Italia paene[2] est īnsula; Italia paenīnsula[3] est. Sicilia et[4] Corsica īnsulae sunt. Viae et silvae et īnsulae et paenīnsulae in Eurōpā sunt. Silvae et viae in īnsulā Britanniā sunt.

Thought Questions.—1. How many islands are mentioned in this passage? 2. How many peninsulas?

---

[1] *Britain.* The meaning of proper nouns and adjectives is usually so clear that they are not listed in the lesson vocabularies; if necessary, they may be looked up in the Latin-English Vocabulary at the end of the book.

[2] *almost.*

[3] Can you obtain the meaning of this word from its English derivative and from the meaning of **paene** and **īnsula**?

[4] *and.*

9

7.   How to Read Latin

Read through a Latin sentence, trying to get the meaning of each word as you come to it. Sometimes an English word derived, or formed, from the Latin word, will give you the clue; sometimes you will have to guess from the rest of the sentence. Some words are purposely used in the Latin passages which have not been explained in the lesson vocabularies. If you cannot guess their meaning, look them up in the Latin-English Vocabulary at the end of the book. Pay careful attention to the endings. When you understand the passage, answer the thought questions; then translate into good English. Do not always use the English meanings of the Latin words as given in the vocabulary, but find English words of like meaning which exactly fit the sentence.

8.   Sentences

The Latin and English passages above are made up of **sentences** —that is, groups of words which express thoughts.

Each sentence consists of two parts: the **subject,** about which something is said, and the **predicate,** which says something about the subject.

9.   Nouns

(*a*) A **noun** is a word that names a person, place, or thing. It happens that the subject of each sentence in the Latin passage just studied is a noun.

(*b*) Nouns are **singular** in number when they mean one person or thing: *island*, īnsula. They are **plural** when they mean more than one: *islands*, īnsulae. Note that Latin nouns, like English nouns, are changed to show plural number. Pick out the singular and the plural nouns in the second paragraph of **1.**

(*c*) The use of a noun in a sentence determines its **case.** In English we sometimes change the ending to show the case: *the boy's hat.* In Latin the cases are distinguished by their endings.

10

10.   Nominative Case as Subject and Predicate

(*a*) In Latin, as in English, the subject of a sentence is in the **nominative** case.

(*b*) A noun used in the predicate after a linking verb (*is, are, seem*, etc.) to complete its meaning is in the nominative. This is called the **predicate nominative.**

(a)   (b)   (a)   (b)
Britannia est īnsula,   Britain is an island.

11.   Nominative Case Endings

The case endings for the nominative, singular and plural, of some nouns are as follows:

	SINGULAR	PLURAL
Examples:	–a	–ae
	via	viae

12.   English Word Studies

The following are English words, borrowed from the Latin, which have kept their Latin nominative endings, both singular and plural. Consult the dictionary for the English pronunciation and meaning of these **loan words.** (Observe that in English –ae is usually pronounced ē, as in *me*.)

alumna, alumnae; antenna, antennae (or **antennas,** when used in radio); **larva, larvae; minutiae** (singular rare)

13.   Vocabulary

NOUNS
īn′sula, *island*	(insulate)	**est,** *is*
sil′va, *forest, woods*	(Pennsylvania)	**sunt,** *are*
vi′a, *way, road, street*	(viaduct)	**nōn,** *not*

Note.—The words in parentheses are English derivatives of the Latin words. Be sure that you understand these derivatives and can use them in English sentences. Enter the above Latin words in a notebook and find additional derivatives. Your teacher will give you directions about the notebook.

14.   SICILIA

Sicilia est īnsula magna in Eurōpā. Magna est fāma Siciliae.[1]
Fortūna Siciliae nōn magna est. In Siciliā est Mōns[2] Aetna.
Aetna est magna. Fāma Aetnae magna est.

Viae in Siciliā nōn bonae sunt. Viae novae nōn longae sunt.
5 Silvae magnae in Siciliā nōn sunt.

Thought Questions.—1. Where is Mt. Etna? 2. Are there good roads
in Sicily?

Mons Aetna

15.   Adjectives

An **adjective** is a word used
to describe or limit the meaning
of a noun. We say that an adjective **modifies** its noun. Pick
out the adjectives in the second
paragraph of 1.

In English, an adjective is not
changed to show number and
case. *This* and *that*, however,
change in the plural to *these* and
those.

In Latin, an adjective shows
by its ending both the number
and the case of the noun which
it modifies.

1. **Silva magna,** *a large forest.*
2. **Silvae magnae,** *large forests.*

An adjective may be used
directly with a noun, as in the
above examples, or in the predicate, as follows:

---

[1] *of Sicily.*   [2] *Mt*

Via. A street scene in old Pompeii

1. **Via longa est bona,** *A long street is good.*
2. **Viae longae sunt bonae,** *The long streets are good.*

16. **Position of Adjectives**

In English the adjective almost always precedes the noun it modifies; we rarely use such expressions as *the house beautiful, Captains Courageous.*

In Latin the adjective precedes only in sentences in which it is more important or emphatic than the noun.

17. **Exercises**

(*a*) (*Read in Latin and get the meaning; then translate into English.*) 1. Īnsula est magna. 2. Via est nova. 3. Viae sunt longae. 4. Viae longae sunt bonae. 5. Fortūna est bona. 6. Via bona est longa. 7. Fāma est bona. 8. Crēta est īnsula.

(*b*) (*Supply Latin words with the correct endings for the English words.*) 1. Longa Īnsula est (*large*). 2. Īnsulae sunt (*long*). 3. Fortūna magna est (*good*). 4. Īnsula nova est (*long*). 5. Eurōpa nōn est (*island*).

Fortuna

(c) (*Copy these sentences and add the correct endings.*) 1. Īnsula nov__ est magn__. 2. Viae bon__ sunt nov__. 3. Magn__ est fām__. 4. Viae nov__ sunt bon__. 5. Fortūn__ est nov__.

18. Vocabulary

Nouns

fā′ma, *report, fame* (famous)
fortū′na, *fortune* (fortunate)

Adjectives

bo′na, *good* (bonus)
lon′ga, *long* (longitude)
mag′na, *large, great* (magnify)
no′va, *new, strange* (novice)

19. English Word Studies

From what Latin word is *insular* derived? Explain this sentence: *Puerto Rico is an insular possession of the United States. Isolation* is derived from the same Latin word; what is meant by a policy of *isolation* for the United States? From what Latin word is *innovation* derived? Use *innovation* in an English sentence. What is a *bonbon* and from what Latin word does it come? Use *magnitude* in an English sentence and tell from what Latin word it is derived.

The name *Aetna* occurs forty-four times in the Chicago telephone directory as the name of business houses, factories, etc. Do you know of any so named in your community or elsewhere?

14

20. ROSAE

Puella parva Rōmāna est.
Rosās[1] in corbulā[2] portat; rosās
amat. Multae rosae in corbulā
sunt. Corbula parva est sed[3]
5 rosae magnae sunt. Puellam parvam accūsātis quod[4] rosās portat?
Nōn accūsāmus: puella bona est.
Puellam amāmus. Ubi rosās
puella parat? Puella eās[5] in silvā
10 magnā parat. Ubi silva est? In
īnsulā longā silva est. In īnsulā
viae sunt multae et bonae.

Puella

Thought Questions.—1. Why do
we not blame the girl? 2. Where does
she get the flowers?

21. Verbs

(*a*) A **verb** is a word used to tell something about a subject
and is therefore the whole predicate or part of it:

He *carries*, **Portat;** The girl *is* small, **Puella** parva *est.*

Pick out the verbs in the third paragraph of **1.**

(*b*) **Tense** is time. The **present tense** represents an act as
taking place now.

(*c*) The **first person** represents the person speaking (*I, we*),
the **second person** the one spoken to (*you*), the **third person**
the person or thing spoken about (*he, she, it, they*). Verbs are
sometimes changed to show person: *I have, he has.* Sometimes
they are changed to show **singular** or **plural number**: *I am,*

---

[1] *roses.*   [2] *basket.*   [3] *but.*   [4] *because.*   [5] *them.*

15

Rosae. Cupids are put to work selling flowers in this Pompeian wall painting.

we are. But in English the distinction of person and number is usually made only by use of the personal pronouns (*I, you,* etc.): *I have, they have.*

(*d*) In Latin, the personal pronoun subjects are usually omitted, and **personal endings** show person and number. The commonest endings are:

1*st person*	–ō (or –m)= *I*	–mus = *we*
2*d person*	–s = *you*	–tis = *you*
3*d person*	–t = *he, she, it*	–nt = *they*

22. Infinitive

The **infinitive** is a form of the verb before which *to* is usually placed in English:[1] *to go.* In Latin, the present infinitive of all regular verbs ends in –re: accūsāre, parāre.

23. Present Stem and Present Tense

The present tense of a verb is formed by adding the personal endings to the **present stem.** This is obtained by dropping the infinitive ending –re: accūsā(re). The hundreds of verbs in Latin

---

[1] The preposition *to* introducing the infinitive is omitted, however, after the verbs *bid, dare, feel, hear, let, make, need, see,* and the auxiliary verbs *can, may, must, shall,* and *will*

are divided, according to the present stem, into four classes called **conjugations**. The present stem of the first conjugation ends in –ā. Thus **portō, portāre** (present stem **portā–**) is conjugated in the present as follows:

SINGULAR	PLURAL
por'tō, *I carry, am carrying, do carry*	portā'mus, *we carry, are carrying, do carry*
por'tās, *you carry, are carrying, do carry*	portā'tis, *you carry, are carrying, do carry*
por'tat, *he, she, it carries, is carrying, does carry*	por'tant, *they carry, are carrying, do carry*

(*a*) **Remember** that all vowels are shortened before –nt and final –m or –t and that –ā– disappears entirely before final ō in the first singular.

(*b*) **Observe** the three ways to translate each Latin verb form —**common, progressive,** and **emphatic.** In English, when *am* and *do* are used as auxiliary verbs, they have no Latin equivalent. Note the difference between **Portat,** *He is carrying,* and **Nauta est,** *He is a sailor.* One cannot say **Est portat.** There are no such auxiliary verbs in Latin.

(*c*) **Remember** that when a noun is used as subject it takes the place of *he,* etc.: **Portat,** *He carries;* **Puella portat,** *The girl carries.*

| DON'T SAY | *The girl she carries.* |
| SAY | *The girl carries.* |

Practice.—Give the present of the verbs **accūsō** and **amō,** translating each form in three ways.

17

24. **Exercises**

(*a*) 1. Accūsō; parās; portat, 2. Portāmus; accūsātis; amant.
3. Multae puellae sunt parvae et bonae. 4. Ubi est Longa Īnsula? 5. Īnsula nova est parva. 6. Ubi est silva magna?

(*b*) 1. Puella (*is preparing*). 2. Puellae (*are carrying*). 3. Ubi
sunt (*large forests*)? 4. Ubi est (*the little girl*)?

(*c*) 1. Via bon__ est nov__. 2. Vi__ sunt bon__. 3. Ubi sunt
puell__ parv__? 4. Portā__ (*we*); para__ (*they*); accūsā__ (*you,
plur.*); ama__ (*she*).

25. **Vocabulary**

NOUN
puel′la, *girl*

ADJECTIVES
par′va, *small*
mul′ta, *much;* plur., *many*
(multitude)

CONJUNCTION[1]
et, *and*

VERBS
accū′sō, accūsā′re, *blame, accuse*   (accusation)
a′mō, amā′re, *love, like* (amiable)
pa′rō, parā′re, *get, get ready,
prepare*   (prepare)
por′tō, portā′re, *carry* (porter)

ADVERB[1]
u′bi, *where*

26. **English Word Studies**

(*a*) The following are additional loan words, borrowed from
the Latin first declension, often found in high-school textbooks
of science:

amoeba, amoebae (or amoebas); nebula, nebulae (or nebulas);
papilla, papillae; vertebra, vertebrae (or vertebras)

Use the above in English sentences.

(*b*) A "porter" is one who *carries* things. What is a *portable*
stove? What does it mean to *import* things? What is an *amateur*?
What is meant by *amity* among nations?

---

[1]For definitions of conjunction and adverb see 547, 545.

18

Via Appia. The open and closed umbrellas of pine and cypress

LESSON IV

27. VIAE BONAE

Via Appia in Italiā est. Nōn nova est sed[1] fāma eius[2] est magna. Causa est quod[3] via est longa et bona. Viae Rōmānae erant[4] bonae. Viae Rōmānae vēram fāmam habent.[5] Ubi sunt malae[6] viae? Multae viae Americānae sunt malae, sed[1] America multās bonās viās parat. Novās viās amāmus. Nautae aquam, nōn viās [5] probant. Aquam in viīs[7] nōn probāmus. Ubi sunt bonae viae? Multam māteriam in viīs[7] portāmus. Nautae māteriam portant?

Thought Questions.—1. Why is the Appian Way famous? 2. Of what do sailors approve?

28. Gender

In English, and sometimes in Latin, **gender** is a distinction in the form of words corresponding to a distinction of sex. It is shown by change of word (*father*, **pater**; *mother*, **māter**), by

---

[1] *but.*   [2] *of it.*   [3] *because.*   [4] *were.*   [5] *have.*
[6] *bad.*   [7] *on the roads.*

19

change of endings (*master*, **dominus**; *mistress*, **domina**), or by use of a prefix (*he-goat*, *she-goat*). *Father*, *master*, *he-goat* are **masculine**; *mother*, *mistress*, *she-goat* are **feminine**. This use of gender is known as **natural gender**.

In English, nouns that are the names of sexless things are **neuter**.

In Latin, however, many nouns are regarded as masculine or feminine which are neuter in English: **via** (f.), *way*; **numerus** (m.), *number*. This use is known as **grammatical gender**. It is determined, not by the meaning of the word, but largely by its ending.

Nouns of the first declension are feminine (except a few which refer to males).

29.   **Accusative: Direct Object**

The **direct object** is the word which is directly acted upon by the verb. It is put in the **accusative** (objective) case. In spite of its name it has nothing to do with accusing.

In Latin, the endings of the accusative in the first declension are:

	SINGULAR	PLURAL
	–am	–ās
Examples:	viam	viās

1. **Anna Clāram amat**, *Anna loves Clara.*
2. **Clāra Annam amat**, *Clara loves Anna.*
3. (*a*) *I saw **him**.*   (*b*) *He saw **me**.*

Observe in the above sentences:

(*a*) In Latin, the accusative of a noun is distinguished from the nominative by its ending.

(*b*) In English, as seen in 1 and 2, a noun does not show by its ending whether it is used as subject or as object. Its case depends upon the word order and sense. Personal pronouns, however, have separate forms for the accusative, as seen in 3 (*a*) and (*b*).

20

Caution.—A noun is not always in the accusative when it is used with or after a verb. **Est** and **sunt** are forms of the linking verb *be* and take the same case after them as before them. They serve as a sign of equality (=):

Italy is a country, **Italia est terra.**

Query.—Why is it incorrect to say in English, *It is* him?

30.　　　Practice

(*a*) Give the nominative plural and the accusative, singular and plural, of **īnsula, fortūna, mā-teria, aqua.**

(*b*) Give the Latin for *you* (sing.) *approve, they are accusing, we do prepare.*

Via in Italia. A street in Ostia, the seaport of ancient Rome

(*c*) Pick out the direct objects in the following sentences:

1. My brother saw many clowns in the circus. 2. John's father is a rich man. 3. This boy found a dollar last week. 4. The butcher sold me two pounds of pork.

(*d*) Translate the words in italics:

1. I see a beautiful *island*. 2. She is a very nice *girl*. 3. Do you like the *woods?* 4. They are going to pave this *street*. 5. I saw several *sailors*.

31.　　　Verb and Subject

1. **Nauta aquam portat,** *The sailor carries water.*
2. **Viam parāmus,** *We are preparing a way.*
3. **Anna et nauta causās probant,** *Anna and the sailor approve the reasons.*

21

Observe that:

(*a*) The verb in each of the above sentences shows the person and number of its subject by its personal ending (review **21,** *d*).

(*b*) Two singular subjects connected by **et** require a plural verb (see sentence 3).

(*c*) The verb stands last.

32.   **Exercises**

(*a*) 1. Nautās accūsō. 2. Causās bonās probātis. 3. Multam māteriam parāmus. 4. Fāmam et fortūnam probās. 5. Nautae multās causās probant. 6. Puella et nauta multam aquam portant. 7. Causae sunt multae et vērae.

(*b*) 1. (*Water*) portāmus. 2. Puella (*many reasons*) probat. 3. Puellae (*Anna*) accūsant. 4. Anna (*the girls*) accūsat.

(*c*) 1. Naut__ (*plur.*) accūsāmus. 2. Aqu__ porta__ (*he*). 3. Ubi sunt silv__? 4. Naut__ (*sing.*) accūsā__ (*you, plur.*). 5. Causam bon__ probā__ (*we*).

33.   **Vocabulary**

NOUNS		VERB	
a′qua, *water*	(aquarium)	pro′bō, probā′re, *test, prove, ap-*	
cau′sa, *cause, reason*	(causal)	*prove*	(probation)
māte′ria, *matter, timber*			
	(material)	ADJECTIVE	
nau′ta, m., *sailor*	(nautical)	vē′ra, *true*	(verify)

34.   **English Word Studies**

(*a*) How does a *nautical* mile differ from an ordinary mile? What is an *aquarium*? Explain this sentence: "I cannot question his *veracity*." There is an *Appian Way* in Cambridge, Mass.

(*b*)   **Latin Phrases in English**

Fortuna caeca est, *Fortune is blind.*

Magna Charta, the *Great Paper*, or document, which is the cornerstone of English liberty.

materia medica, *material,* such as herbs, used in making *medicines.*

22

35. **Roman Roads and Travel**

While the Romans had no railroads, automobiles, steamships, or airplanes, they had better facilities for getting about than the modern world had until the introduction of steamships and steam railroads a hundred years ago. This was due to their wonderful system of roads. Only in the last few years, as a result of automobile travel, have our roads begun to compare with the Roman roads. Road engineers still admire the ancient Roman highways. The secret of these roads was that they were built like walls (cf. **viam mūniō, 187, 6**).

The Romans were such excellent road builders because they saw the need of having good highways in order to maintain communication with the various parts of their extensive empire. Even in the early days when Rome was conquering Italy, it started its policy of road construction. The most important road in Italy, the Appian Way (cf. p. 19), was built by Appius Claudius in 312 B.C. It led to Capua, the most important city in southern Italy. Later it was extended across Italy to Brundisium, the seaport from which travelers sailed to Greece and the Orient. Parts of the Appian Way and of other Roman roads are in use today.

Horses, mules, carriages or omnibuses, and litters were used by travelers who did not wish to go on foot. Along all the roads there were milestones to indicate distances. Often there were benches on which the weary traveler might rest. Watering troughs for horses and fountains for men were provided. Of course travel was slow. Fifty to sixty miles a day was fast time for people in a great hurry. Ordinarily, twenty-five to thirty-five miles was a fair

Model of a Roman freighter. Can you make one like it?

daily average. A trip that we now make comfortably in a night while asleep in a Pullman car took ten or twelve days.

If the roads were better than ours, the hotel accommodations were much worse. In fact, there were only small inns, which were usually dirty and uncomfortable. The wealthier classes stayed overnight at country villas belonging to themselves or their friends, or in the town houses of people they knew. It was not uncommon for rich Romans to have half a dozen or more villas scattered throughout Italy.

Travel by water was avoided as much as possible. Roman ships were small sailing vessels which were also equipped with oars (pp. 23, 254). Sailing was dangerous, and the boats stayed near the shore as much as possible.

Questions for Discussion.—1. The Romans were great road builders —why? 2. Can you judge a people or a community by its roads? 3. What effect has rapid transportation had on the development of the United States?

Read Showerman, pp. 485–502; Davis, pp. 454–456; McDaniel, pp. 168–178; Johnston, pp. 309–315; Mills, pp. 424–429.[1]

---

[1] For full titles of these books see 626.

Bar, or soda fountain (without soda!), in an inn at Herculaneum

LESSON V

36. PUELLAE RŌMĀNAE

Puellae Rōmānae[1] Rōmam et Italiam amābant. Puellae Americānae Americam amant. Puellae Rōmānae erant magnae et parvae, bonae et malae.[2] Puellae Americānae sunt magnae et parvae, bonae et malae. Parva puella Rōmāna pūpās[3] amābat et portābat. Parva puella Americāna pūpās amat et portat. Pūpās amābās?   5

Fīliae Rōmānae patrēs[4] amābant; patrēs erant agricolae. Agricolae terram lātam et plānam amābant. Pīrātae[5] terram vāstābant. Fīliae agricolārum[6] pīrātās accūsābant. Ubi pīrātae terrās plānās et lātās vāstant?

Thought Questions.—1. In what way were Roman girls like American girls? 2. Why did the girls blame the pirates? 3. What is your answer to the last sentence?

Read Showerman, pp. 112–114; Davis, pp. 190–191; Johnston, § 102.

---

[1] *Roman*, an adjective. **Rōma** is a noun: *Rome.*   [2] *bad.*   [3] *dolls.*   [4] *fathers.*
[5] *pirates.*   [6] *of the farmers.*

Parvae puellae Romanae pupas amabant. Two rag dolls and a jointed doll of terra cotta, once dearly loved by Roman girls, now in the Toronto Museum, where modern girls can see them and through them understand their Roman cousins of long ago

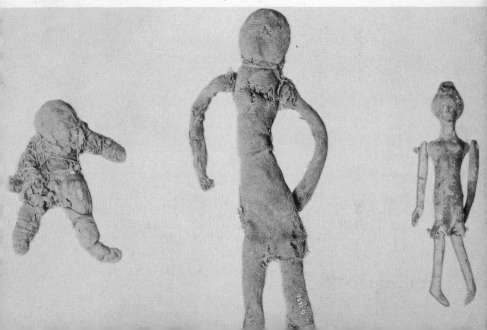

City Hall, New Orleans, in classic style, like many public buildings everywhere

37. Imperfect Tense

The Latin **imperfect** tense, like the English progressive past, shows *continuous*, *habitual*, or *repeated* action (or being) in past time. It is so called because it often represents incomplete acts not because anything is wrong with it.

In Latin, the imperfect tense is formed by adding the tense sign –bā– to the present stem and then attaching the personal endings, which you already know:

SINGULAR	PLURAL
portā'bam, *I was carrying, did carry, carried*	portābā'mus, *we were carrying,* etc.
portā'bās, *you were carrying,* etc.	portābā'tis, *you were carrying,* etc.
portā'bat, *he, she, it was carrying,* etc.	portā'bant, *they were carrying,* etc.

Observe that the personal ending for the first person singular is –m (not –ō as in the present tense).

Practice.—(*a*) Give the imperfect of **amō, accūsō, vāstō,** with meanings.

(*b*) Give the Latin for *he approved, we were preparing, you* (sing.) *carried, they are getting.*

38. Exercises

(*a*) 1. Nautam accūsābāmus. 2. Causās bonās probātis. 3. Viae erant lātae et plānae. 4. Nauta fīliam amābat. 5. Fīlia nautam

26

amābat. 6. Terrās multās vāstābātis. 7. Agricolae aquam et
māteriam portābant.

(*b*) 1. Nautae īnsulās (*were
laying waste*). 2. Agricola terram
plānam (*loved*). 3. Viae novae
erant (*wide*). 4. Puellae aquam
(*were carrying*).

(*c*) 1. Terr___ amābat. 2. Terr___
est lāt___ et plān___. 3. Terr___
(*sing.*) vāstā___ (*we were*). 4.
Nautae aqu___ ama___ (*pres.*).
5. Anna et Clāra puell___ bon___
era___.

Stock Exchange, New York, in
Roman style. Banks, too, often
have the form of temples.

39. **Vocabulary**

NOUNS

agri′cola, m., *farmer*
fī′lia, *daughter* (filial)
ter′ra, *land, earth* (territory)

ADJECTIVES

lā′ta, *wide* (latitude)
plā′na, *level* (plane)

VERBS

vās′tō, vāstā′re, *lay waste* (devastate)
e′rant, *they were*

40. **English Word Studies**

(*a*) From what Latin words are *latitude, terrestrial, subterranean*
derived? What is *terra cotta?*

(*b*) The following, now regarded as English words, have been
adopted from the Latin without change in the nominative singular.
Their plurals sometimes end in –ae, but usually in –s, like most
English nouns:

area, arena, aurora, camera, formula

27

Archives Building, Washington, D. C.—another public building which is a Roman temple. The style of the columns is Corinthian.

The Memorial to Benito Juarez, the Abraham Lincoln of Mexico, in Mexico City. The columns are in the Doric style.

FIRST UNIT REVIEW (LESSONS I–V)

41. Nominative and Accusative

1. What case does the subject take? Give its endings. What case does the direct object take? Give its endings. Give the Latin for the words in italic type:

(a) I saw *large islands.* (b) He had *a good reason.* (c) *Anna* loved the sailor. (d) *Farmers* like *level country.*

2. Give the Latin for the underscored words:

(a) The streets are wide. (b) Anna is a good girl. (c) It was a large island. (d) My daughters are small.

42. Vocabulary

The English meanings of these Latin words will be found with corresponding numbers on the following page. After learning the list both ways, ask someone to test you by reading the words in the Latin list. As each word is read, give the English meaning.

NOUNS

1. agricola	5. fīlia	10. puella
2. aqua	6. fortūna	11. silva
3. causa	7. īnsula	12. terra
4. fāma	8. māteria	13. via
	9. nauta	

ADJECTIVES

14. bona	17. magna	20. parva
15. lāta	18. multa	21. plāna
16. longa	19. nova	22. vēra

VERBS

23. accūsō	26. est	29. probō
24. amō	27. parō	30. sunt
25. erant	28. portō	31. vāstō

ADVERBS
32. nōn   33. ubi

CONJUNCTION
34. et

29

43. Vocabulary

Nouns

1. *farmer*	5. *daughter*	10. *girl*
2. *water*	6. *fortune*	11. *forest*
3. *cause*	7. *island*	12. *land*
4. *report*	8. *matter, timber*	13. *way*
	9. *sailor*	

Adjectives

14. *good*	17. *large*	20. *little*
15. *wide*	18. *much*	21. *level*
16. *long*	19. *new*	22. *true*

Verbs

23. *accuse*	26. *is*	29. *test*
24. *love*	27. *get*	30. *are*
25. *were*	28. *carry*	31. *lay waste*

Adverbs
32. *not*   33. *where*

Conjunction
34. *and*

44. Nouns and Adjectives

In what number and case are each of the following: **fortūna, īnsulam, terrae, silvās, via**? Give the correct form of **magna** with each of the above words.

45. English Word Studies

(*a*) What is a loan word? How should –ae be pronounced in the English words *alumnae, larvae,* and *vertebrae?*

(*b*) What do you think the following italicized words mean, judging from the Latin words from which they come?

an *accuser, amateur* sport, *filial* love, a *novel* idea, a *portable* typewriter, this *terrestrial* ball, to live in *amity.*

46. Verbs

1. Give the present tense of **amō** and the imperfect tense of **parō** with meanings.

2. *Translate*: sunt, parant, accūsāmus, amābam, portābat, erant, probās, vāstābant.

30

Roma. A model of part of the ancient city, showing the Colosseum, the
Palatine Hill, and the Circus

LESSON VI

47. ## RŌMA

Rōma prīmō[1] parva erat; fōrma Rōmae erat quadrāta.[2] Plāna
nōn erat. Posteā[3] magna et clāra rēgīna[4] terrārum erat. Rōmānī[5]
Rōmam amābant. Agricolae et nautae Rōmam spectābant. Viae
Rōmae erant longae sed nōn lātae. Cōpia aquae bonae erat
magna cūra Rōmānīs.[6] Est cōpia aquae clārae cūra Americānīs[7]? 5
Nunc[8] fāma Rōmae magna est. Rōmam amāmus et ruīnās Rōmae
saepe[9] spectāmus.

Thought Questions.—1. Were Roman roads wide? 2. Do we ever see
Rome? 3. Why is a good water supply important?

48. ### Genitive

In English, possession is shown by the **genitive** (possessive)
case ending in −'s, or by the accusative (objective) with *of: the
boy's father* or *the father of the boy.*

In Latin, the genitive endings of the first declension are:

	SINGULAR	PLURAL
	−ae	−ārum
Examples:	viae	viārum

1. **viae īnsulae,** *the roads of the island.*
2. **viae īnsulārum,** *the roads of the islands.*

---

[1] *at first.*   [2] *square.*   [3] *afterwards.*   [4] *queen.*   [5] *the Romans.*
[6] *to the Romans.*   [7] *to Americans.*   [8] *now.*   [9] *often.*

31

Practice.—Give the Latin nominative, genitive, and accusative, singular and plural, of *water, supply, sailor, land*.

49. <center>Exercises</center>

(*a*) 1. Agricolās amāmus. 2. Fīlia agricolae est parva. 3. Magnās cōpiās īnsulae clārae spectābāmus. 4. Est[1] cōpia aquae. 5. Cūrae Annae erant multae sed parvae. 6. Nautae cōpiam aquae clārae portābant. 7. Fōrma īnsulae erat nova.

(*b*) 1. Causae (*of the sailors*) erant vērae. 2. Cōpiam (*of good water*) portāmus. 3. Anna nautās (*of the large island*) spectābat. 4. Nautae agricolās īnsulārum (*blamed*).

(*c*) 1. Ann__ (*Anna's*) cūrae erant mult__. 2. Magn__ erat cūra naut__ (*of the sailors*). 3. Silvās īnsul__ clār__ spectā__ (*they looked at*). 4. Cōpiam aqu__ bon__ portā__ (*I was carrying*).

50. <center>Vocabulary</center>

NOUNS

cō'pia, *supply, abundance,*
  plur., *forces, troops*　(copious)
cū'ra, *care, concern*　(curator)
fōr'ma, *shape*　(form)

VERBS

e'rat, *he, she, it was*
spec'tō, spectā're, *look at*
　　　　　　　(spectacle)

ADJECTIVE

clā'ra, *clear, famous*　(clarify)

CONJUNCTION

sed, *but*

51. <center>English Word Studies</center>

(*a*) Explain this sentence: *He spoke with great clarity.* With what Latin words do you connect *spectator, inspect, formula, accurate?* What is a *curator?* What is a *copious* portion?

(*b*) The following words have been borrowed without change from Latin. The plural ends in –s:

inertia, insomnia, militia, nausea, saliva

---

[1] Supply *there*, omitted in Latin when it does not refer to place.

32

Ad Europam. The Appian Way, described on page 23, as it looks a few miles from Rome. The picturesque trees, which look like open umbrellas, are of course called umbrella pines.

LESSON VII

52. EURŌPA

Ad Eurōpam nāvigābō; tōta[1] familia nāvigābit. Magnam pecūniam ad Eurōpam portābimus. Multam praedam ad Americam portābimus. Magnās undās spectābimus, sed magnās undās nōn amāmus. Ad īnsulās clārās, Britanniam et Siciliam, nāvigābimus. Familia Galliam,[2] Italiam, Germāniam spectābit. Ad nautās cōpiam pecūniae portābō, et nautae nāvem[3] parābunt. Nāvigābitis ad Eurōpam et praedam ad Americam portābitis?

Thought Questions.—1. Who is going to Europe? 2. Who will see Italy?

---

[1] whole.   [2] Gaul (France).   [3] Accusative singular of **nāvis** (ship).

The **future** tense refers to something that will happen at some future time.

In Latin, the future of the first conjugation is formed by adding the tense sign –bi– (corresponding to *shall* and *will* in English) to the present stem and then attaching the same personal endings as in the present:

SINGULAR	PLURAL
portā′bō, *I shall carry*	portā′bimus, *we shall carry*
portā′bis, *you will carry*	portā′bitis, *you will carry*
portā′bit, *he, she, it will carry*	portā′bunt, *they will carry*

Observe that the future sign –bi– loses i before –ō in the 1st sing. and changes to –bu– before –nt in the 3d plur.

Practice.—(*a*) Give the future indicative, with meanings, of spectō, probō, nāvigō.

(*b*) Tell the form of amātis, accūsābat, vāstābāmus, parant.

Familia. This happy family lived near Bucharest, Rumania, the ancient Roman province of Dacia.

54.   **Exercises**

(*a*) 1. Ubi magnam cōpiam pecūniae parābis? 2. Ad terram novam nāvigābimus. 3. Pecūnia est vēra causa cūrārum. 4. Magnae undae sunt ad īnsulam. 5. Nautae ad īnsulam plānam nāvigābunt. 6. Praedam ad silvam portābunt. 7. Anna cōpiam aquae ad familiam portābit.

(*b*) 1. Fīliam agricolae (*he will love*). 2. Ad terrās novās (*we shall sail*). 3. Undās magnās (*they will look at*). 4. Pecūniam ad familiam agricolae (*I shall carry*).

Pecunia. In early times the Romans had no coins and traded with sheep and oxen (pecus). Later they used bronze bars like this, with the figure of an ox, weighing five pounds. A little change for the pocket!

(*c*) 1. Ubi sunt silv— īnsul— (*of the island*)? 2. Est cōpia māteri— bon—. 3. Cōpiam pecūni— et praed— parā— (*we shall get*). 4. Familia naut— (*sailor's*) ad īnsul— lāt— nāvigā— (*will sail*).

55. Vocabulary

Nouns	Verbs
fami′lia, fami′liae, f.,[1] *family* (familiar)	nā′vigō, nāvigā′re, *sail* (navigation)
pecū′nia, pecū′niae, f., *money* (pecuniary)	Preposition[2]
prae′da, prae′dae, f., *loot* (predatory)	ad, with acc., *to*, *toward* (with verbs of "coming" and "going"); *near*
un′da, un′dae, f., *wave* (undulate)	(with verbs of rest)

56. English Word Studies

From what Latin word does *impecunious* come? Explain it in the sentence: *I never saw a more impecunious person.* From what Latin words are *unfamiliar*, *navigable*, *abundance* derived? An "abundant" harvest is one that overflows in big *waves*. Use *inundate* in a sentence.

---

[1] Memorize the nominative, genitive, and gender, in addition to the meaning, of each noun as printed in all vocabularies.

[2] For definition of preposition see 546.

35

57. **COLUMBUS**

Columbus ad Hispāniam[1] nāvigat. Isabellae, rēgīnae[2] Hispāniae, nūntiat: "Terra nōn plāna est; probābō et terrās novās mōnstrābō." Sed Isabella pecūniam nōn dōnat. Tum[3] amīcus[4] litterās ad Isabellam portat, et Isabella Columbō[5] pecūniam 5 mandat. Columbus amīcō[5] victōriam nūntiat.

Columbus nāvigat, sed via longa est et cūrae multae sunt. Nautae Columbum[6] accūsant; poena nautārum magna est. "Ad terrās novās nāvigābimus," Columbus nautīs nūntiat; "Poenam vōbīs[7] nōn nūntiābō sed praedam dōnābō."

10 Sed subitō[8] nauta clāmat[9] "Victōria!" et terram grātam mōnstrat. Columbus cūram nāvis[10] nautīs mandat et terram novam spectat. Litterās ad Isabellam portat et Isabellae praedam grātam dōnat. Nunc[11] Columbus magnam fāmam habet.[12]

Thought Questions.—1. What does Columbus say to Isabella. 2. What does Columbus do when land is sighted? 3. Look up in an encyclopaedia where Columbus got the idea that the earth was round.

[1] Spain.	[2] queen.	[3] then.	[4] a friend.
[5] Dative.	[6] Accusative.	[7] to you.	[8] suddenly.
[9] exclaims.	[10] of the ship.	[11] now.	[12] has.

Map of the world by Ptolemy, Greek geographer, whose work, translated into Latin, was used by all the early explorers

The ruins of the Roman Forum, gay with flowers

58. Dative: Indirect Object

The noun that shows for whom or what the direct object is intended, is called the **indirect object**, and is put in the **dative** case.

In Latin, the endings of the dative in the first declension are:

Singular	Plural
-ae	-īs
Examples: viae	viīs

Nautae pecūniam dōnō, *I give money to the sailor,* or *I give the sailor money.*

Observe the following points:

(1) In addition to the direct object (**pecūniam,** *money*) in the accusative, an indirect object (**nautae,** *sailor*) to show the receiver may be used.

(2) In Latin the indirect object is expressed by the dative, but in English it may be expressed either by the dative, as in the second translation, or by the accusative with *to* (or *for*).

(3) In English there is no separate form for the dative.

(4) In Latin and English the dative is placed before the accusative.

37

(5) In Latin the genitive and dative singular have the same ending in the first declension.

The indirect object in the dative case is used with verbs of *giving, reporting, telling, showing*, etc.

Caution.—After verbs of motion like "come" and "go," *to* is expressed in Latin by a preposition (**ad** with the acc.):

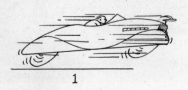

1.   2.

1. He went *to the city* as fast as he could (accusative with **ad**).

2. He told his story *to the officer* and showed *him* his driver's license (datives of indirect object).

59.   **Practice**

(*a*) Give the Latin nominative, genitive, dative, and accusative, singular and plural, of *family, money, care, reason, farmer*.

(*b*) Tell the case to be used in Latin in translating the words in italics:

1. The whole family moved to *California*. 2. I told my *father* what you said. 3. He presented his library to the *city*. 4. We carried our bags to the *station*. 5. I showed *Anna* the book.

60.   **Exercises**

(*a*) 1. Nautīs poenam nūntiābimus. 2. Familiae pecūniam dōnābit. 3. Puellae litterās mandābimus. 4. Agricolīs victōriam grātam nūntiābō. 5. Aquam clāram ad īnsulam parvam portābant. 6. Annae viās silvae mōnstrābō. 7. Anna Clārae magnam pecūniam dōnābit.

(*b*) 1. (*To many families*) pecūniam dōnat. 2. (*To Anna*) poenam nūntiābit. 3. (*To the sailor*) litterās mandābō. 4. (*To the sailors*) viam mōnstrant. 5. (*To many lands*) nāvigābimus.

38

(c) 1. Naut__ (*plur.*) pecūniam dōnābimus. 2. Nautae _____ (*to the islands*) nāvigābunt. 3. Naut__ (*sing.*) litterās mandābō. 4. _____ (*to Anna*) litterās portā__ (*she will carry*). 5. _____ (*to Clara*) pecūniam dōnā__ (*she gave*).

61. Vocabulary

NOUNS

lit′tera, lit′terae, f., *letter* (of the alphabet); plur., *a letter* (epistle) (literary)

poe′na, poe′nae, f., *penalty, punishment* (penal)

victō′ria, victō′riae, f., *victory* (victorious)

VERBS

dō′nō, dōnā′re, *give, present* (donation)

man′dō, mandā′re, *entrust* (mandate)

mōns′trō, mōnstrā′re, *point out, show* (demonstration)

nūn′tiō, nūntiā′re, *report, announce* (pronunciation)

ADJECTIVE

grā′ta, *pleasing, grateful* (gratify)

62. English Word Studies

Try to see the relation between the meaning of the English derivative and the Latin word from which it comes, and then use the derivative in a sentence.

(*a*) An author is a man of "letters," or a "literary" man; a "literal" translation is one that is almost *letter for letter*.

(*b*) A "mandate" is something *entrusted* to a person or a group, as the government of a weak nation.

(*c*) A "novelty" is something *new*.

(*d*) A person who is on "probation" is being *tested*.

In the same way explain *familiar, undulating, navigable*. What is a *penal* institution?

Victoria. A statue in the Carthage Museum

Gallia. The Roman amphitheater at Nîmes, France, now used for bullfights, which are much like the shows held there in ancient times

LESSON IX

63.   **GALLIA**

Cōpiae Rōmānae Galliam occupant et Gallī[1] fortūnās et
familiās silvīs mandant. Sed memoria iniūriārum Galliam ad
pugnam incitat. Gallī[1] Rōmānīs[2] nūntiant:

"Terram nostram[3] cōpiīs occupātis et pugnīs vāstātis. Praedam
5 magnam ad Italiam portātis. Sed pugnābimus et victōriīs vītam
et pecūniam nostram[3] servābimus. Iniūriīs et poenīs nōs[4] ad
pugnam incitātis. Victōriās grātās Rōmae nōn nūntiābitis."

Gallī pugnant, sed multae et clārae sunt victōriae Rōmānae.
Pugnae vītam Gallōrum[5] nōn servant. Ubi est Gallia? Pugnās
10 Gallōrum[5] memoriae mandābitis?

Thought Questions.—1. What did the Gauls do with their families?
2. What did the Romans do to Gaul? 3. Why is France today called a
Latin country?

---

[1] *the Gauls, i.e.* the people of Gaul (**Gallia**).   [2] *to the Romans.*   [3] *our.*
        [4] *us.*   [5] *of the Gauls.*

40

64. **Ablative**

In English, the object of any preposition is in the accusative (objective).

In Latin, the object of some prepositions is in the accusative; of others, in a special case called the **ablative**, the endings of which are:

	SINGULAR	PLURAL
	–ā	–īs
Examples:	viā	viīs

65. **Ablative of Means**

Many ideas expressed in English by a noun preceded by a preposition are expressed in Latin by a noun in the ablative case without a preposition, as the following common type:

Litterīs victōriam nūntiant, *They report the victory by-means-of a letter.*

Observe that **litterīs** (abl.) shows *by what means* they report, and that no preposition is used.

The Colosseum at Rome as it once looked. The colossal statue at the left gave the amphitheater its name—like the tail wagging the dog.

Practice.—Tell the form of **memoriae, vītā, litterārum, pecūniā, victōriam, praedīs; occupābis, servant, incitābāmus, mandābō, dōnās, pugnābitis.**

66. Exercises

(*a*) 1. Pugnīs īnsulam vāstābātis. 2. Aquā vītam agricolārum servābimus. 3. Litterīs magnam victōriam nūntiābit. 4. Memoriā iniūriae nautās incitās. 5. Victōriīs vītam et terram servābant. 6. Magnā pecūniā multās familiās servābitis. 7. Puella memoriae litterās mandābit.

(*b*) 1. (*By the victory*) īnsulam servābimus. 2. (*With money*) nautās incitābāmus. 3. (*With large forces*) īnsulās occupābimus. 4. Memoria iniūriārum nautās (*will arouse*). 5. (*To the family*) victōriam nūntiābō.

(*c*) 1. Victōri___ (*by victory*) terram servā___ (*we saved*). 2. Aqu___ (*with water*) silvam serva___ (*they save*). 3. Pecūni___ nautās incitā___ (*I shall urge on*). 4. Cōpi___ (*with troops*) īnsulam occupā___ (*they will seize*). 5. Agricol___ (*to the farmer*) pecūniam dōnā___ (*I shall give*).

A model of ancient Rome, with Circus Maximus and Colosseum, looking west. The picture on page 31 looks east.

67. Vocabulary

NOUNS

iniū′ria, iniū′riae, f., *wrong, injustice*
    (injurious)
memo′ria, memo′riae, f., *memory*
    (memorial)
pug′na, pug′nae, f., *battle*
    (pugnacious)
vī′ta, vī′tae, f., *life*   (vital)

VERBS

in′citō, incitā′re, *urge on, arouse*
    (excitement)
oc′cupō, occupā′re, *seize*
    (occupation)
pug′nō, pugnā′re, *fight*
    (pugnacity)
ser′vō, servā′re, *save, guard*
    (conservation)

68.   English Word Studies

(*a*) Explain *pugnacious, reservoir, incite*. From what Latin words are *vitamin, preserve, vitality, injury* derived? Give an example of a *conservation* policy in your state.

(*b*)   Latin Phrases in English

    ad nauseam, *to* (the point of) *seasickness* or *disgust*.
    aqua vitae, *water of life*, formerly applied to alcohol.
    Nova Scotia, *New Scotland*, a province in Canada.
    persona grata, a *pleasing* or *acceptable person*.

Ancient and modern Rome, mixed like scrambled eggs. The picture faces east. The slanting street runs through the imperial fora; the Roman Forum is at the right.

Puellae undas spectant.

LESSON X

69.   PUELLAE ET MĀTER

Anna. Ubi est Cornēlia?

Clāra. Ad prōvinciam nunc nāvigat.

Anna. Cūr[1] ad prōvinciam nāvigat?

Claudia. Prōvinciam amat et semper[2] laudat.

5   **Anna.** Puellae, spectāte undās magnās. Fortūna Cornēliae nōn bona est. Cūra mea magna est.

Claudia. Clāra, mōnstrā Annae gemmās[3] tuās novās.

Clāra. Spectā, Anna. Gemmās meās amō.

Anna. Gemmās tuās laudō; magnae et bonae sunt. Meae 10 gemmae parvae sunt.

Māter.[4] Fīliae, portāte aquam ad casam[5] et cēnam[6] parāte. Quīnta hōra nunc est.

Clāra. Aquam portābimus, māter. Quīnta hōra est, Anna. Cēnam parābimus. Valē.[7]

---

[1] *why.*   [2] *always.*   [3] *jewels.*   [4] *mother.*   [5] *house.*
[6] *dinner.*   [7] Imperative: *good-by.*

Thought Questions.—1. Why is Cornelia unlucky? 2. Which girl has the jewels? 3. Which girls are sisters?

70. First Declension: A Summary

ENDINGS		ENGLISH	via longa, *a long way*	
SING.	PLUR.	FORCE	SING.	PLUR.
Nom. –a	–ae	Subj., Pred. Nom.	vi′a lon′ga	vi′ae lon′gae
Gen. –ae	–ārum	Possessive (*of* or *'s*)	vi′ae lon′gae	viā′rum lon-gā′rum
Dat. –ae	–īs	Indir. obj. (*to* or *for*)	vi′ae lon′gae	vi′īs lon′gīs
Acc. –am	–ās	Direct obj.	vi′am lon′gam	vi′ās lon′gās
Abl. –ā	–īs	*from, by, with, in*	vi′ā lon′gā	vi′īs lon′gīs

Observe the following points:

(1) The nominative and ablative singular both end in –a, but the –a is long in the ablative.

(2) The genitive and dative singular and the nominative plural have the same ending (–ae).

(3) The dative and ablative plural have the same ending (–īs).

(4) Most of the endings contain –a, for this is the **A-Declension**, usually called the **first declension**.

Base.—That part of a word to which endings are attached is called the **base**. The base of a noun or adjective is obtained by dropping the genitive singular ending: gen. sing., **viae**, base, **vi–**.

Declension.—To **decline** a noun or adjective is to give all its case forms, singular and plural. That is quite different from declining a second helping of cake.

Practice.—Decline together in all cases, singular and plural, **cōpia magna, silva grāta, victōria parva.**

71. Present Imperative

Verbs thus far studied have been either in the **infinitive mood** or in the **indicative mood**. The latter is used to make statements or ask questions.

45

In provincia Romana. The famous Church of the Madeleine in Paris, just like a Roman temple

Commands are expressed in Latin and English by the **imperative mood.**

The present imperative singular of all conjugations is the present stem of the verb (**23**): **vocā,** *call.* In all conjugations except the third, the plural is formed by adding –te to the singular: **vocāte,** *call.* The imperative usually stands at or near the beginning of the sentence.

Practice.—Form the singular imperative of *fight, praise, carry, report;* the plural imperative of *give, accuse, save.*

72.   Exercises

(*a*) 1. Servā pecūniam tuam et pecūnia tua tē (*you*) servābit. 2. Amā fīliam tuam et fīlia tua tē amābit. 3. Nunc quīnta hōra est; nāvigābimus. 4. Mōnstrāte viam agricolīs. 5. Nautae vītam agricolārum laudant et agricolae vītam nautārum laudant.

46

(*b*) 1. Puellae, (*look at*) undās magnās. 2. (*Arouse*) agricolam et pugnābit. 3. (*Entrust*) fāmam tuam fortūnae. 4. Nautae, nunc ad prōvinciam (*sail*). 5. (*Show*) puellīs litterās tuās.

(*c*) 1. Incitā__ (*imper. plur.*) naut__ (*plur.*). 2. Vāstā__ (*imper. plur.*) prōvinci__ (*sing.*). 3. Laudā__ (*plur.*) puellās. 4. Dōnā pecūniam tuam agricol__ (*sing.*). 5. Agricolae, laudā__ fīliās bon__.

73. <h2 style="text-align:center">Vocabulary</h2>

NOUNS

hō′ra, hō′rae, f., *hour*
prōvin′cia, prōvin′ciae, f., *prov-ince* (provincial)

VERB

lau′dō, laudā′re, *praise* (laudable)

ADJECTIVES

me′a, *my, mine*
quīn′ta, *fifth* (quintet)
tu′a, *your* (referring to one person)

ADVERB

nunc, *now*

74. Latin Words in the Romance Languages

The Romance languages, which are derived from Latin, have borrowed words from it with little or no change. This may be seen at a glance from the following list of eight words selected from the vocabularies of previous lessons.

FRENCH	SPANISH	PORTUGUESE	ITALIAN
accuser	acusar	accusar	accusare
aimer	amar	amar	amare
matériel	materia	materia	materia
terre	tierra	terra	terra
forme	forma	forma	forma
famille	familia	familia	famiglia
lettre	letra	lettra	lettera
province	provincia	provincia	provincia

Judging from the Latin, what does each of these French, Spanish, Portuguese, and Italian words mean? Make a similar column of English words, so far as possible.

(For the relation of Latin to the Romance languages see Appendix, 602–625.)

The Pantheon, a Roman temple famous for its dome, as painted by Pannini in the eighteenth century (Courtesy, National Gallery of Art, Washington, D. C.; Kress Collection)

75. English Word Studies

Give the nominative, genitive, gender, and meaning of the Latin noun suggested by each of the following derivatives:

copious, curate, informal, injure, literature, memorable, pecuniary, penalize, predatory, undulating, pugnacity, vitamin

76. "To" Expressions

Tell whether the dative case or **ad** with the accusative will be needed to express the **to** idea in the following:

I hurried *to school*. The teacher explained the problem *to me*. When I went *to class*, the teacher sent me *to the board* and I showed *the class* how to work it.

77. Vocabulary

NOUNS

1. cōpia	5. hōra	9. pecūnia	13. pugna
2. cūra	6. iniūria	10. poena	14. unda
3. familia	7. littera	11. praeda	15. victōria
4. fōrma	8. memoria	12. prōvincia	16. vīta

ADJECTIVES

17. clāra	18. grāta	19. mea	20. quīnta	21. tua

VERBS

22. dōnō	25. laudō	28. nāvigō	31. pugnō
23. erat	26. mandō	29. nūntiō	32. servō
24. incitō	27. mōnstrō	30. occupō	33. spectō

ADVERB
34. nunc

PREPOSITION
35. ad

CONJUNCTION
36. sed

Victoria. A stamp issued by New Zealand after the World War. Why don't you make a collection of stamps with ancient buildings and figures and with Latin inscriptions?

78. Vocabulary

NOUNS

1. *supply*	5. *hour*	9. *money*	13. *battle*
2. *care*	6. *wrong*	10. *punishment*	14. *wave*
3. *family*	7. *letter*	11. *loot*	15. *victory*
4. *shape*	8. *memory*	12. *province*	16. *life*

ADJECTIVES

17. *clear*   18. *pleasing*   19. *my, mine*   20. *fifth*   21. *your*

VERBS

22. *give*	25. *praise*	28. *sail*	31. *fight*
23. *was*	26. *entrust*	29. *report*	32. *save*
24. *urge on*	27. *point out*	30. *seize*	33. *look at*

ADVERB
34. *now*

PREPOSITION
35. *to*

CONJUNCTION
36. *but*

A stamp of Tunisia, a French colony in northern Africa, once an ancient Roman colony. It pictures a Roman ship.

79. Cases and Their Uses

(*a*) Decline vīta bona, iniūria mea.

(*b*) State the case required and then give in Latin:

1. *large island* (direct object)
2. *your daughter* (possessive)
3. *little girls* (indirect object)
4. *small waves* (means)
5. *true victories* (direct object)
6. *a new punishment* (subject)
7. *large families* (possessive)
8. *much money* (means)

80. Rapid-Fire Drill

(*a*) *Translate:* occupābō, mōnstrās, dōnā, litterārum, pecūniā, laudābunt, servāre, nāvigātis, incitant.

(*b*) *Translate:* of the victory, with money, we report, he will entrust, you (*sing.*) were showing, they give, he fought.

(*c*) *What forms are:* iniūriīs, prōvinciae, undās, pugnābunt, grātam, spectābātis, hōrīs, tua, mandās?

50

81. Children's Games

Roman children had as good times as our children have in playing games. Even the babies had their rattles. Girls had their dolls (p. 25); boys played various kinds of marble games with nuts (p. 53). The phrase **relinquere nucēs** (*to give up nuts*) meant to grow up, but "grown-ups," even the Emperor Augustus, sometimes played such games. Vacation was the time for marble games. The poet Martial says: "Sadly the boy leaves his marbles and is called back to school by the teacher—the Saturnalia [Christmas] vacation is all over."

Roman toys in the Toronto Museum

Other amusements were spinning tops, walking on stilts (p. 80), flying kites, rolling hoops (p. 54), playing with toy wagons (p. 51) and toy soldiers (p. 69), etc. Among their games were blindman's buff, hide and seek, leapfrog (p. 54), jacks (p. 63). Ball games, some like our tennis and handball, were favorites, especially for men.

For indoor amusement the Romans had a board game which was something like chess or checkers, and another like the many games we have in which as many moves are made on a board as are shown by the throwing of dice (p. 80).

Roman boys and men had their sports—not only swimming, fishing (p. 105), hunting, etc., but also athletic contests: running, jumping, throwing the discus, boxing, wrestling, fencing.

Questions for Discussion.—1. Make a list of games played today that Roman children knew nothing about. 2. In what way, if any, do games and sports have educative value? 3. What other values do sports have?

51

In America. A Latin inscription to the palm goddess in Rio de Janeiro, Brazil

LESSON XI

82.   LINGUA LATĪNA

Patriam amāmus et amābimus. Disciplīnā fāmam patriae augēbimus. Disciplīna nōs[1] nōn terret. Lingua patriae nostrae nōn
Latīna est. Sed linguā Latīnā scientiam[2] nostrae linguae augēmus.
Lingua Latīna prīmō[3] nōbīs[4] nova erat sed nunc nōn terret.
5 Linguam Latīnam laudāmus et semper[5] in memoriā habēbimus.
In Britanniā, in Italiā, in Galliā, in Americīs, in multīs terrīs
et prōvinciīs magistrī[6] linguam Latīnam docēbant et nunc docent
et semper docēbunt. Lingua Latīna magnam fāmam habet.

Thought Questions.—1. When did Latin scare us? 2. Why study
Latin?

83.   **Second Conjugation: Present System**

The verbs that have occurred in previous lessons contain the
stem vowel −ā− and belong to the first conjugation. All verbs
which show the stem vowel −ē− in the **present system** (present,

---

[1] *us.*   [2] *knowledge.*   [3] *at first.*   [4] *to us.*   [5] *always.*   [6]*teachers.*

52

imperfect, and future tenses) belong to the **second conjugation**. The only difference from the first conjugation is in the stem vowel and in the present first singular, which keeps the stem vowel, though shortened: **doceō**.

PRESENT

do'ceō, *I teach, am teaching, do teach*   docē'mus, *we teach, are teaching, do teach*

do'cēs, *you teach,* etc.   docē'tis, *you teach,* etc.

do'cet, *he, she, it teaches,* etc.   do'cent, *they teach,* etc.

IMPERFECT: docē'bam, etc., *I was teaching, did teach, taught,* etc.

FUTURE: docē'bō, etc., *I shall teach,* etc.

Give in full after reviewing **portābam** (37) and **portābō** (53). If you need help, see **585**.

Practice.—(*a*) Conjugate **habeō** in the present tense, **terreō** in the imperfect, and **augeō** in the future, with meanings.

(*b*) Give the singular imperative of *fight, teach;* give the plural imperative of *have, scare.*

(*c*) Translate: *they had, he increases, we showed, he will teach, you (plur.) scare.*

84.   **Exercises**

(*a*) 1. Magnae undae Annam terrēbant. 2. Multās linguās nōn docēbō. 3. Magnam victōriam patriae prōvinciīs nūntiābimus. 4. Magnae undae cūrās nautārum augent. 5. Anna, docē linguās. 6. Victōria cōpiārum cōpiam pecūniae nōn augēbit. 7. Magnam pecūniam et parvam disciplīnam habēbat.

Two marble games, left and right, and a hitting game in the middle

(*b*) 1. Nautae Annam (*were scaring*). 2. (*Love*) linguam patriae tuae. 3. Fīlia linguās (*will teach*). 4. (*Increase*) fortūnam tuam disciplīnā. 5. Pecūniam magnam nōn (*we did have*).

85. Vocabulary

NOUNS	VERBS
disciplī'na, –ae,[1] f., *training, instruction* (disciplinary)	au'geō, augē're, *increase* (augment)
lin'gua, –ae, f., *tongue, language* (linguistic)	do'ceō, docē're, *teach* (docile)
	ha'beō, habē're, *have, hold* (habit)
pa'tria, –ae, f., *fatherland, country*	ter'reō, terrē're, *scare* (terrific)

86. English Word Studies

(*a*) From what Latin words are *terrible, territory, doctrine, document* derived? When is the word *doctor* used to mean one who teaches? What is a *linguist?* What do you think *discipline* means? What is its real meaning, as shown by the derivation?

(*b*) A number of Latin verb forms are preserved as English words. First conjugation: **veto, habitat, ignoramus, mandamus.** Second conjugation: **tenet.** For their meaning, see the dictionary.

The Latin ablative of the first declension is preserved in English in the word **via:** "I am going to New York *via* (by way of) Pittsburgh." The ablative plural is found in **gratis:** "He is giving this *gratis*" (out of favor, *i.e.* for nothing). *Gratis* is a contracted form of **grātiīs.**

---

[1] From now on only the genitive ending will be given instead of the full form.

Rolling hoops and playing leapfrog. This picture and the preceding one are from a stone coffin. They make things a bit more cheerful, don't you think?

87. BRITANNIA

Magna īnsula Britannia in amīcitiā Galliae manēbat. Caesar in Galliā pugnābat et amīcitiam Britanniae et Galliae vidēbat. Cōpiās suās[1] in Galliā auget et ad Britanniam nāvigat. Britan-nōs[2] pugnīs terret sed in Britan-niā nōn manet. Īnsulam videt, nōn occupat, sed glōriam suam[1] auget. Caesar grātiam et amīci-tiam cōpiārum meret,[3] quod[4] magna est vigilia Caesaris.[5] Vic-tōriās multīs litterīs Rōmae nūntiat. Magna est grātia patriae quod[4] Caesar vigiliā patriam ser-vat. Nunc Caesar magnam glō-riam habet.

The famous church of St. Paul's, London, which was struck by a bomb in 1940, was built in the Roman style. Watch for other buildings with Roman domes.

Thought Questions.—1. What did Caesar do in Britain? 2. Why did Caesar win the gratitude of his soldiers?

88. Prepositions of Place: *In*

In the preceding lessons the various uses of the prepositions *with, of, to, for, by* with nouns have been expressed in Latin by means of case endings without prepositions. But certain of these English expressions require the use of corresponding preposi-tions in Latin.

---

[1] *his.* [2] *the Brĭt'ons* (accusative). [3] *wins.*
[4] *because.* [5] *of Caesar.*

In with the ablative= *in* or *on:*

> **in silvā,** *in a forest.*
> **in viīs,** *on the streets.*

89. Sentence Analysis

Before writing the translation of an English sentence into Latin, you may find it helpful to place above every noun the case and number required in the Latin sentence, as follows:

Nom. S.   Acc. S.   Dat. S.
1. The *man* gave a *book* to the *boy*.

Gen. S. Nom. S.   Acc. S. Abl. S.
2. My *friend's son* saved his *life* by *flight*.

90. Practice

(*a*) Decline **magna grātia** and **vīta longa.**

(*b*) Give in Latin:
(1) *true friendship*   in the acc., sing. and plur.
(2) *good memory*   in the gen., sing. and plur.
(3) *a great country*   in the abl., sing. and plur.
(4) *a famous language* in the dat., sing. and plur.

91. Exercises

(*a*) 1. Magnam pecūniam in patriā nunc habēmus. 2. Magna erat grātia puellārum. 3. Nautae in terrā nōn manēbunt. 4. Laudāte vēram amīcitiam. 5. Fāmam et glōriam patriae disciplīnā augēbimus. 6. Multās vigiliās in viīs videō. 7. Multam māteriam in silvīs vidēbitis.

A stamp of the Republic of Lebanon, Syria, showing the ruins of Roman Baalbek (see p. 99), and one of Guatemala, showing a temple

56

(*b*) 1. (*On the streets*) vigiliās vidēbāmus. 2. Multa māteria (*in the forest*) est. 3. Cōpiae (*on the island*) nōn manēbunt. 4. (*In the provinces*) multās silvās vidēbimus.

(*c*) 1. Remain and see my family. 2. They remained in the island. 3. I shall see your daughter on the street. 4. By friendship you will increase your influence.

92.   Vocabulary

Nouns

amīci'tia, –ae, f., *friendship* [*amō*][1]

glō'ria, –ae, f., *glory*   (glorious)

grā'tia, –ae, f., *gratitude, influence* [*grāta*]

vigi'lia, –ae, f., *watchfulness, guard*   (vigilant)

Verbs

ma'neō, manē're, *remain*   (mansion)

vi'deō, vidē're, *see*   (provide)

Preposition

in, with abl., *in, on*

93.   Latin Forms of English Names

Many English names of boys and girls are derived from Latin words (*a*) without, or (*b*) with change:

(*a*) Alma, *fostering;* Clara, *clear, bright;* Leo, *lion;* Stella, *star;* Sylvester, *pertaining to the woods.*

(*b*) Mabel, from **amābilis**, *lovable;* Belle, from **bella**, *beautiful;* Florence, from **flōrentia**, *flourishing;* Grace, from **grātia**, *grace;* Margaret, from **margarīta**, *pearl.*

The following names were in common use among the Romans:

August, Augustus, *venerable;* Rufus, *red-haired;* Victor, *conqueror;* Vincent (**vincēns**), *conquering.*

Other Roman names still used in English are:

Emil and Emily (**Aemilius, Aemilia**); Cecilia (**Caecilia**); Claudia; Cornelius, Cornelia; Horace (**Horātius**); Julius, Julia; Mark (**Mārcus**); Paul (**Paulus**).

See whether any members of your class have names derived from Latin which are not included here.

---

[1] When a new word in the vocabulary is related to a word previously studied, the latter instead of an English derivative is given in brackets.

Via lata est. The Temple of Venus and Rome and the Via del Impero

LESSON XIII

94. SOCIUS

Socius meus Mārcus in Altā Viā habitat. Carrum altum et equum parvum habet. Habēnās[1] tenet et equum incitat. Equus nōs[2] ad silvam portat. Via plāna et lāta est. In viā magnum numerum carrōrum et servōrum vidēmus. Servī in viā labōrant; grātiam patriae merent. Magnum numerum servōrum meōrum līberābō; Mārcus servōs nōn līberābit. Mārcus equum et carrum mihi[3] mandat. Grātiam meam meret, et amīcitiam socī Mārcī memoriā tenēbō.

Thought Questions.—1. What does Marcus have? 2. In what way was Marcus friendly to me? 3. How do Marcus and I differ?

95. Second Declension: Nouns and Adjectives in *–us*

All nouns studied thus far have the genitive singular ending –ae and belong to the first declension. Nouns of the **second**

---

[1] *reins.*   [2] *us.*   [3] *to me.*

declension have the genitive singular ending –ī; the endings of the other cases also are different. Nouns ending in –us in the nominative are masculine.

Adjectives of the first and second declensions are declined in the feminine like nouns of the first declension and in the masculine like those of the second declension.

Review the adjectives already studied (42, 77), placing the masculine ending first, as **bonus** (m.), **bona** (f.).

ENDINGS		ENGLISH FORCE	ser'vus bo'nus, *a good slave* (base, **serv– bon–**)	
SING.	PLUR.		SINGULAR	PLURAL
Nom.–us(ius)	–ī	Subject	ser'vus bo'nus	ser'vī bo'nī
Gen. –ī	–ōrum	Possessive	ser'vī bo'nī	servō'rum bonō'rum
Dat. –ō	–īs	Indir. obj.	ser'vō bo'nō	ser'vīs bo'nīs
Acc. –um	–ōs	Direct obj.	ser'vum bo'num	ser'vōs bo'nōs
Abl. –ō	–īs	With prep- ositions	ser'vō bo'nō	ser'vīs bo'nīs

Observe that:

(*a*) The genitive singular and the nominative plural have the same ending (–ī), just as these cases have the same ending (–ae) in the first declension.

(*b*) The dative and ablative singular have the same ending (–ō), likewise the dative and ablative plural (–īs); the latter is the same as in the first declension.

(*c*) Several of the endings include an –o, for this is the **O– Declension.**

(*d*) Nouns (not adjectives) ending in –ius usually contract –iī to –ī in the genitive singular: **so'ciī** becomes **so'cī.** The accent is not changed. The –i–, being a part of the base, appears in every form: dat. **so'ciō**, etc.

Caution.—The nominative plural does not contract.

(*e*) The nominative singular and plural are preserved in many English words: **alumnus, alumni.** Other examples are given in **100** (*b*).

Carrus

96. Agreement

An adjective is said to agree with its noun in gender, number, and case. Similarly, a verb agrees with its subject (either a noun or a pronoun substitute) in person and number. You see then that the noun is the boss of the sentence, which adjective and verb must obey. Still the adjective has something to say, for it *modifies* the noun.

97.   Practice

(*a*) Decline **carrus parvus, socius meus.**

(*b*) Give in Latin, singular and plural: 1. *a good cart* in the nom.; 2. *a new comrade* in the gen.; 3. *a small number* in the dat.; 4. *a large forest* in the acc.; 5. *a grateful slave* in the abl.

98.   Exercises

(*a*) 1. Amīcitiam sociōrum merēmus. 2. Magnus numerus equōrum est in viā lātā. 3. Sociīs meīs et tuīs carrum novum mōnstrābō. 4. Vidēte magnum numerum carrōrum altōrum in viā. 5. Fīlia mea servōs tuōs laudat. 6. Agricolae, līberāte servōs et merēte grātiam patriae.

(*b*) (*My slaves*) in viīs nōn manent. 2. Agricola (*a large number of wagons*) habet. 3. Amīcitiam (*of my comrades*) merēbō. 4. (*To my slave*) pecūniam dōnābō.

(*c*) 1. Gratitude and friendship are pleasing. 2. I shall see many comrades. 3. You (*sing.*) deserve great fame. 4. Keep (*sing.*) your money and you will have an abundance.

60

99. Vocabulary

NOUNS

car'rus, –ī, m., *cart, wagon* (car)
e'quus, –ī, m., *horse* (equestrian)
nu'merus, –ī, m., *number*
(numerical)
ser'vus, –ī, m., *slave* (servile)
so'cius, so'cī, m., *comrade, ally*
(associate)

VERBS

lī'berō, līberā're, *free* (liberator)
me'reō, merē're, *deserve, earn*
(merit)
te'neō, tenē're, *hold, keep*
(retention)

Equi. Ancient statues in Rome

ADJECTIVE

al'tus (m.), al'ta (f.), *high, deep*
(altitude)

100. English Word Studies

(*a*) From their meanings tell which of the following words come from **servāre** and which from **servus**: *serf, conserve, serve, servant, reserve.* What is an *equestrian?* What does the derivation tell us about the meaning of *social, social service, social security, socialism?*

(*b*) The following are some nouns of the –us type preserved in English in their original form. Note that in English –ī is pronounced like –*i* in *mile:*

SINGULAR	PLURAL
alumnus	alumni
bacillus	bacilli
genius	genii (or geniuses, with different meaning)
gladiolus	gladioli (or gladioluses)
radius	radii (or radiuses)

Adjectives include **bonus** and **quietus** (both nouns in English). What is a soldier's *bonus?* A Christmas *bonus?*

Look up the plurals of **campus, circus, discus, focus, fungus, stimulus** in the dictionary.

61

Poena servorum malorum magna erat. Slaves at the oars of a Roman
warship

LESSON XIV

101. **SERVĪ**

Servī Rōmānī erant captīvī. Rōmānī multīs pugnīs singulās
terrās vāstābant, et magnus erat numerus captīvōrum. Captīvōs
ē Graeciā, ē Galliā, ex Asiā, ex Āfricā in Italiam movēbant. In
familiā Rōmānā erant multī servī, bonī et malī.

5   Dominus[1] servōs vocābat: "Mārce et Stātī,[2] hōra quīnta est;
portāte singulī māteriam dē silvā; Cornēlī, vocā socium et movēte
carrum ā viā et equōs ab aquā."

Servī aquam portābant, vigiliae erant, medicī[3] erant, dē vītā,
dē glōriā, dē amīcitiā docēbant. Multī clārī Graecī erant servī et
10 amīcī Rōmānōrum. Litterae[4] Rōmānōrum memoriam servōrum
amīcōrum servant. Poena servī malī magna erat. Servōs bonōs
Rōmānī līberābant.

---

[1] *the master.*   [2] *Statius* (*Stā′shius*)   [3] *doctors.*   [4] *literature.*

Thought Questions. —
1. How did the Romans get their slaves? 2. Where? 3. Name six things that the slaves did.

102. Vocative Case

In Latin, as in English, the case (**vocative**) used in addressing a person has the same form as the nominative, except in the singular of nouns and adjectives of the second declension

Playing with knucklebones. How do you like the hair, girls?

ending in –**us** and –**ius**. These have –**e**, but in nouns (not adjectives) in –**ius**, –**ie** is contracted to –**ī**:

Ubi estis, Mārce et Lūcī et Claudia? *Where are you, Marcus, Lucius, and Claudia?*

Unless emphatic, the vocative never stands first in the sentence.

103. Exercises

(*a*) 1. Servī malī multam praedam ab īnsulīs portābant. 2. Cornēlī, movē carrōs singulōs dē silvā altā. 3. Mārce, vocā servōs ē silvā; ab īnsulā nāvigābimus. 4. Sociī equōs ē Viā Quīntā movēbunt. 5. In malā fortūnā vērōs amīcōs habēbāmus. 6. Captīvī, portāte māteriam dē silvīs ad aquam.

(*b*) 1. My daughter had a large number of true friends. 2. Brutus, move the prisoners from the island. 3. The allies are now calling forces from many provinces. 4. One-at-a-time[1] they sailed from the island to the new land.

---

[1] Words connected by hyphens are to be expressed by one word in Latin.

Vocabulary

NOUN

captī'vus, –ī, m., *prisoner*
(captivate)

VERBS

mo'veō, movē're, *move*
(movement)

vo'cō, vocā're, *call*   (vocation)

ADJECTIVES

amī'cus, –a, *friendly;* as noun,
friend   [*amō*]
ma'lus, –a, *bad*   (malice)
sin'gulī, –ae, plur., *one at a time*
(singular)

PREPOSITIONS

ā, ab,[1] with abl., *from*
dē, with abl., *down from, from,
about*
ē, ex,[1] with abl., *out of, from*

105.   **Prepositions of Place: *Ab, De, Ex***

ā, ab
dē } used with the ablative=*from.*
ē, ex

Examples: ā viā, (*away*) *from the road.*
dē silvā, (*down*) *from the forest.*
ex aquā, (*out*) *from the water.*

While all three prepositions mean *from*, ab means *away from
the outside;* ex, *out from the inside;* dē, merely *from* when it is not
important to distinguish. Sometimes dē means *down from.*

___
[1] The shorter forms ā and ē are used only before words beginning with a consonant
(except *h*), ab and ex before consonants and vowels.

A great many Latin words are formed by joining prefixes
(**prae**=*in front;* **fīxus**=*attached*) to *root* words. These same
prefixes, most of which are prepositions, are those chiefly used
in English, and by their use many new words are continually
being formed. Thus through them English *lives* and grows—
without them it would be *dead*.

Examples of the prefixes **ab–**, **dē–**, and **ex–** are:

(*a*) **ab–** (**abs–, ā–**): *a-vocation, ab-undance, abs-tain.*

(*b*) **dē–**: *de-fame, de-form, de-ter, de-viate, de-portation.*

(*c*) **ex–** (**ē–, ef–**): *ex-alt, ex-patriation, ex-pect* (from **spectō**), *e-voke.*

Define the above words according to prefix and root. For root
words, see previous vocabularies. Distinguish the meaning of
vocation and *avocation*.

The following are other examples of the prefix **ex–** in English:
ex-cuse, e-dict, ex-empt, ef-fect, e-gress, ex-it.

You will find it helpful to keep a list of prefixes in your notebook and to add after each many examples of their use in English
words.

A house in Pompeii, a city destroyed in 79 A. D. by a volcanic eruption

107.   Slaves

In the earliest days the Romans had few slaves, but as they prospered they came to depend more and more on them to do their work. Slaves did much of the work on the farms and in the industries; these, however, were not nearly as extensive as they are today. Many slaves were obtained by the conquest of foreign nations. A large number came from the Orient and spoke Greek. Many of these became teachers, doctors, musicians, actors, book-keepers, etc. The slave was often superior to the master as a result of heredity and early environment. He was generally of the same race as his master.

The lot of the slave was not as hard as we might imagine, though he was often enough mistreated by a cruel master. Slaves were given an allowance, and the thrifty slave could hope to save enough in the course of years to buy his freedom. Masters often granted freedom out of gratitude for services rendered. Many of these freedmen became very rich and influential. A fine example of the intimate relation of master and slave is that of Cicero and his secretary Tiro, a brilliant man who invented a system of shorthand. Some of Cicero's letters show the greatest affection for Tiro.

The wealthy classes kept large numbers of slaves, all of whom had their special tasks. One might be in charge of polishing the silver, another of writing letters, another of announcing the guests or the hour of the day, etc.

Work for the slave: cleaning this silver mirror from Pompeii

More silver (isn't it beautiful and modern?) for the slaves to polish

Disobedient slaves were punished in various ways. The master had the right to kill a slave, but naturally he was not often inclined to do so, as he would be destroying his own property by doing this. Flogging was a common punishment. Another was to send a city slave to the farm, where the work was harder. Runaway slaves when caught were branded on the forehead with the letter **F**, which stands for **fugitīvus.** You can guess the meaning of the word from the English derivative.

Questions for Discussion.—1. Was slavery an element of weakness or strength in the Roman state? 2. Had it any effect upon the character of Roman citizens? 3. What differences are there between Roman slavery and that which once existed in our country?

Read Showerman, pp. 71–73; Davis, pp. 124–138; McDaniel, pp. 26–40; Johnston, pp. 98–124; Mills, pp. 346 ff.

Magister pueros docet. The boys are reading from rolls.

LESSON XV

108.   **MAGISTER**

Magister noster bonus vir ,est. Puerīs bonīs pecūniam dōnat.
Puer bonus sum. Magister puerōs dē agrīs et silvīs, dē virīs
clārīs, dē glōriā et fāmā patriae nostrae, līberae et sacrae, docet.
Disciplīnam magistrī probō.

5   Carrum parvum, sed nōn equum magister habet. In carrō ad
lūdum[1] venit.[2] Sine[3] equō? Sine equō, nam[4] equus in agrīs manet.
Sed magister carrum nōn movet; carrus sē[5] movet.

Amīcus meus Paulus magistrum nōn amat; magister Paulō
pecūniam nōn dōnat. Sed Paulus pecūniam nōn meret. Malus est
10 in lūdō; puellās terret.

Lūdus[1] noster pūblicus est. Amīcus meus Cornēlius in lūdō
pūblicō nōn est. Amīcī semper erimus, nam[4] amīcitia sacra est.

Lūdī Rōmānī nōn pūblicī erant. Multī magistrī Rōmānī nōn
līberī sed servī erant.

Thought Questions.—1. How does the teacher get to school?
2. Why doesn't Paul like the teacher? 3. Do you think that pupils should
be encouraged to study for prizes and high marks?

---

[1] *school.*   [2] *he comes.*   [3] *without.*   [4] *for.*   [5] *itself.*

109. Second Declension: Nouns and Adjectives in –r

Masculine nouns and adjectives whose base ends in –r omit the ending in –us in the nominative singular. Such words therefore end in –er or –r in the nominative. The genitive singular shows whether –e– is retained before –r in the other forms. In memorizing vocabularies, always note carefully (*a*) the *nominative*, (*b*) the *genitive*, (*c*) the *gender* of every noun. Examples are:

Nom.	ager	noster		puer	liber
Gen.	agrī	nostrī		puerī	līberī
Base	agr–	nostr–		puer–	liber–

(The other forms are regular; if you need help, see **568, 573**)

Note.—(1) Nouns and adjectives like **puer** and **līber** have the –e– throughout; those like **ager** and **noster** have it only in the nominative singular, while **vir** has no –e– at all. Most –er words are like **ager**; no others are like **vir**.

Roman children playing with toy soldiers

(2) The English derivative will usually help determine whether the −e− is retained or not; e.g. *puerile, liberal, miserable; agriculture, sacred, magistrate.*

Practice.—(*a*) Decline **magister amīcus, vir līber.**

(*b*) Tell the form of **equīs, agrum, cōpiārum, nostrī, virō, captīvī, līberōs, sacrā.**

110.   Exercises

(*a*) 1. Incitā, Mārce, equum ad agrum. 2. Magister noster linguam clāram docet. 3. Magister tuus puerō malō pecūniam nōn dōnābit. 4. Magnōs agrōs et virōs līberōs in Americā vidēbitis. 5. Memoria clārōrum nostrōrum virōrum sacra est. 6. Virī nostrī agrōs sociōrum amīcōrum nōn vāstābant. 7. Equōs nostrōs magistrō et puerīs mōnstrābimus.

(*b*) 1. Give Anna the boy's money. 2. Our country is free and sacred. 3. The men were moving the timber out of the forest with horses. 4. I see many horses in the fields of our friends.

111.   Vocabulary

NOUNS		ADJECTIVES	
a′ger, a′grī, m., *field*	[*agricola*]	lī′ber (m.), lī′bera (f.), *free*	
magis′ter, magis′trī, m.,			[*līberō*]
teacher	(Mr.)	nos′ter, nos′tra, *our*	(nostrum)
pu′er, pu′erī, m., *boy*	(puerile)	pū′blicus, pū′blica, *public*	
vir, vi′rī, m., *man*	(virile)		(publish)
		sa′cer, sa′cra, *sacred*	(consecrate)

Four scenes from a boy's life: infancy, babyhood, playtime, school

M·CORNELIO·M·F·PAL·STATIO·P

The Capitol in Caracas, Venezuela. Here too, as everywhere, we find classical architecture.

112. **English Word Studies**

Several Latin words of the –**er** type are in common use in English.

Nouns: **arbiter, cancer, minister, vesper.**

Adjectives: **integer, miser, neuter, sinister** (the first two are used as nouns in English).

Assimilation.—Some prefixes change their final consonants to make them like the initial consonants of the words to which they are attached. This is called **assimilation** (**ad**=*to;* **similis**=*like*).

The prefix **ad**– is generally assimilated. Define the following—all formed from words in the previous vocabularies: *ac-curate, al-literation, an-nounce, ap-paratus, a-spect, as-sociate, ad-vocate.*

Additional examples of assimilation of **ad**– are: *ab-breviate, af-fect, ag-gressive, ac-quire, ar-rogant, at-tend.*

What does *agrarian* mean?

71

Roma. The Temple of Saturn, the Forum, and the Palatine Hill

LESSON XVI

113. ## COLŌNĪ RŌMĀNĪ

Puer Rōmānus sum. Es puer? Colōnī sumus et in agrīs multās hōrās labōrāmus. Estis colōnī? Ubi habitātis? Multī agricolae ad urbem[1] Rōmam migrant. In urbem equō et carrō frūmentum[2] portāmus sed in urbe nōn manēmus. In urbe multī virī habitant sed
5 nōn in agrōs migrant. Agrī nostrī magnī sunt. Līberī sumus, sed labōrāmus; multōs servōs nōn tenēmus. Pecūniam nōn habēmus.

Nūntius pūblicus ad agrōs venit[3] et victōriās cōpiārum nostrārum nūntiat. Nūntiī disciplīnam et animum habent.

Thought Questions.—1. For what purpose do these farmers go to Rome? 2. Why do these farmers have few slaves? 3. In what ways are people in cities today dependent on the farmers?

---

[1] *city* (accusative).   [2] *grain.*   [3] *comes.*

72

The Palatine Hill, where Rome was born

114. ## Present of *Sum*

The verb *to be* is irregularly formed in English and Latin, as well as in other languages, and does not belong to one of the "regular" conjugations. The present infinitive is **esse**. The present indicative is conjugated as follows:

sum, *I am*	su′**mus,** *we are*
es, *you are*	es′**tis,** *you are*
est, *he, she, it is*	su**nt,** *they are*

Review **29, Caution.** Give the Latin in the proper case for the underlined words:

1. They are sailors.
2. We are settlers.
3. They move the prisoners.
4. He is a slave.
5. I teach my friend.
6. You are boys

Exercises

(*a*) 1. Servī estis et in agrīs labōrātis. 2. Animus virōrum est magnus. 3. Māteriam equīs et carrīs dē silvīs ad aquam portābitis. 4. Multī līberī virī in īnsulā magnā habitant. 5. Sociī nostrī numerum magnum captīvōrum in īnsulam movēbant. 6. Colōnī ex Eurōpā migrant et ad līberam Americam nāvigant. 7. Servī equōs nūntī in silvās incitābant.

(*b*) 1. We are messengers of a great victory. 2. The messenger's horse is in our field. 3. The prisoners will carry the timber into the fields. 4. Give the loot to the friendly settlers.

116. Vocabulary

Nouns

a'nimus, –ī, m., *mind, courage*
    (unanimous)
colō'nus, –ī, m., *settler* (colonize)
nūn'tius, nūn'tī, m., *messenger*
        [*nūntiō*]

Preposition

in, with acc., *into;* with abl., *in, on*

Verbs

ha'bitō, habitā're, *live*
    (habitation)
labō'rō, labōrā're, *work*
    (laborious)
mi'grō, migrā're, *depart*
    (migration)
sum, es'se, *be*   (essence)

117. Prepositions of Place: *Ad, In*

   ad with acc. = (*up*) *to*   **in** with acc. = *into*

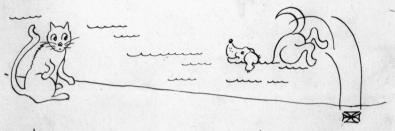

ad aquam   in aquam

Carrōs { ad / in } aquam movent, *They move the carts* { *to* / *into* } *the water.*

Compare a like difference between **ab** and **ex** (**105**).

in aquā

(1) **in** with abl. = *in* or *on*

ın aquam

(2) **in** with acc. = *into*

118. English Word Studies

The prefix **in–** is often assimilated. Define the following, formed from words found in recent vocabularies: *in-gratiate, in-habitant, im-migrant, im-port, in-spect, in-undate.* What is the difference between *emigration* and *immigration?* Additional examples of assimilation of **in–** are: *im-bibe, il-lusion.* Words that have come in through the French often have **en–** or **em–** for **in–** or **im–**: *enchant, inquire* or *enquire.*

What is meant by the *colonial* period of our history? Why do some nations want *colonies?*

The Trojan horse in a Pompeian wall painting. How many men would it hold?

LESSON XVII

119. ## TROIA

Graecī et Trōiānī[1] ad Trōiam[2] pugnābant. Trōiānī barbarī erant, quī[3] in Asiā habitābant. Annōs x pugnant. Tum Ulixēs,[4] clārus Graecus, cōnsilium novum in animō habet. Graecōs signō ēvocat et eīs[5] cōnsilium mandat: "Multam māteriam ex silvā ad castra 5 portāte. Ex māteriā equum altum parāte. Praemium novum barbarīs dōnābimus." Equum parant et in equum virī singulī ascendunt.[6] In equō scrībunt:[7] "Graecī Minervae praemium dōnant." Tum equum ad Trōiam movent. Ad īnsulam parvam nāvigant et frūmentum parant. Vigiliae barbarōrum equum et castra dēserta[8] 10 Graecōrum vident. Equum vocant signum sacrum et in oppidum movent. Nocte[9] Graecī ab īnsulā revertunt[10] et ūnus ex Graecīs[11]

---

[1] the Trojans. [2] Troy. [3] who. [4] Ulys'sēs. [5] to them. [6] climb. [7] write.
[8] deserted. [9] at night. [10] return. [11] one of the Greeks

76

virōs signō ex equō ēvocat. Sociōs in oppidum vocant. Troiam
occupant et vāstant.

Thought Questions.—1. Where
did the Greeks go from Troy?
2. When did they return? 3. How
did the Greeks in the horse know
when to come out? 4. In April, 1940,
German soldiers, disguised as crews
of merchant ships, seized Norwegian
ports. Why did the newspapers call
this a "Trojan horse" trick?

Read Sabin, pp. 277–292; Colum,
pp. 118–121.

120. Neuters of the Second Declension

The second declension contains, in addition to the masculine nouns ending in –us, –er,
and –r, neuter nouns ending in
–um. The only difference between
them and the –us nouns is in the
singular nominative and the
plural nominative and accusative.
Adjectives too have neuter forms.

A modernistic Trojan horse
drawn by a high-school pupil

CASE ENDINGS			sig′num par′vum, *a small sign* (base, **sign– parv–**)			
	SINGULAR	PLURAL	SINGULAR		PLURAL	
Nom.	–um	–a	sig′num	par′vum	sig′na	par′va
Gen.	–ī	–ōrum	sig′nī	par′vī	signō′rum	parvō′rum
Dat.	–ō	–īs	sig′nō	par′vō	sig′nīs	par′vīs
Acc.	–um	–a	sig′num	par′vum	sig′na	par′va
Abl.	–ō	–īs	sig′nō	par′vō	sig′nīs	par′vīs

Note.—(*a*) Neuter nouns and adjectives of all declensions have the
same form in the accusative singular as in the nominative.

77

(*b*) Neuter nouns and adjectives of all declensions end in –ă in the nominative and accusative plural.

(*c*) Neuter nouns (not adjectives) of the second declension ending in –ium usually contract –iī to –ī in the genitive singular: cōnsi'liī becomes cōnsi'lī. The accent is not changed. The –i–, being a part of the base, appears in every form: (dat.) cōnsiliō, etc.

Practice.—(*a*) Decline **frūmentum bonum** and **praemium grātum.**

(*b*) Give in Latin:

(1) *a new standard* in the acc., sing. and plur.

(2) *a famous reward* in the abl., sing. and plur.

(3) *a great plan* in the gen., sing. and plur.

(4) *a small camp* in the dat.

121. **Exercises**

(*a*) 1. Amīcus meus multa praemia merēbit. 2. Cōnsiliō bonō vītam amīcī nostrī servābō. 3. Litterīs virōs barbarōs ad castra ēvocābat. 4. Agricolae frūmentum ex agrīs in castra portābant. 5. Captīvī singulī virīs nostrīs cōnsilium nūntiābant. 6. Castra sociōrum nostrōrum in magnā īnsulā sunt. 7. Fabī, nūntiā signō victōriam amīcīs tuīs.

(*b*) 1. We shall give our friends great rewards. 2. The men were moving the grain with horse and wagon. 3. Our friends saw much grain (*plur.*) in the fields. 4. The colonists will sail from Europe to America.

122. **Vocabulary**

NOUNS

cas'tra, –ō'rum, n., plur., *camp*
  (Lancaster)
cōnsi'lium, cōnsi'lī, n., *plan,*
  advice (counsel)
sig'num, –ī, n., *sign, standard,*
  signal (sign)
frūmen'tum, –ī, n., *grain* (fruit)
prae'mium, prae'mī, n., *re-*
  ward (premium)

ADJECTIVE

bar'barus (m.), –a (f.), –um (n.),
  foreign; as noun, *foreigner, bar-*
  barian (barbarous)

VERB

ē'vocō, ēvocā're, *call out, sum-*
  mon [*vocō*]

78

123. English Word Studies

(*a*) The following are Latin words of the **–um** and **–ium** type preserved in their original form in English:

Singular	Plural	Singular	Plural
bacterium	bacteria	curriculum	curricula (or –ums)
candelabrum	candelabra (or –ums)	spectrum	spectra (or –ums)

(*b*) Latin adjectives and participles used as nouns in English:

Singular	Plural	Singular	Plural
addendum	addenda	memorandum	memoranda
	agenda		(or –ums)
datum	data (remember to	minimum	minima
	say *these* data)		(or –ums)
dictum	dicta (or –ums)	stratum	strata (or –ums)
maximum	maxima (or –ums)		

(*c*) What is a *signatory* to a treaty? Why does **barbarus**, meaning *foreigner*, come to mean *barbarian?* Are all foreigners barbarians? Are we considered barbarians by other nations? Can you give other examples of national prejudice?

(*d*) The Los Angeles telephone directory has ten names under *Troy* and twenty under *Trojan.*

Roman sculpture at Istanbul (formerly Constantinople), Turkey. Surrounded by his court, the Roman emperor Constantine is watching a show. He seems to have washed his face too hard.

Picking grapes while walking on stilts. Can you do it? From a Pompeian wall painting

Dice players in an inn quarreling; in another picture, the innkeeper is chasing them out. From a Pompeian wall painting

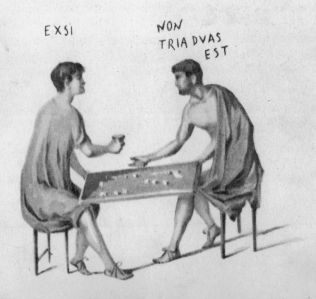

EXSI   NON
TRIA DVAS
EST

124.   Agreement of Adjectives and Nouns

An adjective in Latin must agree with its noun in gender, number, and case. This agreement is shown by endings. In order, therefore, to modify nouns of different genders, every adjective thus far studied has a threefold declension as follows:

magnus, magna, magnum, etc. (For full declension see 573.)

Caution.—Since **nauta** and **agricola** are masculine though belonging to the first declension, an adjective to agree with either must have the second declension forms, as **nauta bonus, nautae bonī,** etc.

Practice.—(*a*) Decline in full **līber** and **novus.**

(*b*) Decline **nūntius sacer, via sacra, bellum sacrum.**

125.   Vocabulary

NOUNS

1. ager	8. cōnsilium	14. lingua	20. puer
2. amīcitia	9. disciplīna	15. magister	21. servus
3. animus	10. equus	16. numerus	22. signum
4. captīvus	11. frūmentum	17. nūntius	23. socius
5. carrus	12. glōria	18. patria	24. vigilia
6. castra	13. grātia	19. praemium	25. vir
7. colōnus			

ADJECTIVES

26. altus	29. līber	32. pūblicus
27. amīcus	30. malus	33. sacer
28. barbarus	31. noster	34. singulī

VERBS

35. augeō	39. habitō	43. mereō	47. teneō
36. doceō	40. labōrō	44. migrō	48. terreō
37. ēvocō	41. līberō	45. moveō	49. videō
38. habeō	42. maneō	46. sum	50. vocō

PREPOSITIONS

51. ā, ab	52. dē	53. ē, ex	54. in

81

126. Vocabulary

NOUNS

1. *field*	8. *plan*	14. *tongue*	20. *boy*
2. *friendship*	9. *training*	15. *teacher*	21. *slave*
3. *mind*	10. *horse*	16. *number*	22. *sign*
4. *prisoner*	11. *grain*	17. *messenger*	23. *comrade*
5. *cart, wagon*	12. *glory*	18. *fatherland*	24. *watchfulness*
6. *camp*	13. *gratitude*	19. *reward*	25. *man*
7. *settler*			

ADJECTIVES

26. *high, deep*	29. *free*	32. *public*
27. *friendly*	30. *bad*	33. *sacred*
28. *foreign*	31. *our*	34. *one at a time*

VERBS

35. *increase*	39. *live*	43. *deserve*	47. *hold*
36. *teach*	40. *work*	44. *depart*	48. *scare*
37. *call out*	41. *free*	45. *move*	49. *see*
38. *have*	42. *remain*	46. *be*	50. *call*

PREPOSITIONS

51. *from*	52. *from, about*	53. *out of, from*	54. *in, on; into*

127. English Word Studies

1. Give and define three English nouns which retain Latin nominative forms, singular and plural, of the first declension; three of the second declension, masculine; three of the second declension, neuter.

2. Give prefix and Latin root word from which the following are derived, and define:

defame, approve, advocate, invocation, immigrant, emigrant, avocation, vocation, deter

3. Choose the word in parentheses which in your opinion most nearly gives the meaning of the underlined word. Tell why you select it.

(*a*) amicable relations (friendly, social, free, hostile)

(*b*) a <u>puerile</u> act (poor, childish, manly, effeminate)

(*c*) a <u>docile</u> creature (wild, untamed, stubborn, easily taught)

(*d*) an animal's <u>habitat</u> (habit, appearance, living place, color)

(*e*) a <u>migratory</u> bird (singing, wandering, tame, nocturnal)

128.   Verbs

Conjugate in full, with meanings, (*a*) **migrō** in the present, (*b*) **maneō** in the imperfect, (*c*) **doceō** in the future.

129.   Rapid-Fire Drill

(1) *What forms are:* tenent, socī, vigiliīs, nūntiī, docēbitis, nūntī, habēbis, habitāre, amīce?

(2) *Translate:* he increases, they have, we live, he was teaching, I shall remain, they are calling, you (*sing.*) deserve, you (*plur.*) will see, call out (*sing.*), remain (*plur.*).

130.   Sentences

(*a*) Choose the right words in the parentheses to complete the sentences correctly. Give your reason for each choice and translate.
1. Agricola (agrōs, agrī) habet. 2. Agrī sunt (magnī, magnōs). 3. Agricolae (in agrōs, in agrīs) labōrant. 4. In īnsulā (multī colōnī, multōs colōnōs) vidēbō. 5. In patriā nostrā (multās agricolās, multōs agricolās) habēmus.

(*b*) There is one word wrong in each of the following sentences. Correct it and then translate.
1. Servus, portā aquam. 2. Amīcī meī sunt multī et vērōs. 3. Agricola est bona. 4. Colōnī multōs servōs habēbat.

Italian stamp in honor of the two thousandth anniversary (1930) of the poet Virgil's birth, with a quotation from Virgil about farmers

131.   BELLUM ET VICTŌRIA

Colōnī equīs et carrīs frūmentum ad castra portābant. Sociīs arma et frūmentum dōnāre parābant. Virī pugnāre et augēre numerum captīvōrum barbarōrum mātūrābant. Cōpiae sociōrum multōs agrōs vāstābant et colōnīs praedam multam dōnābant. Sociōs ob[1] auxilium et cōnsilium laudāre mātūrant: "Sociī bonī, 5

Virī pugnāre maturabant et signa portabant.

semper amīcī erimus. Auxilium et signa amīcitiae vestrae[2] grāta sunt. Magna est concordia nostra in bellō. Concordia nostra barbarōs terrēbit. Patriam nostram 10 līberāre dēbēmus."

Novum erat multōs nūntiōs, equōs, et carrōs in viīs vidēre. Longum erat bellum, sed magnae erant victōriae cōpiārum. 15 Patria victōriās memoriā tenēre dēbet.

Thought Questions.—1. How did the allies aid the colonists? 2. Where were messengers seen? 3. What made up for the length of the war?

132.   Imperfect and Future of *Sum*

Review the present tense of the verb **sum** (114). The imperfect and future tenses of **sum** are likewise irregular in their habits:

---

[1] *on account of*   [2] *your.*

e'ram, *I was*   erā'mus, *we were*
e'rās, *you were*   erā'tis, *you were*
e'rat, *he, she, it was*   e'rant, *they were*

FUTURE

e'rō, *I shall be*   e'rimus, *we shall be*
e'ris, *you will be*   e'ritis, *you will be*
e'rit, *he, she, it will be*   e'runt, *they will be*

Caution.—Do not say *You was*.

133.   Infinitive Used as Subject

(*a*) The infinitive is a verbal noun, and as such it may be used as the subject of a verb; as

    Amīcōs habēre grātum est, *To have friends is pleasing.*
    (Cf. **Errāre hūmānum est,** *To err is human.*)

Note.—Though the infinitive is a noun, it is not declined. It is in the neuter gender. Therefore the predicate adjective must also be neuter, as **grātum** in the example above.

(*b*) The infinitive may be used as a predicate nominative; as

    Vidēre est crēdere, *To see is to believe.*

134.   Infinitive Used as Object

With many verbs the infinitive may be used as direct object, like other nouns; as

    Servōs līberāre parat, *He prepares to free the slaves.*

Note.—This is sometimes called the **complementary infinitive** because in a sense it *completes* the meaning of the main verb.

135. **Exercises**

(*a*) 1. Magnum numerum equōrum in agrīs vidēre grātum erat.
2. Pecūniam habēre est multās cūrās habēre. 3. Puerō praemium
nostrum mōnstrāre mātūrāmus. 4. Nūntiī praemiīs animōs nautārum incitāre parābant. 5. Cōpiae signa et arma ad terram novam
portāre mātūrant. 6. Amīcī nostrī frūmentum habēre dēbent.
7. Bonum erit concordiam et auxilium in bellō habēre.

(*b*) Complete the following in Latin: 1. Es (*my friend*). 2. Erunt
(*our friends*). 3. Erāmus (*comrades*). 4. Erit (*a farmer*). 5. Erat (*a
sailor*).

(*c*) 1. It was pleasing to see the courage and harmony of the
colonists. 2. Slaves, hasten to increase the supply of grain. 3. The
messenger ought to report the plan of war to the men. 4. It is
bad to owe money.

136. **Vocabulary**

NOUNS

ar'ma, –ō'rum, n., plur., *arms,*
  weapons   (armor)
auxi'lium, auxi'lī, n., *aid;* plur.,
  reinforcements   (auxiliary)
bel'lum, –ī, n., *war*
           (belligerent)

concor'dia, –ae, f., *harmony*
           (concord)

VERBS

dē'beō, dēbē're, *owe, ought* (debt)
mātū'rō, mātūrā're, *hasten*
           (maturity)

137. **English Word Studies**

(*a*) What is meant by large *armaments?* Why is a person called
bellicose? What is an *auxiliary* engine on a sailing ship? Five organizations listed in the Chicago telephone directory are called
Concordia; can you guess why? Do you know any by that name?

(*b*)   **Latin Phrases in English**

de novo *anew,* literally, *from a new* (start).
multum in parvo, *much in little.*
in memoriam, *to the memory* (of)—the title of a poem by Tennyson.

Spartacus, captivus Romanorum

LESSON XIX

138. **SPARTACUS**

Spartacus erat clārus servus, captīvus* Rōmānōrum. Sociōs
ēvocat et ad bellum incitat: "Ō sociī, Rōmānī nōn sunt aequī.
Puer eram in oppidō meō, et vīta grāta semper erat. Magna erat
concordia in patriā nostrā. Populus aequus erat. Silvās et agrōs
semper amābam; līber eram. Vērum amīcum habēbam, puerum 5
bonum et grātum. Sed Rōmānī patriam meam vāstant; mē et
amīcum meum ex patriā portant. Nunc post[1] multōs annōs vir sum
et in arēnā pugnō. Hodiē[2] in hōc[3] oppidō virum occīdī[4]—et erat
amīcus meus! Estisne virī? Populum Rōmānum nōn amātis.
Iniūriās nōn merēmus. Nōnne nunc hōra est? Ad arma! Pugnāte! 10
Vocāte sociōs ad auxilium! Servōs līberābimus et ad patriam
migrāre mātūrābimus."

Thought Questions.—1. What happened to Spartacus and his boy-
hood friend? 2. How did the friend die?

Read Showerman, pp. 72–73; Guerber (*Story*), pp. 167–170; Tappan,
pp. 139–140. If you want to read an interesting novel about Spartacus,
read *The Gladiators*, by Arthur Koestler (New York, Macmillan, 1939).

---

[1] *after*   [2] *today.*   [3] *this.*   [4] *I killed.*

In Latin a question is regularly introduced by an interrogative word—either a pronoun (**quis,** *who?* **quid,** *what?*) or adverb (**ubi,** *where?* etc.), or the particle –**ne.** The latter is therefore a kind of question mark at the beginning of a sentence and cannot be translated. It is never used alone but is always attached to the first word in the sentence. Such attached words are called **enclitics.** As the enclitic becomes part of the preceding word, the word accent may shift: **īnsulam'ne.**[1]

When **nōn** is used in a question, it is put first and the enclitic –**ne** is attached to it.

140.   Conversation: A Geography Lesson

M. = **Magister,** *teacher*   **D.** = **Discipulī,** *pupils*

M. Spectāte, discipulī. **D.** Spectāmus, magister.

M. Ubi est Italia? **D.** In Eurōpā Italia est.

M. Estne Italia lāta? **D.** Italia longa sed nōn lāta est.

M. Īnsulamne vidētis? **D.** Corsicam vidēmus.

5 **M.** Estne Corsica magna īnsula? **D.** Parva, nōn magna īnsula est Corsica.

M. Quid in Siciliā vidētis? **D.** Aetnam vidēmus.

M. Magnam īnsulam mōnstrō; Britannia est. Colōnī ex Britanniā ad Americam migrābant.

10 **M.** Eratne Gallia prōvincia? **D.** Gallia erat prōvincia imperī[2] Rōmānī.

M. Nōnne magna erat glōria Galliae? **D.** Magna erat glōria Galliae.

✓ **M.** Discipulī, quis oculōs bonōs habet? **Lūcius.** Ego.[3]

15 **M.** Mōnstrā discipulīs Rōmam. **Lūcius.** Rōma in Italiā est.

Note.—Ask questions and make statements similar to the above, using the map on page 260 or a large wall map.

---

[1] There was a tendency to avoid attaching an enclitic to a word ending in a short vowel and having a short penult. Thus **Corsi'cane** would not be used but the enclitic would be attached to some other word in the sentence.

[2] *Empire.*   [3] *I.*

Questions to Be Answered in Latin.—1. Eurōpane est in Italiā? 2. Estne Italia īnsula? 3. Ubi est Rōma? 4. Estne Italia prōvincia?

141.   Vocabulary

ae′quus, −a, −um, *even, just, calm*   (equality)
op′pidum, −ī, n., *town*
po′pulus, −ī, m., *people*   (popular)
sem′per, adv., *always*   (sempiternal)

142.   English Word Studies

(*a*) What is *popular* government? Use *depopulate* in a sentence. What is meant by the sentence: "I listened to his attacks with *equanimity*"? Give three more derivatives of **aequus**.

(*b*) Give ten derivatives of **nūntiō, portō, probō, spectō,** and **vocō** found by attaching one of the prefixes **ad−, dē−, ex−,** or **in−**.

The Bank of England, "the old lady of Threadneedle Street," in a
Roman dress

Nomen oppidi Chicago est. The Museum of Science and Industry in
classic garb

LESSON XX

143. ### VIRGINIA ET VĒRA

Virginia et Vēra sunt duae puellae quae[1] in oppidō nostrō
vītam grātam agunt. Estne oppidum in Eurōpā? In Eurōpā nōn
est; in Americā est, et puellae Americānae sunt. Nōmen oppidī
"Chicago" est. Agisne vītam grātam in tuō oppidō?

5 Virginia ad Vēram accēdit: "Multī virī oppidum nostrum
accūsant. Nōn aequum est. Nōnne oppidum et populum dēfendere dēbēmus? Nōnne in hōc[2] animum nostrum pōnere dēbēmus?" Vēra respondet: "Quī[3] videt oppidum nostrum id[4]
semper dēfendit et laudat. Quī[3] accēdit inimīcus[5] excēdit amīcus "

10 Quot[6] litterās nōmen "Virginia" habet? Nōmen "Virginia"
octō litterās habet; nōmen "Vēra" quattuor habet. Littera prīma
ambōrum[7] "V" est; littera ultima "a" est. Nōmen "Virginia"
longum est; nōmen "Vēra" nōn longum est. Puella Virginia
parva est; Vēra magna est, sed Vēra semper Virginiae cēdit.

15 Cēdisne amīcō tuō? Puella parva habet nōmen magnum; puella
magna habet nōmen parvum. Estne aequum nōmen "Alta" in
puellā nōn altā pōnere? Estne Clāra clāra?

Thought Questions.—1. What does Virginia think that she and Vera
should do? 2. Which of the girls more often has her way?

---

[1] *who.*   [2] *on this.*   [3] *he who.*   [4] *it.*   [5] *unfriendly.*   [6] *how many.*   [7] *both.*

90

144.   Third Conjugation

(*a*) Verbs of the **third conjugation** have the stem vowel –ĕ–. Note the difference of stem vowel in:

1*st Conj.* (*Long-A Verbs*): Pres. stem **portā–** (from infin. **portāre**)
2*d Conj.* (*Long-E Verbs*): Pres. stem **docē–** (from infin. **docēre**)
3*d Conj.* (*Short-E Verbs*): Pres. stem **pōnĕ–** (from infin. **pōnĕre**)

(*b*) The short vowel –e– of the third conjugation changes to –i– in forming the present tense, except in the third person plural, where it becomes –u–. In the first person singular it disappears before –ō–. Short –e– is lengthened in the imperfect tense.

PRESENT	(*I place*, etc.)
pō′nō	pō′nimus
pō′nis	pō′nitis
pō′nit	pō′nunt

For the full conjugation of the imperfect (**pōnēbam**, etc., *I was placing*, etc.) see **586.**

Conundrum.—How is the present tense of the third conjugation like a conceited person? (Answer: *I* predominates, *u* (*you*) is there but comes last.)

(*c*) The short stem vowel –e– in third conjugation verbs changes to short –i– before –te in forming the plural imperative: sing., **accēde**; plur., **accēdite**, *approach.*

Practice.—(*a*) Conjugate **agō** and **dēfendō** in the present and imperfect tenses.

(*b*) Form the present imperative, singular and plural, of the above verbs, and of **vocō** and **videō**.

(*c*) Give the Latin for *he departs, he moves, he hastens, we are defending, you* (plur.) *approach.*

145.   Exercises

(*a*) 1. Semper, puerī, agite vītam bonam. 2. Colōnī ex agrīs in oppida excēdēbant. 3. Equōsne tuōs, Cornēlī, in aquam agis? 4. Ubi praedam pōnitis? In viā praedam pōnimus. 5. Agricolae

91

ad oppidum nostrum nōn accēdunt. 6. Ad īnsulam cēdēbāmus et castra dēfendere parābāmus.

(b) 1. He was living a good life. 2. The slave is-getting-ready to put the grain into the wagon. 3. Ought we not to increase the number of farmers in the fields? 4. Is he not living a long life?

146.   Vocabulary

a'gō, a'gere, *drive, do, discuss, live* or *spend* (time)   (agent)
cē'dō, cē'dere, *move, retreat, yield*   (accede)
  accē'dō, accē'dere, *approach* (w. **ad**)
  excē'dō, excē'dere, *depart*
dēfen'dō, dēfen'dere, *defend*   (defendant)
pō'nō, pō'nere, *put, place*   (postpone)

147.   English Word Studies

We have seen that many English nouns and adjectives have

The Shedd Aquarium in Chicago is in the Doric style.

preserved their original Latin forms. A great many more have preserved the base of the Latin word. Others again consist of the Latin base plus silent –**e**. The following are examples:

base: *form, public, sign;* base plus –**e**: *cause, fortune, fame, cure*

The same rule is illustrated in the following words in which changes in the base have taken place:

base: *letter* (**littera**), *number* (**numerus**), *car* (**carrus**), *clear* (**clārus**); base plus –**e**: *single* (**singulī**)

Give five other examples of this rule from nouns and adjectives already studied.

Alba Domus. The White House at Washington with its Ionic columns

LESSON XXI

148. VIR QUĪ PATRIAM REGIT

Estne aequus vir quī[1] patriam nostram regit? Officium virī quī populum regit est patriam semper cōnsiliō et armīs dēfendere et servāre, in bellō virōs ad pugnam ēvocāre. Magnam concordiam in patriā habēre dēbēmus. Bonīs virīs patriam, magnam nostram cūram, mandāre dēbēmus. Bonōs virōs probāmus, 5 malōs accūsāmus. Vir quī populum regit semper labōrat; vītam dūram agit. Multī virī ad eum[2] accēdunt et litterās mittunt. Labōrāsne semper et vītam dūram agis?

Vir quī patriam regit in albā domō[3] habitat. In quō[4] oppidō habitat? Semperne ibi manet? Quattuor aut octō aut duodecim 10 annōs ibi manet. Tum excēdit et alium virum ad Albam Domum mittimus. Vidēbisne Albam Domum? Multī puerī et puellae eam[5] spectant. Ūnus ex puerīs[6] fortasse[7] erit vir quī in Albā Domō habitābit. Fortasse tū[8] eris ille[9] vir! Exspectāsne hoc[10]? Sī[11] labōrābis, fortasse hoc[10] praemium, officium nōn parvum, me- 15 rēbis. Disciplīnā, pretiō fāmae, parā regere patriam. Patria exspectat.

Thought Questions.—1. What is the President's duty? 2. Who sees the White House?

---

[1] who. [2] him. [3] white house. [4] what. [5] it. [6] one of the boys.
[7] perhaps. [8] you. [9] that. [10] this. [11] if.

93

1. **Multī virī, amīcī familiae meae, in oppidō sunt,** *Many men, friends of my family, are in the town.*

2. **Nautīs, amīcīs nostrīs, pecūniam dōnāmus,** *We give money to the sailors, our friends.*

Observe that **amīcī** (1) describes the subject **virī** and stands in direct relation to it and is therefore in the nominative while **amīcīs** (2) describes **nautīs,** the indirect object, and is therefore in the dative. No verb is involved. This construction is called **apposition.** A noun in apposition with another noun (or pronoun) is in the same case.

Practice.—(*a*) Give the Latin for the words in italics: I saw John, my *friend.* Have you heard the story of Spartacus, the *slave?* We lived in Australia, a large *island.* I told it to Mr. Jones, *my teacher.*

(*b*) Decline **officium nostrum** and **populus aequus.**

(*c*) Conjugate **exspectō** and **mittō** in the present and imperfect tenses.

The Capitol at Washington—Roman in its Corinthian columns and its dome

150. **Exercises**

(*a*) 1. Mārcus, agricola Rōmānus, in agrīs nunc nōn labōrat. 2. In Americā, patriā nostrā, semper habitābimus. 3. Vir aequus, amīcus puerōrum et puellārum, populum patriae nostrae regit. 4. Patriam dēfendere est officium virōrum. 5. Agricolae ad oppidum cēdunt et nūntium exspectant. 6. Mittite auxilia ad Rōmānōs, sociōs nostrōs.

(*b*) 1. Did the boys see our friend, the sailor? 2. It is the duty of the prisoner, a public slave, to drive the horses. 3. Are you sending aid to our allies, the Roman people? 4. Our friends, the sailors, were departing.

Italian stamp in honor of Virgil (cf. p. 83), with a quotation from the Aeneid, his greatest poem

151. **Vocabulary**

exspec′tō, exspectā′re, *look out for,* *await*	[*spectō*]
mit′tō, mit′tere, *let go, send*	(admittance)
offi′cium, offi′cī, n., *duty*	(office)
re′gō, re′gere, *guide, rule*	(regent)

152. **English Word Studies**

(*a*) Many English verbs preserve the Latin base with or without silent –e: (*a*) *cede, evoke;* (*b*) *defend, laud.*

Give five other examples of this rule from verbs that you have studied.

(*b*) Show how *admit* and *emit* get their meanings from **mittō;** then use them in English sentences. Explain by derivation: *demote, deter, invocation, equity.* Give three derivatives of **cēdō.**

Roma magna et pulchra est. The ruins of the imperial fora

LESSON XXII

153. ROMĀNĪ

Quondam[1] Rōma, oppidum Italiae, parvum erat. Rōmānī, populus firmus, oppidum mūniēbant quod arma capere et patriam dēfendere parābant. Victōriīs magnīs patriam servābant et augēbant. Magna praemia Rōmānī accipiēbant, quod officium faciē-
5 bant. Magnum numerum colōnōrum in aliās terrās mittēbant. Multās terrās barbarās capiēbant, prōvinciās faciēbant et aequē[2] regēbant. Barbarī linguam Latīnam accipiunt. Rōmānī frūmentum ex aliīs terrīs in Italiam portābant. Ad Britanniam, Hispāniam, Āfricam, Graeciam, Asiam nāvigābant et oppida mūniēbant.
10 Nunc Rōma magna et pulchra est. Multī Americānī ad Italiam veniunt et viās pulchrās et templa inveniunt. Mātūrābisne in Italiam venīre et ruīnās[3] Rōmānās invenīre?

Thought Questions.—1. Why were the Romans rewarded? 2. What do visitors to Italy see?

Read Guerber (*Story*), pp. 11–13; Harding, pp. 7–12.

---

[1] *once.* [2] *justly.* [3] Use the English derivative.

154. Third Conjugation: Verbs in -iō

In certain forms of a few important verbs of the third conjugation, –i– is inserted before the stem vowel. This occurs in the first person singular of the present tense (which explains the term "–iō verbs") and the third person plural. It occurs throughout the imperfect tense, with lengthening of the stem vowel. Compare the following model of an –iō verb with **pōnō** (**144,** *b*):

PRESENT	(*I take*, etc.)
ca'piō	ca'pimus
ca'pis	ca'pitis
ca'pit	ca'piunt

Note.—(*a*) The imperfect is **capiēbam**, etc.

(*b*) The imperative is like that of other verbs of the third conjugation: **cape, capite.** (The imperative singular of **faciō** is **fac.**)

155. Fourth Conjugation

Most verbs ending in –iō belong to the **fourth conjugation** and are distinguished by the stem vowel –ī–.

Verbs of the fourth conjugation are called Long-I Verbs, because they retain long –i– throughout their conjugation except where long vowels are regularly shortened (**23,** *a*). Note by contrast that –iō verbs of the third conjugation have short –i– throughout.

PRESENT	(*I fortify*, etc.)
mū'niō	mūnī'mus
mū'nīs	mūnī'tis
mū'nit	mū'niunt

Note.—(*a*) The imperfect is **mūniēbam**, etc.

(*b*) The imperative is **mūnī, mūnīte.**

Practice.—Conjugate and give all possible meanings of the present and imperfect tenses of **accēdō, inveniō, faciō.**

156. Exercises

(*a*) 1. Ubi estis, puerī et puellae? Venīmus, magister.
2. Nōnne aequum est semper amīcōs dēfendere? 3. In agrīs
frūmentum, magnum auxilium, invenīmus. 4. Castra mūniēbant
et virōs ēvocābant, quod pugnāre parābant. 5. In oppidō equōs
inveniunt et multam praedam capiunt. 6. Virī magna praemia
accipiunt, quod officium faciunt.

(*b*) 1. We were fortifying the camp. 2. It is pleasing to find
money. 3. We do not find Marcus, the son of our friend.
4. Marcus is not receiving a reward because he was a bad boy.

157. Vocabulary

ca'piō, ca'pere, *take, seize*   [*captīvus*]
   acci'piō, acci'pere, *receive*
fa'ciō, fa'cere, *do, make*   (efficient)
mū'niō, mūnī're, *fortify*   (munitions)
quod, conj., *because*
ve'niō, venī're, *come*   (convene)
   inve'niō, invenī're, *come upon, find*

158. Latin and English Word Formation: Vowel Changes

When a Latin word is compounded with a prefix, short –a–
or short –e– in the root is usually "weakened" to short –i–
before a single consonant except –r–. The English derivatives
show the same change. Long vowels are not affected; for example:

From **agō**, Latin **ex-igō, ab-igō, red-igō**, etc.; English *exigency*, etc.
From **habeō**, Latin **pro-hibeō, ex-hibeō**, etc.; English *prohibit*, *ex-hibit*, etc.
From **teneō**, Latin **con-tineō, re-tineō**, etc.; English *continent*, *retinue*, etc.

Illustrate the rule further by compounding **capiō** and **faciō**
with **ad–, dē–, ex–,** and **in–.** Give English derivatives of these
compounds in further illustration of the rule.

Ad locum altum. A Roman temple in Baalbek, Syria (see p. 56)

LESSON XXIII

159. **AMĪCITIA**

Mārcus, amīcus meus, fīlius est vīcīnī[1] nostrī. Nōn in oppidō sed in agrīs habitāmus.

Mārcus praemium accipit: equum et carrum. Carrus parvus est et pretium carrī nōn magnum erat. Prīmō[2] equus carrum dūcere nōn vult.[3] Sed Mārcus equum docet, et disciplīna multum efficit. 5 Nunc equus carrum dūcit. Mārcus māteriam in carrō pōnit. Prīmō[2] in viā plānā, tum ad locum altum, terminum agrōrum, equum agere mātūrat. In eō[4] locō puer malus dē viā nōn cēdit et equum terret et ego[5] ex carrō paene[6] cadō. Sed Mārcus equum tenet et mē[7] servat. Ad terminum vītae meae nōn veniō. Nōnne 10 Mārcō grātus esse dēbeō et praemium dōnāre? Pretium parvum erit. Perīculum amīcōs firmōs efficit.

Thought Questions.—1. Why did the wagon cost little? 2. Why is the speaker grateful to Marcus?

---

[1] *neighbor.* [2] *at first.* [3] *does not want.* [4] *that.*
[5] *I.* [6] *almost.* [7] Accusative of **ego.**

160. Word Order

We have observed that the words in a Latin sentence show their connection with one another by means of endings, regardless of position (unlike English). They may therefore be shifted rather freely without obscuring the relationship. The normal order is:

SUBJECT

NOUN—*adjective* (*genitive, appositive*)

PREDICATE

ablative—indir. obj.—dir. obj.—*adverb*—VERB

(*a*) **Remember,** therefore, that the normal order of words is as follows:

1. Adjectives usually follow their nouns, but adjectives of quantity and size precede: **virī bonī; multī virī.**

2. Possessive adjectives (**meus, tuus,** etc.) follow their nouns, unless emphatic.

3. A genitive follows its noun.

4. An indirect object stands before a direct object.

5. A word used to ask a question usually stands first, as in English.

6. The verb stands last. Forms of the linking verb are often placed in the middle of a sentence, as in English.

7. For **nōnne,** see 139.

(*b*) But this normal order is far less regular in Latin than the normal order is in English. The shifted order serves to bring out varying shades of emphasis. This is done also in English, though to a less extent, largely in imitation of the Latin. Emphasis is gained particularly by:

1. Putting the emphatic words *first* in the sentence.

2. *Separating* the emphatic word from the word to which it belongs.

The former is common in English: *Great is the glory of the Lord!*

100

161. Exercises

(*a*) 1. Ad locum altum veniunt et magnam silvam vident.
2. Ad terram sociōrum cōpiās dūcēbāmus. 3. Multōs equōs habēre dēbēmus, sed magnum est pretium. 4. Magister tuus concordiam nōn efficit, quod puerī sunt malī. 5. Vocā, Mārce, virōs ad arma et mūnī loca plāna.
6. Ubi est terminus agrōrum Mārcī, amīcī nostrī?

A floor mosaic, made of colored bits of stone, from Pompeii

(*b*) 1. The price of instruction is small, but the rewards are great. 2. Great is the fame of our teacher. 3. We are coming to the boundaries of our fields. 4. They are hastening to lead the horses to water.

162. Vocabulary

dū′cō, dū′cere,[1] *lead, draw*	(reduce)
effi′ciō, effi′cere, *make (out), bring about*	[*faciō*]
lo′cus, -ī, m., *place;* plur., lo′ca, n.[2]	(local)
pre′tium, pre′tī, n., *price*	(precious)
ter′minus, -ī, m., *end, boundary*	(terminal)

163. English Word Studies

(*a*) Explain by derivation: *location, efficiency, terminate, invention.*

(*b*)   **Latin Phrases in English**

ad astra per aspera, *to the stars through difficulties* (motto of the state of Kansas).

ad infinitum, *to infinity, i.e.* without limit.

ex animo, *from the heart* (sincerely).

Experientia docet, *Experience teaches.*

---

[1] The imperative singular is dūc.
[2] When used in this original sense, **locus** changes gender in the plural.

Via in oppido. Street with shops in Herculaneum today

Puella accipit. A Roman wineshop as it may have been

164.   English and Latin Word Studies

1. Give prefix and Latin root word from which the following are derived: **excipiō, adigō, ērigō, afficiō;** *allocation, depopulate, exigency, efficient.*

2. Make Latin words out of **ad–** and **capiō, in–** and **pōnō, ad–** and **teneō, dē–** and **mereō.**

3. The first word in each of the following lines is a Latin word. From among the last four words in each line pick the one which is an English derivative of the first word:

pōnō	pone	pony	exponent	put
mittēmus	mitten	mitto	send	remit
populus	poplar	population	pope	pop
capit	cap	cape	decapitate	recipient
dūcō	conduct	paint	duck	deuce
aequum	equestrian	equine	equity	equip

165.   Vocabulary

NOUNS

1. arma
2. auxilium
3. bellum
4. concordia
5. locus
6. officium
7. oppidum
8. populus
9. pretium
10. terminus

ADJECTIVE

11. aequus

VERBS

12. accēdō	16. cēdō	20. efficiō	24. inveniō	28. pōnō
13. accipiō	17. dēbeō	21. excēdō	25. mātūrō	29. regō
14. agō	18. dēfendō	22. exspectō	26. mittō	30. veniō
15. capiō	19. dūcō	23. faciō	27. mūniō	

ADVERB

31. semper

CONJUNCTION

32. quod

Vocabulary

Nouns

1. *arms*
2. *aid*
3. *war*
4. *harmony*
5. *place*
6. *duty*
7. *town*
8. *people*
9. *price*
10. *end*

Adjective

11. *even, just*

Verbs

12. *approach*
13. *receive*
14. *drive, do*
15. *take*
16. *move, yield*
17. *owe, ought*
18. *defend*
19. *lead*
20. *bring about*
21. *depart*
22. *await*
23. *do, make*
24. *come upon*
25. *hasten*
26. *send*
27. *fortify*
28. *put*
29. *rule*
30. *come*

Adverb

31. *always*

Conjunction

32. *because*

The baths of Caracalla, Rome, as they once were. See page 114.

167. Nouns and Adjectives

(a) Decline **multum auxilium, populus clārus, concordia vēra.**

(b) Give in Latin the singular and plural of the following in the case required:

my duty (nom.)
a good place (dat.)
a small price (acc.)
a sacred land (gen.)
our friend (abl.)
a just man (nom.)

A wall painting in Pompeii

168   Verbs

(a) Decide which form of **sum** translates the English in the first column:

they were	erāmus	sunt	erant	sumus
you will be	erās	eris	estis	erātis
you are	eris	erāmus	erātis	es
he was	erant	erat	erit	erāmus
we are	erāmus	sumus	estis	erimus
they will be	erunt	erant	erit	sunt
we were	erant	erimus	sumus	erāmus

(b) Give the third plural of the following verbs in the present, imperfect, and future: **sum, exspectō, dēbeō, mittō, efficiō, veniō.**

(c) I. *Give tense, person, and number, and translate:* regunt, pōnit, erunt, mātūrātis, mittēbat, erās, faciēbās, es, exspectābimus, eris, dūcēbant, invenīmus, veniunt, accēdit, laudābunt.

II. *Give in Latin:* he will be; I was fortifying; they were approaching; you (*sing.*) await; we were; they do; they received; you (*plur.*) did come; we shall be; they will hasten; they will be; he leads; we are defending; he was departing; he takes.

Roman children's tunics from Egypt, now in the Royal Ontario Museum, Toronto

GLIMPSES OF ROMAN LIFE

169.   Dress

The most obvious difference between ancient and modern clothing was that civilized men did not in the old days wear trousers. These garments were worn only by barbarians. After the barbarians destroyed the Roman Empire, their garb became the fashion for all Europe. The same is true of the mustache (without beard). No Roman ever wore one, and it was just as much the mark of the barbarian as trousers were. Down to the second century A.D. most Romans were smooth shaven.

All Roman men wore as an outer garment a long shirt called a tunic, made of white wool. Senators and knights had crimson stripes down the front and back. A belt was worn over this, and the upper part was bloused out over the belt. When a Roman was engaged in some active occupation, he pulled his tunic up to his knees. Such a garment alone was worn in the house.

Over the tunic the Roman citizen might wear the toga. This garment was the official dress of Roman citizens, and only citizens were allowed to wear it. It was made of white wool. The toga worn by boys and magistrates had a crimson border. When boys grew up, they changed to the plain white toga. Important citizens always wore this garment when appearing in public, but the ordinary Roman wore it much less frequently.

The toga was really a sort of blanket which was thrown over the left shoulder, pulled across the back and under the right arm, and again thrown over the left shoulder. It was not fastened in any way, and it must have been quite a trick to learn to wear it.

Roman women also wore a tunic. Over this the married women wore a **stola,** a long dress with a flounce at the bottom. For street wear a shawl, called a **palla,** was used.

Wool was the chief material for clothing; next came linen. Silk was rare and expensive, while cotton was almost unknown.

In the house men and women wore sandals or slippers; outdoors they wore shoes. Those of magistrates were red. No stockings were worn, though in cold weather old and sickly people sometimes wound cloth around their legs, like the puttees of soldiers.

Hats were rarely worn, except on journeys. Such as there were had broad brims and were flat. Women often wore ribbons and elaborate pins in their hair. Styles in hairdressing changed constantly as with us, but bobbed hair was unknown among adult women.

A Roman lady using nature's mirror—a garden pool. From a modern painting

Questions for Discussion. — 1. What was the distinctive garment of Roman men? Of women? 2. When did the Romans begin to wear mustaches and trousers?

Read Showerman, pp. 56–64; McDaniel, pp. 81–93; Johnston, chap. VII; Mills, pp. 309–312.

Pluto Proserpinam ad inferos ducit. Drawn by Willy Pogany

LESSON XXIV

170. CERĒS ET PRŌSERPINA

Cerēs, dea frūmentī, et fīlia Prōserpina[1] in Siciliā habitābant. Quondam[2] Prōserpina et aliae puellae in agrīs erant. Locum commodum inveniunt et flōrēs[3] variōs legunt. Ōtium grātum est; magnum erat studium puellārum.

5 Plūtō, deus īnferōrum,[4] Prōserpinam videt et amat. Equōs incitat et ad locum accēdit ubi puellae sunt. Puellae fugiunt. Prōserpina fugere mātūrat, sed Plūtō valet et eam[5] capit, in carrō pōnit, ad īnferōs dūcit.

Cerēs nocte[6] ex agrīs venit. Fīliam exspectat, sed Prōserpina 10 nōn venit. Magna est cūra deae. Ad multa loca, ad terminōs terrae Cerēs accēdit. Ōtium nōn invenit.

Quod Cerēs Prōserpinam nōn invenit, in agrīs nōn labōrat.

---

[1] *Proser'pina.* [2] *once.* [3] *flowers.* [4] *those below, i.e.* the shades in Hades.
[5] *her.* [6] *at night.*

Flōrēs nōn sunt, frūmentum in agrīs nōn est. Populus vītam dūram agit et deam accūsat quod pretium frūmentī magnum est. Multī agricolae dīcunt:

"Quid[1] agēmus? In agrīs labōrāmus sed frūmentum nōn habēmus. Deī nōn aequī sunt; officium nōn faciunt."

Iuppiter, quī deōs et virōs regit, iniūriās populī videt et deae agrōrum nūntiat:

"Prōserpina valet sed Plūtō eam habet. Mercurium nūntium ad īnferōs mittam. Mercurius fīliam tuam ad tē[2] dūcet. Sed nōn semper in terrā Prōserpina manēbit. Ita commodum erit: partem[3] annī in terrā, partem sub terrā aget."

Ita Iuppiter concordiam efficit. Cerēs fīliam accipit. Prōserpina partem annī in terrā, partem sub terrā agit. Cum[4] lībera in terrā est, multōs flōrēs et magnam cōpiam frūmentī. vidēmus, quod Cerēs grāta in agrīs est et magnum est studium deae. Sed cum Prōserpina ad īnferōs excēdit, Cerēs trīstis[5] est, et flōrēs variī nōn sunt.

Thought Questions.—1. What was Proserpina doing when Pluto came? 2. What happened to the flowers after Proserpina left? 3. On what terms did Proserpina go back to her mother?

Read Sabin, pp. 43–47; Guerber, pp. 183–187, 194–195; Bulfinch, pp. 58–64; Harding (*Greek Gods*), pp. 48–51; Baker, pp. 127–136.

171.   Third Conjugation: Future

The future sign of verbs of the first and second conjugations is –bi– (53). The future sign of verbs of the third and fourth conjugations, however, is –ē–. The –ō verbs of the third conjugation, in forming the future, substitute –ē– for the stem vowel –ĕ–, except in the first singular (–am).[6]

pō′nam, *I shall place*	pōnē′mus, *we shall place*
pō′nēs, *you will place*	pōnē′tis, *you will place*
pō′net, *he will place*	pō′nent, *they will place*

---

[1] *what.*   [2] *you.*   [3] Accusative singular of **pars**.   [4] *whenever.*   [5] *sad.*
[6] The third singular and plural have –ĕ–, according to rule (23, *a*).

Practice.—(*a*) Give the present of **mittō**, the imperfect of **cēdō**, and the future of **dēfendō**.

(*b*) Tell the form of **fugit, valēbis, efficit, dūcēmus, docēmus, accipitis, mūniunt, migrābat, agent.**

172. Exercises

(*a*) 1. Valēsne, fīlia mea? Valeō. 2. Puerī bonī magnam fāmam ex studiīs accipiunt. 3. Multās hōrās in ōtiō nōn agēmus sed semper labōrābimus. 4. Puerī nōn excēdent sed puellās dēfendent. 5. Cōpiae nostrae ē castrīs nōn fugiunt. 6. Litterās ad Mārcum, amīcum meum, mittam.

(*b*) 1. Did the girls remain in a suitable place? 2. We shall remain in the town and send a messenger. 3. They fortify the camp and will call reinforcements from the province.

173. Vocabulary

com′modus, –a, –um, *suitable, convenient*	(commodity)
fu′giō, fu′gere, *flee*	(fugitive)
ō′tium, ō′tī, n., *leisure*	(otiose)
stu′dium, stu′dī, n., *eagerness, interest;* plur., *studies*	(studious)
va′leō, valē′re, *be strong, be well*	(valid)
va′rius, –a, –um, *changing, varying*	(variety)

174. English Word Studies

(*a*) Why does the plural of **studium** mean *studies?* What are *commodities* and why are they so called? Can you explain the name *Ceresota* flour? Give three more derivatives of **varius.**

(*b*) Latin Phrases in English

auxilio ab alto, *by aid from* (*on*) *high.*

ex officio, *out of* (*as a result of*) *one's duty* or *office; e.g.* a president of an organization may be a member of a committee *ex officio* (pronounced "offishio") as a result of his office as president.

Montani semper liberi, *Mountaineers* (*are*) *always free* (motto of the state of West Virginia).

victoria, non praeda, *victory, not loot.*

110

Germani Marcum capiunt. Lucius equum incitat.

LESSON XXV

175. **LŪCIUS ET MĀRCUS**

Rōmānī cum Germānīs, populō firmō et dūrō, bella perpetua
gerēbant. Ōtium semper bellō cēdit, et nunc bella perpetua geri-
mus. Quondam[1] Rōmānī et Aquītānī, sociī Rōmānōrum, cum Germānīs pugnābant. Germānī pugnam nōn aequē incipiunt, et
Rōmānī cum sociīs fugiunt. Lūcius, clārus Aquītānus, ex equō 5
virōs Rōmānōs et Aquītānōs in Germānōs incitābat. Servus Lūciō
clārē nūntiat: "Germānī frātrem[2] tuum Mārcum capiunt!" Lūcius
frātrem amābat. Perīculum Mārcī Lūcium magnā cūrā afficit.
Lūcius equum incitat, armīs Germānōs terret, frātrem servat,
fugit. Sed equus nōn valēbat: Lūcius frātrem sōlum[3] in equō 10
pōnit, et ad castra Aquītānōrum et Rōmānōrum equum incitat.
Tum sōlus Germānōs exspectat. Multī Germānī accēdunt. Lūcius
firmus cēdere incipit, auxilium exspectat—sed auxilium nōn
venit—ē vītā excēdit. Mārcus videt et equum in Germānōs in-
citat—et vītam āmittit.[4]   15

Varia et dūra est fortūna bellī et variē virōs afficit, sed glōriam
semper laudāmus.

Thought Questions.—1. Who was Marcus' brother? 2. Who was
killed?

---

[1] *once.*   [2] *brother.*   [3] *alone.*   [4] *loses.*

111

176. Formation of Adverbs

In English, adverbs are usually formed from adjectives by adding the suffix *–ly:* adj., *clear;* adv., *clearly.*

In Latin, adverbs are likewise formed from adjectives. As a rule, adverbs are formed from adjectives of the first and second declensions by adding –ē to the base:

adj., **clārus**	**līber**
adv., **clārē**	**līberē**

Practice.—Form adverbs from **pūblicus, grātus, commodus,** and **aequus.** Give the Latin for *harshly, truly, firmly.*

177. Ablative of Accompaniment

As you already know, the means *with which* something is done is expressed by the ablative without a preposition (**65**): *They*

From Caesar's forum, with three columns of the Temple of Venus, to the Colosseum

fought with arms, **Armīs pugnābant.** When, however, *with* means *together with* or *along with*, the preposition **cum** is used with the ablative. This expresses **accompaniment: Cum servō venit,** *He is coming with the slave.*

Caution.—When tempted to use **cum** (*with*), be sure that *with* means accompaniment or association. In the following English sentences determine when **cum** should be used and when it should be omitted:

(*a*) *Anna is **with the sailor.***

(*b*) *Soldiers fight **with weapons;** generals fight **with armies;** both soldiers and generals fight **with their enemies.***

Virō pugnat.   Cum virō pugnat.

178.   **Exercises**

(*a*) 1. Cum cōpiīs īnsulārum bellum dūrum et perpetuum gerēmus. 2. Armīs oppida dēfendent et cum sociīs pugnābunt. 3. Magister dūrus puerōs malōs poenā aequē afficit. 4. Nautae terram firmam clārē vidēre incipiēbant. 5. Nautae, pūblicē līberāte captīvōs. 6. Servus cum magnā cōpiā pecūniae fugit; nōn ōtium sed dūrās cūrās invenit. 7. In amīcitiā firmā et perpetuā cum sociīs nostrīs manēbimus.

(*b*) 1. It is not just to carry on war with friends. 2. A bad boy afflicts the family with constant care. 3. The settlers began to flee with (their) families. 4. We shall send reinforcements with grain and defend the island with troops.

113

Pennsylvania Station, New York, is not unlike the Roman baths on
page 104.

179. Vocabulary

affi′ciō, affi′cere, *affect, afflict with*	[*faciō*]
cum, prep. with abl., *with*	
dū′rus, –a, –um, *hard, harsh*	(durable)
fir′mus, –a, –um, *strong, firm*	(firmness)
ge′rō, ge′rere, *carry on*	(belligerent)
inci′piō, inci′pere, *take to, begin*	[*capiō*]
perpe′tuus, –a, –um, *constant*	(perpetuity)

180. Latin and English Word Formation

The preposition **cum** is often used as a prefix in Latin and English but always in the assimilated forms **com–**, **con–**, **col–**, **cor–**, **co–**. It usually means *together* rather than *with*.

Define the following words, all formed from verbs which you have studied: *convoke, collaborate, commotion, convene*. What is a political *convention?*

Give five other English words formed by attaching this prefix to Latin verbs, nouns, or adjectives already studied.

114

Graecia. The Acropolis Hill, with the Parthenon Temple, at Athens

LESSON XXVI

181. **VĪTA ANTĪQUA**

Poētae multa[1] dē deīs et virīs antīquīs docent. Multās fābulās
dē clārīs Graecīs et Rōmānīs et dē perpetuā glōriā Rōmānōrum ā
magistrō tuō audiēs et ex librīs trahēs. Fortasse studia tē[2] ad Graeciam et Italiam trahent. Ibi templa deōrum et loca clāra vidēbis dē
quibus[3] poētae scrībunt. Tum verba poētārum commodē memoriā 5
tenēbis. Italia multās antīquās ruīnās continet. Multa[1] dē vītā
antīquōrum Graecōrum et Rōmānōrum inveniēs et audiēs sī[4] cum
amīcīs ad Italiam nāvigābis et ibi manēbis. Multī Americānī ex
Eurōpā variās rēs[5] Rōmānās portant. Fortasse magister tuus rēs
Rōmānās habet et puerīs et puellīs mōnstrāre incipiet. Librī tuī 10
Latīnī multās novās fābulās dē clārīs Rōmānīs continēbunt. Sī
puerī tardī nōn erunt, librōs accipient. Nōnne verba mea puerōs
tardōs afficient?

---

[1] *many things.*   [2] *you* (accusative).   [3] *which.*   [4] *if.*   [5] *things.*

Thought Questions.—1. How will you learn about the Romans? 2. What four things do the ancient poets tell about?

182. Future of Third (–*iō*) and Fourth Conjugation Verbs

Verbs of the fourth conjugation form the future by adding –ē– directly to the present stem (long –i– of the stem is shortened, however, since it precedes another vowel). Verbs of the third conjugation ending in –iō closely resemble fourth conjugation verbs in the future tense; the reason for this is the insertion of –i– (154):

	I shall fortify, etc.		*I shall take*, etc.
mū′niam	mūniē′mus	ca′piam	capiē′mus
mū′niēs	mūniē′tis	ca′piēs	capiē′tis
mū′niet	mū′nient	ca′piet	ca′pient

The Finnish Diet, or parliament, at Helsinki, in Roman style. Every part of the world has been affected by classical art and civilization.

Practice.—(*a*) Give the future tense of **incipiō** and **audiō**.

(*b*) Give the Latin for *they will affect, we shall hear, you* (plur.) *will receive, they will draw, it will contain.*

(*c*) Tell the form of **invenietis, audīs, faciam, vidēbunt, parābat.**

183. **Exercises**

(*a*) 1. Equōs in locō lātō et commodō continēbimus. 2. Nautae nostrī ex aquā virōs trahent et servābunt. 3. Armīsne oppidum dēfendere incipiēmus? 4. Magister tardōs puerōs poenā pūblicē afficiet. 5. Colōnī ex agrīs frūmentum portābunt et magnam pecūniam accipient. 6. Equī carrōs agricolārum tardē trahēbant. Carrī frūmentum continēbant.

(*b*) 1. Anna, a good girl, will justly receive a large reward. 2. We shall defend the camp with arms. 3. The boys will not receive the reward, because they are late. 4. The late boys and girls will not hear the words of the famous man.

184. **Vocabulary**

au′diō, audī′re, *hear*	(audience)
conti′neō, continē′re, *hold* (*together*), *contain*	[*teneō*]
tar′dus, –a, –um, *slow, late*	(retard)
tra′hō, tra′here, *draw, drag*	(attraction)
ver′bum, –ī, n., *word*	(verbal)

185. **Latin and English Word Formation**

Most prefixes are prepositions, but a few are not. **Re–** is used only as a prefix in Latin and English; it means *back* or *again*. It sometimes has the form **red–**, especially before vowels. Examples: **retineō,** *hold back;* **reficiō,** *make again;* **redigō,** *drive back.*

In English, **re–** is freely used with all sorts of words: *reduce, revisit, rehash, refill.*

Give seven examples of the prefix **re–** in English words derived from Latin. Explain *revoke, incipient, refugee, audition.*

117

186.   AENĒĀS

The Trojan War was fought over three thousand years ago at Troy, in Asia Minor near the Dardanelles. The story of the war is told by the Greek poet Homer in the *Iliad*. Virgil, the Roman poet, tells part of the story in his *Aeneid* and goes on to tell of the Trojan Aeneas, said to be the son of the goddess Venus. After the fall of Troy Aeneas eventually reached Italy and, according to the story, he and his companions were the ancestors of the Romans.

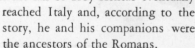

Aeneas patrem portat et filium parvum ducit. Sculpture on a Roman tomb

Troiānī cum Graecīs bellum gerēbant. Graecī Troiam occupant. Aenēās Troiānus arma capit et cum multīs virīs oppidum dēfendere mātūrat. Sed Venus dea, [5] māter Aenēae,[1] eum[2] in mediō oppidō invenit et verba facit:

"Audī sententiam meam. Tenē memoriā familiam tuam. Convocā familiam et amīcōs firmōs [10] et fuge. Novam patriam inveniēs. Cēde fortūnae. Deī Troiam vāstant. Troiānōs poenā dūrā afficient."

Cōnsilium Aenēās nōn grātē [15] audit sed probat. Ad familiam virōs redūcit et amīcōs convocat. Patrem[3] portat et fīlium parvum dūcit. Cum multīs servīs et sociīs ex oppidō fugit. Singulī in [20] locum commodum conveniunt et ibi castra pōnunt. Māteriam

---

[1] Genitive singular.   [2] *him.*
[3] Accusative singular of **pater.**

The baths of Caracalla as they are now (cf. p. 104)

ex silvā portant et nāvēs[1] parant. Tum nāvēs in aquam trahunt
et undīs mandant et migrant. Ad multās īnsulās et terrās novās
veniunt sed patriam novam nōn inveniunt. Vītam dūram agunt. 25
Īra Iūnōnis,[2] rēgīnae deōrum, hoc[3] efficit.

In īnsulā Crētā castra pōnunt. Tum in mediō somnō Aenēās
Penātēs[4] videt et sententiam audit:

"Crēta patria vestra nōn erit. Excēdite, Troiānī. Locus est
quem[5] Graecī Hesperiam, aliī Italiam vocant. Ibi terminum cūrā- 30
rum perpetuārum inveniētis. Ibi in ōtiō et concordiā habitābitis
et magnum oppidum pōnētis et mūniētis."

Ita Troiānī cōnsilium novum capiunt. Castra movent et ad
Italiam nāvigant.

Thought Questions.—1. What did Venus tell Aeneas to do? 2. Whom
does Aeneas take with him from Troy? 3. Why didn't Aeneas stay in
Crete?

Read Sabin, pp. 331–333; Gayley, pp. 346–350; Bulfinch, pp. 262–263;
Guerber, pp. 360–364.

---

[1] Accusative plural of **nāvis**.   [2] *of Juno.*   [3] *this.*
[4] Accusative plural: *Penā'tēs.*   [5] *which* (accusative).

187.   Idioms

Every language contains set phrases or fixed expressions with meanings which cannot be translated literally. For example, we say, *How are you?* when we really mean, *How do you feel?*

Certain set phrases occur in Latin which are peculiar to it and cannot be translated literally into English. These fixed expressions are said to be **idiomatic.** The following should be memorized and entered in the notebook under the general heading "Idioms":

1. **grātiās agō,** *thank,* with dat. (literally, *act gratitude*)
2. **grātiam habeō,** *feel grateful,* with dat. (lit., *have gratitude*)
3. **vītam agō,** *live a life* (lit., *act life*)
4. **bellum gerō,** *wage* or *carry on war*
5. **castra pōnō,** *pitch camp* (lit., *place camp*)
6. **viam mūniō,** *build a road* (lit., *fortify a road:* roads were built like walls)
7. **verba faciō,** *speak, make a speech* (lit., *make words*)
8. **memoriā teneō,** *remember* (lit., *hold in memory*)
9. **cōnsilium capiō,** *adopt a plan* (lit., *take a plan*)

Latin inscription in the Library of Congress, Washington

188. Exercises

(*a*) 1. Pōnite castra, puerī, in agrīs et ibi agite līberam vītam. 2. Magistrō nostrō grātiam habēmus et līberē grātiās agēmus. 3. Puerōs ex mediā silvā in oppidum redūcam. 4. Rōmānī multās longās viās in Italiā mūniēbant. 5. Puerōs singulōs convocābimus et sententiās audiēmus. 6. Virī ex multīs terrīs convenient et verba facient.

(*b*) 1. The boys and girls feel grateful and will thank the teacher. 2. We ought to feel grateful to your friends. 3. The boys will find water and pitch camp. 4. We shall remember the teacher's words about duty.

189. Vocabulary

conve'niō, convenī're, *come together*	[*veniō*]
con'vocō, convocā're, *call together*	[*vocō*]
i'bi, adv., *there*	
me'dius, –a, –um, *middle, middle of*	(mediator)
redū'cō, redū'cere, *lead back*	[*dūcō*]
senten'tia, –ae, f., *feeling, opinion, motto*	(sentence)

190. English Word Studies

A friend is a person whom you know well, love dearly, and treat familiarly. How many English words can you call friends, according to this definition? If you will trace English words back to their Latin roots, you will gain many new friends. For example: A "sentence" in grammar is a single, complete *opinion* or expression. A judicial "sentence" is a judge's *opinion*. A "convention" *comes together* in an "auditorium" to *hear* the speaker. A "mediator" settles disputes by taking a *middle* position. A spiritualistic "medium" is supposed to take a *middle* position between the unseen spirit and the "audience" who *hear*. A "studious" person is one who is *eager* to learn. An "alarm" is a call *to arms* (**ad arma**). To "repatriate" a person is to bring him *back* to his *fatherland*. Learn to look carefully at the *make-up* of every strange English word and you will often detect an old Latin friend *in disguise*.

What is a *convocation?* What did Disraeli mean when he said that Gladstone was "inebriated with the exuberance of his own *verbosity*"?

The New York telephone directory lists twenty-six firms called *Venus;* the Indianapolis directory six. Why is this a popular name?

121

Forum Romanum—looking through the Arch of Septimius Severus to the Arch of Titus

LESSON XXVIII

THE STORY OF LUCIUS

191. **Forum Rōmānum**

Quondam puer parvus Lūcius in Italiā habitābat. Dē glōriā patriae multa audiēbat. Magister Lūciō reliquīsque puerīs loca clāra Rōmae mōnstrābat. In medium Forum Rōmānum cum puerīs properābat. In hunc[1] locum populus Rōmānus conveniē-
5 bat. Ibi virī amīcōs vidēbant et aedificia[2] pūblica templaque spec-
tābant. Ibi nūntiī populum convocābant et magnās victōriās nūntiābant. Ibi virī clārī in rōstrīs[3] verba pūblicē faciēbant et sententiās dēfendēbant.

Magister multa dē patriā in Forō docēbat. Puerī magistrō mag-
10 nam grātiam habēbant, quod Forum amābant. Ē Forō Lūcius reliquīque cum magistrō in Sacram Viam properābant et tabernās[4]
spectābant. Cupitisne[5] plūra[6] dē Lūciō audīre?

---

[1] *this.*　　　[2] *buildings.*　　　[3] *the rostra* (speakers' platform).　　　[4] *shops.*
[5] *desire.*　　　[6] *more.*

122

The Arc de Triomphe, Paris, a triumphal arch in Roman style

Thought Questions.—1. Where did the Romans meet their friends? 2. Why were the boys grateful to their teacher?

192. Hints for Reading

The first step in reading Latin is to follow the order of words, separating them into groups according to their sense and grammatical relation. Such word groups or phrases should be read and understood as units.

After translating **Forum Rōmānum** with due regard to the word groups in each sentence, practice reading the entire passage aloud in the Latin with as much expression as you can.

193. Substantives

A noun is sometimes called a **substantive**.

A **pronoun** is a word used instead of a noun, as *he*, which takes the place of the name of some person, or *that*, which takes the place of the name of a thing. Pronouns, too, are substantives.

Other words also may at times be used substantively. We have already noted the substantive use of the infinitive (**133, 134**).

Sometimes an adjective is used substantively without a noun. The masculine refers to persons, the neuter to things:

(*a*) **Nostrī** (**virī**) **veniunt,** *Our* (*men*) *are coming.*
(*b*) **Multa audiēs,** *You will hear many* (*things*).

194. Conversation

(See *map of the Roman world* on pp. 260 and 261.)

M. = **Magister**   **D.** = **Discipulī**

M. Spectāte, puerī et puellae. **D.** Spectāmus, magister.

M. Ubi oppida vidētis? **D.** In Āfricā et in Asiā et in Eurōpā multa oppida vidēmus.

M. In mediā terrā aquam vidētis. Illam[1] aquam "Medi-terrā-
5 neum Mare"[2] vocāmus.

M. Ibi est Lūsitānia—vidētisne? **D.** Vidēmus.

M. Ubi est Hibernia? **D.** Hibernia est īnsula in Ōceanō Atlan-ticō.

M. Multī virī multōrum populōrum in Eurōpā habitant.

10 **M.** Ubi pugnābant Sociī in Bellō Magnō? **D.** Sociī in Galliā pugnābant.

Questions to Be Answered in Latin.—1. Ubi habitāmus? 2. Nōnne officium nostrum est patriam dēfendere? 3. Ubi est Graecia?

195. Vocabulary

pro′perō, properā′re, *hasten*
-que, conj., *and* (translated before the word to which it is joined)
re′liquus, –a, –um, *remaining, rest* (*of*)   (relic)

196. English Word Studies

What does the English word *forum* mean? What use of the Roman Forum gave this meaning to our word (see **197**)? Can you find any organizations or groups today which use the name *Forum*?

What is a *Hibernian*? How did the *Mediterranean* Sea get its name?

---

[1] *that.*   [2] *Sea.*

124

GLIMPSES OF ROMAN LIFE

197.   The City of Rome

The Romans tell us that Rome was founded in 753 B.C. The first settlement was on the Palatine Hill, named after Pales, the goddess of shepherds. This was natural because the first settlers were shepherds. As the city grew, it spread to the near-by hills and the valleys between them. In the course of time it came to be known as the "City of the Seven Hills." These hills are neither high nor extensive. The Palatine is only 142 feet above the level of the Tiber River—about the height of a ten-story building.

Below the Palatine Hill was the valley which came to be known as the Forum. At first a marshy district, it became the market place of Rome, then its chief shopping and business district, and finally the civic center. In its final development it was a rectangular paved space surrounded by temples, law courts, senate house, and other public buildings. At one end was a speakers' platform called the *rostra* because it was ornamented with the beaks of ships (**rōstra**) captured in a war fought in the fourth century B.C.

The Palatine, because of its nearness to the Forum, became the residence district for the statesmen and wealthy people of the city.

The Palatine Hill from Romulus and Remus Square on the Aventine Hill

Hence it was natural that the first emperors had their homes there. Eventually the whole imperial administration was centered on this hill, and the emperor's buildings covered it completely. So the hill which was named after the patron goddess of the shepherds who built their rude huts there came to be the site of magnificent buildings. Thus it happens that our word *palace* is derived from the name of the hill.

Another hill near the Forum, the Capitoline, got its name from the famous temple of Jupiter known as the Capitolium, because it was the "head" (**caput**), or chief temple of that god. From it the Capitol at Washington gets its name, as well as the Capitols of the various states. The hill also had on it a fort and the temple of Juno Moneta. In connection with this a mint for coining money was later established, and thus from the word **monēta** we get our words *money* and *mint*.

The streets of Rome were narrow and crooked. In the early days they were unpaved. Only during the last part of the first century B.C. (99–1) did Rome begin to become beautiful.

In the early days the people of Rome got their water from wells, springs, and the Tiber River, which winds its way along one side of the city in the shape of the letter S. In 312 B.C. Appius Claudius built the first aqueduct, which brought pure water from a distance. There were many street fountains (pp. 13, 364), and eventually many houses were piped for running water.

For better administration the emperor Augustus divided the city into fourteen regions, or wards. One feature of this arrangement was the reorganization and extension of the police and fire department (**vigilēs,** *watchmen*). Previously fire protection had been so poor that private fire companies were organized. These bought up burning houses at bargain prices and then proceeded to extinguish the fire.

In early days a wall known as the Servian wall was built around the city. But Rome soon outgrew this. In the third century A.D. the wall of Aurelian was built.

A gate in the wall of Aurelian. The battlements are medieval. The pyramid is an ancient tomb, in imitation of the Egyptian.

At its height, Rome had a population of more than a million. The modern city has been growing rapidly in recent years, and has again reached this figure. In 1938 it had 1,266,233 people and had once again become the largest city in Italy.

Rome has been one of the most important cities of the world for a longer time than any other. For hundreds of years it was the capital of the great Roman Empire, then it continued its importance as the seat of the papacy, and in recent generations it has become also the capital of one of the larger nations of Europe. Even in ancient times it received the name of the "Eternal City" (**urbs aeterna**), and it seems that this name has been justified.

Questions for Discussion.—1. What is a civic center? Describe the one in your town, or in a town you have visited, and compare it with that of ancient Rome. 2. Compare the development of Rome and of Washington, D. C. 3. Compare the development of the water supply of Rome with that of some American town.

Read Showerman, pp. 14–28; Mills, pp. 293–301.

Ira Neptuni magna est. Neptune chases the winds away from the Trojan fleet. From a sketch by Rubens

LESSON XXIX

198.   **AD ITALIAM**

In magnīs undīs nāvēs[1] Troiānōrum volvuntur;[2] Sed Troiānī ex mediīs undīs servantur et ad Actium[3] properant; ibi inveniunt Helenum Troiānum, quī terram regēbat. Helenus Troiānōs convocat et verba pauca facit:

5   "Longa est via ad Italiam, ad quam[4] accēdere parātis. Accēdite ad Siciliam et nāvigāte ab Siciliā ad Italiam fīnitimam. Dūrum est semper nāvigāre, sed Fāta viam invenient."

Sententia Helenī grātē accipitur, et Aenēās Helenō grātiās agit. Castra moventur nāvēsque[1] undīs committuntur. "Italiam, Ita-
10 liam videō!" clāmat nauta et terram mōnstrat. In terrā equī clārē

---

[1] Nominative plural.   [2] *are tossed.*   [3] *Actium (Ak'shium).*   [4] *which.*

videntur. "Signum proelī sunt equī," dīcit Anchīsēs;[1] "equīs bellum geritur. Proelium committere nōn dēbēmus." Nōn ibi manent sed ad Siciliam fīnitimam nāvigant. Aetna eōs[2] terret et ab Siciliā fugiunt.

Tum Iūnō ad Aeolum, qùi ventōs regit et continet, venit dīcit- 15 que:

"Sī ventī dūrī in nāvēs[3] Troiānōrum mittentur, magnam grātiam habēbō et magna praemia tibi[4] dōnābō."

Aeolus ventōs in nāvēs mittere mātūrat. Altīs undīs Troiānī terrentur. Arma virīque in undīs sunt. Tum Neptūnus, deus un- 20 dārum, ventōs audit et ad locum venit ubi nāvēs sunt. Īra Neptūnī magna est; ventī lātē fugiunt. Paucī Troiānī āmittuntur; reliquī ad terram veniunt et servantur. Sed in quā[5] terrā sunt? Nōn sciunt.[6]

Thought Questions.—1. Where does Helenus tell the Trojans to go? 2. What does Juno ask Aeolus to do? 3. What does Neptune do? . **Read** Sabin, pp. 334–336; Bulfinch, pp. 264–266; Guerber, pp. 364–366.

199.   Voice: Active and Passive

A verb is in the **active voice** when it shows that the subject acts:

Vir accūsābit, *The man will accuse.*

When the verb shows that the subject is acted upon, it is in the **passive voice:**

Vir accūsābitur, *The man will be accused.*

He is kicking.   He is being kicked.

---

[1] Father of Aeneas; pronounced *Ankī'sēs* in English.   [2] *them.*
[3] Accusative plural.   [4] *to you.*   [5] *what.*   [6] *know.*

Observe that voice is shown in Latin by endings.

Note.—The linking verb **sum** has no voice, for it merely indicates existence.

200. Progressive and Passive Verb Forms in English

Be careful to distinguish between active progressive forms and true passive verb phrases, both of which employ the verb *to be*.

Active (progressive): *He is seeing* (**videt**); *They were calling* (**vocābant**).

Passive: *He is seen* (**vidētur**); *They were called* (**vocābantur**).

Practice.—Tell which of these verbs are passive: *he called, we were cold, he was laughing, they were found, you are being beaten, he is fighting, they will be scolded, he will praise, you will be invited, it was being written, we were reading, she was sent.*

The state Capitol at Little Rock, Arkansas, an excellent example of the Roman style. What other buildings are like it?

201.   Passive Voice of the Four Conjugations

The passive personal endings, which are substituted for the active,[1] are:

PERSONAL ENDINGS		PRESENT	
–r	–mur	por′tor, *I am carried*	portā′mur, *we are carried*
–ris	–minī	portā′ris, *you are carried*	portā′minī, *you are carried*
–tur	–ntur	portā′tur, *he is carried*	portan′tur,[2] *they are carried*
		Similarly **doceor, pōnor, mūnior, capior** (see **585–588**).	

IMPERFECT	
portā′bar, *I was being carried, was carried*	portābā′mur, *we were being carried,* etc.
portābā′ris, *you were being carried,* etc.	portābā′minī, *you were being carried,* etc.
portābā′tur, *he was being carried,* etc.	portāban′tur, *they were being carried,* etc.
Similarly **docēbar, pōnēbar, mūniēbar, capiēbar** (see **585–588**).	

FUTURE	
portā′bor, *I shall be carried*	portā′bimur, *we shall be carried*
portā′beris, *you will be carried*	portābi′minī, *you will be carried*
portā′bitur, *he will be carried*	portābun′tur, *they will be carried*
Similarly **docēbor, pōnar, mūniar, capiar** (see **585–588**).	

Observe that **r** occurs in five of the six passive endings.

Practice.—(*a*) Conjugate **accipiō** in the present passive, **dēfendō** in the imperfect passive, **inveniō** in the future passive.

---

[1] But in forms ending in –ō in the active (as **portō** and **portābō**), the passive ending –r is *added to*, not *substituted for*, the active ending. The –ō– becomes short.

[2] For the vowel shortened before –ntur, see **23** (*a*).

A Greek temple in Sicily. The Temple of Concord, in Doric style, at Agrigento. Sicily and southern Italy were settled by Greeks.

(*b*) *Translate:* we shall be accused, he is being taught, it was not approved, they will be sent, it will be received, he will be heard, you (*sing.*) are moved, they are ruled, you (*plur.*) will be seen, we are awaited.

202.   **Exercises**

(*a*) 1. Reliquī nautae ad prōvinciam mittentur. 2. Rōmānī proelium cum fīnitimīs nunc committunt. 3. Americam, terram līberōrum, amāmus et laudāmus. 4. Paucī virī in fīnitimīs agrīs oppidīsque vidēbantur. 5. Multa praemia reliquīs puerīs puellīsque dōnābuntur. 6. Captīvī ad oppidum redūcentur et proelium committētur.

(*b*) 1. They will receive a few words of advice. 2. A few words of advice will be received. 3. Are the-rest-of the boys working in the fields? 4. The-rest-of the men will be sent to the island.

132

commit′tō, commit′tere, *join together*, *commit*, *entrust;*
  proe′lium commit′tō, *begin battle*   [*mittō*]
fīni′timus, −a, −um, *neighboring;* fīni′timus, −ī, m., *neighbor*
pau′cī, −ae, −a, *few*   (paucity)
proe′lium, proe′lī, n., *battle*

204.   Latin and English Word Formation

We have seen how Latin and English words are formed from
others by the use of prefixes. There are other ways of forming new
words. These we shall discuss later. For the present it is sufficient
to recognize the roots that words have in common. Note the relationship and review the meanings of the following words which
have occurred in the preceding vocabularies:

(*a*) amīcus and amīcitia, (*b*) nāvigō and nauta, (*c*) nūntiō and
nūntius, (*d*) capiō and captīvus (a "captive" is one who is *taken*),
(*e*) pugna and pugnō, (*f*) puer and puella, (*g*) habeō and habitō (to
"inhabit" a place is to keep on *having* it).

From now on try to associate new Latin words with those you
have already had, as well as with English derivatives which you
find.

Can you tell why Boston and Seattle have more firms named
Neptune (five each) listed in their telephone directories than other
cities have?

Italian stamp for the Virgilian celebration of 1930 (cf. p. 83). Aeneas
is shown landing in Italy. In the quotation from the Aeneid Aeneas is
greeting the land which the Fates have promised him and which will
be his home and country.

Cupid, the rascal, poses as Iulus, son of Aeneas, and Dido falls in love.

LESSON XXX

205. AENEAS IN AFRICA EST

Aenēās sociōs convocat et verba facit:

"In terrā nōn nōtā sumus. Sed deī praesidium nostrum sunt. Deīs vītam committite. Neque terra neque aqua nōs[1] terret. Inveniēmus viam aut faciēmus. Italia nostra erit. Ibi et terminus
5 malōrum nostrōrum et ōtium perpetuum ā Troiānīs invenientur. Ibi patria erit et nova Troia."

Tum Aenēās cum sociō ūnō ex castrīs excēdit. Loca explōrāre mātūrat. Venus māter eum[2] videt et appellat. Nōmen oppidī, quod[3] appellātur Carthāgō et in Āfricā est, et nōmen rēgīnae, quae[4] est
10 Dīdō, Aenēae[5] Venus nūntiat. Via ā deā Aenēae mōnstrātur. Aenēās prōcēdit et magnum oppidum videt. In mediō oppidō templum est. Ad templum rēgīna Dīdō cum paucīs sociīs venit. Ibi sunt reliquī Troiānī quōs[6] undae ab Aenēā[7] sēparāverant.[8]

Dīdō mala Troiānōrum audit et dīcit:

---

[1] *us.*   [2] *him.*   [3] *which.*   [4] *who.*   [5] Dative.   [6] *whom.*
[7] Ablative.   [8] Use the English derivative in the past perfect tense (*had—*).

134

"Auxiliō meō aut in Italiam aut in Siciliam commodē veniētis, 15
amīcī. Sed sī in nostrā patriā manēre grātum est, oppidum nostrum vestrum est, et praesidium habēbitis."

Tum magna cēna ā rēgīnā parātur. Aenēās nūntium ad fīlium,
quī Iūlus[1] appellātur, mittit; nūntius dīcit:

"Venī ad oppidum, Iūle. Pater tē[2] exspectat."   20

Sed in locō Iūlī Venus deum Amōrem[3] mittit. Sed et Aenēās
et reliquī Troiānī deum[4] crēdunt esse Iūlum. Tum Amor rēgīnam
afficit, et Dīdō Aenēam amāre incipit.

Thought Questions.—1. How does Aeneas find out where he is?
2. Whom does he see at the temple? 3. Why does Aeneas send for Iulus?
Read Sabin, pp. 335–336; Guerber, pp. 366–367.

206.   Ablative of Personal Agent

A **transitive** verb is one in which the action expressed by the
verb passes over to a receiver, which is the direct object:

        Anna aquam portat, *Anna is carrying water.*
        Puer virum videt, *The boy sees the man.*

An **intransitive** verb is one whose action does not pass over to
a receiver and therefore cannot have a direct object:

        Anna labōrat, *Anna is working.*
        Puer excēdit, *The boy departs.*

In English, and generally in Latin, only transitive verbs are
used in the passive voice.

Let us see what happens when the two sentences containing
transitive verbs are turned around and the verb becomes passive:

        Aqua ab Annā portātur, *The water is carried by Anna.*
        Vir ā puerō vidētur, *The man is seen by the boy.*

Observe that in both English and Latin (*a*) the direct object
of the active verb becomes the subject of the passive verb; (*b*) the
subject of the active verb becomes the object of a preposition
(**ab,** *by*), indicating the agent.

---

[1] *Iulus* (Īyū'lus).   [2] *you.*   [3] *Love*, a Roman god.
[4] **deum . . . Iūlum:** *believe the god to be Iulus.*

Caution.—The ablative of personal agent must be carefully distinguished from the ablative of means, both of which are frequently translated with *by*. Remember that *"means" refers to things*, while *"agent" refers to a person*. Furthermore, the ablative of means *never* takes a preposition, while the ablative of personal agent is never used without the preposition **ā (ab)**. This preposition means *by* only when used before a noun referring to a person and with a passive verb.

Oppidum a Consilio capitur. Mr. Consilium is quite a fellow to pick up a town just like that.

1. **Oppidum cōnsiliō capitur,** *The town is taken by strategy* (**means**).
2. **Oppidum ā nostrīs capitur,** *The town is taken by our men* (**agent**).

Practice.—(*a*) Tell which expresses means and which personal agent:

1. He was praised *by all*. 2. I was hit *by a stone*. 3. She will be summoned *by messenger*, he *by letter*. 4. The note had been written *by hand* and not *with a typewriter*. 5. This book was bought *by me with my own money*.

(*b*) Change the following from active to passive, or from passive to active, and translate:

1. Vir servum vidēbat. 2. Oppida ā populō reguntur. 3. Puerī verba tua exspectābant. 4. Reliqua pecūnia ab amīcō meō accipiētur.

(*c*) Turn back to **183** and put into the passive (*a*) 2, 4, 5, 6.

207.   Agreement

In both English and Latin, when two singular subjects are connected by *or* (**aut**), *either . . . or* (**aut . . . aut**), *neither . . . nor* (**neque . . . neque**), the verb is in the singular: *Neither the boy nor the girl is in the forest*, **Neque puer neque puella in silvā est.**

(*a*) 1. Puer equōs dūcit; equī ā puerō dūcuntur. 2. Magister puerōs puellāsque docēbat; puerī puellaeque ā magistrō docēbantur. 3. Aut puerī aut virī equōs ad agrōs redūcent. 4. Neque servus neque equus in viīs vidēbitur. 5. Multa praemia ā reliquīs puerīs puellīsque grātē accipientur. 6. Neque praesidium neque auxilium ā sociīs nostrīs mittitur. 7. Mārcus amīcus[1] vērus ā multīs appellābātur.

(*b*) 1. The men see few horses; few horses are seen by the men. 2. The girls were scared by the bad boys. 3. The grain is being carried by wagon to the town. 4. Neither water nor grain is being carried by the-rest-of the men.

209. Vocabulary

appel'lō, appellā're, *call*   (appellate)
aut, conj., *or;* aut . . . aut, *either . . . or*
et . . . et, conj., *both . . . and*
ne'que (or nec), conj., *and not, nor;* ne'que . . . ne'que, *neither . . . nor*
praesi'dium, praesi'dī, n., *guard, protection*
rēgīna, –ae, f., *queen*

210. English Word Studies

(*a*) What is meant by taking an *appeal* to a higher court? Why is such a court called an *appellate* court? Find one other derivative of appellō.

(*b*) Latin Phrases in English

consilio et armis, *by counsel and by arms.*
In Deo speramus, *In God we trust* (motto of Brown University).
magnum bonum, *great good.*
terra firma, *solid earth* (as opposed to water).
via media, *a middle way* or *course.*
Explain Victoria regina.

---

[1] Observe that the predicate nominative (10, *b*) may be used with other verbs than sum.

Aeneas meets Venus. This tapestry in the Cleveland Museum of Art was made in the seventeenth century for an Italian cardinal.

211.   **English Word Studies**

1. What is wrong with this sentence:

"This is the first time in a month that I have set foot on *terra cotta*"?

2. Define according to derivation: *relic, digest, Mr., doctor, libel, appellation, mediation, retardation* (look up in the dictionary if necessary).

3. Give prefix and Latin root word from which the following are derived: **redigō, concipiō, attrahō, committō;** *respect, component, incorrigible, exhibit.*

212.   **Vocabulary**

NOUNS

1. ōtium
2. praesidium
3. proelium
4. rēgīna
5. sententia
6. studium
7. verbum

ADJECTIVES

8. commodus
9. dūrus
10. fīnitimus
11. firmus
12. medius
13. paucī
14. perpetuus
15. reliquus
16. tardus
17. varius

VERBS

18. afficiō
19. appellō
20. audiō
21. committō
22. contineō
23. conveniō
24. convocō
25. fugiō
26. gerō
27. incipiō
28. properō
29. redūcō
30. trahō
31. valeō

ADVERB

32. ibi

PREPOSITION

33. cum

CONJUNCTIONS

34. aut
35. aut . . . aut
36. et . . . et
37. neque
38. neque . . . neque
39. -que

139

Populus convenit. The people patriotically refill the Roman treasury during the Second Punic War. A painting by Sciuti

213.   Vocabulary

NOUNS

1. *leisure*
2. *guard*
3. *battle*

4. *queen*

5. *opinion*
6. *eagerness*
7. *word*

ADJECTIVES

8. *convenient*
9. *hard*
10. *neighboring*

11. *strong*
12. *middle (of)*
13. *few*
14. *constant*

15. *remaining*
16. *slow*
17 *changing*

VERBS

18. *affect*
19. *call*
20. *hear*

21. *join together, entrust*
22. *contain*
23. *come together*
24. *call together*

25. *flee*
26. *carry on*
27. *begin*
28. *hasten*

29. *lead back*
30. *draw*
31. *be strong*

ADVERB

32. *there*

PREPOSITION

33. *with*

CONJUNCTIONS

34. *or*
35. *either . . . or*

36. *both . . . and*
37. *. .nor*

38. *neither . . . nor*
39. *and*

1. Form and translate adverbs from **lātus, līber,** and **perpetuus.**

2. Conjugate **trahō, incipiō,** and **audiō** in the future, active and passive.

3. *Translate:* gerit, geret, incipient, incipiunt, properābō, fugiam, audīris, audiēris, afficiuntur, mittentur, conveniēmus, continēbitur, convocābuntur, invenientur.

4. *Give in Latin:* they will hear, they will be heard, I shall see, I shall be seen, he will begin, she will be heard, we shall be called together, it will draw, they will be led back, he was being taught, you (*sing.*) will flee, you (*plur.*) will be affected.

5. Give the Latin for the following in the singular and plural in the case required:

great interest (nom.), *a good price* (gen.), *varying opinion* (dat.), *a small guard* (acc.), *a neighboring place* (abl.).

Italian stamp for Virgil (cf. p. 83). The scene is in the Lower World (see p. 223), where Anchises is prophesying the glories of Rome to Aeneas.

I. Complete and translate:

1. Rēgīna (*by many*) vidēbitur. 2. (*We are called*) amīcī bonī. 3. Multa bella cum multīs populīs ā Rōmānīs (*were carried on*). 4. Verba magistrī ā paucīs (*are heard*). 5. Puer ex aquā ā virō (*will be dragged*).

II. Translate first in the active, then in the passive, making the subject the agent "by whom" and the direct object the subject:

1. Few find leisure. 2. The men will receive aid. 3. The teacher will praise the girls. 4. The boy scares the horses. 5. Many will hear my words.

The death of Dido. From a tapestry in the Cleveland Museum of Art

LESSON XXXI

216. AENEĀS ET DĪDŌ

Ad Annam sorōrem[1] Dīdō properāvit: "Anna soror," dīcit, "animus meus miser perīculīs terrētur; Aenēam amō. Quid[2] agam?"

Anna respondet: "Aenēās est bonus vir. Prō Troiā pugnāvit sed 5 patriam āmīsit; nunc prō nostrā patriā multōs annōs pugnābit. Populī fīnitimī nōn sunt amīcī. Terminī nostrī ab Aenēā proeliīs dēfendentur."

Aenēās in Āfricā cum rēgīnā manet. Dīdō Troiānum per medium oppidum dūcit et eī[3] oppidum mōnstrat.

10 Tum Iuppiter Mercurium nūntium ad Aenēam mīsit. "Annum in hōc[4] locō ēgistī," Mercurius dīcit. "Verba deī memoriā nōn tenēs; properā in Italiam cum sociīs tuīs, ubi fīlius tuus reget. Ibi ōtium habēbis."

---

[1] Accusative: *sister.*   [2] *what.*   [3] *to him.*   [4] *this.*

Aenēās sociōs convocāvit. Sociī frūmentum in nāvēs[1] portāvērunt. Dīdō Aenēam appellāvit: 15
"Cūr fugis? Dūrus es; iniūriam facis. Magnum est perīculum
nostrum. Ā populīs fīnitimīs agrī nostrī vāstābuntur, oppidum
āmittētur. Praesidium nostrum esse dēbēs. In concordiā perpetuā
habitābimus."   .
   Aenēās respondet: "Deum Mercurium vīdī. Officium meum est 20
ad Italiam nāvigāre. Dūrum est, sed deus imperat."
   Aenēās tardē excessit et ad nāvēs vēnit. Sociī convēnērunt et
nāvēs in aquam trāxērunt. Tum nāvēs undīs ventīsque commīsērunt. Dīdō misera nāvēs vīdit et sē[2] interfēcit.[3]
   Troiānī ad Italiam migrāvērunt et patriam novam invēnērunt. 25
Dīdō vītam āmīsit, Aenēās patriam invēnit. Ita[4] librī poētārum
docent.

   Thought Questions.—1. What does Mercury tell Aeneas to do?
2. What argument did Dido use to persuade Aeneas to stay in Carthage?
Read Sabin, pp. 337–338; Gayley, pp. 350–352; Bulfinch, pp. 266–268.

217.   The Perfect Tense

   In English, the **past** tense refers to an action that is completed:
*He **went** yesterday.*
   The **present perfect** refers to an action that is completed, but
from the point of view of the present: *He **has just gone.*** One
cannot say *He has gone yesterday.*
   In Latin, the **perfect** tense is used like both the past and the
present perfect of English, though it more often corresponds to
the past.

218.   The Perfect Stem

   In Latin, the **perfect stem** is found by dropping the personal
ending –ī from the perfect active: āmīsī, āmīs–. As we shall see,
several tenses are formed from the perfect stem.
   Note.—All verbs of the first conjugation thus far studied form the

---

[1] Accusative plural.   [2] *herself.*   [3] *killed.*   [4] *so.*

143

perfect stem by adding −v to the present stem: **properā−**, **properāv−**. No rules, however, can be given for forming the perfect stem of verbs of the other conjugations. Hereafter the first person singular of the perfect active will be given in the vocabularies as the third form. This should be memorized.

219.   Perfect Active

The following endings (used in no other tenses) are added directly to the perfect stem in forming the **perfect active**:

PERFECT ENDINGS	FIRST CONJUGATION	SECOND CONJUGATION
−ī	portā'vī, *I carried, I have carried, I did carry*	do'cuī, *I taught, I have taught, I did teach*
−istī	portāvis'tī, *you carried*, etc.	docuis'tī, *you taught*, etc.
−it	portā'vit, *he carried*, etc.	do'cuit, *he taught*, etc.
−imus	portā'vimus, *we carried*, etc.	docu'imus, *we taught*, etc.
−istis	portāvis'tis, *you carried*, etc.	docuis'tis, *you taught*, etc.
−ērunt	portāvē'runt, *they carried*, etc.	docuē'runt, *they taught*, etc.

Similarly **posuī, mūnīvī, cēpī** (see 586–588).

Practice.—(*a*) Conjugate the following in the perfect active: **convocō** (**convocāv−**), **agō** (**ēg−**), **excēdō** (**excess−**), **dēfendō** (**dēfend−**), **mittō** (**mīs−**), **trahō** (**trāx−**), **accipiō** (**accēp−**), **videō** (**vīd−**), **fugiō** (**fūg−**), **veniō** (**vēn−**).

(*b*) Translate: *to lose, he has departed, we have entrusted, we shall be heard, they will be called.*

220.   Exercises

(*a*) 1. Āmīsimus; nūntiāvit; augēbis; occupāvistis; āmittitur; ēvocāminī. 2. Puer in viā librum āmīsit. 3. Ex oppidō excessimus et ad agrōs silvāsque properāvimus. 4. Multī vītam in bellō āmīsērunt sed magnam glōriam accēpērunt. 5. Multōs annōs in perīculō ēgimus; nunc ōtium habēmus. 6. Multī captīvī ā puerīs prō castrīs vidēbuntur.

(*b*) 1. Were the girls being scared by the horses? 2. Where

144

were the boys? 3. They saw the danger clearly and fled to the woods. 4. I have entrusted the care of the money to guards.

221. Vocabulary

āmit′tō, āmit′tere, āmī′sī, *let go, lose*	[*mittō*]
an′nus, –ī, m., *year*	(annual)
li′ber, li′brī, m., *book*	(library)
mi′ser, mi′sera, mi′serum, *unhappy, poor*	(misery)
perī′culum, –ī, n., *danger*	(perilous)
prō, prep. with abl., *in front of, before, for*	

222. English Word Studies

(*a*) As a prefix **prō–** has its prepositional meanings, with the additional one of *forward*. Define the following derivatives of words which you have already studied:

> *provoke, prospect, produce, proceed*

What is an *annuity?* Tell which of the following are derived from **liber, librī,** and which from **līber, –a, –um:** *liberty, librarian, liberal, liberate.*

(*b*) **Latin Phrases in English**

> pro bono publico, *for the public good.*
> pro forma, *for (as a matter of) form.*
> pro patria, *for (one's) country.*

Mercury in modern style at Rockefeller Center, New York

The grotto of the Sibyl at Lake Avernus in Italy

LESSON XXXII

223.   AENĒĀS AD ĪNFERŌS[1]

Aenēās fīlius Anchīsae[2] fuit, quī[3] in Siciliā ē vītā excessit. Tum
Anchīsēs in somnō ad fīlium vēnit et fīlium vocāvit: "Venī, fīlī,
ad īnferōs, ubi sum. Sibylla[4] viam nōvit et tē[5] dūcet."

Aenēās in Italiam prōcessit, ubi Sibylla habitābat. Cōnsilium
5 Sibyllae erat: "Sī in silvā rāmum[6] aureum inveniēs, tē[5] ad īnferōs
dūcam et sine[7] perīculō redūcam." Ita Aenēās in silvam properāvit. Auxiliō Veneris[8] rāmum invēnit et cum Sibyllā ad īnferōs
dēscendit. Ibi multa nova vidēbat et nōscēbat.

Tum ad magnam silvam vēnērunt. Ibi erat Dīdō. Aenēās
10 rēgīnam vīdit et appellāvit: "Vērumne nūntius nūntiāvit?

[1] *the Lower World* (cf. **170,** n. 4).   [2] *Ankī'sēs* (gen.).   [3] *who.*
[4] *the Sibyl* (a prophetess).   [5] *you* (acc.).   [6] *branch.*
       [7] *without.*   [8] Genitive of **Venus.**

Vītamne āmīsistī? Causane fuī? Invītus[1] ex patriā tuā excessī sed ita deus imperāvit." Sed rēgīna verbīs lacrimīsque Aenēae nōn movētur. Neque Aenēam spectāvit neque respondit sed in silvam fūgit.

Aenēās tardē ex silvā excessit et locum vīdit ubi malī poenā 15 afficiēbantur. Tum Aenēās Sibyllaque in Ēlysium[2] prōcessērunt. Ibi animae[3] bonōrum in concordiā vītam agēbant. Iniūriae et bella aberant. Ibi Anchīsēs erat. Grātus fīlium accēpit et nūntiāvit: "Clārōs Rōmānōs . quī posteā in terrā erunt et glōriam populī tuī mōnstrābō. Rōmānī malōs superābunt et 20 populōs aequē regent."

Thought Questions.—1. What did Aeneas need to go safely into the Lower World? 2. Whom did he see there?

Read Sabin, pp. 338–341.

224.   Perfect of *Sum*

The verb **sum** is conjugated regularly in the perfect:

fu'ī, *I was, I have been*	fu'imus, *we were, we have been*
fuis'tī, *you were, you have been*	fuis'tis, *you were, you have been*
fu'it, *he was, he has been*	fuē'runt, *they were, they have been*

Practice.—Tell the form of erātis, āmīsistī, accipiētis, fuī, vīdimus, vidēmus, dūcet, fūgī, āfuērunt.

225.   How the Perfect and Imperfect Differ

The Latin perfect tense must be carefully distinguished from the imperfect, which always refers to action or being as *repeated*, *customary*, or *continuous*, like the English progressive past. In the following sentences the first group would be in the perfect in Latin, the second in the imperfect:

---

[1] *unwillingly.*   [2] *Elȳ'sium*, the heaven of the Greeks and Romans.   [3] *souls.*

PERFECT

1. *I saw John yesterday.*
2. *I went to camp last summer.*
3. ***Did** you ever **live** in Louisville?*
4. *The alarm clock **rang** and I got up.*

IMPERFECT

1. *I saw John frequently.*
2. *I **used to go** to camp every summer.*
3. ***Did** you **live** in Boston long?*
4. *The alarm clock **kept on ringing,** but I did not get up.*

The perfect tense is used much more often in Latin than the imperfect. In translating the English past into Latin, use the perfect unless there is a clear reason for using the imperfect.

226.   Exercises

(*a*) 1. Multī puerī aberant. Nōnne valēbant? 2. Paucī (of us) labōrābāmus, sed reliquī puerī in castrīs semper manēbant. 3. Agricolārum fīliī et fīliae multa dē agrīs et equīs nōvērunt. 4. Magistrī fīlius multa dē librīs nōvit, sed agrī fīlium agricolae

148

docent. 5. Multī virī servī fuērunt; nunc līberī sunt. 6. Prō patriā ad pugnam prōcessērunt; prō patriā et arma et frūmentum parāvērunt; prō patriā labōrāvērunt et pecūniam dōnāvērunt.

(*b*) 1. We are the sons of free (men) and love our native land. 2. We know much about many lands and peoples. 3. Many wagons were being got ready by the farmers. 4. The farmer has spent many years in the fields.

227. Vocabulary

fī′lius, fī′lī, m., *son*   [*fīlia*]
nōs′cō, nōs′cere, nō′vī, *learn;* in perf. tense, "have
  learned" = *know*
prōcē′dō, prōcē′dere, prōces′sī, *go forth, advance*   [*cēdō*]
ab′sum, abes′se, ā′fuī, *be away, be absent*   [*sum*]

228.   Latin and English Word Formation

We have already studied the preposition **in** used as a prefix (**118**). There is another prefix **in–**, used chiefly with adjectives and nouns, which has an entirely different meaning and must be carefully distinguished from the former. It is a negative prefix (like "un–"), as in *injustice*. It is assimilated like the other prefix **in–**, e.g. *il-legal, im-moral, ir-regular*. Define the following derivatives of words which you have already studied:

  immemorial, immaterial, inglorious, ingratitude, illiberal, illiteracy, infirm

Tell which of the two prefixes (preposition or negative) is used in each of the following:

  inhabit, invalid, invoke, induce, invariable, inequality, inundate, immovable, impecunious

The prefix **dis–** in English and Latin means *apart*, but sometimes it is purely negative like **in–**. Distinguish carefully from **dē–**. It is either assimilated or left unchanged, as follows:

  dis-inter, dis-locate, dis-arm, dif-fuse, di-vert, di-stant, dis-similar

Define the first three of these words, derived from words in previous vocabularies.

Model of Trajan's harbor at Ostia, the seaport of Rome, in the Museum of Science and Industry, Chicago. Ostia is near Latinus' country.

LESSON XXXIII

229. **AENĒĀS ET LATĪNUS**

Aenēās ad Italiam nunc vēnerat. Terra fīnitima ubi Troiānī castra posuerant ā bonō Latīnō regēbātur. Lāvīnia, fīlia Latīnī, ā Turnō amābātur, sed deī verbīs signīsque mātrimōnium nōn probāverant et Latīnum retinuerant.

5 "Vir veniet quī[1] Lāvīniam in mātrimōnium dūcet. Terra Latīnī ā populō novō regētur." Haec[2] fuērunt verba deōrum, et Latīnus audīvit.

---

[1] *who.*   [2] *these.*

150

Aenēās nūntiōs et dōna commoda ad portās oppidī Latīnī dīmīsit. Nūntiī dīxērunt:

"Properāmus concordiam amīcitiamque efficere. Bellum nōn 10 gerēmus in populum Latīnī nec cōpiās ad proelium prōdūcēmus."

Latīnus ad portās prōcessit et dōna accēpit retinuitque; tum respondit:

"Sī Aenēās nōn fuerit inimīcus, tum amīcitia nostra erit perpetua."

15

Tum Latīnus equōs integrōs prōdūxit et nūntiōs cum equīs et dōnīs ad castra Troiāna dīmīsit. Troiānī amīcitiam concordiamque effēcerant—Aenēās et Latīnus nunc nōn inimīcī erant sed sociī.

Thought Questions.—1. Who wanted to marry Lavinia? 2. Why didn't he? 3. Did the Trojans attack the country of Latinus?

Read Gayley, pp. 362–367; Guerber, pp. 372–374.

230.   Past Perfect Active

Ostia in Chicago. An ancient column from Ostia on Chicago's lake front

The **past perfect** tense (sometimes called pluperfect) refers to an action that was completed before a certain time in the past: *He had gone* (before something else happened).

In Latin, the past perfect is formed by adding the tense sign **-erā-** to the perfect stem, together with the personal endings used throughout the present system. It is equivalent in form to the various forms of the imperfect tense of **sum** added to the perfect stem of the given verb:

151

portā'veram, *I had carried*	portāverā'mus, *we had carried*
portā'verās, *you had carried*	portāverā'tis, *you had carried*
portā'verat, *he, she, it had carried*	portā'verant, *they had carried*

Similarly **docueram, posueram, mūnīveram, cēperam.**
(For full conjugation see 585–588.)

Note.—(*a*) The future perfect tense refers to an action completed before a certain time in the future: *He will have gone* (before something else will happen). In Latin, it is formed by adding the tense sign –eri– to the perfect stem, together with the personal endings used throughout the present system: **portāverō**, etc. (cf. 584–588).

(*b*) The three tenses, perfect, past perfect, and future perfect, which are based upon the perfect stem, form the **perfect system**.

Practice.—(*a*) Conjugate in the perfect: **videō, –ēre, vīdī; cēdō, –ere, cessī; efficiō, –ere, effēcī;** in the past perfect: **moveō, –ēre, mōvī; incipiō, –ere, incēpī.**

(*b*) Tell the form of **dīmīserō, prōdūxerat, retinuistī, nōvērunt, prōcesserimus, āmīserātis, docueram.**

Two stamps issued in Italy in 1935 for the two thousandth anniversary of the birth of Horace, one of Rome's most widely loved poets, a particular favorite in the United States. Both have quotations from his poems. The upper has a picture of the Colosseum.

(*a*) 1. Parvī puerī linguam retinēre dēbent. 2. Magister puerōs dīmīsit, quod fōrmās verbōrum nōn nōverant. 3. Nautae nostrī perīculum vīderint. 4. Integrae cōpiae nostrae bellum gerere incēpērunt et prō populīs līberīs pugnāvērunt. 5. Barbarī prō portīs castrōrum cōpiās prōdūxerant. 6. Carrī ex silvā vēnerant et ad oppidum tardē prōcēdēbant.

(*b*) 1. The slave deserved a large reward, because he had saved the life of our son. 2. Marius had fought in Gaul for (his) native land. 3. We had seen strange lands, towns, and peoples.

232.   Vocabulary

dīmit′tō, dīmit′tere, dīmī′sī, *let go, send away*	[*mittō*]
inimī′cus, –a, –um, *unfriendly;* as noun, *enemy*	[*amīcus*]
in′teger, –gra, –grum, *untouched, fresh*	(integer)
por′ta, –ae, f., *gate*	(portal)
prōdū′cō, prōdū′cere, prōdū′xī, *lead forth* or *out*	[*dūcō*]
reti′neō, retinē′re, reti′nuī, *hold* (*back*), *keep*	[*teneō*]

233.   Latin and English Word Formation

We have seen that prefixes are so called because they are attached to the beginnings of words (**106**). Particles which are attached to the ends of words are called **suffixes** (**sub**, *under, after;* **fīxus**, *attached*). Like the Latin prefixes, the Latin suffixes play a very mportant part in the formation of English words.

The suffix **–ia** usually has the form **–y** in English. Give the English forms of the following words found in the preceding vocabularies: **memoria, glōria, familia, iniūria.**

What must be the Latin words from which are derived *colony, luxury, perfidy?*

Some **–ia** nouns drop the **–ia** entirely in English: *concord, vigil, matter* (from **māteria**).

You will find it useful to list suffixes in your notebook, together with many examples of their use in English words.

234.   LŪCIUS PILAM ĀMITTIT

Lūcius. Mārce, venī ad nōs.

Mārcus. Mēne vocās, Lūcī?

Lūcius. Tē vocō. Pilam[1] meam novam āmīsī. Dā[2] nōbīs auxilium. Sī et nōs et tū pilam petēmus nōs eam[3] inveniēmus. Sed sine auxiliō tuō numquam[4] ea ā nōbīs inveniētur.   5

Mārcus. Ubi pilam āmīsistī? Quid faciēbās?

Roman boy with ball and turtle

Lūcius. In herbā āmīsī. Ego et Cornēlius lūdēbāmus. Is pilam nōn āmīsit; ego āmīsī.

Mārcus. Invēnī pilam tuam, 10 Lūcī! Cape.

Lūcius. Magnam grātiam tibi prō beneficiō tuō habeō, Mārce. Beneficium tuum semper memoriā tenēbō. Nunc tē nōn 15 dīmittēmus: lūde nōbīscum. Dubitāsne? Tē vincam!

Mārcus. Grātiās agō; nōn dubitō. Vōbīscum lūdere cupiō. Sed mē nōn vincēs quod integer 20 sum.

Lūcius. Cupisne pilā aut gladiīs lūdere?

Mārcus. Retinēte gladiōs vestrōs. Inimīcī nōn sumus. Pilā 25 lūdere cupiō.

Thought Questions.—1. Who lost the ball? 2. Who found it? 3. What was the reward?

---

[1] *ball.*   [2] *give.*   [3] *it.*   [4] *never.*

In English, personal pronouns are used to show the person of the verb: *I am*, *you are*. In Latin, as we have seen (21), personal endings are used instead. When, however, emphasis or sharp contrast in subjects is desired, the Latin employs the personal pronouns **ego** (*I*) and **tū** (*you*). **Is** and **ea** serve as the personal pronouns of the third person (*he* and *she*). The full declension of hese will be given later. Memorize the declensions of **ego** and **tū**:[1]

	SINGULAR	PLURAL
Nom.	e′go, *I*	nōs, *we*
Gen.	me′ī, *of me*	nos′trum, *of us*
Dat.	mi′hi, *to (for) me*	nō′bīs, *to (for) us*
Acc.	mē, *me*	nōs, *us*
Abl.	mē, *with (from, etc.) me*	nō′bīs, *with (from, etc.) us*

	SINGULAR	PLURAL
Nom.	tū, *you*	vōs, *you*
Gen.	tu′ī, *of you*	ves′trum, *of you*
Dat.	ti′bi, *to (for) you*	vō′bīs, *to (for) you*
Acc.	tē, *you*	vōs, *you*
Abl.	tē, *with (from, etc.) you*	vō′bīs, *with (from, etc.) you*

236.   Possessive Adjectives

From the base of **ego** (me–), **nōs** (nostr–), **tū** (tu–), and **vōs** (vestr–), the possessive adjectives **meus**, **noster**, **tuus**, and **vester** are derived.

The possessive adjectives follow the noun except when emphatic.

Caution.—Never use the genitives **meī**, **tuī**, **nostrum**, and **vestrum** to show possession; use the corresponding possessive adjectives **meus**, **tuus**, **noster**, and **vester**.

Query.—What is the difference between **tuus** and **vester**?

---

[1] When the preposition **cum** is used with the ablative forms of **ego** and **tū**, it is attached to them: **mēcum**, *with me*; **nōbīscum**, *with us*.

The tomb of President Grant on Riverside Drive, New York, in beautiful
classic design. The lower columns are Doric; the upper, Ionic.

237. Personal Pronoun Test

First copy these sentences. Then translate the underlined
English words into the proper Latin forms.

1. She is my friend; he, my enemy.
2. I shall give you a book.
3. She showed us beautiful flowers.
4. I criticize you; you criticize me.
5. We'll treat you (*plur.*) if you'll treat us.
6. I will show you (*sing.*) the house.
7. He came to us and showed us many pictures.
8. Come with us and we will go with you (*plur.*).
9. He was mentioned by me, but she told me nothing.
10. Your daughter was seen by us with you (*sing.*) on the street.

238. Exercises

(*a*) 1. Ego sum amīcus tuus; is est inimīcus. 2. Cupitisne vidēre nōs, amīcōs vestrōs? 3. Gladium meum retinuī et praesidium integrum prōdūxī. 4. Fīlius meus in perīculum mēcum properāre nōn dubitāverat. 5. Ego sum miser sine tē; tū misera es quod tēcum nōn maneō. 6. Multa beneficia ā tē, amīce, accēpī.

(*b*) 1. We are Americans; you are foreigners. 2. Come (*plur.*) with us; we are your friends, not your enemies. 3. I desire to present the sword to you (*sing.*).

239. Vocabulary

benefi'cium, benefi'cī, n., *kindness*   [*faciō*]
cu'piō, cu'pere, cupī'vī, *desire*   (cupidity)
du'bitō, dubitā're, dubitā'vī, *hesitate, doubt*   (indubitable)
e'go, me'ī, *I*   (egoist)
gla'dius, gla'dī, m., *sword*   (gladiator)
is, *he, it;*[1] ea, *she, it*[1]
si'ne, prep. with abl., *without*   (sinecure)
tū, tu'ī, *you*
ves'ter, ves'tra, ves'trum, *your* (referring to two or more persons)

240. English Word Studies

(*a*) Why is a *gladiolus* so named? How does a *miser* feel? What does *inimical* mean? What is an *integer?* From their meanings tell which of the following words come from **porta** and which from **portāre:** *report, portiere, transport, port.*

(*b*) Latin Phrases in English

Et tu, Brute, *You too,* *Brutus* (said by Caesar on receiving the deathblow from his friend, Brutus).

inter nos, *between us.*

Pax vobiscum, *Peace (be) with you!*

Te Deum, *Thee, God (we praise);* the name of a hymn.

---

[1] The word *it* is used to translate **is** and **ea** when the noun referred to is masculine or feminine in Latin but neuter in English (**28**).

157

No, this is not a modern building but a model of an ancient apartment house at Ostia, near Rome.

GLIMPSES OF ROMAN LIFE

241.   Signs of the Times

Perhaps nothing gives us quite so intimate a glimpse of a civilization as its signs and posters on walls, in windows, on posts, and the like. We are fortunate in being able to catch such a glimpse of Roman life through the signs found at Pompeii, a city near Naples which was buried by a shower of volcanic ashes from Mt. Vesuvius in 79 A.D. For more than a hundred years digging has been going on in the ruins, and hundreds of notices painted or scratched on house walls have been uncovered. Among them are the scribblings of small boys, who over and over practiced writing the alphabet. Sometimes they started a fable, as "Once upon a time a mouse . . . " Sometimes they quoted lines from Virgil and other poets. They and grown-ups too wrote their names over and over again. A kind of "pig Latin" is represented by **anumurb** for **urbānum,** like "eesay" for "see." There are messages to sweethearts; in one, greetings are sent to a girl whom the lover calls his little fish. Another girl is called the queen of Pompeii, evidently meaning the beauty queen. To another, who is unnamed, there is merely the message **Venus es.** Several run like this: **Helena amātur ā Rūfō.** But another tells about a girl who

158

cannot stand a certain boy. Some of the messages are not very complimentary: "thief" occurs several times. One reads: **Stronnius nīl scit,** "Stronnius knows nothing." In another, one person says hello to another and adds: **Quid agit tibi dexter ocellus?** "How is your right eye?" Apparently the writer is having some fun about a black eye. The owners of houses tried to keep away idlers by such signs as this: **Ōtiōsīs locus hic nōn est. Discēde, morātor,** "This is no place for idlers. Go away, loafer." Sometimes there are New Year's greetings or "Christmas" greetings (**Iō Sāturnālia**). In some cases record is kept of special events, as a birthday or the arrival of the emperor. One writer indicates that he has a cold. One says he (or she) baked bread on April 19; another that he put up olives on October 16; another tells of setting a hen on April 30. One wall lists daily expenditures, as for cheese, bread, oil, and wine. What appears to be a laundry list mentions a tunic (shirt) and a cloak on April 20, a brassière on

Modern painting of an ancient scene: gladiator celebrating after a victory

Believe it or not, this is an ancient Roman scene in spite of the very modern wicker chair.

May 7, two tunics on May 8. No wonder that some unknown wrote: "Wall, I wonder that you have not collapsed from having to bear the tiresome stuff of so many writers."

When we come to formal notices, we find that election posters play a prominent part. These ask support for this man or that because he is deserving or respectable or honest or because he delivers good bread, etc. The supporters include teamsters, tailors, barbers, dyers, and many other groups. One inscription advocates dividing up the money in the public treasury.

Another group of notices advertises the shows of gladiators, similar to our boxing matches. Besides mentioning the number of matches, they often name other attractions, such as awnings to keep the sun off, sprinklers to keep the dust down, animal fights, athletic contests.

Hotels advertised frequently. One offers a dining room with three couches and all conveniences (**commodīs**). In an apartment house (**īnsula**) shops on the ground floor are offered from July 1, and luxurious (**equestria,** suitable for a rich man) upstairs apartments; "see agent of the owner."

Signs offer rewards for return of lost or stolen articles. On one a man says that he found a horse on November 25 and asks the owner to claim it on a farm near the bridge.

Questions for Discussion.—1. What kind of signs are most frequently seen today? 2. What impressions about us would a stranger get from such signs?

Statuae deorum. An ancient statue of Neptune with his trident and a modern statue by Robert Aitken of Jupiter with his thunderbolt and eagle

LESSON XXXV

242. Q. FABIUS MAXIMUS

Bellō[1] Pūnicō Hannibal cōpiās cum Rōmānīs pugnāre iubēbat sed Q.[2] Fabius Maximus semper discēdēbat neque in ūnō locō manēbat. Sine victōriīs Hannibal Italiam in prōvinciam redigere nōn poterat.[3]

Maximus perpetuā vigiliā etiam Tarentum, oppidum Italiae, 5 recēpit. Līvius in hōc[4] oppidō fuerat sed oppidum āmīserat et ad arcem[5] cōpiās remōverat. Maximus ad portās oppidī cōpiās prōdūxit et oppidum recēpit; tum is etiam ad arcem prōcessit. Ibi Līvius, superbus quod arcem retinuerat, Fabiō dīxit:[6] "Meā operā[7] Tarentum recēpistī." Fabius respondit: "Certē, Līvī, nam 10 ego recēpī oppidum quod[8] tū āmīsistī."

---

[1] Ablative: in——.   [2] Q.= Quīntus.   [3] *was able.*   [4] *this* (ablative).
[5] *citadel* (accusative).   [6] *said.*   [7] *effort.*   [8] *which.*

161

Statuās deōrum ex oppidō Tarentō Maximus nōn remōvit sed, quod deī inimīcī Tarentīnīs erant, Tarentīnōs in oppidō statuās retinēre iussit.

Thought Questions.—1. How did Maximus weaken Hannibal? 2. How did Livius help in recovering Tarentum?

243.   **Past Perfect of *Sum*[1]**

fu'eram, *I had been*
fu'erās, *you had been*
fu'erat, *he had been*

fuerā'mus, *we had been*
fuerā'tis, *you had been*
fu'erant, *they had been*

Practice.—*Translate* erit, sunt, fuit, erātis, sumus, fuerat, esse, erimus, estis.

244.   **Infinitive Object as in English**

1. Virōs discēdere iussī, *I ordered the men to go away.*
2. Mē labōrāre docuistī, *You taught me to work.*

Observe that (*a*) in English such verbs as *order, teach* (also *wish, forbid*, etc.) take an infinitive as *object*, often with a noun or pronoun in the accusative, which may be regarded as its *subject;* (*b*) in Latin certain verbs of similar meaning take the infinitive with subject accusative.

245.   **Exercises**

(*a*) 1. Fīliōs nostrōs bonōs librōs semper retinēre docēmus. 2. Nōnne bonum est inimīcōs in amīcitiam et concordiam redigere? 3. Deus nōs etiam inimīcōs amāre docet. 4. Servī ex silvā māteriam remōverant et ad oppidum fīnitimum prōcesserant, 5. Magister nōs amīcōs nostrōs dīmittere et ā viā discēdere iussit.

---

[1] For the future perfect see 589.

(*b*) 1. It was good to see our friends. 2. They had hesitated to remove the grain without wagons. 3. The sons of farmers are beginning to go away from the farms (**ager**). 4. Lucius, order the boy to lead out fresh horses.

246. Vocabulary

de′us, –ī, m., *god* (deity)
discē′dō, discē′dere, disces′sī, *go away, depart* [*cēdō*]
e′tiam, adv., *also, even*
iu′beō, iubē′re, ius′sī, *order*
red′igō, redi′gere, redē′gī, *drive back, reduce* [*agō*]
remo′veō, removē′re, remō′vī, *remove* [*moveō*]

In honor of the Olympic Games of 1924 Costa Rica issued this stamp with classical buildings on it. Many countries have issued similar stamps for these games, which originated in ancient Greece.

247. Latin and English Word Formation

The Latin suffix –**ia** usually has the form –**y** in English, as we have seen (**233**). When it is preceded by –**t**–, the combination –**tia** as a general rule has the form –**ce** in English.

Give the English forms of the following words found in the preceding vocabularies: **grātia, sententia, prōvincia.**

What must be the Latin words from which are derived *science, diligence, prudence, absence?*

The *tarantula* (a spider) and the *tarantella* (a dance) both got their names from Tarentum. Look them up in the dictionary.

Latin Verb Forms in English

Present: *deficit*
Perfect: *affidavit, vici*

163

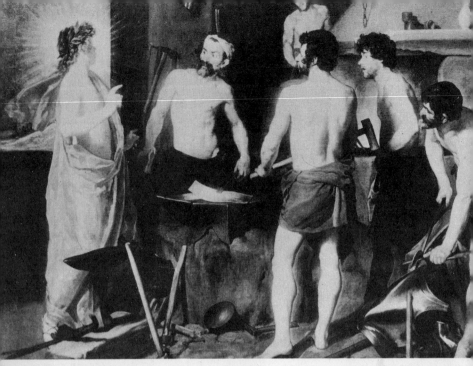

Venus persuades Vulcan to make armor for Aeneas—as Velasquez imagined the scene. It looks like an ordinary blacksmith shop.

LESSON XXXVI

248. AENĒĀS ET TURNUS

Troia ā Graecīs capta erat et Aenēās cum paucīs Troiānīs ad Italiam vēnerat et per terrās barbarōrum cōpiās prōdūxerat. Sed Iūnō inimīca remānsit et multōs barbarōs populōs Italiae contrā Aenēam miserum incitāvit. Ā Turnō Lāvīnia, fīlia rēgis[1] Latīnī, 5 amābātur sed Aenēae[2] dōnāta erat. Turnus bellum gerere nōn dubitāvit. Aenēās bellum nōn grātē suscēpit; ad terminum vītae sub armīs esse nōn cupīvit. Sed causa Troiānōrum ā Fātīs suscepta erat. Aenēās beneficium et auxilium etiam ā Graecīs quī in Italiā habitābant accēpit, quod erant inimīcī Turnō. Per multōs diēs 10 bellum gerēbant, et multa ēgregia exempla virtūtis[3] in proeliīs clārīs prōposita sunt.

---

[1] Genitive singular of **rēx**.   [2] Dative.   [3] *of courage.*

164

Tandem Turnus cōpiās remōvit et sōlus Aenēam ad pugnam ēvocāvit, quod reliquīs exemplum prōpōnere cupīvit. In locō commodō sub portīs oppidī gladiīs pugnāvērunt. Nōn longa fuit pugna, quod Venus, māter Aenēae, fīliō gladium e reliqua ēgregia 15 arma dōnāverat quae[1] deus Vulcānus fēcerat. Fāta iusserant auxilium ad Turnum nōn mittī;[2] itaque Iūnō aberat. Turnus vītam āmīsit, et cōpiae Turnī discessērunt.

Thought Questions.—1. Why did Turnus carry on war with the Trojans? 2. Why did Aeneas defeat Turnus?

Read Sabin, pp. 341–342; Gayley, pp. 367–372; Bulfinch, pp. 290–292.

249. Perfect Participle

A **participle** is that part of a verb which is used like an adjective.

The **perfect passive participle** in Latin is declined like **magnus, –a, –um.** In the first conjugation it is regularly formed by adding **–tus** to the present stem: **portā-tus.** It agrees, like an ordinary adjective, with a noun or pronoun in gender, number, and case: **litterae plicātae,** *the folded letter.* The perfect participle represents an act as having taken place before the time indicated by the main verb.

The perfect participle of each new verb will hereafter be given in the vocabularies as the fourth form. The four forms given are called the **principal parts.**

250. Perfect System Passive

In English, all the passive tenses are **compound,** consisting of two or more words.

In Latin, the tenses of the present and perfect systems thus far studied have been single or **simple** in form. In the passive, however, the three perfect tenses are compound, and are formed by combining the perfect participle of the given verb with the present, imperfect, and future tenses of **sum** to form the perfect, past per-

---

[1] *which.*   [2] *to be sent.*

fect, and future perfect tenses, respectively. In the compound tenses the participle really modifies the subject and therefore agrees with it in gender, number, and case.

251. Perfect Passive

In English, the past passive is formed by using the past tense of *to be* (i.e. *was*) as an auxiliary or helping verb with the past participle.

In Latin, the perfect passive is formed by using the *present* tense of **sum** as an auxiliary with the perfect participle.

portā′tus (–a, –um)	sum, *I was, have been carried* es, *you were, have been carried* est, *he was, has been carried*	portā′tī (–ae, –a)	su′mus, *we were, have been carried* es′tis, *you were, have been carried* sunt, *they were, have been carried*

Similarly **doctus sum, positus sum, mūnītus sum, captus sum.**

(For full conjugation see 585–588.)

An example of the charming wall paintings in Pompeii. Similar ones were used elsewhere but more have been preserved in Pompeii.

Like Costa Rica (p. 163), Uruguay issued stamps for the Olympic Games of 1924. This one shows a famous Greek statue, the "Victory of Samothrace," now in the Louvre at Paris. Victory has lost her head—as victories sometimes do.

VRVGVAY · MCMXXIV· 2 ⅚ JVEGOS OLIMPICOS

252. Past Perfect Passive

In English, the past perfect passive is formed by using the past perfect tense of *to be* (i.e. *had been*) as an auxiliary with the past participle.

In Latin, the past perfect passive is formed by using the *imperfect* tense of **sum** (*i.e.* **eram**) as an auxiliary with the perfect participle (cf. the formation of the corresponding active tense by adding the imperfect tense of **sum** to the perfect stem: **portāveram**):[1]

portā′tus (–a, –um)	e′ram, *I had been carried* e′rās, *you had been carried* e′rat, *he had been carried*	portā′tī (–ae, –a)	erā′mus, *we had been carried* erā′tis, *you had been carried* e′rant, *they had been carried*

Similarly **doctus eram, positus eram, mūnītus eram, captus eram.**
(For full conjugation see **585–588**.)

Practice.—(*a*) Conjugate in the perfect passive **trahō, –ere, trāxī, trāctus; videō, –ēre, vīdī, vīsus;** in the past perfect passive: **moveō, –ēre, mōvī, mōtus; agō, –ere, ēgī, āctus.**

(*b*) *Translate:* they have been seen; I had been dragged; you had been moved; driven; having been seen.

---

[1] The future perfect passive consists of the participle and the future of **sum: portā′tus e′rō** (cf. **584–588**).

167

The barefoot boy had his troubles
even in ancient times.

253. Exercises

(*a*) 1. Ēgregium exemplum
beneficī ā magistrō vestrō prōpositum est. 2. Arma carrīs ad
castra portāta erant. 3. Equī ab
agricolā per silvam ad aquam
āctī erant. 4. Ēgregiumne exemplum amīcitiae memoriā tenētis?
5. Causam populī suscipere est
officium bonōrum. 6. Vir ā puerō
sub aquam trāctus erat, sed et vir
et puer servātī[1] sunt.

(*b*) 1. The rest of the books
had been removed by the teacher.
2. The farmer's son had seen few
towns, but he knew much about
horses. 3. My son had presented
an excellent example. 4. He had
been taught by good teachers.

254. Vocabulary

ēgre′gius, –a, –um, *distinguished, excellent* (egregious)
exem′plum, –ī, n., *example* (exemplify)
per, prep. with acc., *through*
prōpō′nō, prōpō′nere, prōpo′suī, prōpo′situs, *put forth, offer* [*pōnō*]
sub, prep., *under, close to;* with acc. after verbs of motion; with
   abl. after verbs of rest
susci′piō, susci′pere, susce′pī, suscep′tus, *undertake* [*capiō*]

255. Latin and English Word Formation

The preposition **sub,** used as a prefix in Latin and English,
means *under, up from under:* **sus-tineō,** *hold up;* **succēdō,**
come up. It is regularly assimilated before certain consonants:

---

[1] Note that the participle is plural because it refers to both **vir** and **puer.**

sup-port, suc-ceed, sug-gest, sus-ceptible, suf-fer, sur-rogate, sus-tenance, sus-pend, but *sub-mit, sub-trahend.* We use it freely in English to form new words: *sub-let, sub-lease.*

Per usually remains unchanged when used as a prefix.

Explain by derivation the meaning of *permanent, permit, sustain, suspect.* What is meant by being *susceptible* to colds?

Why are iron and steel mills named after *Vulcan?* Why does the name *Vulcan* occur more often in the Pittsburgh telephone directory than that of any other Roman god? What do you infer from the fact that Buffalo, Chicago, Cleveland, Philadelphia, and Pittsburgh are among the cities that have the name *Vulcan* in their telephone directories four or more times?

Factories too use a modified classical architecture. This is the Edwards plant at Norwalk, Connecticut. It manufactures electric signaling devices.

The destruction of the children of Niobe, by the English painter
Richard Wilson. This picture, in the Boston Museum, was shown at
the New York World's Fair in 1940.

LESSON XXXVII

256.   NIOBĒ

Niobē,[1] rēgīna superba, in Graeciā habitābat. Avus erat Iuppiter, quī deōs virōsque regēbat, et hoc[2] superbiam rēgīnae augē-
bat. Niobē erat superba etiam quod septem fīliōs et septem fīliās
habēbat.

5   Apollō deus erat fīlius Lātōnae, et Diāna erat fīlia. Aliōs
līberōs Lātōna nōn habēbat.

Sacra[3] Lātōnae ā populō suscipiēbantur. Superba Niobē adfuit
et rogāvit:

"Cūr sacra mātrī[4] duōrum līberōrum suscipitis? Hoc[5] nōn per-
10 mittam. Etiam Niobē dea est; xiv, nōn duōs, līberōs habet.
Lātōna glōriam nōn meret—Niobē esse prīma dēbet. Vōbīs lībe-
rīsque vestrīs exemplum ēgregium prōpōnō. Sī[6] sententia mea ā
vōbīs nōn probāta erit, poenā afficiēminī."

---

[1] Nī'obē.   [2] this.   [3] sacred rites.   [4] for the mother.   [5] this.   [6] if.

Superba verba rēgīnae ā Lātōnā audīta sunt. Fīlium vocāvit et
officium permīsit:

"Tē iubeō septem fīliōs Niobae interficere."

Prīmus fīlius adfuit et interfectus est, tum reliquī. Niobē septem fīliōs nunc per linguam superbam āmīserat, tamen remānsit
superba quod fīliae remānsērunt. Itaque Lātōna iussit etiam fīliās
septem ēdūcī et ā Diānā interficī. Singulae fīliae ē vītā discessē- 20
runt, et Niobē misera in saxum dūrum mūtāta est. Poenā magnā et
aequā affecta erat.

Thought Questions.—1. Give three reasons for Niobe's pride.
2. Who was Diana's brother? 3. Why were Niobe's children killed?

Read Sabin, pp. 13–15; Gayley, pp. 99–103; Bulfinch, pp. 117–120;
Guerber, pp. 93–96.

257.   Practice

(*a*) Conjugate in the perfect passive: āmittō, –ere, āmīsī,
āmissus; retineō, –ēre, retinuī, retentus; redigō, –ere, redēgī,
redāctus; in the past perfect passive: cupiō, –ere, cupīvī, cupītus; iubeō, –ēre, iussī, iussus; nōscō, –ere, nōvī, nōtus.

(*b*) Tell the form and translate: ēductī sumus, susceptum
erat, permissum erit, trāctī erātis, mōtus es, āctī erant, vīsae
estis, iussae sunt, portātus erō, prōpositum est.

258.   Present Infinitive Passive

In English, the present infinitive passive is formed by using the
auxiliary *to be* with the past participle.

In Latin, the present infinitive passive is formed by changing
the active infinitive ending –re to –rī:

Active: portā're, *to carry;*   docē're; mūnī're
Passive: portā'rī, *to be carried;* docē'rī; mūnī'rī

Note.—In the third conjugation, final –ĕre is changed to –ī:

Active: pō'nere, *to place;* ca'pere
Passive: pō'nī, *to be placed;* ca'pī

Practice.—Form and translate the present passive infinitive of videō, agō, trahō, suscipiō, ēdūcō, moveō, appellō, and inveniō.

This stamp was issued by the government of Transjordan, east of Palestine, under British mandate. The picture shows Roman ruins at Jerash.

259. **Exercises**

(*a*) 1. Nōnne dūrum est sub aquā remanēre? 2. Vītam līberōrum meōrum tibi permittere nōn dubitāvī. 3. Equī ex oppidō per agrōs lātōs ēductī erunt. 4. Pecūnia merērī et servārī ā puerīs puellīsque dēbet. 5. Puerī adfuērunt prīmī, quod puellae tardae fuērunt. 6. Verbīs bonōrum virōrum semper incitārī et regī dēbēmus.

(*b*) 1. The troops had been ordered to seize the fortified town. 2. The boys are absent, but the girls are present. 3. We have ordered the boys to be dismissed. 4. The children ought to be called together and praised by the teacher.

260. **Vocabulary**

ad′sum, ades′se, ad′fuī, adfutū′rus,[1] *be near, be present*　[*sum*]
ēdū′cō, ēdū′cere, ēdū′xī, educ′tus, *lead out*　[*dūcō*]
lī′berī, –ō′rum, m., *children*　[*līber*]
permit′tō, permit′tere, permī′sī, permis′sus, *let go through, allow, entrust* (with dat.)　[*mittō*]
prī′mus, –a, –um, *first*　(primary)
rema′neō, remanē′re, remān′sī, remānsū′rus,[1] *remain*　[*maneō*]

---

[1] A few verbs lack the perfect participle; some of these have the future active participle in –ūrus, which appears as the fourth principal part.

(*a*) According to telephone directories, New York has thirty-one firms named *Apollo*, St. Louis seven; New York has twenty-seven named *Diana*, St. Louis three. Do you know of any firm or product with these names?

What is a *primary* school? A political *primary?*

The word *education* is often wrongly derived from **ēdūcere**. As you can see, the derivative of **ēdūcere** would be *eduction*. *Education* comes from a related word, **ēdŭcāre**, *to bring up*. Etymologically then if you are well educated you are well brought up.

(*b*)   Latin Phrases in English

Dei gratia, *by the grace of God* (seen on Canadian coins).

Deo gratias, *thanks to God*.

per annum, *by (through) the year*.

sic semper tyrannis, *thus always to tyrants* (motto of the state of Virginia).

sub rosa, *under the ròse, i.e.* in concealment.

Monticello, Virginia, the home of Thomas Jefferson, designed by himself. The Doric columns and Roman dome are no accident, for Jefferson was a good classical scholar and helped introduce classical architecture and other phases of ancient civilization in the United States.

Types of decoration used on ancient walls at Pompeii

262. English Word Studies

(*a*) Find and use in sentences as many English derivatives as possible from **servō, moveō, dūcō, capiō.** For example: from **servō** is derived *conservation*, used as follows: *The **conservation** of our forests is a necessity.*

(*b*) Pick out from **263** the Latin words from which each of the following is derived: *primitive, permission, beneficiary, exemplary, proposition, librarian, inimical, integration, commiserate, retention, reproduce.*

263. Vocabulary

NOUNS

1. annus
2. beneficium
3. deus
4. exemplum
5. fīlius
6. gladius
7. liber
8. līberī
9. perīculum
10. porta

ADJECTIVES

11. ēgregius
12. inimīcus
13. integer
14. miser
15. prīmus
16. vester

PRONOUNS

17. ego
18. is, ea
19. tū

VERBS

20. absum
21. adsum
22. āmittō
23. cupiō
24. dīmittō
25. discēdō
26. dubitō
27. ēdūcō
28. iubeō
29. nōscō
30. permittō
31. prōcēdō
32. prōdūcō
33. prōpōnō
34. redigō
35. remaneō
36. removeō
37. retineō
38. suscipiō

ADVERB

39. etiam

PREPOSITIONS

40. per   41. prō   42. sine   43. sub

Vocabulary

NOUNS

1. *year*	4. *example*	8. *children*
2. *kindness*	5. *son*	9. *danger*
3. *god*	6. *sword*	10. *gate*
	7. *book*	

ADJECTIVES

11. *distinguished*	13. *untouched*	15. *first*
12. *unfriendly*	14. *unhappy*	16. *your*

PRONOUNS

17. *I*	18. *he, she*	19. *you*

VERBS

20. *be away*	25. *depart*	30. *entrust*	35. *remain*
21. *be present*	26. *hesitate*	31. *go forth*	36. *remove*
22. *lose*	27. *lead out*	32. *lead forth*	37. *hold back*
23. *desire*	28. *order*	33. *offer*	38. *undertake*
24. *send away*	29. *learn*	34. *reduce*	

ADVERB

39. *also*

PREPOSITIONS

40. *through*	41. *for*	42. *without*	43. *under*

265.   First Conjugation: Principal Parts

Verbs of the first conjugation generally form the perfect stem by adding –v to the present stem (218, Note) and form the perfect participle by adding –tus to the present stem (249). Review the following verbs, whose principal parts are regular:

accūsō, amō, appellō, convocō, dōnō, dubitō, ēvocō, exspectō, habitō, incitō, labōrō, laudō, līberō, mandō, mōnstrō, nāvigō, nūntiō, occupō, parō, portō, probō, pugnō, servō, spectō, vāstō, vocō

266.   Forms

1. Give the Latin for *I, me, we, us, with me, with us; you* (as sing. subject and object), *you* (as plur. subject and object), *of you* (sing. and plur.), *with you* (sing. and plur.).

Our South American neighbors have the same Roman background as we. Here is the cathedral in Buenos Aires, Argentina, with its Corinthian columns and its sculptured pediment.

2. Give in Latin the singular and plural of *great danger* and *my son* used (*a*) as subject, (*b*) as direct object, (*c*) as indirect object.

3. Give the Latin for *seen, having been driven, undertaken*.

4. (*a*) Give the present passive infinitive of **appellō, āmittō, removeō,** and **audiō.** (*b*) Translate *to undertake, to be undertaken; to order, to be ordered; to lead forth, to be led forth*.

5. Give (*a*) the active first singular of **iubeō** and (*b*) the passive third plural of **permittō** in six tenses, translating each tense form.

6. (*a*) Translate **fuerant, fuistī, iusserāmus, discessit, remōvī, retinuistis, cupīvimus, ēdūxerat, prōpositum est, remōtus erat, dubitāverō.** (*b*) Give in Latin *he had been, she had been seen, it has been presented, he has remained, it will be entrusted, they have been, we had been sent away*.

177

THE STORY OF LUCIUS (*Cont.*)

267.   **Lūdus**

Lūciumne in memoriā habētis? Lūcius reliquīque puerī Rōmānī ā magistrō in pulchrum Forum Rōmānum ēductī erant. Nunc iterum dē Lūciō audiētis, quod bonī puerī puellaeque fuistis. Dē lūdō Lūcī nunc agēmus. Lūdus est locus ubi magister puerōs puellāsque docet. Prīmus lūdus vocābātur "lūdus litterārum." In 5 Lūcī lūdō puellae ob variās causās nōn erant, et paucī puerī. Rōmānī līberōs in pūblicum lūdum nōn mittēbant quod lūdī pūblicī nōn erant. Sed tamen pretium disciplīnae erat parvum. Puerī pecūniam et praemia ad magistrum portābant. Servī puerōs ad lūdum ante aurōram dūcēbant 10 et lanternam librōsque portābant. Nōnne dūrum erat multās hōrās in lūdō agere? Servī in lūdō manēbant et puerōs ad familiās redūcēbant. 15

Sleepyhead. Perhaps a schoolboy, with his lantern

WHAT ROMAN BOYS STUDIED

Etiam magister servus erat. Litterās et verba et numerōs docēbat. Lingua lūdī erat Latīna, quod puerī Rōmānī erant. Numerōs Lūcius nōn amābat. Magister 20 puerīs fōrmās litterārum mōnstrābat. Tum digitōs puerōrum tenēbat, et litterās faciēbant. Sententiae[1] puerīs ā magistrō mōnstrābantur. Exemplum sen- 25

[1] *mottoes.*

tentiae est: "Ibi semper est victōria ubi concordia est." Sententiās pulchrās semper amābat Lūcius et in memoriā tenēbat. Dīligentiā et studiō praemia merēbat.

BAD LUCK

Tardī discipulī poenā afficiēbantur, sed Lūcius semper prīmus veniēbat, quod ad lūdum properābat neque in viīs remanēbat. 30 Sed mala fortūna vēnit. Pecūnia Lūciō permissa erat et ad magistrum portābātur. In viā pecūniam āmīsit et tardus fuit. Magister puerōs appellāverat, et reliquī puerī responderant, "Adsum!" Tum magister Lūcium appellāvit. Puerī respondērunt, "Abest!" Tum vēnit Lūcius sine pecūniā et magister puerīque dē pecūniā 35 āmissā audīvērunt. Magister dūrus Lūcium miserum ā puerīs sublevārī[1] iussit et poenā eum[2] affēcit, quod pecūniam āmīserat et tardus fuerat.

FOUND!

Magister discipulōs dīmīsit et singulī excessērunt. Lūcius cum servō discessit et pecūniam in viā sub carrō invēnit. Ad lūdum 40 properāvit et magistrō pecūniam dōnāvit. Magister bonō puerō grātiās ēgit et ob dīligentiam laudāvit.

Thought Question.—What differences are there between your school and that of Lucius?

268.   **Conversation: School**

Magister. Discipulōs appellābō. Anna. **Anna.** Adsum.
M. Marīa. **Marīa.** Adsum.
M. Mārcus. **Discipulī.** Abest.
M. Ubi est Mārcus? **D.** Ad lūdum nōn vēnit. (Etc.)
M. Grātane erat vīta puerōrum Rōmānōrum? **D.** Nōn grāta erat 5 vīta puerōrum Rōmānōrum, quod puerī Rōmānī ante aurōram in lūdum dūcēbantur.
M. Ubi puerī Rōmānī labōrābant? **D.** In lūdō puerī Rōmānī labōrābant.

---

[1] *to be lifted up.*   [2] *him.*

M. Multĭne puerī in lūdō fuērunt? **D.** Paucī puerī in lūdō fuērunt.

Questions to Be Answered in Latin.—1. Ubi nunc estis? 2. Estne grātum in lūdō esse? 3. Pecūniamne tuam āmīsistī? 4. Ubi librum tuum Latīnum āmīsistī? 5. Tardusne in lūdum vēnistī? 6. Semperne tardus in lūdum veniēs?

269. How to Study a Latin Paragraph

Do not turn to the vocabulary at the end of the book for a word you do not know. Read an entire paragraph before you look up a word. There are three ways to find the meaning of a word *without looking it up:*

Jupiter looks down on the modern home in Roman style of Walter H. Mayer at Chiwaukee, Wis. (cf. p. 344).

1. *English derivatives* (nearly every Latin word has at least one English derivative).

2. *Related Latin words* (if you know the meaning of re- and dūcō, you know the meaning of redūcō).

3. *Sensible guessing.*

Use the vocabulary merely to verify results. In this way you will save time and gain a better command of Latin.

270. Hints for Developing "Word Sense"

No word in any language, except a few prepositions, etc., has the same meaning at all times. While words, as a rule, have one general meaning, they may have several *shades of meaning*, which

180

depend entirely upon their context or surroundings. In translating a Latin word, therefore, it is necessary to derive its exact meaning · (as opposed to its general or "vocabulary" meaning) from its context or setting; for example,

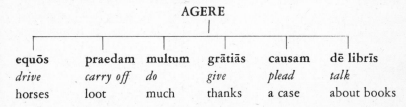

AGERE

equōs	praedam	multum	grātiās	causam	dē librīs
drive	*carry off*	*do*	*give*	*plead*	*talk*
horses	loot	much	thanks	a case	about books

The above are only a few of the meanings of **agō**. From now on, when translating do not confine yourself to the meanings given to words in the vocabulary, but select the one best suited to the context. In this way you will learn to express yourself in good English.

271.   Vocabulary

dīligen′tia, –ae, f., *diligence*   (diligent)
lū′dus, –ī, m., *school*
ob, prep. with acc., *toward, on account of, for*
pul′cher, –chra, –chrum, *beautiful*   (pulchritude)

272. English Word Studies

Make a diagram similar to that in **270** but substitute six derivatives of **agere** with their meanings for the six Latin words.

Find derivatives for the following new words in **267**: iterum (l.3), aurōra (l.10), lanterna (l.11).

Find an English derivative for every word in lines 16–21 of **267** except **etiam, erat, et, quod.**

Statue of a young Roman in the Metropolitan Museum

273. Roman Schools

Even before going to school some Roman children learned the alphabet by playing with letters cut out of ivory, as ours do from their blocks. They started to school at about the same age as our children. The schools were quite different, however. They were very small private schools, usually run by slaves for small fees. Work began early in the morning. The children were taken to and from school by slaves called **paedagōgī**, a Greek word which means those who "lead (take) children." They did no teaching but merely kept their children in order. Our word pedagogue is derived from this word.

In the elementary school, called the **lūdus litterārum,** the three R's formed the basis of the curriculum. For reading the Romans had to depend at first on the Twelve Tables of the law. In the third century B.C. a school teacher translated the *Odyssey* from Greek for the use of his pupils. Later other works of literature were used.

Tablet with Greek spelling exercise, styli, inkwell, wax tablets

Writing was practiced on wax tablets, consisting of wooden boards covered with a thin layer of wax. The writing was done by scratching the wax with a pointed stylus made of metal or bone. The other end of this was flat for erasing, or rather smoothing over the wax. The Romans also wrote with pen and ink on papyrus, a kind of paper made out of thin strips of a reed which grew in Egypt. Most books were made out of rolls of this material. But it was expensive, and school children used only the backs of old books and loose sheets for their "scratch paper." Parchment came to be used instead of wax-covered wood for tablets. Eventually a number of these were put together to form a book of our kind, and the papyrus roll went out of fashion.)

Arithmetic was complicated by the fact that the Romans did not have the Arabic system of numerals with its zero. Multiplication and division were impossible. The Romans had two helps in their arithmetic: an elaborate system of finger counting and the abacus, or counting board, similar to those used as toys by children today and those which you may see in Chinese laundries.

More advanced education prepared boys for the one respected profession in ancient Rome, that of law and public life. Hence the secondary school, called the **schola grammaticī** (*school of the grammarian*), specialized in language, composition, rhetoric, and public speaking. But the course was also a broadly cultural one and included literature, both Greek and Latin. Most educated Romans learned to speak and write Greek fluently.

The college course in the **schola rhētoricī** (*school of the rhetorician*) was still more technical in preparation for a career in which public speaking, whether in a law court or a legislative body, played a very important role. For graduate work students could go to such university centers as Athens or Rhodes and listen to lectures by leading philosophers and rhetoricians.

(Although the aim of the schools beyond the elementary stage was the narrow one of preparing citizens for public service, the practical Romans felt that a liberal training in literature and philosophy was the best system for attaining their purpose.)

Questions for Discussion.—1. What educational advantages do you have that a Roman boy did not have? 2. Compare books and writing material then and now. 3. What sort of education should our government officials have?

Read Showerman, pp. 194–202; Davis, pp. 191–204; McDaniel, pp. 70–76; Johnston, pp. 85–95; Mills, pp. 323–330.

Puer Romanus a servo ad ludum ducitur.

LESSON XXXIX

274. LŪDĪ RŌMĀNĪ ET AMERICĀNĪ

Inter lūdōs Rōmānōs et nostrōs similitūdō[1] nōn magna est. In lūdīs Rōmānīs inter puerōs erant nūllae puellae, in nostrīs sunt multae; puerī Rōmānī ad lūdum ā servīs dūcēbantur, nōs sōlī venīmus; magistrī Rōmānī servī erant, nostrī līberī sunt; lingua lūdōrum Rōmānōrum erat Latīna, lingua lūdōrum nostrōrum est Anglica. Ob dīligentiam et studium puerīs Rōmānīs praemia pulchra dabantur, nunc puerī Americānī "A" merent. Tardī discipulī Rōmānī poenā afficiēbantur, sed tardī discipulī poenā semper afficiuntur. Ob variās causās vīta discipulōrum nostrōrum grāta est, sed etiam puerī Rōmānī lūdum librōsque amābant. Magna pecūnia lūdīs nostrīs datur et beneficia disciplīnae pūblicae ad omnēs[2] puerōs puellāsque pertinent. Nōnne est

---

[1] *likeness* (nominative feminine). [2] *all.*

officium pūblicum pecūniam dare et lūdīs auxilium submittere?
Rōmānī lūdīs auxilium nōn submittēbant, neque beneficia disciplīnae pūblicae ad puerōs Rōmānōs pertinēbant.

Thought Questions.—1. How do our schools resemble Roman
schools? 2. How did the boys get to school?

275.   Principal Parts

The principal parts of the model verbs of the four conjugations
and of **sum** are as follows:

CONJUGATION	PRES. INDIC.	PRES. INFIN.	PERF. INDIC.	PERF. PART.
I	portō	portāre	portāvī	portātus
II	doceō	docēre	docuī	doctus
III	(a) pōnō	pōnere	posuī	positus
	(b) capiō	capere	cēpī	captus
IV	mūniō	mūnīre	mūnīvī	mūnītus
Irregular Verbs	sum	esse	fuī	futūrus[1]
	absum	abesse	āfuī	āfutūrus

276.   Tense Stems

The many different forms of every Latin verb are built upon
only **three stems**. These are obtained from the principal parts
as follows:

1. To find the **present stem**, drop –**re** from the present infinitive active: **portā–**, etc.

2. To find the **perfect stem**, drop –**ī** from the perfect indicative
active: **portāv–**, etc.

3. To find the **participial stem**, drop –**us** from the perfect participle: **portāt–**, etc.

Query.—What tenses are formed (a) upon the present stem, (b) upon
the perfect stem, (c) with the perfect participle?

---

[1] *See* **260**, footnote 1.

(*a*) 1. Officium pūblicum est puerīs puellīsque disciplīnam dare. 2. Castra in altō locō inter oppidum et silvam erant. 3. Ob multās causās concordia inter līberōs esse dēbet. 4. Ob amīcitiam auxilium submīsimus. 5. Ob magnum perīculum cōpiae nostrae colōnīs arma permīsērunt.

(*b*) 1. On-account-of the danger we did not desire to sail to Europe. 2. The fields had been laid waste and the town seized by the slaves. 3. He has been aroused by the messenger's harsh words. 4. We have furnished reinforcements to the scared provinces.

278. Vocabulary

dō,[1] da're, de'dī, da'tus, *give* (dative)

in'ter, prep. with acc., *between, among*

perti'neō, pertinē're, –ti'nuī, –tentū'rus, with ad, *pertain to* [*teneō*]

submit'tō, submit'tere, –mī'sī, –mis'sus, *let down, furnish* [*mittō*]

279. Latin and English Word Formation

As a prefix in Latin and English, **inter–** has its usual meanings. It is rarely assimilated. It is used rather freely in English to form new words: *inter-class, inter-state, inter-scholastic*, etc.

As a prefix **ob–** has the meaning *towards* or *against*. It is regularly assimilated before certain consonants: *oc-cur, of-ficial, o-mission, op-ponent;* but *ob-tain, ob-serve, ob-durate, ob-vious.*

Explain by derivation the meaning of *intercede, opponent, intervene, obvious.*

What are *data?* What is meant by *pertinent* facts?

---

[1] **Dō** is irregular in three parts—perfect **dedī**, and ă in **dare** and **datus**. The a is short in all indicative forms except the present tense, second person singular, and in the plural imperative.

Pulchra templa deorum. Two temples in Rome, at the ancient cattle market, near the Tiber River. Both temples, like many others in Rome and elsewhere, were Christian churches during the Middle Ages.

LESSON XL

280.   TEMPLA DEŌRUM

Silvae erant prīma templa deōrum. Prīmō[1] virī in agrīs habitābant et Nātūram colēbant. Posteā virī quī in oppidīs habitābant templa pulchra in altīs locīs ad glōriam deōrum pōnēbant. Templa saepe in altīs locīs posita sunt. Cūr? Quod haec[2] loca fīnitima caelō erant, in quō deī habitābant.   5

"Nātūra est pulchra," hominēs[3] dīxērunt. "Etiam loca sacra ad quae convenīmus et in quibus deōrum beneficia petimus pulchra esse dēbent. Ad fortūnam nostram pertinet deīs templa dare. Deīs grātiam habēmus ob frūmentum quō vītam sustinēmus et ob auxilium perpetuum quod nōbīs submīsērunt."   10

Itaque Graecī et Rōmānī ob beneficia deōrum magna et pulchra templa faciēbant quae erant grāta deīs. Statua aut deī aut deae semper in templō pōnēbātur.

In Graeciā et Italiā ruīnae templōrum multōrum et pulchrōrum videntur. Templum clārum Athēnae, appellātum Parthenōn, ob 15

---

[1] at first.   [2] these.   [3] men.

fōrmam pulchram semper laudātum est. Nōnne fuērunt multa templa Rōmāna inter pictūrās[1] quās vīdistī? Cūr pictūrās templōrum et Graecōrum et Rōmānōrum, quae in multīs librīs inveniuntur, nōn spectātis?

20   In templīs virī auxilium deōrum petēbant. Virī malī quōrum vīta in perīculō erat saepe ad templa fugiēbant, quod neque ex templīs removēbantur neque ibi poenam sustinēbant.

Thought Questions.—1. Where were the first temples? 2. Why? 3. How can we find out what the ancient temples looked like?

Read Harding (*Greek Gods*), pp. 8–9.

281.   **The Relative Pronoun** *Quī*

The pronouns *who, which, what,* and *that* in English are called **relative** pronouns because they *relate* or refer to some preceding word, called their **antecedent.**

There is only one relative pronoun in Latin, declined as follows:

	SINGULAR			PLURAL		
	M.	F.	N.	M.	F.	N.
Nom.	quī	quae	quod	quī	quae	quae
Gen.	cuius[2]	cuius	cuius	quōrum	quārum	quōrum
Dat.	cui	cui	cui	quibus	quibus	quibus
Acc.	quem	quam	quod	quōs	quās	quae
Abl.	quō	quā	quō	quibus	quibus	quibus

English Meanings in Singular and Plural

	M. AND F.	N.
Nom.	who, which, that	which, that
Gen.	of whom, whose, of which	of which, whose
Dat.	to (for) whom, which	to (for) which
Acc.	whom, which, that	which, that
Abl.	by, etc., whom, which	by, etc., which

[1] Use the English derivative.

[2] Note that the genitive singular is alike in all genders, likewise the dative singular, and that the accusative singular, masculine and feminine, ends in –m, as in English *whom*. The nominative singular feminine is like the nominative plural neuter.

188

Even in far-off New Zealand the Town Hall at Dunedin, with its columns and pediment, is in the familiar Roman style. One touch of ancient Rome makes the whole world kin.

282. Relative Pronouns as Used in English

While *that* as a relative can be used to refer to both persons and things, *who* always refers to persons and *which* to things. In other words, *which* is the neuter of *who*. *Which* and *that* do not change form to indicate case, while *who* does:

Nom. who   Gen. whose   Dat. and Acc. whom

283. The Relative Pronoun as Used in Latin

When a sentence contains two or more subjects and predicates, the separate parts are called **clauses**. A **relative clause** is introduced by a relative pronoun.

In the following sentences the antecedent and relative are underlined. Give the number and gender of each:

1. (*a*) **Puella abest; puellam accūsō,** *The girl is absent; the girl I accuse.*
   (*b*) **Puella quam accūsō abest,** *The girl whom I accuse is absent.*
2. **Oppidum quod vīdit erat parvum,** *The town which he saw was small.*
3. **Castra ex quibus vēnimus erant magna,** *The camp from which we came was large.*

189

4. **Virum cui librum dedī vīdistī,** *You saw the man to whom I gave the book.*

5. **Puer cuius librum habeō est amīcus noster,** *The boy whose book I have is our friend.*

Observe that the relative pronoun agrees with its antecedent in gender and number, but its case depends upon its use in its own clause.

Note.—The relative may be omitted in English but never in Latin: *The man (whom) I saw,* **Vir quem vīdī.**

Practice.—Give in Latin the proper form of the underlined English words:

1. I saw the horses that were on the road.
2. The boy whom I visited is my cousin.
3. Have you seen the girl to whom I gave the books?
4. The man by whom we were robbed has been arrested.
5. Where is the road by which we came?
6. I know the town in which the president was born.
7. The land from which our parents came is beautiful.
8. Have you ever seen the islands to which we sailed two years ago?
9. All the men to whom we spoke were greatly pleased by your action.
10. All the girls whom I have invited have accepted, but one girl whose mother is sick may not be able to come.

284. Exercises

(*a*) 1. Vir cui pecūniam permīsī amīcus meus erat. 2. Cūr nōn fortūnam quam Nātūra vōbīs dedit sustinētis? 3. America ob iniūriās quās accēperat bellum suscipere nōn dubitāvit. 4. Cūr pecūniam puerō vīsō ā tē in viā nōn dedistī? 5. Librōs quī ad fāmam et fortūnam pertinent puerī amant. 6. Via quā vēnimus pulchra erat.

(*b*) 1. The boy whom I saw in the woods is approaching. 2. He endured constant dangers on-account-of (his) enemies. 3. I saw the boy whose book I lost.

190

cūr, interrog. adv., *why*
nātū′ra, –ae, f., *nature* (natural)
pe′tō, pe′tere, petī′vī, petī′tus, *seek, ask* (petition)
quī, quae, quod, *who, which, that*
susti′neō, sustinē′re, –ti′nuī, –ten′tus, *hold up, maintain, endure* [*teneō*]

286. Word Study: Intensive Prefixes

Most of the Latin prepositions which are used as prefixes in Latin and English may have intensive force, especially **con**–, **ex**–, **ob**–, **per**–. They are then best translated either by an English intensive, as *up* or *out*, or by an adverb, as *completely, thoroughly, deeply*. Thus **commoveō** means to *move greatly*, **permagnus**, *very great*, **obtineō**, to *hold on to*, **concitō**, to *rouse up*, **excipiō**, to *catch, receive*.

Explain *component, confirmation, evident, elaborate*. What is meant by *conservation* of natural resources? What is a political *conservative*? What is a *contract*?

Ruins of a Greek building in Doric style at Paestum in southern Italy. This town furnished ancient Rome with roses in winter.

Colosseum. A view from the air. Most of the missing stone was used to build palaces in modern Rome.

LESSON XLI

287.   **COLOSSĒUM**

Lūdōs et pompās populus magnō studiō spectābat. In Italiā, Āfricā, Galliā cōnservantur theātra et amphitheātra Rōmānōrum, in quibus lūdī etiam nunc habentur. Nātūra virōrum varia est sed paucī lūdōs nōn amant. Cōnservāsne pictūrās Colossēī Rōmānī
5 quās invenīs?

Captīvī et servī in mediā arēnā pugnāre cōgēbantur. Populus Rōmānus studium lūdōrum numquam intermīsit. Multī captīvī cum magnō animō pugnābant et lībertātem[1] obtinēbant. Multī malī virī etiam prō vītā pugnābant et poenam in arēnā sustinēbant.
10 Ōlim duo gladiātōrēs[1] in arēnā Rōmānā pugnābant. Tum inter gladiātōrēs vēnit sine gladiō vir bonus aequusque, quī petīvit: "Cūr pugnātis? Proelium intermittite; nam amīcī estis. Malum exemplum prōpōnitis." Gladiātōrēs verbīs nōn permōtī sunt sed virum bonum interfēcērunt. Servī virum ex arēnā trahere incipiē-

---

[1] Use the English derivative.

bant. Tum populus īrā permōtus est, quod vir erat Tēlemachus, 15
quī amīcus miserīs semper fuerat et magnam fāmam obtinuerat.
Numquam posteā gladiātōrēs in Colossēō pugnāvērunt.

Thought Questions.—1. To what use are some ancient theaters put
today? 2. What two classes of people fought in the amphitheaters?

Read Showerman, pp. 349–351; Davis, pp. 401–406; Mills, pp. 313–
316.

288.   Second Conjugation: Principal Parts

The following are verbs already studied, but whose principal
parts have not been given in full. Memorize their principal parts
and give the three stems of each:

dēbeō	dēbēre	dēbuī	dēbitus
habeō	habēre	habuī	habitus
mereō	merēre	meruī	meritus
terreō	terrēre	terruī	territus
valeō	valēre	valuī	valitūrus
teneō	tenēre	tenuī	tentus
contineō	continēre	continuī	contentus
retineō	retinēre	retinuī	retentus
augeō	augēre	auxī	auctus
maneō	manēre	mānsī	mānsūrus
iubeō	iubēre	iussī	iussus
moveō	movēre	mōvī	mōtus
removeō	removēre	remōvī	remōtus
videō	vidēre	vīdī	vīsus

Note.—It will be seen that no general rule can be given for forming
the perfect and participial stems of verbs of the second conjugation.
The most common type, however, is illustrated by **dēbeō**. Note the other
types, which are arranged in groups.

Practice.—Give a synopsis (see **563**) of **augeō** in the 1st
sing. and **videō** in the 3d plur., active.

In English, the manner of an action is expressed by an adverb or a phrase (*i.e.* a group of words) answering the question *How?* When a phrase is used, a preposition, such as *with*, introduces it.

In Latin, manner is similarly expressed:

1. **Cum studiō labōrat,** *He labors with eagerness (eagerly).*
2. **(Cum) magnō studiō labōrat,** *He labors with great eagerness (very eagerly).*

Note that when an adjective is used, **cum** may be omitted.

Caution.—Be careful to distinguish this latest use of "with" from the "with" studied in section **177** under **Caution.** Distinguish the three different uses of "with" in the following sentences:

(*a*) *I shall go* **with him with the greatest pleasure.**
(*b*) *We can work* **with greater success with this equipment.**
(*c*) **With my auto** *I can cover the distance* **with you with ease.**

290.   Exercises

(*a*) 1. Magnā cūrā silvās nostrās cōnservābimus. 2. Magnā iniūriā tum populus miser regēbātur. 3. Puer quī prīmum locum obtinuerat cum magnā cūrā studiōque labōrāverat. 4. Multī puerī ob bellum studia intermīsērunt. 5. Amīcus noster nōn permōtus est sed aequō animō ad oppidum prōcessit. 6. Frūmentō et pecūniā miserōs līberē sustinuimus.

(*b*) 1. He has been deeply-moved by my words. 2. The teacher carefully taught the boys to save money. 3. The bad boy very carefully removed the teacher's books.

291.   Vocabulary

cōnser'vō, –ā're, –ā'vī, –ā'tus, *save, preserve*   [*servō*]
intermit'tō, intermit'tere, –mī'sī, –mis'sus, *let go, stop, interrupt*   [*mittō*]
obti'neō, obtinē're, obti'nuī, obten'tus, *hold, obtain*   [*teneō*]
permo'veō, permovē're, –mō'vī, –mō'tus, *move (deeply)*   [*moveō*]
tum, adv., *then*

Many English words that seem quite dull and ordinary have very interesting stories locked up within them. The key to these stories is Latin. Use this key and do not lose it. Let us try it now.

The "efficient" person is the one who *accomplishes* (**efficiō**) something—remember this when you hear people talk about "efficiency." A "traction" company is engaged in *drawing* or *hauling* vehicles. What is a "tractor"? What sort of person is a "tractable" person? Politicians should remember that a public "office" is a *duty*. An "office" is also a place where one does his *duty* or *daily work*.

Find the stories in *petition, competition, promotion, demotion, condone, conservative.*

The English form of **Colosseum** is *Coliseum.* It occurs seven times in the San Francisco telephone directory, five in that of New Orleans. What does it mean in English?

The Roman Forum. In front, the temple of Saturn; at the left, the arch of Septimius Severus and the Senate; at the right, the Colosseum

Verus Romanus. Dentatus refuses a bribe.

LESSON XLII

293. ## VĒRUS RŌMĀNUS

Audīvistīne dē Dentātō? "Quis fuit et quid fēcit?" rogās.
Quod Dentātum nōn nōvistī aut memoriā nōn tenēs, vōs monēbō.

Dentātus fuit clārus Rōmānus quī cōpiās prōdūxit atque inimīca oppida castraque variīs modīs cēpit. Modus eius[1] vītae et ab
5 amīcīs et ab inimīcīs probābātur ac laudābātur, nam Rōmānus
bonus erat. Cum[2] officia pūblica intermittēbat, agricola erat atque
in agrīs labōrābat.

Samnītēs,[3] quōs Dentātus cēdere coēgerat, magnam pecūniam
ad clārum virum mīsērunt. "Pecūnia quam coēgimus est tua.
10 Auxilium tuum atque amīcitiam petimus." Tum Dentātus permōtus eōs[4] monuit: "Quod aurum mihi datis? Cōnservāte aurum
vestrum. Nam vērus Rōmānus pecūniam obtinēre nōn cupit sed
eōs[4] quī aurum habent superāre."

Thought Questions.—1. What did Dentatus do when he was not in
public service? 2. What is the point of Dentatus' answer to the Samnites?

---

[1] *his.*   [2] *whenever.*   [3] *Sam'nītes.*   [4] *them.*

Interrogatives

Interrogative pronouns and adjectives are used to ask questions.

I. **Pronoun.**—In English, the interrogative pronoun *who* refers only to persons, *what* refers only to things.

In Latin, the interrogative pronoun corresponding to *who* and *what* is **quis, quid,** declined as follows:

	SINGULAR		PLURAL		
	M. AND F.	N.	M.	F.	N.
Nom.	quis, *who?*	quid, *what?*	quī	quae	quae
Gen.	cu'ius, *whose?*	cu'ius, *of what?*	quō'rum	quā'rum	quō'rum
Dat.	cui, *to whom?*	cui, *to what?*	qui'bus	qui'bus	qui'bus
Acc.	quem, *whom?*	quid, *what?*	quōs	quās	quae
Abl.	quō, *by whom?*	quō, *by what?*	qui'bus	qui'bus	qui'bus

Note.—The plural is translated like the singular.

II. **Adjective.**—In English, the interrogative pronoun *who* cannot be used as an adjective; we cannot say, *Who man?* But *what* may be used as an adjective, referring to persons or things: *What man? What thing?*

In Latin, the interrogative adjective is **quī, quae, quod,** declined like the relative pronoun (**281**). Compare the interrogative **quis** with the relative **quī** and note differences in the singular.

Lapsūs Linguae ("Slips of the Tongue").—Have you ever said, *Who did you see?* Why is *who* incorrect? Give the correct form and translate the sentence into Latin.

Practice.—(*a*) Decline *what ally? what price?*

(*b*) Decide whether the words in italics are pronouns or adjectives, then give the proper Latin form:

1. *Who* were those men? 2. *What* girls came? 3. *What* did he say? 4. *What* towns were destroyed? 5. *Whose* book is that? 6. To *whom* shall I give this? 7. To *whom* shall I go? 8. By *whom* (sing.) was he seen? 9. *What* boys do you mean?

(*a*) 1. Quī puer verbīs bonī virī nōn permōtus est? 2. Quid amīcī tuī fēcērunt atque quod praemium accipient? 3. Quō modō sociī pecūniam coēgērunt? 4. Quod cōnsilium, puellae, ā magistrō vestrō vōbīs datum est? 5. Ā quō vōs puerī magnā cūrā dē perīculīs monitī erātis? 6. Quod fuit pretium librī quem ab amīcō tuō accēpistī? 7. Cui puerō, cui puellae, Nātūra nōn vītam grātam dedit?

(*b*) 1. To whom shall we give the money and present the rewards? 2. By what street did you girls come and whom did you seek? 3. In what manner did you obtain the money which you have?

296.   Vocabulary

atque (ac), conj., *and*
cō′gō, –ere, coē′gī, coāc′tus, (*drive together*), *collect, compel*   [*agō*]
mo′dus, –ī, m., *manner*   (mode)
mo′neō, –ē′re, mo′nuī, mo′nitus, *remind, warn*   (monitor)
nam, conj., *for* (in the sense "because," introducing a verb)
quis, quid, *who, what*

297.   English Word Studies

(*a*) What is a *cogent* reason for doing something? What is an *intermission* in a play? Explain the meaning of *modal, model, admonition*.

(*b*)   Latin Phrases in English

Cui bono? (lit., *to whom for a good?*) *For whose benefit is it? What good is it?*

Ilium fuit, *Ilium has been* (i.e. *no longer exists*), said of Troy (**Ilium**) after its destruction by the Greeks; now applied to anything that is past.

in absentia, *in absence.*

in perpetuum, (*to perpetuity*), *forever.*

sine qua non, *a necessity* (lit., *without which* [*condition it is*] *not* [*possible*]).

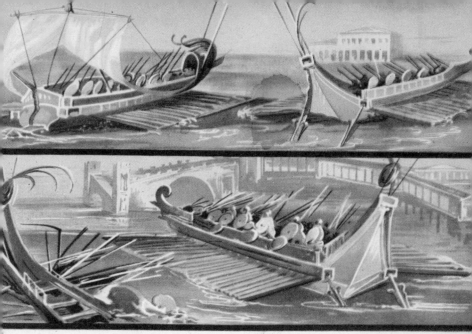

Fortasse trans aquam in Britanniam procedemus. Roman warships in
a Pompeian wall painting

LESSON XLIII

298. PŪBLIUS MĀRCŌ SAL.[1]

A letter which might have been sent by a young Roman from Caesar's
camp in Gaul in 55 B.C. to a friend in Rome.

Sī valēs, bene est; ego valeō. Magnō studiō lēgī litterās tuās
quae cum cūrā scrīptae et plicātae erant.

Rogās dē Galliā ac dē nōbīs cognōscere cupis. Vīta nostra nōn
dūra est. Multī captīvī in castrīs iam coāctī sunt. Caesar multās
pugnās iam pugnāvit et multa oppida mūnīta cēpit. Mox erit 5
dominus Galliae et Galliam in prōvinciam rediget. Sed dominus
aequus erit. Tum cōpiās nostrās trāns Rhēnum ēdūcet et Germānōs terrēbit. Iam eōs[2] monuit. Modum quō bellum gerit
probō. Sententia eius[3] est: "Veniō, videō, vincō." Magnus et

---

[1] For **salūtem dīcit:** *Publius pays his respects to Marcus,* the usual form of greeting
in a letter.

[2] *them.*   [3] *his.*

199

Roman gate in Lincoln, England, about nineteen hundred years old.
Think of the millions who have passed through it. The grocery store
runs smack into it.

10 ēgregius vir est. Fortasse trāns aquam in Britanniam prōcēdēmus,
quae est magna īnsula dē quā nōn ante lēgī aut cognōvī.

Quid Quīntus noster agit? Quae nova officia suscēpit? Cūr
nōn ante scrīpsit? Litterās tuās cum studiō exspectābō. Valē.[1]

Thought Questions.—1. Did Publius have an easy time in Gaul?
2. Has Publius seen Germany yet? Britain?

Read Showerman, pp. 498–499; Davis, pp. 207–209; Johnston, pp.
315–317.

299. Third Conjugation: Principal Parts

Memorize the principal parts of these verbs already studied
and give the three stems of each. No rule can be given for the
formation of the third and fourth parts, but the commonest type
has a perfect ending in –sī. The participle ends in –tus or –sus:

---

[1] *farewell.*

I	cēdō	cēdere	cessī	cessūrus
	(Similarly accēdō, discēdō, excēdō, prōcēdō)			
	gerō	gerere	gessī	gestus
	mittō	mittere	mīsī	missus
	(Similarly āmittō, committō, dīmittō)			
	dūcō	dūcere	dūxī	ductus
	(Similarly prōdūcō, redūcō)			
	regō	regere	rēxī	rēctus
	trahō	trahere	trāxī	trāctus
	dēfendō	dēfendere	dēfendī	dēfēnsus
	agō	agere	ēgī	āctus
	nōscō	nōscere	nōvī	nōtus
II	accipiō	accipere	accēpī	acceptus
	incipiō	incipere	incēpī	inceptus
	cupiō	cupere	cupīvī	cupītus
	faciō	facere	fēcī	factus
	afficiō	afficere	affēcī	affectus
	efficiō	efficere	effēcī	effectus
	fugiō	fugere	fūgī	fugitūrus

Note.—The change or lengthening of the vowel of the perfect and participial stems may be compared with the change of vowel in English *sing*, *sang*, *sung*, etc.

Practice.— Give a synopsis of **mittō** in the third singular and **accipiō** in the first plural passive.

300. **Exercises**

(*a*) 1. Bellum trāns Ōceanum cum victōriā gessimus. 2. Vigiliae ante portam positae erant. 3. Litterās quās scrīpsī plicābō et ad amīcum meum mittam. 4. Bonus est dominus noster, quod populum cum concordiā regit. 5. Linguam Latīnam cum studiō legere incipimus, quod multa nova verba iam cognōvimus. 6. Litterae ā tē scrīptae cum cūrā plicātae erant.

(*b*) 1. The new words ought always to be learned. 2. I do not know the boy who lives across the street. 3. The poor prisoners had been dragged across the fields. 4. Marcus, who wrote the letter which you are reading?

301.   Vocabulary

an′te, adv. and prep. with acc., *before* (of time or place)
cognōs′cō, cognōs′cere, cognō′vī, cog′nitus, *learn;* perf.
   tense, "have learned" = *know* [*nōscō*]
do′minus, –ī, m., *master* (dominate)
iam, adv., *already*
le′gō, le′gere, lē′gī, lēc′tus, *gather, choose, read* (legible)
pli′cō, –ā′re, –ā′vī, –ā′tus, *fold* (application)
scrī′bō, scrī′bere, scrīp′sī, scrīp′tus, *write* (Scripture)
trāns, prep. with acc., *across*

302.   Latin and English Word Formation

Ante– has its regular meaning and form when used as a prefix. **Trāns–** (or **trā–**, as in **trā-dūcō**) means *through* or *across*.

Importance of the Verb.—The most important part of speech in Latin for English derivation is the verb, and the most important part of the verb is the *perfect participle*. This form is also the most important for Latin word formation. Therefore *learn carefully* the principal parts of every verb.

By associating Latin word and English derivative, you can make the English help you in your Latin, and *vice versa*. You can often tell the conjugation or the perfect participle of a Latin verb by the help of an English derivative. The English word *mandate* shows that **mandō** has **mandātus** as its perfect participle and is therefore of the first conjugation. Similarly *migrate, donation, spectator*, etc. The word *vision* helps one remember that the perfect participle of **videō** is **vīsus**. Similarly *motion* from **mōtus**, *missive* from **missus**, *active* from **āctus**. Give derivatives from **lēctus, nōtus, ductus.** Explain *election, deposit, complication, domineer*.

In compounds short **–a–** becomes short **–e–** before two consonants (cf. **158**): **captus, acceptus.** Give two examples each from compounds of **capiō** and **faciō**.

202

303. English Word Studies

1. Find and use in sentences as many English derivatives as possible from **vocō, videō, mittō,** and **faciō.** Remember the importance of the perfect participle.

2. The first word, printed in bold face type, in each of the following lines is a Latin word. From among the last five words in each line pick the one which is an English derivative of the first word.

dō dough	dote	do	dot	dative
moneō money	remain	admonition	moan	remind
cōgō cog	incognito	cognate	cogency	concoct
petō pet	compete	petal	petite	impede
legō leg	log	collect	lag	lick

304. Vocabulary

NOUNS

1. dīligentia
2. dominus
3. lūdus
4. modus
5. nātūra

ADJECTIVE

6. pulcher

PRONOUNS

7. quī
8. quis

VERBS

9. cognōscō
10. cōgō
11. cōnservō
12. dō
13. intermittō
14. legō
15. moneō
16. obtineō
17. permoveō
18. pertineō
19. petō
20. plicō
21. scrībō
22. submittō
23. sustineō

ADVERBS

24. cūr
25. iam
26. tum

PREPOSITIONS

27. ante
28. inter
29. ob
30. trāns

CONJUNCTIONS

31. atque, ac
32. nam

The parliament buildings of Victoria, the capital of British Columbia, Canada, are in classical style.

305. Vocabulary

NOUNS

1. *diligence*
2. *master*
3. *game, school*
4. *manner*
5. *nature*

ADJECTIVE

6. *beautiful*

PRONOUNS

7. *who*
8. *who?*

VERBS

9. *learn*
10. *collect, compel*
11. *save*
12. *give*
13. *stop*
14. *gather, read*
15. *remind, warn*
16. *hold, obtain*
17. *move deeply*
18. *pertain to*
19. *seek*
20. *fold*
21. *write*
22. *furnish*
23. *maintain*

ADVERBS

24. *why*
25. *already*
26. *then*

PREPOSITIONS

27. *before*
28. *between, among*
29. *on account of*
30. *across*

CONJUNCTIONS

31. *and*
32. *for*

306. Principal Parts

1. Give the four parts of the following verbs: **mittō, cēdō, dūcō, agō, faciō.**

2. Give in Latin the principal parts of the following verbs: *defend, flee, have, be, see, remain, increase, learn.*

Forms

1. Give a synopsis of **moveō** in the 2d sing., act.; **agō** in the 3d sing., pass.; **accipiō** in the 3d sing., pass.

2. Decline **quae nātūra, quod signum, quī dominus.**

3. Supply the missing words in the right form and translate: (*a*) (*To whom*) librum dabō? (*b*) (*What*) librōs lēgistī? (*c*) (*Whom*) petis? (*d*) (*Who*) litterās scrīpsit? (*e*) (*By whom*) litterae scrīptae sunt? (*f*) (*Who*) venient?

308.   "With" Ablatives

See **65, 177, 289,** and then decide whether the "with" phrase in each sentence expresses (*a*) means, (*b*) manner, or (*c*) accompaniment:

1. Artists paint *with colors;* poets *with words.* 2. The soloist sang *with deep feeling.* 3. She spoke *with a smile.* 4. I spent the evening *with friends.* 5. My uncle farms *with a tractor.* 6. We shall talk over matters *with him.* 7. It is *with regret* that I leave those *with whom* I have been so closely associated. 8. All supported the cause *with enthusiasm and money.*

No. 5   No. 3

Don't be like these people: The uncle (5) wrongly used cum and paying the penalty; the girl (3) picked the wrong ablative.

309. Food and Meals

(The easiest way to give an idea of Roman foods is by listing some important foods which were unknown to the Romans: potatoes, tomatoes, bananas, oranges, sugar, coffee, tea. Butter was rarely used, except externally as a sort of salve or cold cream. Milk and cheese were freely used. Instead of sugar, honey was used for sweetening.) The extensive use of honey made beekeeping a very important occupation. Wheat bread baked in round loaves (see figure on this page) was the "staff of life." Cabbage, onions, beans were among the chief vegetables. Apples, pears, grapes, olives were the chief fruits. The **mālum Persicum** (from which our word *peach* is derived) was, as its name shows, originally brought from Persia.

(Much use was made of salads of various kinds, as is true in Italy today. Hence one reason for the importance of olive oil. This was used also in cooking, instead of butter, and in lamps.

The favorite meat was pork. Various kinds of fowl and birds were eaten, even peacocks by the wealthy classes. Fish and oysters became extremely popular.)

Besides milk and water the chief drink of the Romans was wine. There were many grades of native and imported wines. They were usually mixed with water when drunk at meals.

Scene in a bakery in Pompeii. The round loaves are creased so that they can be broken more easily. The boy seems hungry.

Breakfast was a simple meal, chiefly of bread. In the country, dinner (**cēna**) was at noon, but in the city this was postponed till early evening. Instead there was a luncheon (**prandium**) at midday or somewhat earlier.

The dinner consisted of a course of relishes (lettuce, onions, eggs, oysters, asparagus, etc.), called the **gustus** (*taste*), followed by the chief course (meat, fish, or fowl and vegetables), then the dessert, called the **secunda mēnsa** (*second table*), of fruit, nuts, and sweets. The Latin expression **ab ōvō usque ad māla**, *from eggs to apples*, meaning from beginning to end, shows what the usual relishes and desserts were. Wine was served with the meal. Tobacco was unknown.

The guests reclined on couches instead of sitting on chairs. There were couches along three sides of the rectangular table, each with room for three people. As the guests reclined on their left elbows, only their right hands were free. Forks were rarely used. Food was taken up with the fingers or with spoons. Meat was cut up before being served. Though much use was made of the fingers, we may well imagine that people of culture ate quite as daintily as we do who have forks to help us.

Questions for Discussion.— 1. Where did we originally get the important foods which the Romans knew nothing about? 2. Name the order of meals and describe a Roman dinner. 3. How would you arrange a Roman banquet in your Latin club or school?

Read Showerman, pp. 124–136; McDaniel, pp. 120–136.

This artist's drawing, based on existing remains at Pompeii, gives a good idea of a Roman shop. Is the boy's mouth watering?

Plinius et puer

LESSON XLIV

310. PLĪNIUS ET PUER

Plīnius,[1] cuius facta bona certē iam ante multīs nōta fuērunt, litterās scrīpsit quās etiam nunc legere possumus. Quondam ad oppidum parvum in quō nātus[2] erat vēnit. Ibi inter multōs virōs amīcum nōtum cum fīliō cernit. Plīnius ā puerō petīvit: "Disci-
5 pulusne es?" Puer respondit: "Discipulus Mediōlānī[3] sum." Plīnius commōtus rogāvit: "Cūr nōn hīc[4]?" Puer respondit: "Nōn possum, nam magistrōs nōn habēmus." Tum Plīnius amīcō dīxit[5]: "Verbīs fīlī tuī commōtus sum. Certē lūdum hīc habēre potestis atque dēbētis. Cognōsce cōnsilium meum. Ego nōn
10 līberōs habeō sed tertiam partem[6] pecūniae quam dabitis parātus sum dare."

Thought Questions.—1. Where did Pliny see his friend? 2. Why did the boy go to school in another town? 3. What was Pliny's offer?

---

[1] *Pliny.*   [2] *born.*   [3] *at Milan.*   [4] *here.*   [5] From **dīcō.**   [6] Accusative.

311. Participles Used as Adjectives and Nouns

Perfect participles of many verbs came to be used as simple adjectives, just as in English: **parātus**, "prepared," *ready;* **nōtus**, "known," *familiar;* **certus**, "decided," *sure.* A participle, like any adjective, may be used substantively: **factum**, "having been done," *deed.*

312. Conjugation of *Possum*

Possum is a compound of **sum** and is therefore **irregular**. It has no passive voice. Review the conjugation of **sum**. **Possum** = **pot(e)+sum**. **Pot-** becomes **pos-** before all forms of **sum** which begin with **s-**. The perfect tenses are regular.

PRESENT

pos'sum, *I can, am able*	pos'sumus, *we can, are able*
pot'es, *you can, are able*	potes'tis, *you can, are able*
pot'est, *he can, is able*	pos'sunt, *they can, are able*
Imperfect pot'eram, etc., *I could, was able*	Future pot'erō, etc., *I shall be able*

(For full conjugation see **590**.)

Practice.—(*a*) Give the form and the meaning of **potuerās, poterātis, potuērunt, possunt, poterit, posse**.

(*b*) Translate *you could, they had been able, we shall be able, he can, they could*.

313. Exercises

(*a*) 1. Amīcus certus in malā fortūnā cernitur. 2. Perīcula vītae bonum virum commovēre nōn poterunt. 3. Linguam Latīnam et legere et scrībere possum. 4. Facta virōrum clārōrum semper nōta erunt et laudābuntur. 5. "Facta, nōn verba" sententia nostra esse dēbet. 6. Ante bellum patria nostra nōn parāta erat; nam magnās cōpiās nōn habēbāmus.

(b) 1. Few men can neither read nor write. 2. We came across the fields, because the road was not familiar. 3. They had not been able to come on-account-of the bad streets. 4. My motto is: "Always ready." Is it yours?

314. Vocabulary

cer'nō, –ere, crē'vī, crē'tus, (*separate*), *discern, see*	(discretion)
cer'tus, –a, –um, *fixed, sure*	[*cernō*]
commo'veō, –ē're, –mō'vī, –mō'tus, *disturb*	[*moveō*]
fac'tum, –ī, n., *deed*	[*faciō*]
nō'tus, –a, –um, *known, familiar*	[*nōscō*]
parā'tus, –a, –um, *prepared, ready*	[*parō*]
pos'sum, pos'se, po'tuī, ——, *can, be able* (with infinitive)	[*sum*]
ter'tius, –a, –um, *third*	(tertiary)

315. English Word Studies

(a) Explain *commotion, certificate, notorious, tertiary.*

(b) Latin Words and Phrases in English

de facto, *from* or *according to fact, actual;* as a de facto government, one which is actually in operation, even if not recognized as legal.

erratum (plur. errata), *error.*

terra incognita, *an unknown land.*

Translate ante bellum.

Model of the Roman aqueduct at Nîmes, France, made by pupils of the Edward D. Libbey High School, Toledo, Ohio, under the direction of Mrs. P. Emerson Burton

Wall built by the Romans at Chester, England. The town was originally
a Roman camp.

LESSON XLV

316.   **COLŌNĪ AMERICĀNĪ**

Dē factīs colōnōrum quī ē Britanniā ad Americam vēnērunt
multa certē nōvistī. Commōtī patriam relīquērunt et terram novam
petīvērunt. Multī antecessērunt, reliquī posteā ad terram petītam
trānsportātī sunt. In locīs altīs stetērunt et terram novam grātē
crēvērunt. Etiam puerīs puellīsque Rōmānīs "colōnī" nōtī erant. 5

Cōpiae ā Rōmānīs in Britanniam trānsportātae sunt et bella ibi
gessērunt. Vālla fēcērunt atque viās mūnīvērunt. Tum colōnōs
trādūxērunt et agrōs captōs et oppida occupāta colōnīs dedērunt.
Per colōnōs in Britanniam trāductōs lingua Latīna Britanniae data
est. Semper cōpiae antecēdunt, tum colōnī veniunt.   10

Rōmānī oppida in Britanniā mūnīvērunt—Londīnium, Eborā-
cum, Lindum; nunc appellantur London, York, Lincoln. Multae

211

ruīnae Rōmānae etiam nunc in Britanniā stant et cernī possunt. Quis nōn cupit ad Britanniam nāvigāre et ibi ruīnās relīctās 15 vidēre?

Thought Questions.—1. How did the Roman colonists get farms? 2. Are there any traces of Roman buildings in England?

317. Fourth Conjugation: Principal Parts

Memorize the principal parts of the following verbs, which have occurred in previous lessons:

audiō	audīre	audīvī	audītus
veniō	venīre	vēnī	ventūrus
conveniō	convenīre	convēnī	conventūrus
inveniō	invenīre	invēnī	inventus

318. Numerals: How Lucius Learned to Count

Ūnus[1] puer et ūnus puer sunt **duo** puerī; duo librī et ūnus liber sunt **trēs** librī; duo equī et duo equī sunt **quattuor** equī; trēs carrī et duo carrī sunt **quīnque** carrī; quattuor oppida et duo oppida sunt **sex** oppida; sex dominī et ūnus dominus sunt **septem** dominī; quīnque nautae et trēs nautae sunt **octō** nautae; septem agrī et duo agrī sunt **novem** agrī; sex puellae et quattuor puellae sunt **decem** puellae.

Summary: **ūnus, duo, trēs, quattuor, quīnque, sex, septem, octō, novem, decem.**

319. Exercises

(*a*) 1. Multum frūmentum in Eurōpam trānsportātum est. 2. Nūntium mīsimus ad Marium, quī sine auxiliīs antecesserat. 3. Ob equōs et carrōs in viā stāre nōn possumus. 4. Ubi pecūnia quam āmīserās inventa est? 5. Servī trāns agrōs equōs territōs trādūcere nōn potuērunt. 6. Ob quās causās colōnī agrōs relīquērunt?

---

[1] *one.*

(*b*) 1. How did you hear about your friend's injury? 2. Marius ordered our forces to be led-across. 3. We ought to work with eagerness. 4. Why do you stand in the middle (of the) street?

320. Vocabulary

antecē′dō, –ere, –ces′sī, –cessū′rus, *go before*   [*cēdō*]
relin′quō, –ere, relī′quī, relīc′tus, *leave (behind), abandon*   (relinquish)
stō, stā′re, ste′tī, statū′rus, *stand*   (station)
trādū′cō, –ere, –dū′xī, –duc′tus, *lead across*   [*dūcō*]
trānspor′tō, –ā′re, –ā′vī, –ā′tus, *transport*   [*portō*]

321. The Latin Influence upon English

Latin words have kept coming into English continuously from the b▬▬▬ng of the language down to the present moment. Julius Caesar twice invaded Britain, but the Romans did not conquer the island until a century later. For four hundred years the Romans ruled Britain, and the language of the towns at least became Latin. When the Angles and Saxons invaded Britain in the fifth century and gave their name (*Angle-land, Eng-land*) and language to the island, they adopted a number of Latin words. Even before that they had come into contact with the Romans in northern Germany and borrowed some Latin words. So you see that one may say that Latin affected English even before English existed as a separate language.

As the Romans in Britain found it necessary to build many military camps, which developed into towns, the word **castra** is to be found in a number of town names, many of which have been used in our country also. So *Chester* (Pa.), *Ro-chester* (N. Y.), *Man-chester* (N. H.), *Wor-cester* (Mass.), *Lan-caster* (Pa.). What other names with these endings can you give?

We have seen a similar evolution in the United States where frontier forts, erected originally as defenses against the Indians, became trading posts, out of which have grown flourishing cities, such as Fort Dodge (Ia.), Fort Scott (Kan.), and Fort Worth (Tex.).

A Roman wedding as shown on a Roman wall painting

LESSON XLVI

322.   MĀRCUS PŪBLIŌ SAL.[1]

An answer to the letter in 298.

Adductus litterīs ā tē, Pūblī, in Galliā scrīptīs, respondēbō, nam multa nova sunt. Quid putās? Quīntus noster fīliam tertiam Rūfī in mātrimōnium dūxit! Ego nōn potuī hoc[2] prōvidēre; Quīntus mē nōn cōnsuluit. Tūne hoc prōvīdistī? Tenēsne me-
5 moriā puellam, parvam ac timidam? Nōn iam timida est; nunc pulchra est, ā multīs amāta.

Scrīpsistī dē Caesaris[3] ēgregiīs victōriīs. Cum magnō studiō litterās tuās lēgī, nam Gallia semper fuit terra nova et nōn nōta mihi. Paucī nūntiī dē Galliā vēnērunt, quī fugam Gallōrum nūn-
10 tiāvērunt. Caesar victōriīs suīs glōriam et fāmam armōrum Rōmānōrum augēbit. Nōn iam timēbimus Gallōs in fugam datōs. Alpēs, quae inter nōs et Gallōs stant, nunc Rōmam ā perīculō dēfendunt, nam Gallī timidī trāns Alpēs cōpiās nōn trānsportā-
bunt. Cōpiās trāductās removēre dūrum erit.

---

[1] See **298.**   [2] *this.*   [3] Genitive singular.

Sī Caesar mē cōnsulit, librum "Dē Bellō Gallicō" scrībere dēbet. 15
Sī liber ab eō[1] scrībētur, ā multīs legētur; etiam post multōs annōs
cum cūrā et dīligentiā legētur.

Litterae tuae nōn longae erant. Cūr longās litterās nōn scrībis?
Multa nova vīdistī atque vidēbis. Valē.[2]

Thought Questions.—1. What girl was pretty? 2. Where did Caesar
win victories?

323.   Participles Used as Clauses

The participle, although not much used in English, is exceedingly common in Latin. It often serves as a *one-word substitute* for
a subordinate clause, introduced in English by *who*, etc., *when
ever*, *since* or *because*, *although*, and *if*. At other times it is best
eginni ... ated by a coördinate clause. The meaning of the Latin sentence as a whole will always determine the exact meaning of the
participle. Always translate the participle *literally* before attempting to expand it into a clause. Note the various translations in the
following:

Relative   1. **Oppida *capta* vīdī,** *I saw the towns* **which had been
                captured** (lit., *the captured towns*).
Temporal   2. ***Convocātī* ad proelium dūcentur,** *After they have been
                called together, they will be led to battle* (lit., *having been
                called together*).
Causal   3. ***Territī* nōn prōcessērunt,** *Because they were scared, they
                did not advance* (lit., *having been scared*).
Coördinate 4. **Librum *lēctum* tibi dabō,** *I shall read the book and give
                it to you* (lit., *the book read*).

Observe that (*a*) the *perfect* participle denotes time *before* that
of the leading verb; (*b*) it agrees like an adjective with some noun
or pronoun in gender, number, and case.

324.   Exercises

(*a*) 1. Malus puer, ab amīcīs monitus, verbīs addūcī nōn iam
potest. 2. Monitī vōs dē perīculō cōnsulere nōn poterāmus.

---

[1] *him.*   [2] *farewell.*

Ancient Rome as represented in the moving picture "Ben Hur"

3. Captīvī nōn parātī gladiōs cēpērunt et sociōs nostrōs in fugam dedērunt. 4. Rōmānī multa oppida occupāta relīquērunt. 5. Pecūnia, ā mē in viā āmissa, ab amīcō meō inventa est. 6. Perīculum prōvīsum nōs nōn terruit.

(*b*) Substitute a participle in the proper agreement for the words within parentheses:

1. Numerus librōrum (*which I consulted*) magnus fuit. 2. Multōs librōs lēgī (*because I had been influenced*) ā magistrīs meīs. 3. Quattuor librōs (*after reading them*) ēmī. 4. Liber bonus (*if read*) cum cūrā semper amīcus vērus erit.

(*c*) 1. I saw the girl who had been scared[1] by you. 2. The boys read the book because they had been influenced by the teacher's words. 3. I have read the letter written by my son.

325. ✓   Vocabulary

addū'cō, –ere, addū'xī, adduc'tus, *lead to, influence*   [*dūcō*]
cōn'sulō, –ere, –su'luī, –sul'tus, *consult*   (consultation)
fu'ga, –ae, f., *flight;* in fu'gam dō, *put to flight*   [*fugiō*]
nōn iam, adv., *no longer*
prōvi'deō, –ē're, –vī'dī, –vī'sus, *foresee*   [*videō*]
ti'midus, –a, –um, *timid*   (timidity)

[1] Express in two ways.

216

326. The Latin Influence upon English (*Cont.*)

In the preceding lesson we saw that a number of Latin words came into English as a result of the Roman occupation of Britain. Other examples are *wall* (from **vāllum**), together with place names like *Walton* (*Walltown*); *port* (from **portus,** *harbor*), together with place names like *Portsmouth; street* (from **strāta**); *Lin-coln* (from **colōnia,** *colony*); cf. *Cologne*, the name of a German city, which was an ancient Roman colony.

A century and a half after the Angles and Saxons settled in England, Pope Gregory sent missionaries to convert the island to Christianity. As the missionaries spoke Latin, they introduced a number of Latin words into English, especially words dealing with the Church, e.g. *temple* (**templum**), *disciple* (**discipulus**), *bishop* (**episcopus**).

Explain *cologne, Stratford, antecedent, relic, providence*.

The beautiful Lincoln Memorial in Washington, D. C., in the simple Doric style. The festoons at the top are often found on Roman buildings.

A bad spill in a circus race. From the moving picture "Ben Hur"

LESSON XLVII

THE STORY OF LUCIUS (*Cont.*)

327. Circus

Dē "lūdō" in quō magister docēbat lēgistis. Sed erat etiam "lūdus"[1] in quō ōtium agēbātur; nam puerī Rōmānī nōn semper labōrābant sed etiam lūdēbant. Dictum est: "Puerī puerī erunt."

"The Parade's Coming"

Fēriae[2] erant. Lūcius, amīcus noster parvus, ad lūdōs pūblicōs 5 in Circō factōs ā servō adductus est. Multī ad Circum conveniēbant; nam populus lūdōs amābat. Nōn paucī ante aurōram vēnerant. Lūcius et servus loca commoda beneficiō amīcī invēnērunt et exspectāvērunt. Sed quid audiunt? Servus clāmat: "Pompa venit! Pompa venit!" Pompa per Forum et Sacram Viam ad Circum prō-10 cesserat et nunc per portam in Circum prōcēdēbat. In pompā fuērunt deōrum fōrmae, virī, puerī, equī, quadrīgae,[3] aurīgae.[4]

---

[1] See Vocabulary.　　　　　　　　[2] *holidays.*
[3] Quattuor equī quī carrum trahunt "quadrīgae" appellantur.
[4] "Aurīgae" sunt virī quī quadrīgās agunt.

The Chariot Race: "They're Off!"

Pompa per Circum ēducta est; Lūcius cum studiō exspectāvit.
Tum sex quadrīgae, ad portam redāctae, signum exspectāvērunt.
Signum datum est et equī ā portā missī sunt.

15   Inter aurīgās fuit Pūblius, quī magnam fāmam ob multās victōriās habuit. Erat amīcus familiae Lūcī nostrī, et Lūcius multa dē
Circō ā Pūbliō cognōverat. Nunc Lūcius cum reliquīs Pūblium
magnō studiō spectābat.

Publius Handicapped at the Start

Sed Pūblius habuit ūnum equum quī erat novus et timidus et
20 tardus; reliquae quadrīgae antecessērunt. Lūcius magnā cūrā
affectus, malam fortūnam amīcī nōn prōvīderat. Sed victōria nōn
āmissa erat; nam septem spatia erant.

Two Chariots Out of the Race

In mediō Circō erat longa spīna.[1] Terminī spīnae "mētae"
appellātī sunt. Magnum erat perīculum aurīgārum ad mētās. Ita-
25 que in prīmō spatiō nec prīmus
nec secundus aurīga quadrīgās ā
mētīs regere potuit. Ēiectī[2] per[3]
terram equīs trāctī sunt atque
iniūriās accēpērunt. Servī virōs
30 ad spīnam portāvērunt et auxilium dedērunt.

Quadrigae. Model made in the Libbey High School, Toledo, Ohio, Mrs. P. Emerson Burton, teacher

Publius Still Last

Nunc erant quattuor quadrīgae. Sex spatia restābant, sed
Pūblius antecēdere nōn poterat.
35 Quīnque, quattuor spatia restābant. Pūblius ultimus erat. Duo
spatia restābant; populus clāmā-

---

[1] *wall.*   [2] From ēiciō.   [3] *over.*

bat et cōnsilium multum Pūbliō dabat sed nōn audiēbātur.
Pūblius magnā cūrā equōs regēbat et etiam retinēbat, sed populus
40 nōn cognōverat. Ūnum spatium restābat; Lūcius commōtus
lacrimās retinēre nōn potuit. Fortūna inimīca erat.

"AND THE LAST SHALL BE FIRST!"

Sed quid vidēmus? Pūblius antecēdit! Nōn iam equōs retinet
sed incitat. Ūnus equus, "Parātus" appellātus (nam semper parātus erat), integer fuit et properāre incipit. Nōn iam Pūblius erat
45 ultimus; iam tertium, iam secundum locum tenet. Ūnus aurīga
ante Pūblium restat. Aequī sunt—deī sunt bonī!—prīmus ad
mētam ultimam Pūblius venit et praemia victōriae accipit! Et
Lūcius—quid faciēbat? Clāmābāt: "Iō! Iō! Pūblius! Parātus!
Clāra victōria!"

50 Nōnne grāta erat vīta puerōrum Rōmānōrum? Sed etiam nunc
in circō quadrīgās vidēre potestis; nam circum pompamque ā
Rōmānīs accēpimus.

Thought Questions.—1. What was the route of the parade? 2. How
many laps were there in the race? 3. How many chariots?

328.	Vocabulary

clā'mō, –ā're, –ā'vī, –ā'tus, *shout, cry out*   (clamor)
pom'pa, –ae, f., *parade*   (pomp)
spa'tium, spa'tī, n., *space, time; lap*   (spacious)
ul'timus, –a, –um, *farthest*   (ultimate)

329.	English Word Studies

Explain the title of Elgar's march "*Pomp and Circumstance*."
What derivative of **circus** shows how **circus** got its meaning?
Explain by etymology: *declamation, claim, reclamation, expatiate,
ultimatum, delude.*

A circus race as an ancient sculptor saw it

GLIMPSES OF ROMAN LIFE

330.   **Amusements**

The chief amusements for the people as a whole were the circus, the gladiatorial shows, and the theater. The oldest and most popular was the circus with its races, fully described in the "Story of Lucius" (see figures p. 218 ff.). The races were the main thing; gradually various side shows and acrobatic exhibitions were added to fill in the time between races. The modern circus is descended from the ancient, but the chariot races no longer have the same prominence. Even the circus parade which precedes the performance today is borrowed from the Romans, who called it a **pompa.**

The circus games were held at public expense on holidays. They took place in the valley between the Palatine and Aventine. Originally the people sat on the hillsides; later magnificent stands seating 200,000 people were built. Other circuses were built in Rome and elsewhere, but the original Circus Maximus remained the chief one.

For the interest these games created we may compare our baseball and football games. There were various racing clubs, distinguished by their colors, like our schools and colleges; we are reminded also of the "Red Sox" and "White Sox" of baseball. Drivers were popular heroes and often became rich. Their records and those of the horses were carefully kept. One man is said to have won 3559 races. This reminds us of the attention given to the number of home runs made by famous baseball players.

The theater was another important place for amusement. In imitation of Greek custom, Roman theaters were semicircular and open to the sky. The actors usually wore masks which indicated what kind of part the actor was playing. Women's parts were played by men. Both comedies and tragedies were given. The most famous writers of comedies were Plautus and Terence, whose plays are still in existence.

The gladiatorial contests were rather late importations from Etruria, the country to the north of Rome. At first they consisted

The stage of the Roman theater at Sabratha, Libya, northern Africa. It is partly restored but even so it is one of the finest in existence.

of sword fights between two men—fencing matches with swords instead of foils. Curiously enough, these fights took place at funerals. Later on they became very popular. Fights between men and animals (like the Spanish bullfights) were added, as well as fights between animals. Sometimes very elaborate shows were put on. They were held in open-air amphitheaters. Many Roman towns all over the world had their theaters and amphitheaters. The famous Colosseum at Rome (pp. 41, 192), which had room for 50,000 people, was not built until 80 A.D.

Questions for Discussion.—1. What modern sports compare with the circus games of the Romans in popular appeal? 2. In what ways did the Roman theater differ from ours? 3. What were the good and the bad features of the gladiatorial contests? What modern sports have similar features?

Read Showerman, pp. 308–351; Davis, pp. 374–406; Guerber (*Story*), pp. 142–145; Johnston, chap. IX.

The theater of Marcellus at Rome, built in the reign of Augustus. At the left is the Capitoline Hill.

The rocks that Polyphemus threw at the departing Ulysses, so they say,
near Catania, Sicily. Don't you believe it? Well, here are the rocks.

LESSON XLVIII

331. **ULIXĒS**

Ulysses (or Odysseus) was one of the Greeks who fought in the
Trojan War. His many wanderings before he returned to his home in
Ithaca, an island west of Greece, are described by Homer in the *Odyssey.*

Ulixēs, dux Graecus quī in bellō Troiānō pugnāverat, post
pācem ad Ithacam, in quā īnsulā habitāverat, properāvit. Sed multa
mala miser sustinuit nec salūtem invēnit. Cūrīs dūrīs pressus
decem annōs in multīs terrīs ēgit.

5   Post pācem ā Troiā cum multīs mīlitibus Ulixēs nāvigāverat.
Ad ultimam terram Lōtophagōrum[1] accessit. Paucī mīlitēs Graecī
lōtum ēdērunt[2] et amāvērunt; et ducem et sociōs nōn iam memoriā tenuērunt. Ulixēs mīlitēs nōn relīquit sed ad nāvēs redūxit.

Tum ad Siciliam ventīs āctus est. In Siciliā habitāvērunt Cy-
10 clōpēs,[3] hominēs altī et dūrī quī singulōs oculōs[4] habuērunt.
Neque deōrum neque hominum lēgēs timuērunt. Ulixēs cum
paucīs hominibus in hōc[5] locō frūmentum petīvit. Magna spē-
lunca[6] inventa est in quā multum frūmentum fuit. Tum vēnit
Cyclōps[7] quī appellātus est Polyphēmus. Ovēs[8] in spēluncam ēgit.

---

[1] *Lotus-eaters.*   [2] *ate the lotus.*   [3] *Cyclō'pēs.*   [4] *one eye apiece.*   [5] *this.*
[6] *cave.*   [7] *Cyclops.*   [8] *sheep.*

Polyphēmus Graecōs vīdit et dīxit: "Ā quō locō venītis? Quī [15] hominēs estis? Quid petitis?" Ulixēs respondit: "Nōs Graecī sumus. Ego Nēmō[1] appellor. Auxilium tuum petimus."

Polyphēmus duōs hominēs cēpit et ēdit; tum somnum cēpit. Graecī sude[2] oculum Polyphēmī pressērunt, quī clāmāvit et sociōs convocāvit. "Quid est?" rogant. "Quis tē vulnerāvit?" [20] Polyphēmus respondet: "Nēmō mē vulnerāvit." Itaque reliquī Cyclōpēs discessērunt. Polyphēmus Graecōs petīvit sed nōn invēnit quod sub ovibus ligātī ex spēluncā excessērunt.[3] Līberātī ad nāvēs properāvērunt atque in fugā salūtem invēnērunt.

Thought Questions.—1. How long did it take Ulysses to reach home? 2. Why did not the other Cyclopes help Polyphemus? 3. What does the term "lotus-eater" mean when applied to anyone today?

Read Sabin, pp. 307–312; Gayley, pp. 318–323; Bulfinch, pp. 241–244; Guerber, pp. 337–345; Colum, pp. 156–167.

332. Third Declension: Masculine and Feminine Nouns

The genitive singular of nouns of the **third declension** ends in **-is;** the base is obtained by dropping this ending. All three genders are found among nouns of the third declension, and no general rule can be given. The gender, as well as the nominative and genitive singular, must therefore be learned from the vocabulary. Masculine and feminine nouns are declined alike, as follows:

ENDINGS		**mīles,** *soldier* (base, **mīlit-**)		**lēx,** *law* (base, **lēg-**)	
SING.	PLUR.	SING.	PLUR.	SING.	PLUR.
Nom. —[4]	-ēs	mī′les	mī′litēs	lēx	lē′gēs
Gen. -is	-um	mī′litis	mī′litum	lē′gis	lē′gum
Dat. -ī	-ibus	mī′litī	mīli′tibus	lē′gī	lē′gibus
Acc. -em	-ēs	mī′litem	mī′litēs	lē′gem	lē′gēs
Abl. -e	-ibus	mī′lite	mīli′tibus	lē′ge	lē′gibus

[1] *No-man.*   [2] *with a stake.*

[3] This trick still works: In 1940 two German prisoners escaped from a Canadian prison camp by clinging to the under side of a garbage truck.

[4] The ending of the nominative singular varies. When not omitted, it is usually **-s;** c and g of the base combine with **-s** to form **-x.**

Ulysses makes fun of Polyphemus. A painting by the famous English artist Turner

(*a*) **Observe** that the dative and ablative plural are alike; this is true of all declensions. The nominative and accusative plural also are alike in the third declension.

Practice.—(*a*) Decline **homō magnus, pāx aequa.**

(*b*) Tell the form of **salūtem, ducum, modum, mīlitibus, lēgī, fugae, ducem, mīlite.**

333.   **Exercises**

(*a*) 1. Dux mīlitēs ēvocātōs ad pugnam prōdūxit. 2. Ob vigiliam praesidī, equī nōn removērī poterant. 3. Magna est glōria mīlitum quī bellō pressī nōn cessērunt. 4. Salūs patriae in armīs mīlitum nostrōrum nōn iam pōnētur, sī pācem aequam efficiēmus. 5. Sine bellō pācem et ōtium et salūtem obtinēre cupimus. 6. Ibi potest valēre populus, ubi lēgēs valent.

(*b*) 1. Many books sent by boys and girls were received by the soldiers. 2. "Safety first!" is a good motto. 3. The general ordered the soldiers to be called-together. 4. Why is he absent? He ought to offer an example and be present.

226

Vocabulary

dux, du'cis, m., *leader, general* [*dūcō*]
ho'mō, ho'minis, m., *man, human being* (homicide)
lēx, lē'gis, f., *law* (legal)
mī'les, mī'litis, m., *soldier* (military)
pāx, pā'cis, f., *peace* (pacifist)
pre'mō, –ere, pres'sī, pres'sus, *press, press hard* (pressure)
sa'lūs, salū'tis, f., *health, safety* (salutary)

335. English Word Studies

(*a*) Explain *illegal, impressive, depression, ducal, militant*. To *salute* a person is to wish him *health*, as we say "*good* morning," not "*bad* morning." To *pay* a person is to *pacify* him. What is a *pacifist?*

Find out why iron works in San Francisco and a steel company in Detroit have the name *Cyclops*.

(*b*) **Latin Phrases in English**

Dux femina facti, *A woman (was) leader in (of) the deed.*
lex scripta, *the written law.*
novus homo, *a new man* (in politics); hence, *an upstart.*
pax in bello, *peace in (the midst of) war.*

Destruction of the ships of Ulysses. An ancient wall painting found in Rome

Circe, regina pulchra, socios Ulixis in animalia vertit. A painting by
the English artist Burne-Jones

LESSON XLIX

336. CIRCĒ

Tum Ulixēs ad rēgnum Aeolī, rēgis ventōrum, nāvigāvit, quī
Ulixī[1] ventōs malōs in saccō ligātōs dedit et dīxit: "Malīs ventīs
ligātīs, nōn iam impediēris et in patriā tuā salūtem inveniēs."

Itaque multōs diēs[2] Graecī sine impedīmentō nāvigāvērunt,
5 ūnō bonō ventō āctī, reliquīs ligātīs. Iam Ithacam clārē cernunt.
Sed nautae dē saccō cūrā affectī sunt quod dē ventīs quī in saccō
erant nihil audīverant. "Praemia et pecūnia in saccō sunt," nauta
dīxit. "Rēx Ulixēs nautīs quī mala sustinuērunt pecūniam dare
dēbet." Itaque, saccō apertō,[3] ventī expedītī Graecōs ad rēgnum
10 Aeolī redēgērunt. Sed nōn iam Aeolus auxilium dat. Ūnam nāvem
Graecī nunc habent, reliquīs āmissīs.

---

[1] Dative.   [2] Accusative plural.   [3] From **aperiō,** *open.*

228

Nunc, impedīmentīs relīctīs, ad īnsulam veniunt quam Circē pulchra regēbat. XX hominēs, ab Ulixe[1] ad rēgīnam missī, pācem praesidiumque lēgum petīvērunt. Ab Eurylochō duce per silvam ad rēgīnam pedibus ductī sunt, quae eōs[2] in animālia[3] vertit. Eury- 15 lochus sōlus in animal nōn versus ad nāvem fūgit et Ulixī omnia[4] dē sociīs impedītīs nūntiāvit. Ulixēs commōtus cum reliquīs auxilium sociīs pressīs dare mātūrāvit. In viā Mercurium deum vīsum cōnsuluit. Mercurius eum[5] monuit et herbam eī[6] dedit. "Hāc[7] herbā," inquit, "vītam tuam servāre et mīlitēs tuōs 20 expedīre poteris." Ulixēs rēgīnam iussit sociōs in hominēs vertere. Circē Ulixis[8] verbīs et factīs territa animālia in hominēs vertit. Rēgīna, quae nōn iam inimīca fuit, magnam ac bonam cēnam parāvit. Sociīs expedītīs, annum ibi Ulixēs mānsit et vītam grātam ēgit. Tum ā sociīs adductus discessit. 25

Thought Questions.—1. What caused the storm which prevented Ulysses from reaching Ithaca? 2. How did Ulysses find out what Circe had done to his men?

Read Sabin, pp. 313–315; Gayley, pp. 324–327; Guerber, pp. 347–349; Colum, pp. 169–173; Bulfinch, pp. 245–247.

337. Ablative Absolute

In English, we sometimes say, *This meeting with your approval, I shall act accordingly.* Because such phrases as "This meeting with your approval" are used loosely and have no direct connection with either the subject or the predicate of the sentence, they are said to be in the **nominative absolute,** *i.e.* they are *absolutely free* in a grammatical sense from the rest of the sentence. The phrase quoted above is equivalent to an adverbial clause: *Since this meets with your approval.*

In Latin, this loose construction is very common, with this difference: the *ablative* is used instead of the nominative. This in-dependent use of the participial phrase is therefore known as the

---

[1] Ablative. [2] *them.* [3] Accusative plural: *animals.*
[4] *everything.* [5] *him.* [6] *to him.* [7] *(with) this.* [8] Genitive.

ablative absolute. The perfect participle is most frequently used in this construction.[1]

In English, there is an active and a passive past participle: *having sent* (act.), *sent* or *having been sent* (pass.). *In Latin, there is only a passive perfect participle.* In Latin, therefore, the ablative absolute with the passive participle is often used where the active participle is employed in English.

Translate the participle *literally* before attempting to expand it into a clause beginning with *when, since, after, because, if, although* (see **323**) or an active participle.

1. *Servō accūsātō* (lit., *the slave having been accused*), **dominus discessit,** *After accusing the slave, the master departed.*

2. *Litterīs nōn missīs* (lit., *the letter not having been sent*), **puer pecūniam nōn accēpit,** *Because he did not send the letter, the boy did not receive the money.*

3. *Oppidīs nostrīs captīs* (lit., *our towns captured*), **bellum gerēmus,** *If our towns are captured, we shall wage war.*

4. *Signō datō* (lit., *the signal having been given*), **dux prōcessit,** *Having given the signal, the general advanced.*

Caution.—The ablative absolute cannot be used when the noun or pronoun with which the participle agrees forms any part of the main sentence (subject or predicate). Compare the follow-

ing sentence with those above and note that the ablative absolute construction cannot be used because the participle in this case must agree with the subject:

Servus accūsātus territus est, *The slave, having been accused, was terrified.*

---

[1]Occasionally a noun, adjective, or present participle is used.

Roman writing materials: papyrus rolls, wax tablets, inkwells, etc.

338. Exercises[1]

(*a*) 1. Dux servōrum, signō datō, equōs ēdūcī iussit. 2. Captīvī miserī, trāctī ad pedēs rēgis, pācem timidē petēbant. 3. Librō āmissō, puella legere nōn potuit. 4. Impedīmentīs in oppidō relīctīs, mīlitēs salūtem petīverant. 5. Hominēs, praedā armīsque impedītī, properāre nōn poterant. 6. Rōmānī, castrīs mūnītīs, Gallōs in fugam vertērunt. 7. Librīs lēctīs, puerī magistrum aequō animō exspectāvērunt. 8. Expedītī ex perīculō Deō grātiam habēre dēbēmus.

(*b*) Translate the words in italics by participles:

1. *After* the money *was given*, the boy was returned to his parents. 2. The boy *having been freed*, everyone was happy. 3. This boy, *sent* to visit his aunt, lost his way. 4. *Having read* the books, we returned them to the library. 5. *After putting* the prisoner in jail, the policeman went home. 6. The boys *having been warned* to stop fighting, the principal went back to his office.

(*c*) 1. The advice of the teacher having been heard, we shall read the book. 2. Having written good letters, the boys will receive rewards. 3. Hindered by bad roads, we have not been able

---

[1] Be careful to distinguish the ablative absolute from other uses of the participle.

to come on foot. 4. After sending a messenger, the king shouted:
"My kingdom for (prō) a horse!"

339.   Vocabulary
li'gō, –ā're, –ā'vī, –ā'tus, *bind*   (ligament)
pēs, pe'dis, m., *foot*   (pedal)
  expe'diō, –ī're, expedī'vī, expedī'tus, (lit., *make the foot free*),
    set free
  impedīmen'tum, –ī, n., *hindrance;* plur., *baggage*
  impe'diō, –ī're, impedī'vī, impedī'tus, (lit., *entangle the feet*),
    hinder
rēx, rē'gis, m., *king*   (regal)
  rēg'num, –ī, n., *royal power, kingdom*
ver'tō, –ere, ver'tī, ver'sus, *turn*   (version)

340.   Latin and English Word Studies

Latin words should not be memorized individually but in
groups—by *families*, so to speak. This is much easier, much more
useful, and much more interesting. For example, there is the word
pēs, the father of its family. From it are derived many other words
in Latin and in English. **Im-pediō** means to *entangle the feet*. An
"impediment" is a *tangle*, something in the way. Transportation
is still a big problem with an army; it is no wonder that the Romans, without railroads or motor trucks, called the baggage train
of the army **impedīmenta**. **Ex-pediō** means to get the *foot out*
of the tangle; therefore in English an "expedient" is a means of
solving a difficulty. To "expedite" matters is to hurry them along
by removing obstacles.

You have already become acquainted with several other
"families" of words (204). Other words which should be grouped
together are **regō, rēgnum,** and **rēx; dō** and **dōnō; dūcō** and
dux; ager and **agricola; cōnsulō** and **cōnsilium.** Show how the
members of these families are related.

What is the meaning of *ligature, ligament, obligation, pedestrian?*
Why is *Aeolian* the name of an organ company? What do you
really mean when you say "I am much *obliged*"?

341. English Word Studies

1. Make a sketch map of England (not including Scotland) and indicate on it names of towns derived from Latin **castra** (as many as you can). Then see how many of these town names are found in the United States and in how many states.

2. The first word in each of the following lines is a Latin word. From among the last five words in each line pick the one which is an English derivative of the first word.

stāre	status	stair	stare	star	stay
hominī	homely	home	hominy	homicide	hum
mīles	mile	militant	mill	millinery	million
premō	supreme	premises	premonition	express	prime
clāmō	clam	clamp	clammy	inclement	exclaim
pāx	pace	packs	Pacific	impact	pass

342. Vocabulary

Nouns

1. dux
2. factum
3. fuga
4. homō
5. impedīmentum
6. lēx
7. mīles
8. pāx
9. pēs
10. pompa
11. rēgnum
12. rēx
13. salūs
14. spatium

Adjectives

15. certus
16. nōtus
17. parātus
18. tertius
19. timidus
20. ultimus

Verbs

21. addūcō
22. antecēdō
23. cernō
24. clāmō
25. commoveō
26. cōnsulō
27. expediō
28. impediō
29. ligō
30. possum
31. premō
32. prōvideō
33. relinquō
34. stō
35. trādūcō
36. trānsportō
37. vertō

Adverb

38. nōn iam

233

Vocabulary

NOUNS

1. *leader*
2. *deed*
3. *flight*
4. *man*
5. *hindrance*
6. *law*
7. *soldier*
8. *peace*
9. *foot*
10. *parade*
11. *kingdom*
12. *king*
13. *health, safety*
14. *space*

ADJECTIVES

15. *sure*
16. *known*
17. *prepared*
18. *third*
19. *timid*
20. *farthest*

VERBS

21. *influence*
22. go before
23. *discern*
24. cry out
25. *disturb*
26. *consult*
27. set free
28. *hinder*
29. *bind*
30. *can*
31. *press*
32. *foresee*
33. leave behind
34. *stand*
35. *lead across*
36. *transport*
37. *turn*

ADVERB

38. *no longer*

Pompeian wall painting showing a fight at the amphitheater between Pompeians and visitors from a neighboring town—like a fight between spectators at a football game

1. (*a*) Decline **rēx magnus, lēx bona.**

(*b*) What is the case of **ducum, hominī, mīlitibus, pācem?**

2. Give a six-tense synopsis of **possum,** 3d plur., translating each tense form.

345.   Numerals

1. (The teacher assigns a number—"Ūnus," "Duo," "Trēs," etc., to each of ten pupils. The following questions and others like them should be answered by the pupil whose number furnishes the correct answer.)

Magister. Quot (*how many*) sunt duo et quattuor?

Discipulus "Sex." Duo et quattuor sunt sex.

M. Quot sunt quattuor et quīnque? **D. "Novem."** Quattuor et quīnque sunt novem.

Note.—A competitive game can be made by having two sets of ten (or less) and scoring one for the side whose representative answers first.

2. Give the Latin word for the missing numeral represented by the ?

(*a*) III+V= ?	(*c*) IV+ ?=X	(*e*) X− ?=VIII
(*b*) XII÷III= ?	(*d*) II×V= ?	(*f*) VI−I= ?

346.   Participles

(*a*) Substitute a Latin participle in the right gender, number, and case for the words in italics:

1. Puerī (*although they were called*) nōn vēnērunt. 2. Fīliōs virī (*who has been accused*) nōvimus. 3. Perīcula (*if foreseen*) mē nōn terrent. 4. Librum (*after I had read it*) ēmī. 5. Puellae (*because they had been scared*) fūgērunt.

(*b*) Translate the ablative absolute in each of the following sentences into good English:

1. **Pecūniā inventā,** he will rejoice. 2. **Litterīs scrīptīs,** I took a walk. 3. **Auxiliō missō,** they can still win. 4. **Auctōritāte āmissā,** he was still king.

The rock near Corfu that was once the Phaeacian ship—so they say.

LESSON L

347. SĪRĒNĒS ET PHAEĀCIA

Tum ad Sīrēnēs[1] Ulixēs vēnit. Sīrēnēs corpora avium[2] et capita puellārum habuērunt. Carmina pulchra canēbant, quibus nautae affectī nāvēs ad saxa vertēbant. Hōc[3] modō vītam āmittēbant.

Sed Ulixēs dē Sīrēnibus ā Circē[4] monitus erat. Perīculō prōvīsō, 5 aurēs[5] sociōrum cērā clausit, sed nōn suās. Iussit manūs[6] pedēs- que suōs ad nāvem ligārī. Hōc modō carmina Sīrēnum clārē audīvit neque vītam āmīsit.

Ubi ad Siciliam vēnērunt, sociī Ulixis occīsī sunt et Ulixēs sōlus ad īnsulam āctus est in quā habitābat rēgīna pulchra cui[7] nōmen 10 erat Calypsō. Rēgīna Ulixem nōn dīmīsit. Itaque Ulixēs ibi octō annōs—longum temporis spatium—remānsit. Sed tum Iuppiter rēgīnam iussit Ulixī nāvem parāre. Hōc[3] factō, Ulixēs expedītus rēgīnam relīquit.

Sed nāvis undīs frācta est ad īnsulam; nōmen īnsulae erat 15 Phaeācia.[8] Vulneribus impedītus homō miser vix potuit corpus in silvam fīnitimam ad flūmen trahere, ubi somnum cēpit.

Interim Nausicaa,[9] rēgis Phaeāciae fīlia, cum aliīs puellīs carrō ad flūmen prōcēdēbat, quod in flūmine vestēs lavāre cupīvit; nam tempus mātrimōnī aderat. Ubi vestēs in flūmine lāvērunt, labōre 20 intermissō, Nausicaa pilam[10] ad reliquās puellās in ōrdine iaciē-

---

[1] *the Sī'rens.*   [2] *of birds.*   [3] *this* (ablative).   [4] *Ablative.*   [5] *ears.*   [6] *hands.*
[7] *whose.*   [8] *Phaeacia* (*Fēā'shia*).   [9] *Nausic'āă.*   [10] *ball.*

236

bat. Clāmōribus puellārum ab Ulixe audītīs, Ulixēs pilam ex flūmine servāvit. Puellae timidae fugere incipiunt, quod Ulixēs ob mala atque vulnera quae sustinuerat nōn pulcher erat. Sed Nausicaa nōn territa ante Ulixem stetit et eī[1] grātiās ēgit. Vestibus plicātīs, ad oppidum in ōrdine prōcessērunt. Ulixēs ab rēge Al- 25 cinoō[2] acceptus est, cui factīs clārīs nōtus fuit. Paucōs diēs Ulixēs in Phaeāciā mānsit. Tum Alcinous Ulixem ad patriam Ithacam mīsit. Itaque post xx annōs Ulixēs sōlus sine sociīs ad patriam vēnit.

Ulixe in Ithacā vīsō, Neptūnus nāvem in quā Ulixēs trāns- 30 portātus erat ante portum Phaeāciae in saxum vertit. Portus īnsulae hōc[3] impedīmentō clausus est neque posteā Alcinous et hominēs īnsulae nāvigāre potuērunt.

Thought Questions.—1. How did Ulysses manage to hear the Sirens without danger? 2. Why did Nausicaa go to the river? 3. Why did the girls run away?

Read Sabin, pp. 316–320; Gayley, pp. 328–331; Guerber, pp. 350–353, 355–357; Colum, pp. 135–142, 174–181; Bulfinch, pp. 251–257.

348.   **Third Declension: Neuter Nouns**

	ENDINGS		corpus, *body* (base, corpŏr–)	
	SINGULAR	PLURAL	SINGULAR	PLURAL
Nom.	—	–a	cor′pus	cor′pora
Gen.	–is	–um	cor′poris	cor′porum
Dat.	–ī	–ibus	cor′porī	corpo′ribus
Acc.	—	–a	cor′pus	cor′pora
Abl.	–e	–ibus	cor′pore	corpo′ribus

Observe that the nominative and accusative singular of neuter nouns are alike, and that the nominative and accusative plural both end in –a.

Practice.—(*a*) Decline nōmen clārum. (*b*) Tell the form of flūmina, capitum, lēgēs, tempus, flūminī, nōmine, rēgibus.

---

[1] (*to*) *him.*   [2] *Alcinous (Alsin′o-us).*   [3] *this.*

Exercises

(*a*) 1. Litterae quās fīlia mea scrīpsit nec caput nec pedem habent. 2. Quae nōmina flūminum Galliae cognōvistis? 3. Corpore hominis inventō, puer magistrum vocāvit. 4. Pāce factā, ōrdō in Eurōpā nōn reductus est. 5. Ob tempus annī frūmentum trānsportāre nōn poterāmus. 6. Rēx, victōriā barbarōrum territus, cōpiās trāns flūmen trādūxit.

(*b*) 1. The river which you see is deep. 2. Horses have large bodies but small heads. 3. (There) were many wounds made with a sword on the sailor's body. 4. Since the river is closed, grain can no longer be transported.

350. Vocabulary

ca′put, ca′pitis, n., *head*	(capital)
clau′dō, –ere, clau′sī, clau′sus, *close*	(clause)
cor′pus, cor′poris, n., *body*	(corporation)
flū′men, flū′minis, n., *river*	(fluid)
nō′men, nō′minis, n., *name*	(nominate)
ōr′dō, ōr′dinis, m., *order, rank*	(ordinary)
tem′pus, tem′poris, n., *time*	(temporal)
vul′nus, vul′neris, n., *wound*	(vulnerable)

351. English Word Studies

(*a*) Many English words preserve the original Latin forms of the third declension:

SINGULAR	PLURAL	SINGULAR	PLURAL
apex	apexes or apices	index	indexes or indices
appendix	appendixes or appendices	vertex	vertexes or vertices
genus	genera		viscera (singular rare)
stamen	stamens or stamina (with difference of meaning)		

Nouns with their plurals in –s are **consul**, **ratio**, and many nouns in –or: **doctor, actor, factor, labor, victor,** etc.

(*b*) Explain *contemporary, invulnerable, decapitate, capitalism, capital punishment.* What is a *corporation?* What is meant by *incorporated?* State two ways in which *siren* is used today.

LESSON LI

PĒNELOPĒ

Ulixēs, nāvī et sociīs āmissīs, corpore vulneribus cōnfectō, in patriam pervēnerat. Ad fīnem itineris sed nōn labōrum vēnerat. Et cīvēs et hostēs crēdidērunt Ulixem nōn iam vīvum esse.

Prīmus pāstor, cuius nōmen erat Eumaeus, Ulixem vīdit sed nōn cognōvit. Ab Eumaeō Ulixēs multa dē uxōre Pēnelopē et fīliō Tēlemachō audīvit. Tēlemachus ab īnsulā tum aberat, quod Pēnelopē eum[1] trāns mare ad ultima rēgna cīvitātēsque Graeciae mīserat, in quibus locīs itinera faciēbat et Ulixem petēbat. Per multōs annōs nūllam fāmam dē Ulixe Pēnelopē accēperat. Interim multī ducēs rēgēsque cupiditāte rēgnī Ulixis adductī dē montibus Ithacae et ē fīnitimīs īnsulīs convēnerant et rēgīnam in mātrimōnium petēbant. Cīvēs hōs[2] hostēs ē fīnibus Ithacae sine auxiliō ad montēs redigere nōn poterant. Itaque Pēnelopē, capite submissō, dīxit:

"Ubi vestem quam faciō cōnfēcerō, nōn iam dubitābō in mātrimōnium darī."

Itaque exspectāvērunt. Sed cōnsilium Pēnelopae fuit tempus trahere. Itaque nocte retexēbat[3] vestem quam multā dīligentiā texuerat. Post trēs annōs hominēs cōnsilium Pēnelopae cognōvērunt, et Pēnelopē accūsāta vestem cōnficere coācta est.

Penelope weaving. Drawn by Willy Pogany

---

[1] *him.* [2] *these.* [3] *unwove.*

Hōc[1] tempore Ulixēs nāvī ad īnsulam trānsportātus est. Eōdem[2] tempore Tēlemachus ā Minervā monitus ad Ithacam properāvit. Ibi ad mare ab Ulixe vīsus atque cognitus est. Ulixēs Tēlemachum ad oppidum antecēdere iussit. Ab Ulixe monitus Tēlemachus 35 neque mātrī neque aliīs dē patre nūntiāvit.

Thought Questions.—1. Who was Telemachus' father? 2. Why was Telemachus away when Ulysses arrived in Ithaca? 3. How did Penelope deceive the suitors?

Read Sabin, pp. 320–322; Guerber, pp. 357–359; Colum, pp. 186–187; Bulfinch, p. 189.

353. Third Declension: *I*–Stem Nouns

The important group of nouns which have –ium instead of –um in the genitive plural are called *i*–stem nouns. In addition to this difference, neuters ending in –e have –ī instead of –e in the ablative singular, and –ia in the nominative and accusative plural. The classes of masculine and feminine i–stem nouns are:

1. Nouns ending in –is having no more syllables in the genitive than in the nominative: **cīvis.**
2. Nouns of one syllable whose base ends in two consonants: **pars** (gen. part–is), nox (gen. noct–is).

	cīvis, *citizen* (base, cīv–)		mare, *sea* (base, mar–)	
	SING.	PLUR.	SING.	PLUR.
Nom.	cī'vis	cī'vēs	ma're	ma'ria
Gen.	cī'vis	cī'vium	ma'ris	ma'rium
Dat.	cī'vī	cī'vibus	ma'rī	ma'ribus
Acc.	cī'vem	cī'vēs[3]	ma're	ma'ria
Abl.	cī've	cī'vibus	ma'rī	ma'ribus

Practice—(*a*) Decline **nāvis bona, mare pulchrum.**

(*b*) Give the singular and plural in Latin in the case required: *high mountain* (gen.), *long journey* (acc.), *good citizen* (dat.), *neighboring enemy* (abl.), *our end* (nom.).

---

[1] *at this.*   [2] *at the same.*   [3] Occasionally –īs is used in the accusative plural.

240

354. Exercises

(*a*) 1. Parvā nāvī colōnī trāns mare lātum ad Americam migrāvērunt. 2. Ad fīnem itineris longī vēnērunt. 3. Ob numerum hostium quī in montibus erant cīvēs in castrīs remānsērunt. 4. Bonī cīvēs officia pūblica suscipere nōn dubitant. 5. Altōs montēs et flūmina alta in Eurōpā vīdī.

(*b*) 1. We have made a long journey but can now see the end. 2. If[1] the sea is closed, the enemy's ships will not be able to transport reinforcements. 3. I have ordered the citizens to close the gates of the town. 4. By whom was a ship seen on a mountain?

Pensive Penelope

355. Vocabulary

*cī′vis, cī′vis,[2] cī′vium, m., *citizen* (civic)

cōnfi′ciō, –ere, –fē′cī, –fec′tus, (*do thoroughly*), complete, exhaust (cf. "do up") [*faciō*]

*fī′nis, fī′nis, fī′nium, m., *end;* plur., *borders, territory* (final)

*hos′tis, hos′tis, hos′tium, m., *enemy*,[3] usually plur. (hostile)

i′ter, iti′neris, n., *journey, road, march* (itinerary)

*ma′re, ma′ris, ma′rium, n., *sea* (marine)

*mōns, mon′tis, mon′tium, m., *mountain* (mount)

*nā′vis, nā′vis,[4] nā′vium, f., *ship* (navy)

---

[1] Use ablative absolute.
[2] Nouns marked with an asterisk (*) are i–stem nouns. The genitive plural of such nouns is always given in these vocabularies.
[3] *National enemy,* differing from **inimīcus,** *personal enemy.*
[4] The ablative singular ends in –ī.

241

The State Capitol at Olympia, Washington, in the Roman style

356.   **English Word Studies**

(*a*) Many Latin **i**–stem nouns ending in –**is** are preserved in their original form in English. The original plural in –**es** is pronounced like "ease":

axis	axes
basis	bases

Distinguish **axes** from *axes* (plural of *ax*), **bases** from *bases* (plural of *base*).

(*b*) Why do you suppose that a firm in New York is called *Penelope* Frocks?

(*c*)   **Latin Phrases in English**

de jure, *according to right*, as a **de jure** government; cf. **de facto** (**315,** *b*).

Fata viam invenient, *The Fates will find a way.*

me iudice, *in my judgment* (lit., *I being judge*).

per capita, *by heads* or *individuals.*

pro tem. (pro tempore), *for the time, temporarily.*

Tempus fugit, *Time flies.*

242

Sure-shot Ulysses shoots the suitors.

LESSON LII

357. FĪNIS LABŌRUM

Ulixēs, rēx fortis Ithacae, ad portās oppidī quod rēxerat stābat, ā multīs cīvibus vīsus, sed nōn cognitus, quod vestēs sordidās gerēbat. In oppidum facilī itinere prōcessit. Multōs servōs vīdit ā quibus nōn cognitus est. Canis tamen Ulixis dominum cognōvit et gaudiō[1] affectus ē vītā excessit. Ubi Ulixēs ad rēgīnam adduc- 5 tus est, omnēs procī[2] eum[3] hostem appellāvērunt et discēdere iussē- runt. Sed Pēnelopē, quae eum nōn cognōverat, vestibus sordidīs permōta eum manēre iussit et cibum eī[4] dedit.

Pēnelopē vestem cōnfēcerat et nunc tempus aderat quō iūs erat marītum dēligere. Iussit magnum arcum[5] pōnī ante procōs[2] 10 quem Ulixēs clārus ante xx annōs tetenderat. Tum nūntiāvit:

"Homō quī arcum Ulixis fortis tendere poterit marītus meus erit; marītus novus pār Ulixī esse dēbet. Ita iūs est."

Itaque singulī in ōrdine arcum cēpērunt sed tendere nōn po-

---

[1] joy.   [2] suitors.   [3] him.   [4] to him.   [5] bow.

243

15 tuērunt quod Ulixī parēs nōn fuērunt. Tum Ulixēs arcum petīvit. Omnēs rīsērunt,[1] sed Pēnelopē iussit arcum Ulixī darī. Id[2] quod reliquī nōn facere poterant—arcum tendere—Ulixī facile erat. Tum in procōs arcum tendit, quōs in fugam dedit. Tēlemachus et Eumaeus auxilium dedērunt. Ulixēs omnēs portās oppidī claudī 20 iusserat, ob quam causam procī ex oppidō ad montēs fugere nōn potuērunt. Salūte petītā, nōn inventā, omnēs interfectī sunt. Hōc[3] modō rēgnum et uxōrem Ulixēs recēpit et in lībertāte pāceque vītam ēgit. Nōn iam nāvibus itinera trāns maria faciēbat.

Thought Questions.—1. Why was Ulysses not recognized? 2. Why did everyone laugh when Ulysses asked for the bow? 3. What do we mean when we say of a person, "He cannot bend Ulysses' bow"?

Read Sabin, pp. 322–323; Colum, pp. 233–254; Bulfinch, pp. 258–261.

358. Adjectives of the Third Declension

The adjectives thus far studied, such as **magnus, −a, −um** and **sacer, −cra, −crum,** have been declined like nouns of the first and second declensions. Many adjectives, however, belong to the third declension. With the exception of one important class, which will be studied later, almost all adjectives of the third declension are i–stems. They are divided into classes according to the number of forms which are used in the nominative singular to show gender, as follows:

Libertas—Statue of Liberty in New York harbor

1. **Two endings**[4]—masculine and feminine in −is, neuter in −e: **fortis, forte.**

2. **One ending**—one form for all genders: **pār.**

---

[1] From **rīdeō**.   [2] *that.*   [3] *this.*

[4] A few adjectives in −er have *three endings* in the nominative singular, one for each gender: **celer, celeris, celere.**

Artists' restorations of the ancient lighthouses at Alexandria, Egypt, and Dover, England. The former had a statue; compare with the Statue of Liberty, which too was once used as a lighthouse. See also page 253, and, for the liberty idea, page 252.

Adjectives of the third declension have –ī in the ablative singular, –ium in the genitive plural, and –ia in the neuter nominative and accusative plural. Note particularly that the ablative singular, unlike that of most i–stem *nouns*, ends in –ī.

	SINGULAR		PLURAL	
	M. AND F.	N.	M. AND F.	N.
Nom.	for′tis	for′te	for′tēs	for′tia
Gen.	for′tis	for′tis	for′tium	for′tium
Dat.	for′tī	for′tī	for′tibus	for′tibus
Acc.	for′tem	for′te	for′tēs[1]	for′tia
Abl.	for′tī	for′tī	for′tibus	for′tibus
Nom.	pār	pār	pa′rēs	pa′ria
Gen.	pa′ris	pa′ris	pa′rium	pa′rium
Dat.	pa′rī	pa′rī	pa′ribus	pa′ribus
Acc.	pa′rem	pār	pa′rēs[1]	pa′ria
Abl.	pa′rī	pa′rī	pa′ribus	pa′ribus

[1] Occasionally –īs is preferred to –ēs (353, footnote 3).

245

Practice.—(*a*) Decline **lībertās pār, iter facile.**

(*b*) Give in Latin: *brave boys* (acc.), *every citizen* (abl.), *all towns* (gen.), *equal right* (acc.), *brave enemies* (dat.).

359. Exercises

(*a*) 1. Pretium lībertātis est vigilia. 2. Servus fortibus factīs lībertātem obtinuit. 3. Omnia maria nāvibus hostium clausa erant. 4. Nōvistīne, amīce bone, hominem quem in nāvī vīdimus? 5. In nostrā patriā omnēs cīvēs sunt līberī et parēs. 6. Facilī itinere inventō, dux omnēs cōpiās dē montibus dūcere mātūrāvit.

(*b*) 1. All free men love peace. 2. Nature has given us many beautiful (things). 3. Citizens, it will not be easy to defend the freedom of our country on the sea. 4. We ought not to undertake a long journey now.

360. Vocabulary

fa′cilis, fa′cile, (lit., "do-able"), *easy*	[*faciō*]
for′tis, for′te, *strong, brave*	(fort)
iūs, iū′ris, n., *right*	(jury)
līber′tās,[1] lībertā′tis, f., *freedom*	[*līber*]
om′nis, om′ne, *all, every*	(omniscient)
pār, gen. pa′ris, *equal* (with dat.)	(parity)
ten′dō, -ere, teten′dī, ten′tus, *stretch*	(tendon)

361. English Word Studies

A number of English nouns and adjectives preserve the nominative singular, and a few the nominative plural of Latin adjectives of the third declension: **par, pauper, simplex, duplex,** etc.; **September,** etc.; **amanuensis.** Neuter forms occur in **simile, facsimile, insignia** (singular rare), **regalia** (singular rare), **forte** (singular only). The dative plural is preserved in **omnibus** (a vehicle *for all*) and the ablative singular in **velocipede** (a vehicle *with swift foot*). This word shows that in the third declension most *adjectives* have –ī in the ablative, while most *nouns* have –e.

---

[1] All nouns ending in –tās are feminine

LESSON LIII

362. ## RŌMULUS ET REMUS

Silvius Proca, rēx fortis Albānōrum,[1] Numitōrem et Amūlium fīliōs habuit. Numitōrī rēgnum relīquit, sed Amūlius, Numitōre ē cīvitāte pulsō, rēxit. Rhēa Silvia, fīlia Numitōris, geminōs,[2] Rōmulum et Remum, habuit. Amūlius puerōs in Tiberī flūmine pōnī iussit. Sed aqua geminōs in siccō[3] relīquit. Lupa[4] accessit et 5 puerōs aluit.[5] Posteā Faustulus, pāstor rēgis, puerōs invēnit. Post multōs annōs Rōmulō et Remō dīxit: "Numitor est avus vester." Adductī pāstōris verbīs, geminī Amūlium gladiō interfēcērunt et Numitōrī, quem Amūlius ē cīvitāte pepulerat, rēgnum dedērunt.

Posteā oppidum mūnīvērunt in locō in quō inventī erant, quod 10 dē nōmine Rōmulī Rōmam appellāvērunt.

Rōmulus Remusque parēs erant, sed Rōmulō nōn facile erat Remō cēdere. Remō interfectō, Rōmulus sōlus Rōmānōs rēxit et omnibus iūra dedit.

Thought Questions.—1. How was Amulius related to Numitor? 2. To Rhea Silvia? 3. To Remus?

Read Sabin, pp. 100–103; Guerber (*Story*), pp. 22–27.

363. The Right Word in the Right Place

Faustulus Romulum et Remum invenit. A painting by Rubens. One still reads stories of babies nourished by wolves and other animals.

We have observed from a study of **agō** (**270**) that a Latin word may have many shades of meaning, which are suggested by the context. In

---

[1] *Albans.*   [2] *twins.*
[3] *on dry ground.*   [4] *wolf.*
          [5] *fed.*

translating, therefore, do not confine yourself to the "vocabulary" meaning of the word but select the particular meaning demanded by English usage. Observe the varying translation of **magnus, –a, –um** when used with the following nouns:

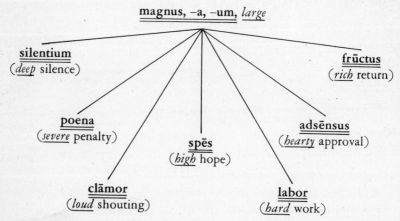

magnus, –a, –um, *large*

silentium
(*deep* silence)

frūctus
(*rich* return)

poena
(*severe* penalty)

adsēnsus
(*hearty* approval)

spēs
(*high* hope)

clāmor
(*loud* shouting)

labor
(*hard* work)

Exercise.—(*a*) Combine **magnus, –a, –um** with each of the following nouns already studied and translate freely: **perīculum, studium, pecūnia, pretium.**

(*b*) How does **altus, –a, –um** differ when applied to rivers and mountains?

(*c*) Translate **puella pulchra** and **homō pulcher.**

364.   Exercises

(*a*) 1. Post multōs annōs Rōmānī iūra cīvitātis omnibus dedērunt. 2. Flūmina omnia Italiae ex montibus ad mare tendunt. 3. Ego aut viam inveniam aut faciam. 4. Post oppidum erat mōns altus, in quō multī fortēs mīlitēs hostium pulsī erant. 5. Poteruntne hostēs, montibus occupātīs, posteā iter facere? 6. Dēbēmusne, pāce factā, numerum nāvium augēre?

(*b*) 1. Equal rights of citizenship were given to many brave Gauls. 2. After a long journey my friend is approaching (**ad**) the end of life. 3. The road stretches through the mountains. 4. Is it not pleasing to all men to see friends?

cī′vitās, cīvitā′tis, f., *citizenship*, *state*   [*cīvis*]
pel′lō, –ere, pe′pulī, pul′sus, *drive*, *defeat*   (repulsive)
post, prep. with acc., *behind* (of place); *after* (of time)
  post′eā, adv., *afterwards*

366.   English Word Studies

(*a*) The suffix –tās is usually found in nouns formed from adjectives. Its English form is –ty, which is to be carefully distinguished from –y (233).

What must be the Latin words from which are derived *commod-
ity*, *integrity*, *liberty*, *publicity*, *timidity*, *variety?* Note that the letter
preceding the ending is usually –i–.

(*b*)   **Latin Phrases in English**
ad fin. (ad finem), *near the end* (of the page).
P.S. (post scriptum), *written after* (at the end of a letter).

Translate the motto of the University of Texas (supply **est**): **Disciplina
praesidium civitatis.** The Los Angeles Public Library has on it the
inscription **in libris libertas.**

Romulus and Remus on an Italian stamp. This ancient bronze wolf
once stood on the Capitoline Hill in Rome, where, as Cicero tells us,
it was damaged by lightning. You can see where the lightning struck
on the left hind leg. The original twins disappeared, and the present
ones were added in the fifteenth century.

Sicilia. A Doric Greek temple of Juno at Agrigento

LESSON LIV

367.   **CĪNEĀS ET PYRRHUS**

Pyrrhus erat rēx Ēpīrī. Cīneās,[1] quī erat lēgātus in Pyrrhī castrīs
et reliquōs lēgātōs amīcitiā et virtūte superābat, cōnsiliīs Pyrrhī
nōn probātīs, cum multā lībertāte rēgem monēbat. Quondam Pyrrhus dīxit: "In Italiam prōcēdere et cīvitātem Rōmānam cum
5 celeritāte superāre parō."

Cīneās, "Superātīs Rōmānīs," inquit, "quid est tibi in animō[2]
facere, rēx fortis?"

"Italiae fīnitima est īnsula Sicilia," inquit rēx, "quam facile erit
armīs occupāre."

10 Tum Cīneās, "Occupātā Siciliā," inquit, "quid posteā faciēs?"

Pyrrhus tum respondit: "Posteā trāns mare in Āfricam mīlitēs
meōs celerēs trānsportābō et hostēs, quī celeritāte et virtūte mīlitibus meīs nōn parēs sunt, pellam."

---

[1] *Cineas* (*Sin'eas*).   [2] quid ... animō, *what do you intend?*

Cīneās, "Pulsīs hostibus," inquit, "quid tum faciēs?" "Post haec[1] bella, Cīneā,"[2] inquit Pyrrhus, "pāce cōnfirmātā, vītam in 15 ōtiō agam."

Celer Cīneās respondit: "Cūr nōn etiam nunc pācem cōnfirmāre potes atque in ōtiō vītam agere? Quid tē impedit?"

Thought Questions.—1. What were Pyrrhus' plans? 2. What did Cineas want Pyrrhus to do? 3. What do you think of his argument? 4. What are some of the causes of war?

368.   Ablative of Respect

1. **Equī et hominēs nōn sunt parēs celeritāte,** *Horses and men are not equal in swiftness.*

2. **Puer erat vir factīs,** *The boy was a man in deeds.*

3. **Numerō, nōn animō superāmur,** *We are surpassed in number, not in courage.*

Observe the following points:

(*a*) The ablative expresses the respect in which the meaning of an adjective, a noun, or a verb is true.

(*b*) No preposition is used in Latin, though in English we use the preposition *in.*

369.   Exercises

(*a*) 1. Puer erat celer pede sed studiīs ab omnibus superābātur. 2. Servī cum magnā celeritāte ad flūmen fūgērunt. 3. Nōn omnēs puerī dīligentiā et celeritāte parēs sunt. 4. Omnēs hostēs ē fīnibus nostrīs certē pellēmus. 5. Pāx et amīcitia cum cīvitātibus fīnitimīs ā Rōmānīs cōnfirmātae sunt. 6. Colōnī ex patriā migrant et in variīs terrīs cīvitātem petunt.

(*b*) 1. We cannot all be swift of foot. 2. He was king in name, but he did not have a kingdom. 3. Does a horse excel a boy in swiftness? 4. (Now that) peace has been established,[3] free citizens will maintain the freedom of the state.

---

[1] *these.*   [2] Vocative.   [3] See 337.

ce'ler, ce'leris, ce'lere, *swift*   (celerity)
    cele'ritās, celeritā'tis, f., *swiftness*
cōnfir'mō, –ā're, –ā'vī, –ā'tus, *make firm, encourage, establish*   [*firmus*]
su'perō, –ā're, –ā'vī, –ā'tus, *overcome, excel*   (insuperable)
vir'tūs, virtū'tis, f., *manliness, courage*   [*vir*]

371.   Latin Phrases in English

Arma non servant modum, *Arms (war) do not preserve restraint.*

Dominus providebit, *The Lord will provide.*

Ense petit placidam sub libertate quietem, *With the sword she seeks quiet peace under liberty* (motto of the state of Massachusetts). President Roosevelt quoted this in 1939 to show the need of arms to preserve peace and liberty.

extempore, *without preparation* (lit., *according to the time*).

Fortes Fortuna adiuvat, *Fortune aids the brave.*

in omnia paratus, *prepared for all things.*

Vanitas vanitatum et omnia vanitas, *Vanity of vanities, and all (is) vanity* (from the Vulgate, or Latin translation of the Bible, *Ecclesiastes,* I, 2).

Virtute et armis, *By courage and by arms* (motto of the state of Mississippi).

Libertas. Two coins showing the Roman idea of Liberty. Both figures hold the liberty cap. The word "Augusta" implies that the liberty was granted by the emperor. The initials are for "senatus consulto," by decree of the Senate. Compare with the Statue of Liberty on page 244.

372. English Word Studies

(*a*) Give the Latin noun suggested by each of the following: *civil, finish, submarine, navigate, author, corpulent, legislate, nominal, decapitate.*

(*b*) Give the Latin verb suggested by each of the following: *expedite, press, verse, attention, repellent.*

(*c*) Give the Latin adjective suggested by each of the following: *omnipresent, celerity, facilitate, disparity, fortitude.*

(*d*) Find and use in sentences as many English derivatives as possible from **parō, teneō, agō,** and **scrībō.**

Coin showing lighthouse at Messina, Sicily, with statue of Neptune (cf. p. 244)

373. Vocabulary

NOUNS

1. caput	6. fīnis	11. lībertās	16. ōrdō
2. celeritās	7. flūmen	12. mare	17. tempus
3. cīvis	8. hostis	13. mōns	18. virtūs
4. cīvitās	9. iter	14. nāvis	19. vulnus
5. corpus	10. iūs	15. nōmen	

ADJECTIVES

20. celer   21. facilis   22. fortis   23. omnis   24. pār

VERBS

25. claudō   27. cōnfirmō   28. pellō   29. superō
26. cōnficiō   30. tendō

ADVERB

31. posteā

PREPOSITION

32. post

374. **Vocabulary**

Nouns

1. *head*	6. *end*	11. *freedom*	16. *order*
2. *swiftness*	7. *river*	12. *sea*	17. *time*
3. *citizen*	8. *enemy*	13. *mountain*	18. *courage*
4. *state*	9. *journey*	14. *ship*	19. *wound*
5. *body*	10. *right*	15. *name*	

Adjectives

20. *swift*	21. *easy*	22. *strong, brave*	23. *all*	24. *equal*

Verbs

25. *close*	27. *make firm*	28. *drive*	29. *overcome*
26. *complete*			30. *stretch*

Adverb	Preposition
31. *afterwards*	32. *after*

375. **Summary of Ablative Uses**

The uses of the ablative may be grouped under three heads:

I. The **true** or **"from"** ablative (ab, *from*, and **lātus**, *carried*), used with the prepositions **ab**, **dē**, or **ex**—if any preposition is

Navis. A Roman ship shown in a mosaic floor at Ostia. Mosaic floors, made of bits of colored stone, were frequently used in Roman buildings.

used. The ablative of agent (with **ab**) belongs here.

II. The **associative** or "with" **ablative,** used with the preposition **cum** — if any preposition is used. The ablatives of means, accompaniment, and manner belong here.

III. The **place** or "in" **ablative,** used with the prepositions **in** or **sub** — if any preposition is used.

Every ablative construction may be put into one of these groups. Sometimes the use is literal, as, *I am going **with** you.* Sometimes it is figurative, as, *I shall buy a book **with** the money.*

Nueces County Building at Corpus Christi, Texas, in Ionic style

376.   Forms

(*a*) Decline **dux fortis, lībertās nostra, omnis mīles, rēx magnus, nāvis pulchra.**

(*b*) Give the following in Latin:
1. *a small ship*   in the nom., sing. and plur.
2. *an easy journey*   in the gen., sing. and plur.
3. *a good citizen*   in the dat., sing. and plur.
4. *a brave enemy*   in the acc., sing. and plur.
5. *the deep sea*   in the abl., sing. and plur.

(*c*) Give the genitive and the accusative, singular and plural, of **tempus, cīvis, corpus, fīnis, hostis, mare, nāvis, flūmen.**

(*d*) Give the synopsis of **impediō,** 3d plur., act.; **premō,** 1st plur., pass.; **superō,** 3d sing., act.; **videō,** 2d plur., pass.; **fugiō,** 2d sing., act.

Iuppiter, rex deorum   Iuno, regina deorum

LESSON LV

THE STORY OF LUCIUS (*Cont.*)

377.   **Deī**

Rōmānī multōs deōs habuērunt. Deōs in omnibus locīs vīdērunt—in terrā, in agrīs, in frūmentō, in montibus, in silvīs, in undīs maris, in aquā flūminum, in omnī nātūrā. Nōn omnēs parēs
auctōritāte erant, nam magnī deī erant et parvī deī, deī deaeque.
5 Inter magnōs deōs prīmus auctōritāte erat Iuppiter, rēx atque
pater deōrum hominumque, quī in caelō habitābat et fulmine
malōs terrēbat. Iūnō erat uxor Iovis[1] et rēgīna deōrum. Venus erat
pulchra dea amōris. Mārs, deus bellī, arma pugnāsque amābat.
Auctor populī Rōmānī vocābātur. Mercurius, celer nūntius deō-
10 rum, omnēs celeritāte superābat. Neptūnus erat deus maris, quī

---

[1] Genitive singular of **Iuppiter**.

256

A mosaic shrine in a house at Pompeii

equōs in undīs regēbat. Reliquī magnī deī erant Cerēs, dea frūmentī, Minerva, dea sapientiae, Diāna, dea silvārum, Vulcānus,
deus ignis, Apollō, quī omnia prōvidēbat et quem hominēs cōn-
sulēbant, Bacchus, deus vīnī.

STRANGE GODS

Lūcius noster nōmina omnium magnōrum et multōrum par- 15
vōrum deōrum cognōverat—quod nōn facile erat; nam magnus
erat numerus deōrum deārumque. Etiam "terminus agrōrum" deus
erat. Concordiam, Victōriam, Salūtem, Pācem, Fortūnam, Virtūtem Rōmānī deās vocāvērunt, quod sacrae erant et ā Rōmānīs
amābantur. Etiam pecūnia ā Rōmānīs amābātur et dea erat, sed 20
tamen (ita scrībit auctor Rōmānus, Iuvenālis[1]) nōn in templō
habitāvit.

---

[1] *Jū'venal.*

257

Erant etiam deī familiārēs, prīmī quōs Lūcius cognōverat. Lār familiāris erat deus quī familiam cōnservābat. Penātēs erant deī 25 quī cibum servābant. Vesta erat dea focī, in quō cibus parābātur. Ad focum erant parvae fōrmae deōrum. Ibi, omnibus līberīs et familiāribus convocātīs, pater Lūcī deīs grātiās agēbat et cibum dōnābat. Quondam nōn multus cibus erat, sed tamen pater deīs dōnābat. Lūcius ā patre petit: "Cūr cibus deīs ā tē datur? Nōn 30 multum habēmus." Pater respondit: "Cibō datō, deī hominibus magna beneficia et longam vītam dabunt."

Thought Questions.—1. Who was Juno's husband? 2. Why did the Romans have so many gods?

378. Vocabulary

auc′tor, auctō′ris, m., *maker, author* (authorize)
    auctō′ritās, auctōritā′tis, f., *authority, influence*
familiā′ris, –e, *of the family, friendly;* as noun, m., *friend* [*familia*]
pa′ter, pa′tris, m., *father* (paternal)

379. English Word Studies

Jupiter is found in the telephone directories of New York, St. Louis, and Milwaukee; *Juno* in the first two.

Mars occurs four times in Cleveland and Chicago, once in Dallas. Watch out for cartoons representing Mars.

Mercury occurs twenty-six times in New York, eleven in Chicago, eight in Los Angeles, etc.

Minerva is found twice in Denver, fourteen times in New York. For the other gods see **190, 204, 255, 261, 445.**

Jupiter prophesies Roman greatness in a quotation from the Aeneid on an Italian stamp in honor of Virgil.

380.　　　　　　Roman Religion

In the oldest form of the Roman religion there was a god or spirit for almost everything—even for the hinges of the door. Essentially this was a religion of the family. The worship came to center about the household god known as the Lar (*plural*, Lares). Other household gods of importance were Vesta, goddess of the hearth, the Penates, gods of the food supply, and the Genius, or guardian spirit of the head of the house. This family worship remained the most vital part of Roman religion.

There were many other gods. In course of time, as Greek influence increased, some of these were identified with the chief Greek gods: Jupiter with Zeus, Mars with Ares, etc. These gods all had their special functions: Neptune was god of the sea, Ceres was the goddess of grain, etc.

The identification of the Greek and Roman gods illustrates a common practice among the Romans, that of borrowing gods from other people. First they borrowed from their neighbors, later from people farther away. So in the course of time various religions were introduced from Egypt, Asia Minor, and Persia.

Among the Romans religion was the business of the state. Temples were built and restored by the government, and the priests, including the **pontifex maximus**, or chief priest, were government officials.

One important phase of the official religion was the attempt to determine the will of the gods in various ways. The augurs were a

Ceres tops the Board of Trade, Chicago.

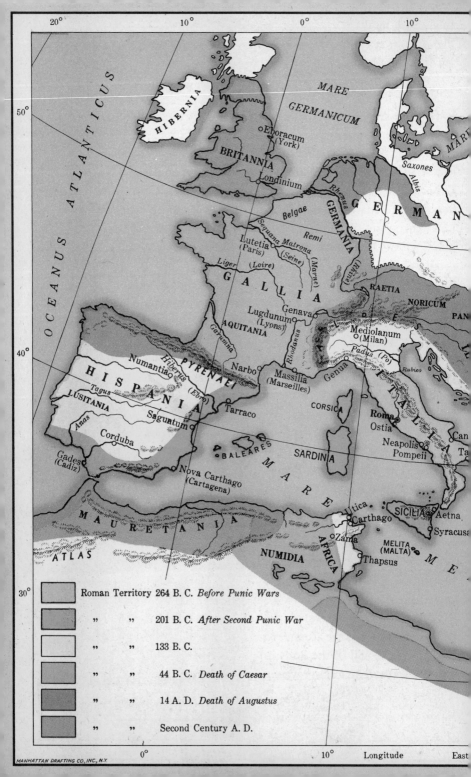

OCEANUS ATLANTICUS

MARE GERMANICUM

HIBERNIA

BRITANNIA

o Eboracum (York)

Londinium

Saxones

Albis

GERMANIA

Belgae

Rhenus

GERMAN

Remi

Seguana (Seine) Matrona (Marne)

Lutetia (Paris)

Liger (Loire)

GALLIA

RAETIA

NORICUM

PAN

Lugdunum (Lyons)

Genava

AQUITANIA

Garumna

Rhodanus

Mediolanum (Milan)

Padus (Po)

Rubico

Narbo

Massilia (Marseilles)

Genua

ITALIA

HISPANIA

Numantia

Hiberus (Ebro)

PYRENAEI

Tagus

LUSITANIA

Anas

Corduba

Saguntum

Tarraco

CORSICA

Roma

Ostia

Neapolis

Pompeii

Can

Ta

Gades (Cadiz)

BALEARES

SARDINIA

Nova Carthago (Cartagena)

MARE

MAURETANIA

NUMIDIA

ATLAS

Utica

Carthago

Zama

AFRICA

Thapsus

SICILIA

Aetna

Syracusa

MELITA (MALTA)

ME

MANHATTAN DRAFTING CO., INC., N.Y.

Roman Territory 264 B.C. *Before Punic Wars*

"   "   201 B.C. *After Second Punic War*

"   "   133 B.C.

"   "   44 B.C. *Death of Caesar*

"   "   14 A.D. *Death of Augustus*

"   "   Second Century A.D.

Longitude   East

IMPERIUM ROMANUM

Scale of Miles
0   100   200   300   400

30°   40°   50°   60°

50°

40°

30°

CAUCASUS

MARE CASPIUM

PONTUS EUXINUS
(Black Sea)

ACIA

uvius

THRACIA

salonica

IA

Byzantium
Constantinople)
Bosporus

BITHYNIA

PONTUS

ARMENIA

PARTHIA

Troia

Mare

Athenae

Aegaeum

ta

RHODUS

ASIA

GALATIA

CAPPADOCIA

PAMPHYLIA

CILICIA

LYCIA

Antiochia

CYPRUS

MESOPOTAMIA

ASSYRIA

PHOENICIA

Euphrates

Palmyra

SYRIA

Damascus

Tigris

Babylon

Tyrus

PALAESTINA

Hierosolyma
(Jerusalem)

RANEUM

ETA

Alexandria

ARABIA

AEGYPTUS

Nilus

Greenwich   30°   40°

group of priests whose business it was to determine whether a certain important act (such as a military expedition) would be successful. This they did by watching the flight of birds. Certain movements were supposed to indicate success; others, failure. Many intelligent Romans lost faith in this practice but kept it up in order to influence the more ignorant classes. Another practice, borrowed from the Etruscans, was to examine the entrails of animals for light as to the will of the gods. These two methods were official and were used before important matters were undertaken. Private persons also resorted to numerous unofficial fortune-tellers, such as astrologers.

With so many gods to worship, the Romans naturally had many holidays. Some of these were celebrated with amusements as well as religious observances, as is true of our holidays today. The amusements about which you have read (330) developed in this way.

Questions for Discussion.—1. What part did family worship play in Roman life? 2. What two religious practices of the Romans seem absurd to us? 3. To what extent is astrology practiced today? 4. In what countries today is religion "the business of the state"?

Read Showerman, pp. 280 ff.; McDaniel, pp. 101–105; Tappan, pp. 65–67; Johnston, pp. 395–404; Baker, pp. 193–211.

Altar at Pompeii showing a sacrifice. The priest always covered his head.

381. SĀTURNUS ET IUPPITER

Auctor et prīmus rēx
deōrum Ūranus erat.
Hunc fīlius Sāturnus
ex rēgnō expulit. Ūra-
5 nus hīs verbīs Sātur-
num monuit: "Tempus
auctōritātis tuae nōn
longum erit; nam tū ā
fīliō tuō expellēris."
10 Hīs verbīs territus Sāturnus omnēs fīliōs in
ōrdine dēvorābat. Sed
māter illum quem ante[1]
reliquōs amābat servā-
15 vit. Hic fuit Iuppiter,
ad īnsulam Crētam ā
māter missus. Post

Jupiter hurls his thunderbolt at the snake-
legged Giants. This beautiful medal, made
by the artist Pistrucci, celebrates the victory
at Waterloo. Wellington and Blücher in
classical armor are attended by Victory.

paucōs annōs hic patrem expulit et rēgnum illīus occupāvit.
Sāturnus reliquōs fīliōs reddere coāctus est. Rēgiam[2] in monte
20 Olympō Iuppiter posuit, ex quō in omnēs partēs spectāre poterat.
Frātrēs convocāvit. Neptūnō maris rēgnum, Plūtōnī rēgnum īnferōrum[3] permīsit.

Sed posteā Gigantēs,[4] fīliī Terrae, cum deīs bellum gessērunt.
Illī ad Olympum praecipitēs cucurrērunt sed ā deīs superātī poenīs
25 dūrīs affectī sunt.[5]

Thought Questions.—1. Who was the father of Saturn? 2. Of
Jupiter? 3. Who were the sons of Saturn?

Read Sabin, pp. 90–91; Gayley, p. 59; Guerber, pp. 18–20.

---

[1] *more than.*   [2] *palace.*   [3] *of the shades* (in Hades).   [4] *the Giants.*
[5] Modern version: in 1940 Greek and Italian airplanes fought over Mt. Olympus.

The Demonstratives *Hic* and *Ille*

In English, *this* and *that* are used to point out persons or objects and are therefore called **demonstratives.** They may be used as either adjectives or pronouns; as, *This man certainly did not write that.*

In Latin, **hic** means *this* (*near* the speaker in place or thought), while **ille** means *that* (*more distant* from the speaker). From such expressions as *this man*, *that woman*, etc., the demonstrative adjectives **hic** and **ille** came to be used as substitutes for a third person pronoun *he, she, it.* The personal pronoun, however, is usually not required in Latin.

	SINGULAR			PLURAL		
	M.	F.	N.	M.	F.	N.
Nom.	hic	haec	hoc	hī	hae	haec
Gen.	hu′ius	hu′ius	hu′ius	hō′rum	hā′rum	hō′rum
Dat.	huic	huic	huic	hīs	hīs	hīs
Acc.	hunc	hanc	hoc	hōs	hās	haec
Abl.	hōc	hāc	hōc	hīs	hīs	hīs

	SINGULAR			PLURAL		
	M.	F.	N.	M.	F.	N.
Nom.	il′le	il′la	il′lud	il′lī	il′lae	il′la
Gen.	illī′us	illī′us	illī′us	illō′rum	illā′rum	illō′rum
Dat.	il′lī	il′lī	il′lī	il′līs	il′līs	il′līs
Acc.	il′lum	il′lam	il′lud	il′lōs	il′lās	il′la
Abl.	il′lō	il′lā	il′lō	il′līs	il′līs	il′līs

Observe that both **hic** and **ille** in the plural are declined regularly, like **bonus, –a, –um,** with the exception of the nominative and accusative plural neuter of **hic** (**haec**). Note that **hic** and **ille** resemble **quī** in the genitive singular.

The Pantheon—a temple at Rome (cf. pp. 48, 275)

383.   **Position of Demonstratives**

Demonstrative adjectives regularly precede their nouns in Latin and English: *this boy*, **hic puer**; *that girl*, **illa puella**. Therefore, when *that* precedes its noun, it is a demonstrative adjective (**ille**); when it follows, it is a relative pronoun (**quī**), equivalent to *who* or *which*: *The man **that** I saw was famous*, **Vir *quem*** (not **illum**) vīdī clārus erat.

384.   **Exercises**

(*a*) 1. Haec est mea patria; nam ego cīvis Americānus sum. 2. Hī hominēs sunt patris meī amīcī; illī sunt inimīcī. 3. Hunc cognōvī sed illum ante hoc tempus nōn vīdī. 4. Ille erat dux ducum. 5. Praeceps in illum virum cucurrī, quod illum nōn vīdī. 6. Māter mea huic hominī magnam grātiam habet, quod hic patrem meum servāvit.

(*b*) Supply the right forms of **hic** and **ille** and translate:

1. (*This*) flūmen altum est, (*that*) nōn altum est. 2. (*These*) ho-

mĭnēs laudō, (those) accūsō. 3. (This) puerī patrem et (that) puellae mātrem vīdī. 4. Pecūnia ab (this) puerō āmissa est et ab (that) puellā inventa est.

(c) 1. What is the name of that man? 2. This is my money; that is yours. 3. This boy excels that (one) in (his) studies. 4. When this book has been read,[1] I shall read that (one).

385. Vocabulary

cur'rō, –ere, cucur'rī, cursū'rus, *run*   (current)
expel'lō, –ere, ex'pulī, expul'sus, *drive out*   [*pellō*]
hic, haec, hoc, *this*
il'le, il'la, il'lud, *that*
mā'ter, mā'tris, f., *mother*   (maternal)
prae'ceps, gen. praeci'pitis, *headlong, steep*   (precipice)

386. English Word Study: The Third Declension

The third declension is very important in Latin on account of the number of words which belong to it. Hence more English words are derived from nouns and adjectives of this declension than from any other declension. The English word is usually derived from the base, and not from the nominative. It is therefore doubly important to memorize the genitive, from which the base is obtained. It would be difficult to see that *itinerary* is derived from **iter** if one did not know that the genitive is **itineris.** Examine the words of the third declension studied thus far, and see how many have derivatives from the base. Note the help given for English spelling: *temporal, corporal, military, nominal,* etc.

On the other hand, the English derivative will help you determine the genitive. In the following list of words, a derivative is placed after each; give the genitive: **religiō** (*religion*), **sermō** (*sermon*), **latus** (*lateral*), **rādīx** (*radical*), **orīgō** (*original*), **ēruptiō** (*eruption*), **custōs** (*custody*), **dēns** (*dental*), **mōs** (*moral*).

---

[1] Use ablative absolute.

A LATIN PLAY

VICTŌRIA MĀTRIS

Persōnae

Gāia, *Rōmāna*   Pyrrhus, *rēx Graecōrum*
Mārcus, *parvus fīlius Gāiae*   Mīlitēs Graecī

Locus: in castrīs relīctīs in Campāniā. Tempus: annō CCLXXV ante Christum.

Gāia. Iuppiter, tē vocāmus! Nōbīs et Rōmae auxilium dā!

Mārcus. Māter! Quid dīcis? Cūr pater nōn venit?

Gāia. Pater abest. Nōn veniet.

Mār. Sed cūr nōn cum patre sumus?

Gāia. Ille cum duce Dentātō pugnat—magnum est perīculum 5 Rōmae nostrae. Graecī nunc per Campāniam veniunt.

Mār. Per Campāniam?

Gāia. Sed ad haec castra relīcta fūgimus. In hōc locō nōs nōn invenient.

Mār. Nōn timeō. Cum Graecīs pugnābō.   10

Gāia. Mātrēs et puerī patriae auxilium dare nōn possunt; pugnāre est virōrum officium.

Mār. Vir sum. Possum pugnāre. Nōnne vidēs? (*Gladium relīctum capit.*)

Gāia. Āh, meus puer erit fortis mīles—sed quid est? Pedēs equō- 15 rum audiō.

Vōx Mīlitis Graecī. Castra relīcta sunt; nēmō adest.

Mār. Cūr territa es, māter? Cūr mē tenēs?

Gāia. Graecī sunt! Iuppiter, tē vocāmus! (*Per portam veniunt Pyrrhus et mīlitēs Graecī.*)   20

Pyrrhus. Ho! Quis adest?

Mīles Graecus. Puer cum mātre.

Gāia. Cūr ad hunc locum vēnistis, Graecī? Haec terra, haec castra sunt Rōmāna.

Mīles. Sunt Rōmāna—sed erunt Graeca.   25

267

Mār. Nōn erunt Graeca. Virī Rōmānī sunt fortēs.

Pyr. Oho! Etiam puer fortis est. Fortem puerum petō. Potesne litterās ad castra Graecōrum portāre?

Gāia. Ille nōn portābit; Rōmānus est.

30 **Pyr.** Nōnne omnēs viās cognōvistī, puer? Vidēsne hanc pecūniam? Tua erit—

Gāia. Graecī pecūniam capiunt et patriam relinquunt; nōs sumus Rōmānī.

Pyr. Pyrrhus sum, rēx Graecōrum. Hunc puerum interficere

35 possum. Properāre dēbēmus. Puer litterās portābit. (*Mīlitēs ad Gāiam et Mārcum accēdunt. Gāia gladium relīctum capit et tenet, sed Pyrrhus hunc nōn videt.*)

Gāia. Meus fīlius servus Graecōrum nōn erit.

Mīles. Quid faciētis? Fugere nōn potestis, pugnāre nōn potestis.

40 **Gāia.** Sed hoc facere possum—prō patriā meā!

Mār. Māter! (*Gāia gladiō Mārcum interficit, tum sē.[1]*)

Mīlitēs. Oh! (*Pyrrhus Gāiam et Mārcum spectat.*)

Pyr. Ita mātrēs Rōmānae pugnant. Quid virī facient?

(*Exeunt tardē*)

---

[1] *herself.*

Cur territa es, mater? Cur me tenes?

Milites Romani. From the moving picture "The Sign of the Cross"

LESSON LVII

388. CAEDICIUS FORTIS

Prīmō bellō Pūnicō hostēs locum nātūrā mūnītum occupā-
verant, et perīculum mīlitum Rōmānōrum magnum erat. Aestās
erat, nam Rōmānī semper aestāte, nōn hieme, bella gerēbant.
Dux nihil facere poterat. Tribūnus mīlitum Rōmānus cui[1] nōmen
Caedicius[2] erat, ad ducem hōc tempore vēnit et dīxit, locō quō- 5
dam[3] mōnstrātō:

"Cōpiās tuās servāre poteris sī ad illum locum cccc mīlitēs
currere iubēbis. Hostēs, ubi hōs mīlitēs vīderint, proelium com-
mittent et hōs omnēs interficient. Dum haec faciunt, facile erit
reliquōs mīlitēs ex hōc locō ēdūcere. Haec est sōla via salūtis." 10

"Bonum tuum cōnsilium probō," inquit dux, "sed quis illōs
praecipitēs in mortem certam dūcet?"

"Cūr mē nōn mittis? Mors mē nōn terret," respondit tribūnus.

Itaque dux tribūnō grātiās ēgit et hunc cum cccc mīlitibus contrā hostēs mīsit. Fortēs Rōmānī nihil timuērunt. Neque cessērunt 15

---

[1] *whose.*   [2] *Caedicius (Sēdish'ius).*   [3] *certain.*

269

Rome after the Punic Wars, one of four large maps of colored marble
which show the growth of the Roman Empire (cf. pp. 260-261). These
have been placed on the wall of an ancient building in Rome.

neque fūgērunt sed magnīs cōpiīs hostium superātī sunt. Omnēs
aut vītam āmīsērunt aut vulnera accēpērunt. Interim reliquī mīlitēs
Rōmānī integrī salūtem petīvērunt.

Deī praemium tribūnō ob ēgregium exemplum dōnāvērunt;
20 nam vītam nōn āmīsit. Vulnera multa accēpit sed neque in capite
neque in corde. Illā aestāte hostēs expulsī sunt, et hieme Rōmānī
hostēs nōn iam timuērunt.

Thought Questions.—1. What was Caedicius' suggestion? 2. What
happened to Caedicius?

389.   Ablative of Time When

In English, time is expressed with or without the prepositions
in, *on*, etc.: *last summer*, *in winter*.

In Latin, time when is expressed by the ablative, *usually without
a preposition.*

1. **Illō annō in oppidō mānsimus,** *That year we remained in town.*
2. **Aestāte agrī sunt pulchrī,** *In summer the fields are beautiful.*

Note.—Compare with the ablative of place where (**88**). Observe that
when *at*, *in*, or *on* denotes *time* instead of *place*, no preposition is used.

270

390. Exercises

(*a*) 1. Prō Deō et patriā! Haec clāra verba corda virōrum semper incitāvērunt. 2. Hōc annō nihil timēmus, quod cōpiam frūmentī habēmus. 3. Prōvinciā occupātā, mīlitēs nostrī, paucī numerō sed corde fortēs, auxilia exspectābant. 4. Hic puer et aestāte et hieme labōrat, quod pater māterque pecūniam nōn habent. 5. Quīntā hōrā omnēs servī cum magnā celeritāte fūgērunt. 6. Illā hieme multōs librōs lēgī sed hāc aestāte nihil fēcī.

(*b*) 1. Good citizens fear God and love (their) country. 2. If[1] Marcus is our leader, we shall be able to live in safety this winter. 3. In summer the rivers are not deep. 4. In a few years America will have many ships on every sea.

391.   Vocabulary

aes'tās, aestā'tis, f., *summer*
cor, cor'dis, n., *heart*   (cordial)
hi'ems, hi'emis, f., *winter*
*mors, mor'tis, mor'tium, f., *death*   (mortal)
ni'hil (indeclinable), *nothing*   (annihilate)
ti'meō, –ē're, ti'muī, ——, *fear, be afraid*   (timid)

392.   English Word Studies

(*a*) An *excursion* is a little *run out of* town. What is a *current* of water? *Cursive* writing? A *recurrent* illness? *Concurrent* powers of the federal government and the states? *Discord* is *hearts apart; concord, hearts together.* What is a *cordial* welcome? An apple *core?*

(*b*)   Latin Phrases in English

Alma Mater, *fostering mother,* applied to a school or college.
A.D. (anno Domini), *in the year of our Lord.*
aut Caesar aut nihil, *either Caesar or nothing.*
iustitia omnibus, *justice for all* (motto of the District of Columbia).
Pater Noster, *Our Father, i.e.* the Lord's Prayer, which begins with these words.
primus inter pares, *first among his equals.*

---

[1] Use ablative absolute, omitting a word for *is.*

271

Prisoners brought to a Roman camp

LESSON LVIII

393.   CĪVITĀS RŌMĀNA

Duae partēs cīvitātis Rōmānae, Trōiānī et Latīnī, contra perīcula commūnia pugnāvērunt. Ubi cīvitās concordiā aucta est, rēgēs populīque fīnitimī praedae cupiditāte adductī partem agrōrum Rōmānōrum vāstābant. Paucī ex amīcīs[1] auxilium Rōmānīs sub-
5 mittēbant quod perīculīs territī sunt. Sed Rōmānī properābant, parābant, cum hostibus proelia committēbant, lībertātem patriam-que commūnem armīs dēfendēbant, mortem nōn timēbant. Dum pāx incerta est,[2] dum eī nē spīrāre quidem[3] sine perīculō possunt, cūram perpetuam nōn remittēbant.
10 Dum haec geruntur,[2] eī Rōmānī quōrum corpora ob annōs nōn iam firma erant sed quī bonō cōnsiliō valēbant dē rē pūblicā[4] cōn-

---

[1] ex amīcīs = amīcōrum.   [2] Use the past tense.   [3] nē ... quidem, *not even*.
[4] Translate by the English derivative of this compound noun.

sulēbantur et ob aetātem patrēs aut senātōrēs appellābantur.

Prīmō rēgēs erant, quī lībertātem cōnservābant et rem pūbli-
cam augēbant, sed posteā, quod hī superbī fuērunt, Rōmānī
fēcērunt cōnsulēs.   15

Eō tempore corda omnium Rōmānōrum glōriam spērāvērunt.
Virī fortēs bella amābant, in castrīs aestāte atque hieme labōrābant, nihil timēbant: virtūs eōrum omnia superāverat. Itaque
populus Rōmānus magnās hostium cōpiās paucīs mīlitibus in
fugam dabat, oppida nātūrā mūnīta pugnīs capiēbat. Hostibus 20
superātīs et perīculō remōtō, Rōmānī aequē regēbant. Iūra bellī
pācisque cōnservābant. Hōc modō auctōritās eōrum cōnfirmāta
est. In ultimās partēs mīlitēs eōrum missī sunt. Post tertium
Pūnicum bellum Rōmānī fuērunt dominī omnium terrārum ma-
riumque. Nunc sine cūrā spīrāre et animōs remittere potuērunt. 25

Sed tum fortūna, semper incerta, eōs superāvit. Hī pecūniam
imperiumque, nōn iam glōriam spērāvērunt. Superbī, nōn iam
aequī fuērunt. Iūra lēgēsque nōn iam cōnservāvērunt.

Thought Questions.—1. What were the two parts of the Roman
state? 2. What did the old men do? 3. What caused the decay of Rome?

394.   **The Demonstrative** *Is*

	SINGULAR			PLURAL		
	M.	F.	N.	M.	F.	N.
Nom.	is	e′a	id	e′ī (i′ī)	e′ae	e′a
Gen.	e′ius	e′ius	e′ius	eō′rum	eā′rum	eō′rum
Dat.	e′ī	e′ī	e′ī	e′īs (i′īs)	e′īs (i′īs)	e′īs (i′īs)
Acc.	e′um	e′am	id	e′ōs	e′ās	e′a
Abl.	e′ō	e′ā	e′ō	e′īs (i′īs)	e′īs (i′īs)	e′īs (i′īs)

Practice.—Decline **ea pars, id longum iter, is vir.**

How *Is* **Is Used.**—Instead of pointing, in a forceful way, to a
definite person or thing, as **hic** and **ille** do, **is** usually refers to
somebody or something just mentioned. When used without a
noun, it is usually translated as a personal pronoun, *he, she,* or *it;*

273

Latin inscription on the Department of Justice Building, Washington

therefore, the genitive **eius** may be translated *his*, *her*, *its*, while **eōrum** and **eārum** mean *their*. **Is** often serves as the antecedent of a relative clause; as **Is quī videt probat,** *He who sees approves.*

395.   **Exercises**

(*a*) 1. Dum spīrō spērō.[1] 2. Commūne perīculum concordiam facit. 3. Certa āmittimus dum incerta petimus. 4. Is cui librōs dedī eōs nōn remīsit. 5. Puellās et eārum mātrem in oppidō vīdī 6. Hostibus pulsīs, vigiliam nostram nōn remittēmus. 7. Eī puerī quōs aestāte vīdimus erant eius discipulī.

(*b*) 1. This man is my teacher; that man is her father. 2. She and her father are away. 3. Give him a part of the money. 4. We shall see him and his mother this summer.

396.   **Vocabulary**

commū′nis, –e, *common*	(communistic)
dum, conj., *while*	
incer′tus, –a, –um, *uncertain*	[*cernō*]
is, e′a, id, *this, that; he, she, it*	
*pars, par′tis, par′tium, f., *part*	(partition)
remit′tō, –ere, remī′sī, remis′sus, (lit., *let back*), *relax,* *send back*	[*mittō*]
spē′rō, –ā′re, –ā′vī, –ā′tus, *hope* (*for*)	(despair)
spī′rō, –ā′re, –ā′vī, –ā′tus, *breathe*	(inspiration)

[1] This is one of the mottoes of South Carolina.

397. English Word Studies: The Names of the Months

In early Roman times the year began March 1, and February was the last month. We still use the ancient Roman names of the months. **March** was named after Mars. **April** was the *opening* month (**aperiō**), when the earth seems to open up. **May** is the month when things become *bigger* (**maior**). **June** is Juno's month. **July** was originally called **Quīnctīlis**, the *fifth* month, but was renamed in honor of Julius Caesar after he had the calendar reformed. Similarly **August** was originally **Sextīlis**, the *sixth* month, but was renamed after the Emperor Augustus. **September** was originally the *seventh* month and kept its name even after it later became the ninth; similarly, **October, November, December.** **January** was named after Janus, the god of beginnings. **February** was the time of purification (**fēbrua**), like the Christian Lent.

Model of the Pantheon in the Metropolitan Museum of Art, New York (cf. pp. 48, 265). It was originally built by Agrippa in the reign of Augustus.

398.   MIDĀS

Midās, nōbilis genere, rēx Phrygiae, multīs oppidīs expugnātīs, magnam auctōritātem habuit. Ōlim Sīlēnus, magister deī Bacchī, in agrīs Phrygiae interceptus, ad eum rēgem ductus est. Quod Sīlēnus ab rēge multa beneficia accēpit, Bacchus parātus fuit rēgī dare id quod spērāvit. Midās dīxit: "Sī omnia quae parte corporis 5 meī tetigerō[1] in aurum vertentur, mihi grātum erit."

Hōc factō, omnia commūnia quae rēx tangēbat in aurum vertē-bantur. Terram tangit: nōn iam terra est sed aurum. Aquam tangit: eōdem modō in aurum vertitur. Tum grātiās Bacchō prō magnō praemiō ēgit. 10

Tum rēx cēnam magnam parārī iussit et omnia genera cibōrum in mēnsā pōnī. Haec mēnsa ab eōdem tācta in aurum versa est. Dum magnā celeritāte servī cēnam parant, Midās familiārēs nō-bilēs convocāvit. Grātō animō bonam cēnam quae parāta erat spectāvit. Dum cibum capit, cibus in aurum versus est. Vīnum 15 in mēnsā pōnī iussit. Hoc tangit et nōn iam idem est sed in aurum vertitur. Omnibus amīcīs ēgregia cēna grāta fuit sed nōn rēgī. Inter multōs cibōs edere[2] nōn potuit.

Tandem ad Bacchum, auctōrem malōrum, rēx miser prōcessit et fīnem supplicī petīvit — nam sup- 20 plicium et impedīmentum, nōn iam praemium erat id quod ā deō accēperat. Bacchus iussit eum in flūmine Pactōlō[3] sē[4] lavāre. Prae-ceps rēx ad flūmen cucurrit, ubi 25 sē lāvit, sē remīsit, sine cūrā spīrāvit. Arēna[5] flūminis in au-rum versa est, et etiam nunc in hōc eōdem flūmine aurum est.

Silenus holding the infant Bacchus

---

[1] From tangō.   [2] eat.
[3] Pactō'lus.   [4] himself.   [5] sand.

Built-in couches in a dining room in Pompeii. Cushions were put on top.

Thought Questions.—1. Why did Bacchus reward Midas? 2. How?
3. What is meant by the expression used today, "The Midas touch"?
4. What did Mr. Hoover mean in comparing (1940) the gold buried at
Fort Knox to that acquired by Midas?

Read Sabin, pp. 19–21; Gayley, pp. 157–158; Guerber, pp. 177–179;
Bulfinch, pp. 52–54.

399. The Demonstrative *Īdem*

The demonstrative **īdem** is a compound of **is** and **–dem**, with
slight changes for ease of pronunciation:

	M.	F.	N.
		SINGULAR	
Nom.	ī'dem	e'ădem	i'dem
Gen.	eius'dem	eius'dem	eius'dem
Dat.	eī'dem	eī'dem	eī'dem
Acc.	eun'dem	ean'dem	i'dem
Abl.	eō'dem	eā'dem	eō'dem
		PLURAL	
Nom.	eī'dem (ī'dem)	eae'dem	e'ădem
Gen.	eōrun'dem	eārun'dem	eōrun'dem
Dat.	eīs'dem (īs'dem)	eīs'dem (īs'dem)	eīs'dem (īs'dem)
Acc.	eōs'dem	eās'dem	e'ădem
Abl.	eīs'dem (īs'dem)	eīs'dem (īs'dem)	eīs'dem (īs'dem)

Practice.—Give the Latin in the singular and plural for *the same body* in the acc., *the same summer* in the abl., *the same year* in the gen., *the same punishment* in the nom., *the same part* in the dat.

400. Exercises

(*a*) 1. Eōdem annō lībertās servīs data est. 2. Dux eum ad idem supplicium trahī iussit. 3. Dum omnia timēmus, glōriam spērāre nōn possumus. 4. Hominēs līberī parēsque esse dēbent, quod eundem Deum habent. 5. Hic homō nōbilī genere sed nōn magnīs factīs illum superat. 6. Oppidō expugnātō, Caesar impedīmenta hostium intercēpit.

(*b*) 1. His punishment scared the rest. 2. Their towns were taken-by-assault the same year. 3. He will not send back the same book. 4. When I saw the same boy,[1] I was no longer afraid.

401. Vocabulary

expug'nō, –ā're, –ā'vī, –ā'tus, (lit., *fight it out*), *capture by assault* [*pugnō*]

ge'nus, ge'neris, n., *birth, kind* (generation)

ī'dem, e'ādem, ī'dem, *same* (identity)

interci'piō, –ere, –cē'pī, –cep'tus, *intercept* [*capiō*]

nō'bilis, –e, (lit., "know-able"), *noble* [*nōscō*]

suppli'cium, suppli'cī, n., *punishment* [*plicō*]

402. English Word Studies

(*a*) Explain the word *communism*. **Supplicium** literally means *folding* (or bending) *down* for punishment. Explain *supplication*.

(*b*) **Latin Phrases in English**

Homo proponit, sed Deus disponit, *Man proposes, but God disposes.*

ibid. (ibidem), *in the same place.*

id. (idem), *the same* (*i.e.* as mentioned above).

i.e. (id est), *that is.*

quid pro quo, *something for something* ("tit for tat").

Explain **semper idem, genus homo.**

---

[1] Use ablative absolute.

278

Horatius at the bridge

LESSON LX

403. **HORĀTIUS**

Nunc in locīs commodīs sedēbimus et legēmus dē Horātiō,[1]
virō fortī nōbilīque genere. Sī haec fābula tē dēlectābit,[2] tū ipse
lege eandem sorōribus frātribusque tuīs parvīs (sī frātrēs sorō-
rēsque habēs), quī circum tē sedēbunt et cum magnō studiō
audient.   5

Tarquiniī,[3] ā Rōmānīs pulsī, ā Porsenā,[4] rēge Etrūscōrum, auxilium petīvērunt. Itaque Porsena ipse cum magnīs cōpiīs Rōmam[5]
vēnit. Rōmānī, dē salūte commūnī incertī, territī sunt, quod
magna erat potestās Etrūscōrum magnumque Porsenae nōmen.
Rōmānī quī agrōs colēbant in oppidum migrāvērunt; portās clausē- 10
runt et oppidum ipsum praesidiīs dēfendērunt. Pars urbis Tiberī
flūmine mūnīta est. Pōns sublicius[6] iter hostibus dabat, sed ēgregius vir prohibuit, Horātius Coclēs,[7] illō cognōmine appellātus

---

[1] *Horatius (Horā'shius).*   [2] Translate by the present: *pleases.*
[3] *the Tar'quins,* Etruscan rulers of Rome in the sixth century B.C.
[4] *Por'sena.*   [5] Supply *to.*   [6] *made of piles.*   [7] *Cō'clēs'* ("One-Eye").

The Rotunda (library) of the University of Virginia, modeled after the Pantheon (p. 275) by Thomas Jefferson

quod in proeliō oculum āmīserat. Is, extrēmā pontis parte occu-
15 pātā, cōpiās hostium sōlus sine auxiliō intercēpit et sustinuit et
Rōmānōs quī fugiēbant pontem frangere iussit. Ipsa audācia hostēs
terruit. Ponte frāctō, armīs impedītus, praeceps in Tiberim dēsiluit
et per multa tēla incolumis[1] ad Rōmānōs trānāvit. Eius virtūte oppidum nōn expugnātum est. Grāta ob factum clārum eius cīvitās
20 fuit. Multī agrī eī pūblicē datī sunt. Hōs ad terminum vītae coluit.
Exemplum virtūtis ab eō prōpositum Rōmānī semper memoriā
retinuērunt.

Thought Questions.—1. Why did Porsena come to Rome? 2. How
was he prevented from entering the city? 3. How did Cocles get his name?
4. Is the destruction of bridges important in modern warfare?

Read Haaren and Poland, pp. 58–60; Guerber (*Story*), pp. 73–74;
Harding, pp. 35–39; Mills, pp. 67–68; Macaulay's *Lays of Ancient Rome*,
"Horatius."

A Latin Pun

Equus in stabulō est sed nōn ēst, The horse *is* in the stable but does
not *eat* (**est** means *is;* **ēst** means *eat*).

---

[1] *unharmed*

280

In English, compound pronouns are formed by joining *-self* to *my, your, him, her, it*, and the plural *-selves* to *our, your, them*. These compounds may be used in an intensive or emphatic sense; as, *I saw the man myself*.

In Latin, the pronoun **ipse** is a compound of **is** (394) and the intensive particle **–pse**, and therefore has purely intensive force: **Ipse hominem vīdī**, *I saw the man myself*. Note that **ipse** may be used alone in the nominative to emphasize an omitted subject. It is declined like **ille** (382), except in the neuter nominative and accusative singular.

	SINGULAR		
	M.	F.	N.
Nom.	ip′se	ip′sa	ip′sum
Gen.	ipsī′us	ipsī′us	ipsī′us
Dat.	ip′sī	ip′sī	ip′sī
Acc.	ip′sum	ip′sam	ip′sum
Abl.	ip′sō	ip′sā	ip′sō

(The plural is regular.)

Practice.—*Translate* frātris ipsīus, suppliciō ipsō, partēs ipsae, hic cīvis ipse, illārum nāvium ipsārum, sorōrī meae ipsī, eiusdem generis, eōrundem auctōrum.

405.   Exercises

(*a*) 1. Nōnne idem ipsī vīdistis, puerī? 2. Frātrēs et sorōrēs eiusdem familiae paria iūra habēre dēbent. 3. Quis est puer ille qu͞ cum sorōre meā sedet? 4. Quae officia soror tua ipsa suscipiet? 5. Ille homō agricola appellātur quod agrōs colit. 6. Deī quōs Rōmānī colēbant multī erant.

(*b*) 1. These (men) are standing; those are sitting. 2. The same winter they saw and heard him themselves. 3. These letters were written by the king himself. 4. We ourselves shall get much money in a few years.

co′lō, –ere, co′luī, cul′tus, *till, inhabit, worship*   (cultivate)

frā′ter, frā′tris, m., *brother*   (fraternal)

ip′se, ip′sa, ip′sum, *self, very*

se′deō, –ē′re, sē′dī, sessū′rus, *sit*   (session)

so′ror, sorō′ris, f., *sister*   (sorority)

407.   English Word Studies: The Norman-French Influence

We saw in earlier lessons (**321, 326**) how Latin words were introduced into English at its very beginning. A very important period of influence was after the Norman conquest of England (1066). The language of the Normans was an old form of French, itself descended from Latin. In the course of a few centuries, the English language underwent striking changes and adopted many French (Latin) words. These sometimes show considerable changes in the original spelling. Especially common is the change of one vowel to two (cf. **507**). Because so many words were borrowed from old French, which was more like Latin than modern French is, English words are often more like Latin in form and meaning than French words are.

Look up the Latin originals of *captain, vizor, homage, duke, peer, treason*. See Scott's *Ivanhoe*, Chap. I, for *pork, beef*, etc. Explain *cult, culture, agriculture, degenerate, infinite, sediment*.

Italian stamp in honor of Horace's two thousandth birthday (cf. p. 152). The quotation from his Odes welcomes the return of spring: the snow disappears, the grass returns to the fields, the leaves to the trees. This ode was a favorite with Thomas Jefferson, who was an excellent Latin scholar and an admirer of all things classical.

In Graecia. Olympia as it was in ancient days

LESSON LXI

408. ### CICERŌ ET TĪRŌ

Cicerō et Tīrō fuērunt Rōmānī clārī, alter maximus[1] ōrātor tōtīus Italiae, alter fīdus[2] servus. Quod Tīrō dīligentiā sapientiāque Cicerōnī magnum auxilium dabat, Cicerō eum tōtō corde amābat. Neuter sine alterō ūllum iter facere cupiēbat.

Cicerō cum Tīrōne in Graeciā fuerat. Ubi in Italiam revertit, 5 Tīrō sōlus in Graeciā relīctus est quod aeger[3] fuit. Cicerō ad eum trēs epistulās in itinere ūnō diē[4] scrīpsit. Inter alia haec ipsa scrīpsit:

"Variē litterīs tuīs affectus sum, prīmā parte territus, alterā cōnfirmātus. Hōc tempore tē[5] neque marī neque itinerī committere 10 dēbēs. Medicus tuus bonus est, ut[6] scrībis et ego audiō; sed eum nōn probō; nam iūs[7] nōn dēbet stomachō[8] aegrō darī. Ad illum

---

[1] *greatest.*   [2] *faithful.*   [3] *sick.*   [4] Ablative.   [5] *yourself.*
[6] *as.*   [7] *soup.*   [8] Use the English derivative.

283

et ad Lysōnem[1] scrīpsī. Lysōnis nostrī neglegentiam nōn probō, quī, litterīs ā mē acceptīs, ipse nūllās remīsit. Sed Lysō Graecus est
15 et omnium Graecōrum magna est neglegentia. In nūllā rē[2] properāre dēbēs.

"Curium[3] iussī omnem pecūniam tibi dare quam cupis. Sī medicō pecūniam dabis, dīligentia eius augēbitur. Magna sunt tua in mē officia;[4] omnia superāveris, sī, ut[5] spērō, salūtem tuam
20 cōnfirmātam vīderō. Ante, dum magnā dīligentiā mihi auxilium dās,[6] nōn salūtem tuam cōnfirmāre potuistī; nunc tē nihil impedit. Omnia dēpōne; salūs sōla in animō tuō esse dēbet."

Nōnne dominī bonī illīs temporibus Eurōpam colēbant? Sed aliī malī erant. Omnī aetāte et in omnibus terrīs bonī et malī ho-
25 minēs fuērunt et sunt et semper erunt.

Thought Questions.—1. What was Tiro's relation to Cicero? 2. To whom did Cicero write about Tiro's illness? 3. Use a remark in this letter as a basis for discussion of national and racial prejudices.

409. Declension of Ūnus

The numeral **ūnus** and the other words in the vocabulary of this lesson are irregular only in the genitive and dative singular of all genders. In these cases they are declined like **ipse** (404), in all others like **magnus**. If you need help in declining them, see 576. Like **hic, ille,** and **is,** these adjectives are emphatic and therefore precede their nouns.

Practice.—(*a*) Decline in the singular **alius tuus frāter.**

(*b*) Give the Latin for the following in the genitive and dative singular: *neither sister, the whole town, the other leader, no winter, safety alone, one citizen.*

410. Words Often Confused

I

alius = *another*, implying a group of *three or more*.
alter = *the other*, i.e. *of two* and no more.

---

[1] Tiro was staying at Lyso's house.   [2] *thing.*   [3] *Cu'rius*, a banker.
[4] *services.*   [5] *as.*   [6] With **dum** = **dabās.**

II

tōtus = *whole*, *i.e.* no part missing, not capable of being divided.

omnis = in singular *every*, as opposed to the adj. **nūllus,** *no;* in plural, **omnēs** = *all*, *i.e.* simply a collection of units or parts.

III

nūllus = *not any*, *no*—always an adjective.

nihil = *not a thing*, *nothing*—always an indeclinable noun.

nēmō[1] = *no man*, *no one*—always a noun.

411.   Exercises

(*a*) 1. Sorōrēs meae agrōs montēsque tōtīus īnsulae vīdērunt. 2. Rēx neutrī fīliō rēgnum committet. 3. Is homō ipse ab aliīs ac-

---

[1] See 461.

Ruins of Roman Carthage, in northern Africa, near the modern city of Tunis. Carthage was once Rome's greatest rival and enemy.

cūsātus est sed ab aliīs dēfēnsus est. 4. Cōnsilia alterius ducis alterī nōn erant grāta. 5. Omnēs amīcī eius iam discessērunt et is sōlus nunc manet. 6. Accēpistīne ipse ūlla praemia prō meritīs tuīs? (*See* **193**.) Nūlla accēpī neque ūlla exspectō.

(*b*) 1. To one sister I shall give money, to the other this book. 2. My brother spent part of that same summer alone in the woods. 3. Have you seen my mother and sister? I have seen neither. 4. Every man in our whole country ought to work.

412.   Vocabulary

a'lius, a'lia, a'liud,[1] *other, another*   (alias)
   (a'lius ... a'lius, *one ... another;* a'liī ... a'liī,
   some ... others)
al'ter, al'tera, al'terum,[2] *the other* (of two)   (alternate)
   (al'ter ... al'ter, *the one ... the other*)
neu'ter, neu'tra, neu'trum, *neither* (of two)   (neutral)
nūl'lus, nūl'la, nūl'lum, *no, none*   (nullify)
sō'lus, sō'la, sō'lum, *alone, only*   (solitary)
tō'tus, tō'ta, tō'tum, *whole*   (total)
ūl'lus, ūl'la, ūl'lum, *any*
ū'nus, ū'na, ū'num,[3] *one*   (unit)

Remember that the above adjectives except **alter** have –ī'us in the genitive and –ī in the dative singular of all genders.

413.   English Word Studies: Spelling

Latin words are often very helpful in fixing the spelling of English words. In this lesson we shall consider words in which a double consonant occurs.

If the Latin word has a double consonant, it is usually preserved in English, except at the end of a word: *terrestrial*, but *inter* (from **terra**); *carriage*, but *car* (**carrus**); *rebelled*, but *rebel*

---

[1] Note that the neuter nominative and accusative singular end in –d, not –m (cf. **ille**).

[2] The genitive singular of **alter** ends in –ius.

[3] **Uter**, *which* (of two), and **uterque**, *each, both*, are likewise irregular and belong to this group but are comparatively unimportant.

The Roman theater at Mérida, Spain. Look at the map on pages 260–261 and pick out the countries which are represented by Roman ruins illustrated in this book.

(**bellum**); *remitted*, but *remit* (**remittō**). *Letter* has two *t*'s and *literature* only one in the root because the spelling of Latin **littera** varied.

Many prefixes bring about the doubling of consonants by assimilation. The most important are **ad–**, **con–**, **in–**, **ob–**, **ex–**, and **sub–**. If you will analyze the English word, you can often tell whether the consonant is to be doubled: **con–** and **modus** form **commodus**; prefix **ad–** and you get the English derivative *ac-com-modate* with two *c*'s and two *m*'s. Similarly *commend* has two *m*'s; *re-com-mend* has two *m*'s but only one *c* because **re–** is never assimilated. Other examples of doubling through assimilation are *im-material, ac-celerate, suf-ficient, ef-ficient* (but *de-ficient*, for **dē–** is not assimilated).

Find five more examples of doubling of consonants as a result of assimilation.

The capture and destruction of Carthage by Scipio the Younger in
146 B.C. brought to an end the third and last of the Punic Wars. From a
modern painting

414. English Word Studies

(*a*) Give in Latin words suggested by the derivatives: *cordial, partial, sedentary, fraternity, inspiration, cult, generation, sorority, cursive, remiss, maternal.*

Sedentary

(*b*) Find and use in sentences as many derivatives as possible from **trahō, audiō,** and **premō.**

415. Vocabulary

NOUNS

1. aestās
2. auctor
3. auctōritās
4. cor
5. frāter
6. genus
7. hiems
8. māter
9. mors
10. nihil
11. pars
12. pater
13. soror
14. supplicium

ADJECTIVES

15. alius
16. alter
17. commūnis
18. familiāris
19. incertus
20. neuter
21. nōbilis
22. nūllus
23. praeceps
24. sōlus
25. tōtus
26. ūllus
27. ūnus

PRONOUNS

28. hic
29. īdem
30. ille
31. ipse
32. is

VERBS

33. colō
34. currō
35. expellō
36. expugnō
37. intercipiō
38. remittō
39. sedeō
40. spērō
41. spīrō
42. timeō

CONJUNCTION

43. dum

Vocabulary

Nouns

1. *summer*	4. *heart*	8. *mother*	12. *father*
2. *author*	5. *brother*	9. *death*	13. *sister*
3. *authority*	6. *birth, kind*	10. *nothing*	14. *punishment*
	7. *winter*	11. *part*	

Adjectives

15. *other, another*	19. *uncertain*	22. *no, none*	25. *whole*
16. *the other*	20. *neither*	23. *steep*	26. *any*
17. *common*	21. *noble*	24. *alone*	27. *one*
18. *friendly*			

Pronouns

28. *this*	29. *same*	30. *that*	31. *self*	32. *this, that*

Verbs

33. *till, worship*	36. *capture by assault*	40. *hope*
34. *run*	37. *intercept*	41. *breathe*
35. *drive out*	38. *relax, send back*	42. *fear*
	39. *sit*	

Conjunction
43. *while*

417. Forms

(*a*) Make **hic, ille,** and **īdem** agree as demonstrative adjectives with the following nouns in the case required, as follows:

īnsulae (gen.): **huius, illīus, eiusdem īnsulae**

aestāte	frātrēs (nom.)	patris
auctōrī	genera (nom.)	sorōrem
cor (acc.)	mātrum	supplicium (acc.)

(*b*) Supply the correct form of **is** in the following and translate:
1. (*Him, her, it*) vīdī. 2. (*By him, by her*) vīsus sum. 3. Fīlium (*his, her*) docēbō. 4. Nōvistīne (*their*) patrem? 5. Hunc librum (*to him, to her, to them*) dabō.

(*c*) Decline **nūllus pater, alia aestās.**

Dining room in a Roman house, from a model

LESSON LXII

418. QUĪNTUS CICERŌ ET POMPŌNIA

Pompōnius Atticus erat firmus amīcus M. Cicerōnis. Pompōnia, soror Atticī, erat uxor Quīntī, frātris M. Cicerōnis. Inter Pompōniam Quīntumque nōn semper concordia erat. Ūna gravis causa inter aliās erat haec, quod apud[1] Quīntum auctōritās Stātī[2] valēbat, quem domō[3] expellere nūllō modō potuit. Pompōnia 5 aliēnae auctōritātī cēdere nōn cupīvit. Neuter alterī cēdere potuit. Cicerō Pompōniam accūsāvit, Atticus Quīntum. Cicerō ad Atticum hōc modō scrīpsit:

"Frātrem meum vīdī. Tōtus sermō inter nōs dē tē et sorōre tuā fuit. Verba eius nōn inimīca fuērunt. Tum ad Pompōniam con- 10 tendimus. Quīntus eī amīcā vōce dīxit: 'Pompōnia, tū rogā mulierēs ad cēnam, ego puerōs (fīlium Cicerōnis et frātris eius) rogātūrus sum.' Sed illa, audientibus nōbīs, 'Ego ipsa sum,' inquit, 'in hōc locō hospita.' Hoc dīxit quod īdem Stātius antecesserat et

---

[1] *with.*   [2] *Statius* (*Stā'shius*), a freedman of Quintus.   [3] *from the house.*

291

15 cēnam parārī iusserat. Tum Quīntus, 'Audīsne?' inquit mihi, 'haec semper sustinēre cōgor.' Dīcēs: 'Haec vōx nihil est.' Sed magnum[1] est; verbīs dūrīs atque animō aliēnō eius oppressus et commōtus sum. Ad cēnam illa nōn adfuit; Quīntus ad eam sedentem sōlam cibum mīsit; illa remīsit. Grave vulnus Quīntus accēpit 20 neque ipse ūllam iniūriam fēcit. Cupiēns eam plācāre nōn potuit. Gravibus cūrīs opprimor. Quid factūrī sumus? Contendere dēbēmus inter sorōrem tuam et frātrem meum pācem efficere."

Thought Questions.—1. Who was Atticus' brother-in-law? 2. Of whom was Pomponia jealous?

419. Present Participle

In English, the **present participle** has both an active and a passive form: (*a*) *I saw your brother **reading** a book;* (*b*) *The book now **being read** by your brother is a good one.* In both examples the present participle *modifies a noun.* It is likewise used in making the progressive verb form: *Your brother **is reading.*** Here "reading" does not modify the noun but is a part of the verb and shows a progressive action (see **23**, *b*).

In Latin, the present participle has only the active form. It is

Seal of Hunter College, New York, with head of Minerva and Latin motto

used to modify nouns or pronouns and never combines with the verb **sum** to form verb phrases. *Your brother is reading* becomes in Latin simply **frāter tuus legit.** The present participle, like the present infinitive, represents an act *as taking place at the time indicated by the main verb.*

The present participle of the four conjugations is formed by adding **–ns** to the present stem.

[1] *it is a serious thing.*

292

Cupids run a drugstore in this Pompeian wall painting—but no sand-
wiches or sundaes.

It is declined like a third declension adjective of one ending
(358), with the base ending in –nt–, as follows:

	SINGULAR		PLURAL	
	M. AND F.	N.	M. AND F.	N.
Nom.	por'tāns	por'tāns	portan'tēs	portan'tia
Gen.	portan'tis		portan'tium	
Dat.	portan'tī		portan'tibus	
Acc.	portan'tem	por'tāns	portan'tēs (–īs)	portan'tia
Abl.	portan'te (–ī)		portan'tibus	

Note.—(*a*) The ablative singular ending is regularly –e, but –ī is used
instead whenever the participle is used simply as an adjective. (*b*) In verbs
of the fourth conjugation, and –iō verbs of the third, –ie– appears throughout, forming the base –ient–, as audiēns, audientis; capiēns, capientis.
(*c*) **Sum** has no present participle; that of **possum** is potēns.

420.   Future Active Participle

Latin, unlike English, has a **future active participle**. This is
formed by dropping the –**us** of the perfect participle and adding
–**ūrus, –a, –um**: portātūrus, –a, –um, *going to carry;* futūrus, –a,
–um, *going to be.* It is declined like magnus, –a, –um.

Practice.—Form and translate the participles of **rogō, opprimō,** and **expellō** in the present and future.

421.   Exercises

(*a*) 1. Cūr in hōc locō sine patre tuō mānsūrus es? 2. Vōcēs
amīcōrum rogantium auxilium ā nōbīs audītae sunt. 3. Hieme

nūllōs agricolās in agrīs labōrantēs vidēmus. 4. Rōmānīs prōcē-
dentibus, barbarī fūgērunt. 5. Duo puerī pugnantēs ā magistrō
captī sunt. 6. Hī puerī, suppliciō gravī affectī, ā magistrō expulsī
sunt. 7. Oppressī in aliēnō locō, hostēs cum impedīmentīs ad
montēs contentūrī sunt.

(b) (*Instead of clauses, use participles wherever possible.*)

1. The number of (those) approaching is not large. 2. The
swords given to the other soldiers are heavy (but not long). 3.. He
was accused by you (while he was) defending the public cause.
4. He was going to fold the letter which he had written.

422. Vocabulary

aliē′nus, –a, –um, *another's, unfavorable*   [*alius*]
conten′dō, –ere, –ten′dī, –tentū′rus, *struggle, hasten*   [*tendō*]
gra′vis, –e, *heavy, severe*   (gravitation)
op′primō, –ere, oppres′sī, oppres′sus, *overcome, surprise*   [*premō*]
ro′gō, –ā′re, –ā′vī, –ā′tus, *ask*   (interrogative)
vōx, vō′cis, f., *voice, remark*   [*vocō*]

423. English Word Studies

(a) What is a *neutral?* An *alien?* What is meant by the statement
in the Declaration of Independence "that all men . . . are endowed
by their Creator with certain *unalienable* [usually quoted *inalien-
able*] rights; that among these are life, liberty, and the pursuit of
happiness"?

(b)   **Latin Phrases in English**

in loco parentis, *in place of a parent.*

inter alia, *among other things.*

ipso facto, *by the fact itself, thereby.*

obiter dictum, (*something*) *said by the way* (**ob iter**), *incidentally.*

Timeo Danaos et dona ferentes, *I fear the Greeks even when they
bring gifts* (Virgil).

una voce, *with one voice, unanimously.*

Vox populi vox Dei, *The voice of the people* (*is*) *the voice of God.*

Explain **in toto, vox humana.** Explain the motto in the illustration
on page 292.

Insignia of the Order of the Cincinnati (p. 298). At the left, three senators present a sword to Cincinnatus; at the right, he returns to his plow.

LESSON LXIII

424.   CINCINNĀTUS

Hostēs Minucium,[1] ducem Rōmānum, et cōpiās eius in locō aliēnō magnā vī premēbant. Ubi id nūntiātum est, Rōmānī timentēs vim hostium cupīvērunt Cincinnātum[2] dictātōrem facere, quod is sōlus Rōmam ā perīculō nōn levī prohibēre et cīvitātem servāre poterat. Ille trāns Tiberim eō tempore agrum parvum colēbat. 5 Nūntiī missī eum in agrō labōrantem invēnērunt et cōnstitērunt. Salūte[3] datā acceptāque, Cincinnātus uxōrem parāre togam iussisse dīcitur; nam nōn oportēbat[4] sine togā nūntiōs audīre.

Nūntiī eum dictātōrem appellant et dīcunt: "Mīlitēs nostrī ab hostibus premuntur et cīvēs terrentur. Perīculum nostrum nōn 10 leve est. Hostēs nōn cōnsistent sed mox ad portās nostrās ipsās venient. Auxilium tuum rogāmus." Itaque Cincinnātus, vōcibus eōrum adductus, contrā hostēs contendit. Rōmānī, tēlīs iactīs,

---

[1] *Minucius (Minū'shius)*   [2] *Cincinnatus (Sinsinā'tus)*
[3] *greeting.*   [4] *it was not proper.*

295

The Tiber River and the island, shaped like a boat, at Rome. The temple was a hospital, and a hospital still stands there.

hostēs opprimunt et castra expugnant. Minuciō servātō, Cin-
15 cinnātus dīcitur hostēs sub iugum[1] mīsisse. Tum, nūllīs hostibus
prohibentibus, cōpiās ad urbem redūxit et triumphāvit. Ductī sunt
in pompā ante eum ducēs hostium, capta arma ostenta sunt; post
eum mīlitēs vēnērunt praedam gravem portantēs. Et haec omnia
Cincinnātus magnā celeritāte gessit: dictātūrā in[2] sex mēnsēs
20 acceptā, sextō decimō diē[3] ad agrōs discessit, nōn iam dictātor
sed triumphāns agricola. Eōdem mēnse agricola et dictātor et
iterum agricola fuit.

Thought Questions.—1. Where was Cincinnatus' farm? 2. Who was
with him when the messengers came? 3. How long did he stay away
from his farm?

Read Harding, pp. 65–70; Haaren and Poland, pp. 76–81; Mills, pp.
77–79.

425.   Perfect Active Infinitive

The **perfect active infinitive** is formed by adding –**isse** to the
perfect stem: **portāvisse**, *to have carried;* **docuisse**, etc.

---

[1] *under the yoke, i.e.* an arch of spears. This act signified surrender.
[2] *for.*   [3] *sixteenth day.*

Review infinitive used as subject and object, see **133, 134**; infinitive with subject in the accusative as in English, see **244**.

Practice.—Form the perfect active infinitive of **dīcō, intercipiō, videō, expediō**.

426. Exercises

(*a*) 1. Rōmānī paucās nāvēs ad Britanniam mīsisse dīcuntur. 2. Rēgis fīlia librum scrīpsisse sine auxiliō dīcitur. 3. Prohibēre vim et pācem cōnservāre est nōbile. 4. Ostendite omnibus bonum exemplum. 5. Mīlitēs cōnsistentēs arma levia cum magnā vī iēcisse dīcuntur. 6. Homō malus mē cōnsistere iussit et omnem meam pecūniam dare. 7. Quis dīxit: "Dā mihi lībertātem aut dā mihi mortem"?

(*b*) 1. That king is said to have tilled the fields himself. 2. We cannot breathe under water. 3. I saw your father folding a letter. 4. Those men are said to have sailed to a strange land.

Pompeian wall painting showing a peaceful garden scene: birds, fountains, and all

cōnsis'tō, –ere, cōn'stitī, cōnstitū'rus, *stand still, stop* [*stō*]
dī'cō, –ere, dī'xī, dic'tus,[1] *say, tell* (diction)
ia'ciō, –ere, iē'cī, iac'tus, *throw* (projectile)
le'vis, –e, *light* (in weight) (levity)
*mēn'sis, mēn'sis, mēn'sium, m., *month*
osten'dō, –ere, osten'dī, osten'tus, (*stretch out*), *show* [*tendō*]
prohi'beō, –ē're, –hi'buī, –hi'bitus, *prevent, keep from* [*habeō*]
*vīs, —,[2] f., *force, violence;* plur. vī'rēs, vī'rium, *strength* (vim)

French stamp showing the Pont du Gard, a remarkably well-preserved Roman aqueduct near Nîmes

428. Latin and English Word Studies

(*a*) The suffix –or, when added to the participial stem, indicates the doer of an action: **monitor** (*one who warns*), **scrīptor** (*one who writes*), **inventor** (*one who finds*). It is used in English in the same way.

When the suffix –or is added to the present base of a verb, it usually indicates a state of being or condition: **timor, amor, terror.** It is used in English.

Find five English words which are formed by adding the suffix –or to the stems of verbs that you have studied. Explain *eject, injection, reject, ostentation, prohibition.*

(*b*) The city of Cincinnati was named from the Society of the Cincinnati, formed by army officers at the end of the Revolutionary War. Why do you suppose the Society took that name? What does its motto mean: **Omnia reliquit servare rem publicam?**

---

[1] The imperative singular is dīc.
[2] Genitive and dative singular rarely found (see 572).

A peaceful scene in an ancient home. The loom for weaving is at the right. From a painting by Forti

GLIMPSES OF ROMAN LIFE

429. **How the Roman Made His Living**

In early days nearly every Roman was a farmer and even later farming remained the chief occupation of the Romans, as it is of Americans. It is not surprising therefore that Cincinnatus left his plow to lead the Romans in war and on its successful completion returned to his farm. In the early days many a war was won by the "embattled farmers." Nor is it surprising that farming was considered the foundation of Roman life, as it is of American life, and that the Roman character, like ours, was largely determined by it.

At first farms were small and were worked by the owner and his family. The increased use of slave labor led to increase in the size of farms and to a change in the attitude toward farming.

Industry was not so highly developed among the Romans as among us. There were no large factories. Much of the work was done by hand either at home or in small shops. The spinning of thread and the weaving of cloth were often done at home. The emperor Augustus wore clothing made by slaves under his wife's direction. There were carpenters, workers in metal, masons and bricklayers, makers of tools, wagonmakers, brickmakers, and so on. There were no huge factories for the manufacture of automobiles, telephones, railroad equipment, and hundreds of other articles because they had not been invented. The making of bricks came nearest to being industry in the modern sense.

The free workers were members of what may be called unions, whose chief purposes were to bring the members together for good fellowship and to provide burials for the members who died. Many slaves, too, came to be employed in industry.

The shops were very small—there were no department stores or chain stores. Usually a small room at the front of a private residence was used as a shop. The wares were often displayed outside. Sometimes the shopkeepers cluttered up the sidewalks and streets so much that they interfered with traffic until some strict official prevented this.

Such were the occupations of the poorer classes. Rich men invested their money in the wholesale trade, real estate, loans, government contracts, and foreign trade. The professions, with the exception of law and public life, were not well developed. Doctors and teachers were usually slaves or freedmen, *i.e.* former slaves. Law and politics were largely reserved for the upper classes.

Read Showerman, pp. 225–252; Johnston, pp. 328–355.

Questions for Discussion.—1. What are the chief professions today? 2. What percentage of our people today are engaged in farming? In industry? 3. Have you seen goods displayed on sidewalks? Is this permitted by law? 4. To what did Emerson refer in these lines?

"Here once the embattled farmers stood
And fired the shot heard round the world."

The tomb of Augustus as it was. This emperor introduced a long period
of peace in the Roman Empire—the pax Augusta.

LESSON LXIV

430. **BELLA**

Quae sunt causae bellī? Variī auctōrēs ostendērunt multās esse
causās. Multa bella ob iniūriās gesta esse vidēmus. Haec bella
iūsta fuērunt. Multī populī pugnant quod putant imperium auc-
tōritātemque vī bellōque augērī posse. Hī cupiunt patriam esse
nūllī secundam. Hī sī superantur omnia saepe āmittunt; sī supe- 5
rant, aliēnās terrās occupant. Putāsne bella huius generis iūsta
esse? Multī dīcunt omnia bella iūsta esse, aliī putant nūlla esse
iūsta. Quid dē hōc putās? Possuntne bella prohibērī? Nōvimus
aliōs prō lībertāte, aliōs prō glōriā bella gessisse. Quae fuērunt
causae bellōrum Americānōrum? 10

Horātius,[1] poēta Rōmānus, scrībit dulce esse prō patriā vītam
āmittere. Sī patria in perīculō est, nōnne putās mūnus nostrum
esse eam dēfendere? Scīmus nōn levēs esse labōrēs mīlitum, gravia

---

[1] *Horace.* The exact words of his famous phrase are: **Dulce et decōrum est prō
patriā morī.**

301

eōs accipere vulnera, multōs ad mortem mittī; etiam scīmus eōs
15 nōn dubitāre omnēs labōrēs prō patriā grātō animō suscipere et
sustinēre. Prō hīs mūneribus praemia aequa eīs solvere nōn possumus. Sed praemia nōn exspectant; spērant cīvēs facta sua memoriā tentūrōs esse et aliōs semper parātōs futūrōs esse patriam
dēfendere. Hōc modō praemia solvere possumus.
20 Quis scit bella ūllō tempore cōnstitūra esse? Sed spērāmus
parvō spatiō temporis nōn iam bella futūra esse; spērāmus omnēs
hominēs aliōrum iūra cōnservātūrōs esse. Tum bella nōn iam
erunt, et sine bellīs pāx perpetua cōnfirmābitur.

Thought Questions.—1. Which wars were just? 2. What do soldiers
hope for? 3. What are your answers to the questions asked in the text?

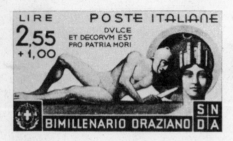

Italian stamp issued for
Horace's two thousandth birthday (cf. pp. 152, 282). His
immortal line on patriotism
(p. 301) is quoted and is illustrated with the picture of a
dying soldier.

431. Perfect Passive and Future Active Infinitive

(*a*) The **perfect passive infinitive** is a compound tense,
formed by using the perfect participle with the present infinitive
esse: **portātus, –a, –um esse,** *to have been carried;* **doctus, –a,
–um esse** (cf. perfect passive indicative: **portātus sum**).

(*b*) The **future active infinitive** is a compound tense, formed
by using the future active participle with the present infinitive
esse: **portātūrus, –a, –um esse,** *to be going to carry;* **doctūrus,
–a, –um esse.**

Note.—There was no future passive infinitive in common use in Latin.

(*c*) **Learn** the infinitives, active and passive, of the model verbs
(584–588) and **sum** (589).

(*b*) Translate the words in italics:

1. I know *him to be* wise. 2. I know the *girl lost* money. 3. I believe the *man to be* trustworthy. 4. They say the *book was read* by few. 5. I hear that your *sister will live* in Detroit.

(*c*) 1. Galba said, "My father is a soldier." 2. We all know that his father is brave. 3. I hear that Galba's brother was a sailor and was not scared by the sea. 4. I think that Galba himself will be a soldier. 5. He himself said, "I am going to be a soldier, for my father is a soldier."

435.   Vocabulary

iūs′tus, –a, –um, *just*	[*iūs*]
la′bor, labō′ris, m., *work, hardship*	[*labōrō*]
mū′nus, mū′neris, n., *duty, service, gift*	(munificent)
pu′tō, –ā′re, –ā′vī, –ā′tus, *think*	(reputation)
sci′ō, scī′re, scī′vī, scī′tus, *know*	(science)
secun′dus, –a, –um, *second*	(secondary)
sol′vō, –ere, sol′vī, solū′tus, *loosen, pay*	(solution)

436.   English Word Study: Spelling

The base of the Latin present participle is –ant, –ent, or –ient, according to the conjugation (419). This is used as a suffix in English, with the same meaning as the participial ending –*ing*.

A common mistake in the spelling of English words is due to the confusion of –ant and –ent. Reference to the Latin partly solves the difficulty:

(*a*) All English words derived from the first conjugation follow the Latin spelling with an –a–: *expectant, emigrant.*

(*b*) All adjectives and most nouns derived from the other conjugations follow the Latin spelling with an –e–: *regent, agent, efficient.*

(*c*) But some *nouns* have an –a–: *tenant, defendant.*

Give eight English words with suffix –ant or –ent derived from Latin words previously studied. Explain *laboratory, omniscient, solvent, absolve, remunerate.*

Coriolanus' wife and child make their appeal to him. A painting by
David. Who wrote a play and who an overture about him?

LESSON LXV

437.   **CORIOLĀNUS**

Mārcius, nōbilis Rōmānus, Coriolōs,[1] oppidum Volscōrum,[2]
expugnāverat. Ob hoc mūnus "Coriolānus" appellātus est.

Post bellum ob variās causās plēbs īrā ācrī permōtus Coriolānum accūsāvit, clāmāns eum esse hostem. Coriolānus, perīculum
5 īnstāre sentiēns, fūgit ad Volscōs quōs ipse superāverat. Volscī
dīcuntur eum benignē[3] accēpisse, nam sēnsērunt eum esse ducem
fortem ac iūstum et Rōmam nōn iam amāre. Etiam spērāvērunt
eum contrā Rōmānōs pugnātūrum esse.

Mox Coriolānus, dux ā Volscīs lēctus, ad urbem Rōmam con-
10 tendit, omnia in itinere vāstāns. Rōmānī, castrīs eius ad urbem

---

[1] *Corī'olī.*   [2] *Volsci (Vol'sī).*   [3] *kindly.*

positīs, bellō īnstantī territī sunt. Lēgātī dē pāce ad Coriolānum missī sunt sed ubi pervēnērunt ab eō remissī sunt. "Mātrem eius ad eum mittēmus," putāvērunt Rōmānī; "sī cūra urbis cor eius nōn tanget, amōre mātris ille certē tangētur, et fīnem labōrum nostrōrum inveniēmus." Itaque māter et uxor Coriolānī cum duōbus 15 parvīs fīliīs ad castra hostium pervēnērunt.

Coriolānus, verbīs ācribus mātris permōtus et lacrimīs omnium tāctus, dīcitur clāmāvisse: "Quid fēcistī, māter? Tū sōla Rōmam servāvistī sed mē vīcistī." Tum iussit Volscōs discēdere. Rōma lacrimīs, nōn armīs servāta erat. Coriolānī facta semper in me- 20 moriā omnium haerēbunt.

Thought Questions.—1. How did Coriolanus get his name? 2. Where did he go when exiled? 3. Why did he spare Rome?

Read Mills, pp. 74–77; Guerber (*Story*), pp. 87–91; Haaren and Poland, pp. 64–71.

438. How Indicative and Infinitive Differ in Tense

> 1. *It was thought that he was present.*
> 2. *He was thought to be present.*

In the first sentence, the verb in the subordinate clause is in the past indicative. In the second sentence, the infinitive *to be* refers to the same time but is in the present tense. The tenses of the **indicative** are determined by their *relation to present time*, but the tenses of the **infinitive** are determined by their *relation to the verbs on which they depend*. This is true in Latin as in English and should be remembered in translating a Latin infinitive into an English "that" clause.

439. How the Tenses of the Infinitive Differ

1. The present infinitive represents time or action as *going on*, from the standpoint of the introductory verb:

$$\left.\begin{matrix} \text{Dīcit} \\ \text{Dīxit} \end{matrix}\right\} \text{ eōs vocāre, } He \left\{\begin{matrix} says \\ said \end{matrix}\right\} (that) \ they \left\{\begin{matrix} are \\ were \end{matrix}\right\} calling.$$

(Change **vocāre** to **vocārī** and translate.)

2. The future infinitive represents an act that will occur *later*, from the standpoint of the introductory verb:

Dīcit } eōs vocātūrōs esse, *He* { *says* } (*that*) *they* { *will* } *call.*
Dīxit } { *said* } { *would* }

3. The perfect infinitive represents time or action as *completed before* that of the introductory verb:

Dīcit } eōs vocāvisse, *He* { *says* } (*that*) *they* { *have* } *called.*
Dīxit } { *said* } { *had* }

(Change **vocāvisse** to **vocātōs esse** and translate.)

Note that the participle in the compound forms of the infinitive must agree with its subject (see 2 above).

Wall painting showing house front and other details from Boscoreale near Pompeii, now in the Metropolitan Museum of Art, New York

440. **Exercises**

(*a*) 1. (*a*) Omnēs scīmus puerōs Americānōs esse ācrēs et fortēs. (*b*) *Substitute* scīvimus *for* scīmus *in* (*a*) *and translate.* 2. Rōmānī dīcēbant Caesarem esse fortem ducem nec superātum esse. 3. Servī spērāvērunt labōrem futūrum esse facilem. 4. Omnēs sēnsimus perīculum īnstāre. 5. Omnēs puerī certē sciunt Columbum ad Americam pervēnisse. 6. Puer nōn clāmāre potuit, quod vōx haesit. 7. Quis dīxit amīcum meum sine frātre pervēnisse?

(*b*) Translate the words which are in italics:

1. He knew *me to be* his friend. 2. He knew that *I was working* hard. 3. We saw that *we would*

not *arrive* in time. 4. We hear that your *father has been sent* to Europe on a secret mission. 5. He said that his *son was being taught* by new methods.

(*c*) 1. Who said that we would not come? 2. The boy thought that (his) father had been saved. 3. My mother wrote that the islands were beautiful. 4. We can prove that our cause is just. 5. The general says that the soldiers of the provinces were brave.

Filius parvus. Statuette in Metropolitan Museum

441.   Vocabulary

ā′cer, ā′cris, ā′cre,[1] *sharp, keen*	(acid)
hae′reō, –ē′re, hae′sī, hae′sus, *stick*	(adhesive)
īn′stō, –ā′re, īn′stitī, ——, *threaten*	[*stō*]
perve′niō, –ī′re, –vē′nī, –ventū′rus, (*come through*), *arrive*	[*veniō*]
sen′tiō, –ī′re, sēn′sī, sēn′sus, *feel, realize*	(sense)
sī, conj., *if*	
tan′gō, –ere, te′tigī, tāc′tus, *touch*	(tangent)

442.   English Word Studies

By addition of the suffix –ia (233) to the base of the present participle, a suffix –antia or –entia is formed which becomes –ance, –ence, –ancy, or –ency in English (cf. the change of –tia to –ce (247): **scientia,** *science*). The difficulty in spelling is again removed by reference to the Latin (cf. 436).

Give eight English nouns with this suffix derived from Latin words previously studied. Explain *coherence, sensitive, consensus, intangible, dissension, inherent.*

---

[1] Cf. 358, footnote 3.

309

THE STORY OF LUCIUS (*Cont.*)

443. ### Virginēs Vestālēs

Etiam cīvitās focum Vestae habuit. Templum Vestae in Forō urbis Rōmae stābat. Ibi sex puellae, Virginēs Vestālēs appellātae, ignem perpetuum Vestae semper servābant. Magna erat glōria Vestālium, et maximē ā populō Rōmānō amābantur. Eīs in viīs urbis vīsīs, omnēs cōnstitērunt atque dē viā cessērunt. Facile erat eās cognōscere, quod omnēs semper albās vestēs gessērunt, neque ūlla alia mulier vestem eiusdem generis gessit. In Circō loca ēgregia eīs dabantur. Sed dūrum fuit supplicium Vestālis quae mala fuit: ea vīva sub terrā posita est.

Home of the Vestal Virgins in the Roman Forum. On the side are the statues of the chief Vestals. At the left, the lofty Basilica of Maxentius; at the right, a church built into the temple of Venus and Rome

Their chief explains their duties to the Vestals. Their dress shows why they were called the first nuns. A painting by Leroux

EXACTING DUTIES

Iūlia, soror Lūcī, Vestālis erat et multa dē vītā Vestālium dīcē- 10
bat. Cum reliquīs Vestālibus in Ātriō[1] Vestae ad templum habitāvit sed saepe patrem et mātrem et frātrēs vidēbat. Dīxit vītam
Vestālium grātam esse sed labōrem numquam facilem esse: eās
omnia magnā cūrā dīligentiāque facere cōgī. Dīxit Vestālēs ligna[2]
in focō eōdem modō semper pōnere et omnia certīs hōrīs in ōrdine 15
facere. Itaque spatium disciplīnae longum erat. Puellae sex annōrum, ā patribus mātribusque Vestae datae, prīmōs decem annōs
discipulae ēgērunt, tum decem annōs in officiīs ēgērunt et posteā
parvās puellās docuērunt. Tamen post trīgintā annōs lībertās
eīs data est et eae ad amīcōs familiāsque redīre[3] potuērunt, sed 20
multae in Ātriō Vestae mānsērunt. Sex sōlae Vestālēs in Ātriō ūnō
tempore habitāvērunt.

MISFORTUNE

Quondam Iūlia, aquam sacram portāns, vīdit aliam Vestālem
ante portam sedentem flentemque et ad eam cucurrit. Causā petītā,
illa respondet, vōce haerente: "Sīvī[4] ignem sacrum exstinguī; 25
vigiliā cōnfectā, somnō oppressa sum." Iūlia, corde malā for-

---

[1] _ā'trium, house._   [2] _wood._   [3] Infinitive of **red-eō,** _go back._   [4] _I let._

tūnā amīcae tāctō, tamen illī nūllum cōnsilium dare potuit. Itaque illa pontificī omnia dīxit, et hic eam verberāvit—nihil aliud
facere potuit, quod ita lēgēs iussērunt.

RIGHT OR WRONG

30 Hōc audītō, Lūcius ācrī vōce respondit illam miseram nōn me-
rēre ob lassitūdinem poenā afficī et ōtium habēre dēbēre, sed eius
soror, Iūlia, quae aliam sententiam habuit, respondit: "Etiam
amīca mea ipsa quae verberāta est sentit supplicium aequum
fuisse. Mūnera nostra gravia sunt. Sī multā cūrā mūnera nōn effi-
35 ciēmus, perīculum grave īnstābit. Itaque poena neglegentiae
ācris esse dēbet. Sī ego ignem exstinguī sinam[1] (quod spērō numquam futūrum esse), gravem poenam, etiam mortis, solvere
dēbēbō."

Thought Questions.—1. How would you explain the origin of the
custom of keeping the sacred fire burning? 2. How many Vestals were
there all together, including those in training?

Note.—If you want to know more about the Vestals, read the fascinat-
ing novel, *The Unwilling Vestal*, by Edward Lucas White.

444. Vocabulary

num'quam, adv., *never*
respon'deō, –ē're, respon'dī, respōn'sus, *answer*   (response)
ta'men, adv., *nevertheless*
***urbs, ur'bis, ur'bium,** f., *city*   (suburban)

445. English Word Studies

(*a*) What is an *urban* community? What are the *suburbs* of a
city? What is meant by an *urbane* person? What is a *correspondent?*
Explain the difference between *adhesion* and *cohesion*.

(*b*) *Vesta* as the name of a firm is found three times in the
Chicago telephone directory, twice in Kansas City, etc. Why was it
chosen for the name of a battery?

---

[1] From **sinō:** *I let.*

446.   The House and Its Furniture

The Roman town house was different from ours and more like that of southern Europe today. As glass was expensive, there were few windows on the street. The typical house, as found in numerous examples at Pompeii, consisted of two parts, front and rear. The front consisted of a large room, called the atrium, surrounded by small bedrooms. The atrium had an opening in the roof for light and air. The roof sloped down to the opening. Below the opening there was a basin into which the rain fell. This cistern, as we may call it, furnished the soft water for washing, so necessary in a country where most of the water is hard. At the corners of the basin there were often columns extending to the roof.

As the house was built directly on the street, it had no front yard. The heavy front door opened into a hall leading into the atrium. On one side of the hall there might be a small shop, usually rented out to people who did not live in the house. On the other side there was the room of the doorkeeper (iānitor). Very often there was a place for a watchdog. Sometimes a fierce dog was painted on the wall or depicted in mosaic on the floor of the hall.

Atrium of a house at Herculaneum, with wooden screen or movable partition

Opposite the entrance was the study or office (tablīnum) of the master of the house, placed so that he could keep an eye on what was going on. Here he kept his safe. Often there were also upstairs rooms.

The rear of the house surrounded a garden. Because of the columns which ran all around the garden this part was called the peristyle. It was often very pretty. Charming fountains and statuary were usually to be seen in the garden. Kitchen, bathroom, dining rooms were in this part of the house. There were often two dining rooms, one on the shady side for summer, the other on the sunny side for winter.

The walls were covered with elaborate paintings (p. 166, etc.). Rugs and draperies were in common use. The floors were usually covered with stone flags or mosaic, as in Italy today, instead of wood. There was not much furniture. Chairs were few, and many of them were without backs. On the other hand, there were many couches, used like easy chairs, not only for reading and resting but also at the dinner table. There were many kinds of tables and stands, often very beautiful. Many small lamps of bronze or clay were placed everywhere, some on stands, some on large, elaborate candelabra. These burned olive oil. Glass chimneys were unknown. The light was so poor that people went to bed early and got up early. Candles were also used.

Kitchen utensils and dishes were made of bronze, silver, or earthenware. Those made of earthenware were chiefly red in color and were decorated with engraved lines.

Besides the town houses just described, there were country homes (**vīllae**) which were more elaborate. In Rome there were also apartment houses, called **īnsulae** because they were "islands" surrounded by streets. Most Romans lived in such houses, which were often five or six stories high. They were remarkably like modern apartment houses. Many were flimsily built for speculation and were an easy prey for fires.

Questions for Discussion.—1. In what ways did Roman houses differ from ours? 2. How did the poor lighting facilities affect the daily life of the people? 3. How does climate affect the types of houses?

Read Showerman, pp. 76–88; Mills, pp. 301–309; McDaniel, pp. 5–13; Johnston, Chap. VI.

ELEVENTH UNIT REVIEW (LESSONS LXII–LXVI)

447. English Word Studies

1. Explain the following and give the Latin words from which they are derived: *omnipotent, alienate, vocal, expulsive, oppressive, diction, ostensible, prohibit.*

2. Find and use in sentences as many English derivatives as possible from **dīcō** and **putō.**

3. The first word in each of the following lines is a Latin word. From among the last five words in each line pick the one which is an English derivative of the first word.

scit	skit	sky	sigh	scientific	sit
tangō	tangerine	tang	intangible	tango	tactics
putātus	putty	put	repute	potato	pot
dīcere	contradict	dixie	dice	decree	decent
gravia	graft	graveyard	gravity	engrave	gray

448. Vocabulary

NOUNS

1. labor	3. mūnus	5. vīs
2. mēnsis	4. urbs	6. vōx

ADJECTIVES

7. ācer	9. gravis	11. levis
8. aliēnus	10. iūstus	12. secundus

VERBS

13. cōnsistō	18. īnstō	22. prohibeō	26. sciō
14. contendō	19. opprimō	23. putō	27. sentiō
15. dīcō	20. ostendō	24. respondeō	28. solvō
16. haereō	21. perveniō	25. rogō	29. tangō
17. iaciō			

ADVERBS

30. numquam   31. tamen

CONJUNCTION

32. sī

Vocabulary

Nouns

1. *work*
2. *month*
3. *duty, service*
4. *city*
5. *force*
6. *voice*

Adjectives

7. *sharp, keen*
8. *another's*
9. *heavy, severe*
10. *just*
11. *light*
12. *second*

Verbs

13. *stop*
14. *struggle, hasten*
15. *say, tell*
16. *stick*
17. *throw*
18. *threaten*
19. *overcome*
20. *show*
21. *arrive*
22. *prevent*
23. *think*
24. *answer*
25. *ask*
26. *know*
27. *feel, realize*
28. *loosen, pay*
29. *touch*

Adverbs

30. *never* 31. *nevertheless*

Conjunction

32. *if*

450. ## Forms

(*a*) Decline **labor ipse, nūlla vox**.

(*b*) Give a synopsis of **timeō** in the 3d plural active; of **remittō** in the 3d singular passive.

(*c*) Form the participles, active and passive, of **dīcō, iaciō, sciō**, and **rogō**.

(*d*) Form the infinitives, active and passive, of **sentiō, intercipiō, tangō**, and **expugnō**.

Very modern wooden shutters in a Pompeian window. These are restored, but the ashes which covered the originals left a perfect cast which made restoration easy.

Spareribs for the lady's dinner. A de luxe Roman butcher shop, with easy chair and footstool. Cleaver and chopping block look very modern. From a sculptured relief

451. Participles and Infinitives

(*a*) Note these differences between Latin and English in expressing indirect statement:

In Latin	*In English*
1. No conjunction is used.	1. "That" is regularly used.
2. The subject is in the accusative.	2. The subject is in the nominative.
3. The verb is in the infinitive.	3. The verb is in the indicative.

(*b*) Translate the words in italics. Be careful to make the participle agree with its noun in gender, number, and case:

1. *Running* water is usually fresh. 2. We saw the boys *running* a race. 3. They heard the sound of men *approaching*. 4. Are they *going to remain?* 5. She was *going to say* something. 6. He forgot to mail the letter *after he had written* it. 7. *When he had heard these words*, he felt encouraged.

(*c*) Complete in Latin these indirect statements and translate: 1. Sciō (*the boys read*) librōs. 2. Spērō (*the boys will read*) librōs. 3. Putō (*the boys have read*) librōs. 4. Dīxit (*the books were being read*) ā puerīs. 5. Dīxit (*the books had been read*) ā puerīs.

317

Labor omnia vincit.

LESSON LXVII

452.   QUATTUOR AETĀTĒS

Prīma aetās erat aurea. Sāturnus erat rēx deōrum hominumque.
Illō tempore poenae lēgēsque aberant, quod omnēs hominēs
iūstī erant. Nūllae nāvēs in marī erant, nec trāns mare lātum hominēs nāvigābant. Bellum numquam erat nec mīlitēs et arma. In
5 ōtiō vītam hominēs agēbant, nam omnēs terrae concordiā et
pāce ligātae sunt. Hominēs in agrīs nōn labōrābant; terra nōn
culta ipsa frūmentum et omnia ūtilia dabat. Urbēs nōn erant. Neque hiems neque aestās erat: semper erat vēr. Flūmina lactis[1] et
vīnī erant. Quod omnēs agrī commūnēs erant, terminī agrōrum
10 nōn erant. Aliēnōs agrōs hominēs nōn cupiēbant.

Sāturnō expulsō, Iuppiter rēx erat. Nunc incipit secunda aetās,
quae ex argentō est, dūrior quam prīma, grātior tamen quam ter-

---

[1] *of milk.*

318

tia. Tum aestās et hiems esse incipiunt; quattuor sunt spatia annī. Tum prīmum in agrīs labōrāre hominēs incipiunt.

Tertia aetās ex aere[1] erat. Dūrior erat quam secunda.　15

Quārta aetās, quae ex ferrō est, dūrissima omnium est. Poenae gravissimae statuuntur, sed hominēs interficiunt et rapiunt. Nautae in omnī marī ad ultima loca nāvigant et ūtilia petunt quae in variīs terrīs continentur. Bellīs numquam intermissīs, hominēs terrās aliēnās vincere mātūrant. Nihil sacrum est; omnia rapiun- 20 tur. Hominēs in agrīs labōrant; nam labor omnia vincit.

Haec dīcunt auctōrēs clārissimī Rōmānī dē quattuor aetātibus. Vergilius[2] putābat iterum aetātem auream futūram esse. Etiam nunc putāmus vītam semper grātiōrem futūram esse. Putātisne condiciōnem fortūnamque populī Rōmānī meliōrem[3] fuisse quam 25 condiciōnem nostram? Quō modō statuistī hanc sententiam vēriōrem esse? Quae erit condiciō hominum post mīlle annōs? Quis hoc prōvidēre potest? Aliī dīcunt: "Tempora mūtantur, et nōs mūtāmur in illīs." Aliī respondent hominēs semper eōsdem fuisse et futūrōs esse. Quae est sententia vestra? Possuntne ambae[4] sen- 30 tentiae vērae esse?

Thought Questions.—1. Why did not men work in the Golden Age?　2. When did they begin?　3. When did crime begin?

453.　　　Comparison of Adjectives

Adjectives are changed to show **degree**. This is called **comparison**. There are three degrees: **positive, comparative, superlative**. The positive is the simple form of the adjective; the others indicate a greater degree.

In English, the comparative is formed by adding –**er** (–**r**) to the positive: *high-er, brave-r*. The superlative is formed by adding –**est** (–**st**) to the positive: *high-est, brave-st*. But adjectives of more than one syllable are often compared by the use of *more* and *most: more skillful, most skillful*.

---

[1] *of bronze.*　　　[2] *Virgil.*　　　[3] *better.*　　　[4] *both.*

In Latin, the endings –ior (m. and f.), –ius (n.) are regularly added to the base of the positive to form the comparative, and –issimus, –a, –um to form the superlative:

POSITIVE	COMPARATIVE	SUPERLATIVE
altus, –a, –um, *high* (base, alt–)	altior, altius, *higher*	altissimus, –a, –um, *highest*
fortis, –e, *brave* (base, fort–)	fortior, fortius, *braver*	fortissimus, –a, –um, *bravest*

Hints for Translating.—The comparative may often be translated *more, too, rather;* the superlative, *most, very, exceedingly.*

454.   Declension of the Comparative

Adjectives are declined as follows in the comparative:

	SINGULAR		PLURAL	
	M. AND F.	N.	M. AND F.	N.
Nom.	al'tior	al'tius	altiō'rēs	altiō'ra
Gen.	altiō'ris	altiō'ris	altiō'rum	altiō'rum
Dat.	altiō'rī	altiō'rī	altiō'ribus	altiō'ribus
Acc.	altiō'rem	al'tius	altiō'rēs	altiō'ra
Abl.	altiō're	altiō're	altiō'ribus	altiō'ribus

Observe that, while comparatives are declined like adjectives of the third declension, they do not have –ī in the abl. sing.,–ium in the gen. plur., or –ia in the nom. and acc. plur. neuter, *i.e.* comparatives are not i–stems.

Remember that in Latin when **quam** is used, the two things compared are in the same case, but in English *than* is followed by the nominative: **Fortiōrem virum quam illum nōn vīdī,** *A braver man than he I have not seen.*

Practice.—(*a*) Compare grātus, –a, –um; nōbilis, –e; clārus, –a, –um; levis, –e; longus, –a, –um.

(*b*) Decline **tardus, –a, –um** in the comparative.

(*c*) Decline **supplicium iūstius.**

320

(*a*) 1. Quid est ūtilius et grātius quam librōs bonōs legere?
2. Novissimum librum ad frātrem meum mittere statuī. 3. Gallī
vīribus corporis Rōmānōs superābant sed nōn erant fortiōrēs virī.
4. Homō dē viīs mē rogāvit; ego respondī hanc esse plāniōrem
quam illam. 5. Eī ostendimus duo itinera per montēs—alterum
facile, alterum longius et incertius. 6. Condiciōnēs pācis dūrissi-
mae ab hostibus victīs semper esse habentur.

(*b*) 1. Why are not the rivers of Italy very long? 2. Even more
severe terms of peace than these will be determined (upon). 3. I
know that that river is swift but not very wide. 4. Nothing is more
useful than water. 5. Does peace have nobler victories than war?

456. Vocabulary

ae′tās, aetā′tis, f., *age*   (eternal)
condi′ciō, condiciō′nis, f., *condition, terms*   (conditional)
quam, conj., *than*
ra′piō, –ere, ra′puī, rap′tus, *carry off*   (rapture)
sta′tuō, –ere, sta′tuī, statū′tus, (*make stand*), *establish, determine*   [*stō*]
ū′tilis, –e, *useful*   (utility)
vin′cō, –ere, vī′cī, vic′tus, *conquer*   (invincible)

Forum of Caesar and Temple of Venus as they were. Julius Caesar
claimed name and descent from Iulus, son of Aeneas, the son of Venus.

Mellon Institute of the University of Pittsburgh in Ionic style

457. English Word Studies

It is important to distinguish different words from the same stem. "Plain" and "plane" both come from **plānus,** *level.* A "plain" is a *level* field; a "plain" person is not above the average *level* in appearance, etc. A "plane" is a *level* surface (hence "plane" geometry); it is also a tool which makes surfaces *level.* "Plane" is therefore used in a more literal, "plain," in a less literal, sense.

A "corpse" is a dead *body* (from **corpus**); a "corps" (pronounced "core") is a *body* of men forming part of an army. The former is literal, the latter, figurative. A "corporation" is a *body* of men united for commercial or other purposes. A "corpuscle" is a little *body* in the blood. "Corporal" punishment is punishment inflicted upon the *body, i.e.* a whipping. Anything "corporeal" has a *body, i.e.* it is not imaginary. Similarly, a "principal" is the *leading* person in a school; a "principle" is a *leading* rule.

In accordance with the above suggestions explain *statue* and *statute; urban* and *urbane; sensory* and *sentiment; respiration* and *inspiration.*

322

458. ### BAUCIS ET PHILĒMŌN

Iuppiter et Mercurius per Phrygiam, quae in Asiā est, iter
fēcērunt, sed nēmō in tōtā illā gente eōs cognōvit. Omnēs eōs
iūdicāvērunt esse humilēs hominēs. Ad mīlle domōs accessērunt;
nam locum somnō aptum petīvērunt. Sed omnēs, hīs vīsīs, domōs
5 celeriter clausērunt. In tōtā regiōne repulsī sunt. Tamen ūna
domus, parva et humilis, eōs nōn reppulit. Ibi Baucis et Philēmōn[1] multōs annōs longae vītae ēgerant. Condiciōne humilī nōn
affectī, paupertātem leviter et fortiter sustinuērunt. Duo tōta
domus[2] fuērunt, et dominī et servī ipsī; nam servōs nōn habuērunt.

10 Cēnam humilem Baucis magnā dīligentiā et celeritāte parāvit;
numquam celerius labōrāverat. Tum, omnibus īnstrūctīs, deōs ad
cēnam vocāvit. Mēnsa, nōn pulchra sed ūtilis, paucīs sed bonīs
cibīs īnstrūcta erat. Vīnum sūmunt, sed semper crātēr[3] vīnum con-
tinēbat. Tum Philēmōn et Baucis, ad mēnsam sedentēs, clārē
15 sēnsērunt deōs adesse. Tum Iuppiter, "Deī sumus," inquit,
"tōtam hanc gentem poenam solūtūram esse statuimus, quod
nēmō nōbīs auxilium dedit, sed
vestra vīta servābitur. Ad montem prōcēdēmus." Itaque Baucis
20 et Philēmōn, hāc ōrātiōne permōtī, ad montem tardē prōcessērunt. Ibi cōnstitērunt et vīdērunt tōtam regiōnem sub aquā
esse, domum suam sōlam ma-
25 nēre. Dum spectant, domus
eōrum in pulchrum templum vertitur.

Tum Iuppiter, "Quid cupitis?"
inquit; "id quod petitis dō-

Baucis and Philemon. The pet
goose goes into the oven. Painting by Lavalley

---

[1] *Baucis (Bau'sis)*, *Philē'mon.*
[2] *household* (predicate nominative).
[3] *bowl.*

30 nābō." Philēmōn, uxōre cōnsultā, respondit: "Nūllum mūnus nōbīs grātius aptiusque est quam esse sacerdōtēs[1] illīus templī et ē vītā eōdem tempore excēdere, quod in concordiā multōs annōs ēgimus." Hoc mūnus accēpērunt.

Post multōs annōs, aetāte gravēs ante sacrum templum stā-
35 bant. Corpora eōrum in arborēs[2] tardē vertuntur; vōcēs haerent; nōn iam spīrant. Neuter ante alterum ē vītā excessit. Multōs annōs hae duae arborēs ante templum stābant.

Thought Questions.—1. What was Jupiter looking for? 2. Why did it take so long to find it? 3. How did Philemon find out that his guests were gods?

Read Sabin, pp. 83–84; Gayley, pp. 77–80; Guerber, pp. 43–44; Bulfinch, pp. 54–57.

459.   Formation of Adverbs

(*a*) For adverbs formed from adjectives of the first and second declensions, see **176**.

(*b*) Adverbs are formed from adjectives of the third declension, as a rule, by adding –iter to the base; as, adj., **fortis**, adv., **fortiter**; adj., **ācer**, adv., **ācriter**.

The **comparison of adverbs** is very similar to that of adjectives:

POSITIVE	COMPARATIVE	SUPERLATIVE
al'tē	al'tius	altis'simē
for'titer	for'tius	fortis'simē

Note that in the comparative degree the adverb always has the same form as the neuter accusative singular of the comparative adjective.

Practice.—Form and compare adverbs from the following adjectives already studied:

longus, ūtilis, levis, clārus, firmus, gravis, vērus

---

[1] *priests.*   [2] *trees.*

(*a*) 1. Sciō hoc flūmen esse longius quam illud. 2. Tardius pervēnimus quod reliquī puerī celerius cucurrērunt. 3. Nostrī fortissimē pugnāvērunt sed ab hostibus repulsī sunt. 4. Pater meus omnia iūstē et celeriter iūdicat. 5. Hī mīlitēs, ē castrīs ēductī, ad proelium ā duce īnstruuntur. 6. Puerī magistrō librum dedērunt, et ille ōrātiōne aptā respondit.

(*b*) 1. We certainly hope that peace has been established among all nations. 2. Our men fight more bravely. 3. No one approves a very long speech. 4. The battle was sharply fought, but few men received severe wounds.

461. Vocabulary

ap′tus, –a, –um, *fit, suitable·* (adapt)
*gēns, gen′tis, gen′tium, f., *people, nation* [*genus*]
hu′milis, –e, *low, humble* (humility)
īn′struō, –ere, īnstrū′xī, īnstrūc′tus, *arrange, provide* [*struō, arrange*]
iū′dicō, –ā′re, –ā′vī, –ā′tus, *judge* (judicial)
nē′mō, dat. nē′minī, acc. nē′minem (no other forms), *no one* [*homō*]
ōrā′tiō, ōrātiō′nis, f., *speech* (orator)
re′giō, regiō′nis, f., *region* [*regō*]
repel′lō, –ere, rep′pulī, repul′sus, *drive back, repulse* [*pellō*]

462. English Word Studies: The Suffix –*iō*

In Latin the suffix –iō is added to verb stems, usually to the participial stem. As this generally ends in –t or –s, words of this origin generally end in –tiō or –siō. The suffix indicates an act or the state which results from an act: ōrātiō is the act of speaking, or the result, *i.e.* a speech. Nouns with this suffix have –iōnis in the genitive. Therefore the base ends in –**n**. The English form of the suffix, which is very common, is –**ion** (–**tion**, –**sion**): *region, oration, session.* It often has the force of the suffix –*ing*.

Give and define ten English words with the suffix –**ion** derived from Latin verbs which you have studied. Look up the origin and meaning of *gentle* and *gentile*.

463.   DAEDALUS ET ĪCARUS

In īnsulā Crētā Mīnōs[1] fuit rēx. Daedalus[2] cum fīliō parvō
Īcarō[2] ibi captīvus fuit. Fugere nōn potuit quod mare prohibuit.
"Neque per terram," inquit, "neque per mare fugere possum,
sed caelum certē nōn clausum est. Illā viā difficillimā prōcēdēmus." Itaque ālās parāvit, simillimās ālīs vērīs avium.[3] Partēs 5
ālārum cērā ligāvit. Īcarus ad patrem stābat, ālās levissimās
tangēbat, opus patris impediēbat. Tandem fīnis labōris difficilis
aderat; ālae parātae erant. Daedalus tempus aptum esse iūdicāvit.
Tum ālās corporī fīlī iūnxit et eum hīs verbīs monuit:

"In mediō caelō prōcēdēmus; nam, sī humilius volābimus,[4] 10
undae ālās graviōrēs facient; sī altius volābimus, ignis ālās ūret[5]
et in mare cadēs."

Daedalus and Icarus

Tum omnēs partēs ālārum
fīliō ostendit et omnia in ōrdine
explicāvit. Perīculum esse sēnsit 15
et fīliō timuit, quī patrī dissi-
millimus erat. Ālīs īnstrūctus
antecessit et fīlium iussit post
volāre.

Agricolae territī ex agrīs eōs 20
vīdērunt; multī putāvērunt eōs
deōs aut deīs similēs esse.
Celerrimē pater fīliusque āera[6]
ālīs pepulērunt.[7] Multās regiōnēs
gentēsque relīquērunt. Tum puer 25
nōn iam timidus patrem ducem
relīquit. Ōrātiōnem patris memoriā nōn tenuit et altius volāvit

---

[1] Mī′nŏs.   [2] Daedalus (Dĕd′alus), Ic′arus.
[3] of birds.   [4] fly.   [5] will burn.
[6] Accusative singular: air.
[7] From pellō: beat.

quod iūdicāvit nihil accidere posse. Sed multa accidērunt celeriter 30
sōl cēram solvit; nōn iam ālae haesērunt. Praeceps puer miser
in mare cecidit; frūstrā[1] nōmen patris clāmāvit. Ab illō posteā
hoc mare nōmen[2] accēpit.

Interim pater, nōn iam pater, in omnibus regiōnibus fīlium
petīvit, nōmen fīlī clāmāvit. Tandem ālās propriās Īcarī in undīs
vīdit sed corpus eius numquam invēnit. 35

Tum ipse ad Siciliam pervēnit et ibi multōs annōs ēgit. Sed
fābula ab aliīs dicta huic dissimilis est: scrībunt eum in Italiam
volāvisse et ibi in templō ālās posuisse. Hōc modō deīs prō
salūte grātiās ēgit.

Prīmus omnium hominum Daedalus per caelum lātum volāvit, 40
sī auctōrēs Graecī et Rōmānī vērum dīxērunt. Nunc multī
hominēs volant, sed nēmō ālīs propriīs. Nāvibus ālās iūnximus.

Thought Questions.—1. In what way did Icarus disobey his
father? 2. Where did Daedalus land? 3. Explain why Oregon has the
motto **Alis volat propriis.**

Read Sabin, pp. 260–261; Gayley, pp. 246–248; Guerber, pp. 253–255;
Bulfinch, pp. 161–163.

464. Comparison of –*er* Adjectives and Their Adverbs

All adjectives ending in **–er** form the superlative by adding
–rimus, –a, –um to the nominative singular masculine of the
positive:

Positive	Comparative	Superlative
lī′ber, lī′bera, lī′berum	lībe′rior, lībe′rius	līber′rimus, –a, –um
ā′cer, ā′cris, ā′cre	ā′crior, ā′crius	ācer′rimus, –a, –um
ce′ler, ce′leris, ce′lere	cele′rior, cele′rius	celer′rimus, –a, –um

[1] *in vain.*   [2] The Icarian Sea.

The corresponding adverbs are formed as follows:

Positive	Comparative	Superlative
lī'berē	lībe'rius	līber'rimē
ā'criter	ā'crius	ācer'rimē
cele'riter	cele'rius	celer'rimē

Practice.—Compare **miser, pulcher, altus.** Form and compare the corresponding adverbs. Decline **illa līberior patria.**

465.   Adjectives with Superlative in –*limus*

The superlative of five adjectives ending in –lis is formed by adding –limus, –a, –um to the base of the positive:

fa'cilis, –e	faci'lior, faci'lius	facil'limus, –a, –um
diffi'cilis, –e	diffici'lior, diffici'lius	difficil'limus, –a, –um
si'milis, –e	simi'lior, simi'lius	simil'limus, –a, –um
dissi'milis, –e	dissimi'lior, dissimi'lius	dissimil'limus, –a, –um
hu'milis, –e	humi'lior, humi'lius	humil'limus, –a, –um

Note.—Other –lis adjectives, such as **nōbilis, –e, ūtilis, –e,** etc., form the superlative regularly—*i.e.* by adding –issimus, –a, –um to the base of the positive: **nōbil–is'simus, –a, –um.**

Interior of a house at Herculaneum

The adverb of **facilis** is **facile**. The adverbs formed from the other adjectives in the preceding list are formed regularly.

In the superlative the corresponding adverbs end in –ē: **facillimē**.

Hungarian stamp with picture of a flyer who might be Icarus. You don't believe it? Seeing is believing: here's the picture.

466. Dative with Adjectives

1. **Hic liber est similis illī,** *This book is similar to that.*

2. **Ille homō est frātrī meō inimīcus,** *That man is unfriendly to my brother.*

Observe that the dative is often used with Latin adjectives whose English equivalents are followed by *to*. The following have already been studied: **amīcus, inimīcus, similis, dissimilis, aptus, grātus.**

467. Exercises

(*a*) 1. Nihil est nōbīs ūtilius quam bonus liber; nam est nōbilissimus amīcōrum, semper firmus et vērus. 2. Humilis homō nec altē cadere nec graviter potest. 3. Rōmānōrum deī dissimillimī nostrō Deō erant. 4. Hic equus similior meō est quam ille. 5. Ille liber difficillimus est, nam pauca clārē explicat.

(*b*) 1. The teacher in a very beautiful speech unfolded the life of Caesar. 2. As the bad men approached, the boys ran more quickly. 3. The places in which our soldiers fell are the most sacred in Gaul. 4. This region is fit for (to) some men, but not for others.

Vocabulary

ca′dō, –ere, ce′cidī, cāsū′rus, *fall* (casualty)
  ac′cidō, –ere, ac′cidī, ——, *fall to, befall, happen* (with dat.)
diffi′cilis, –e, *difficult* [*facilis*]
ex′plicō, –ā′re, –ā′vī, –ā′tus, *unfold, explain* [*plicō*]
iun′gō, –ere, iūn′xī, iūnc′tus, *join (to)* (junction)
pro′prius, –a, –um, (*one's*) *own* (propriety)
si′milis, –e, *like* (similarity)
  dissi′milis, –e, *unlike*

469. English Word Studies

(*a*) Explain *accident, coincidence, proprietor, inexplicable, decadent.* What is meant by the *assimilation* of the foreign population in our country?

(*b*) **Legal Phrases in English**

Lawyers use so many Latin phrases daily that they must be familiar with Latin. A few such phrases are:

subpoena, a summons to court *under penalty* for failure to attend.

ex post facto, *resulting after the fact;* e.g. a law which makes punishable acts committed before its passage.

in forma pauperis, *in the form* (or *manner*) *of a poor man;* to sue as a poor man and so avoid the costs of the suit.

in propria persona, *in one's own person* (not through some one else).

Look through the court records and legal items in the newspapers for other Latin phrases.

Roman cemetery near Ostia. The tombs are all tiny houses. Truly a dead town.

Elephanti maximi—the first tanks. From the film "Scipio Africanus"

LESSON LXX

470. PYRRHUS ET EIUS VICTŌRIA

Rōmānī, quī erant optimī mīlitēs, gentēs quae proximae urbī erant vīcerant et in ulteriōrēs partēs Italiae pervēnerant; summā virtūte contrā maiōrēs cōpiās hostium in extrēmīs ac difficillimīs regiōnibus Italiae pugnāverant. Posteā bellum novī generis, dissimile aliīs, cum Pyrrhō, rēge maximō Ēpīrī, gessērunt. 5

Pyrrhus in Italiam īnferiōrem ā Tarentīnīs, gente pessimā, vocātus est, quī eō tempore cum Rōmānīs pugnābant. Is ad Italiam vēnit et elephantōrum auxiliō Rōmānōs reppulit, quod Rōmānī elephantōs maximōs nōn ante vīsōs timuērunt. Tamen fortiter pugnāvērunt. Peius[1] Pyrrhō victōrī quam victīs Rōmānīs 10 accidit. Plūrimī Pyrrhī mīlitēs cecidērunt. Pyrrhus, ubi plūrima corpora Rōmānōrum interfectōrum vulnera in fronte habēre vīdit, haec verba fēcit: "Cum tālibus[2] mīlitibus tōtum orbem[3] facillimē

---

[1] *a worse thing.*   [2] *such.*   [3] *earth.*

vincere possum!" Familiāribus dē victōriā agentibus dīxit: "Sī
iterum eōdem modō vīcerō, nūllōs mīlitēs in Ēpīrum redūcam."
15 Iūdicāvit hanc victōriam nōn ūtilem esse quod plūrēs mīlitēs
āmīserat.

Thought Questions.—1. What was the cause of Pyrrhus' victories?
2. What is a "Pyrrhic victory"?

Read Harding, pp. 115–119; Guerber (*Story*), pp. 115–118; Mills,
pp. 102–105.

471. Irregular Adjectives Compared

In English, certain adjectives in common use are compared
irregularly, such as *good, better, best; bad, worse, worst.*

In Latin, the following adjectives, among others, are compared
irregularly and should be memorized:

POSITIVE	COMPARATIVE	SUPERLATIVE
bonus, –a, –um (*good*)	melior, melius (*better*)	optimus, –a, –um (*best*)
malus, –a, –um (*bad*)	peior, peius (*worse*)	pessimus, –a, –um (*worst*)
magnus, –a, –um (*large*)	maior, maius (*larger*)	maximus, –a, –um (*largest*)
parvus, –a, –um (*small*)	minor, minus (*smaller*)	minimus, –a, –um (*smallest*)
multus, –a, –um (*much*)	——, plūs[1] (*more*)	plūrimus, –a, –um (*most*)

Exercise.—Find English derivatives of the above adjectives.

Note that adverbs formed from the above adjectives are compared, in general, according to the rule (**459**); exceptions used
in this book are noted in the vocabularies.

Extrēmus and *Summus.*—In English, it is necessary to use
nouns to translate adjectives like **extrēmus** and **summus:** in

---

[1] Gen. **plūris**; there is no masculine and feminine singular, and no dative in any
gender; the plural is **plūrēs, plūra,** gen. **plūrium,** etc. See **578.**

extrēmā ōrātiōne, *at the end of the speech;* summus mōns, *top of the mountain* (cf. reliquī mīlitēs, *rest of the soldiers;* in mediō flūmine, *in the middle of the river*). When thus used, the adjective usually precedes its noun.

472.   Exercises

(*a*) 1. Nōnne spērās proximam hiemem nōn futūram esse dūriōrem quam hanc? 2. Optimī cīvēs patriam semper optimē dēfendent. 3. Pessimī hominēs in ultimās regiōnēs mittī dēbent. 4. Summus mōns ā nōbīs facillimē occupātus est. 5. Puerī ad īnferiōrem partem flūminis ab extrēmīs fīnibus prōvinciae iter facient. 6. Hī puerī territī sunt quod perīculum maximum esse sēnsērunt. 7. Agricolae Americānī maiōrem cōpiam frūmentī habēbunt quod meliōrēs agrōs habent.

(*b*) 1. Can a horse run more swiftly than a man? 2. We shall do this very quickly and well without your aid. 3. Our men fought more bravely than the enemy. 4. The smallest boy is not the worst.

Circus Maximus in all its splendor, with imperial box and Palatine Hill at left

bĕ′nĕ, adv., *well*   [*bonus*]

extrē′mus, –a, –um, *farthest, last, end of*   (extremist)

īnfe′rior, īnfe′rius, *lower*   (inferiority)

pro′ximus, –a, –um, *nearest, next* (with dat.)   (proximity)

sum′mus, –a, –um, *highest, top of*   (summit)

ulte′rior, ulte′rius, *farther*   (ulterior)

474.   English Word Studies

Obverse

Reverse

Seal of the United States, with mottoes. The lower mottoes are based on Virgil: God "has smiled on our undertakings," "a new series of generations."

(*a*) A number of English words preserve the forms of the comparative and superlative of Latin irregular adjectives: *major* (cf. *mayor*), *maximum*, *minor*, *minus*, *minimum*, *plus*, *nonplus*, *inferior*, *superior*, *ulterior*, *prior*, *anterior*, *posterior*, *interior*, *exterior*, *junior*, *senior*.

What is the difference between a *majority* and a *plurality* vote? Between a *majority* and a *minority* report?

(*b*) **Latin Phrases in English**

e pluribus unum, *one out of many* (motto of the United States, found on its coins).

esse quam videri, *to be rather than to seem* (*to be*) (motto of the state of North Carolina).

excelsior, *higher* (motto of the state of New York).

Translate the motto of Oklahoma (also of the University of Illinois and the American Federation of Labor): **Labor omnia vincit**.

LESSON LXXI

475.   PYRRHUS ET FABRICIUS

Fabricius,[1] quī erat īnferior genere quam aliī Rōmānī, tamen ab omnibus amātus est quod optimus fortissimusque mīles erat. Neque amīcōs neque inimīcōs suōs fallēbat. Praemia numquam sūmēbat. Itaque Rōmānī cīvitātis suae salūtem eī crēdidērunt et eum inter aliōs lēgātōs ad Pyrrhum mīsērunt.   5

Multa quae dē Fabriciō et eius summā honestāte Pyrrhus audīverat vēra esse crēdidit. Itaque hunc lēgātum in castrīs suīs cōnspectum bene accēpit. Ad extrēmum eī dīxit: "Cūr nōn in Ēpīrum mēcum venīs et ibi manēs? Quārtam rēgnī meī partem tibi tribuam." Sed Fabricius respondit sē neque partem rēgnī 10 sibi tribuī cupere neque sūmptūrum esse.

Proximō annō Fabricius contrā Pyrrhum pugnāvit. Medicus rēgis mediā nocte ad eum vēnit et dīxit sē prō praemiō Pyrrhum interfectūrum esse. Fabricius, quī nēminem fefellerat, iussit hunc ligātum redūcī ad dominum et Pyrrhō omnia dīcī. Ubi rēx medi- 15 cum ligātum cōnspexit, maximē mōtus dīxit: "Ille est Fabricius quī nōn facilius ab honestāte quam sōl ā cursū[2] suō āvertī potest!"

Thought Questions.—1. Why did the Romans have so much confidence in Fabricius? 2. What offer did Pyrrhus make to Fabricius? 3. What reason did Pyrrhus have for being grateful to Fabricius?

Read Harding, pp. 121–122; Guerber (*Story*), pp. 119–121.

476. Reflexive Pronouns

In English, the pronouns *myself, ourselves*, etc., may be used in apposition with a noun or pronoun for emphasis, like Latin

Pyrrhus

---

[1] *Fabricius (Fabrish'ius).*   [2] Ablative: *course.*

Roman Forum as it was, with rostra, arch of Septimius Severus, and Senate

ipse (404): *I saw him **myself,** Ipse* eum vīdī. They are also used alone as objects of verbs or of prepositions to refer to the subject of the verb; they are then called **reflexive pronouns**: *I saw myself.*

In Latin, the personal pronouns of the first and second persons may be used reflexively, but in the third person Latin has a special reflexive pronoun, **suī,** declined alike in the singular and plural:

Gen. su′ī,		*of himself, herself, itself, themselves*
Dat. si′bi,	*to* " " " "
Acc. sē (sē′sē),	" " " "
Abl. sē (sē′sē),	*with (from,* etc.) " " " "

Query.—Why is **suī** without a nominative?

336

(ego) mē rogō, *I ask myself*	(nōs) nōs rogāmus, *we ask ourselves*
(tū) tē rogās, *you ask yourself*	(vōs) vōs rogātis, *you ask yourselves*
(is) sē rogat, *he asks himself*	(eī) sē rogant, *they ask themselves*

Practice.—Give a synopsis of līberō, 1st sing.; fallō, 2d plur.; interficiō, 3d sing., using the proper reflexive pronoun with each.

478. Reflexive Adjectives

Corresponding to **meus, tuus, noster,** and **vester,** derived from **ego, tū, nōs,** and **vōs,** there is the reflexive adjective **suus, –a, –um,** *his own, her own, its own, their own,* derived from **suī.**

Stamp of Barbados, British colony in the West Indies, showing Britannia holding Neptune's trident and driving his sea horses over the waves

Caution. — Remember that **suus, –a, –um** *always refers to the subject of the verb.* When *his, her,* etc., do not refer to the subject, **eius,** etc., must be used (**394**).

479.   Exercises

(*a*) 1. Crēditisne Deum mare terramque prō sē aut prō nōbīs fēcisse? 2. Frāter eius mātrem suam fefellit et posteā sē interfēcit. 3. Arma sūmēmus et nōs fortiter dēfendēmus contrā pessimōs hostēs. 4. Puerum pessimum currentem vīdī, sed ille crēdidit sē ā mē nōn vīsum esse. 5. Tū tē ipsum fallere semper potuistī sed mē numquam fefellistī. 6. Mūnera pūblica optimīs, nōn pessimīs, hominibus tribuī dēbent.

(*b*) Translate the words in italics:

1. We saw *his* brother. 2. The girl loved *her* mother. 3. They

will defend *themselves* and *us*. 4. You will see *their* friends. 5. He wasted *his* money and *theirs*.

(*c*) 1. We always praise ourselves and accuse others. 2. He says that he himself has four brothers, but he cannot deceive me. 3. Entrust yourselves and all your (possessions) to us. 4. The leader of the enemy, having caught sight of us, killed himself.

480.   Vocabulary

cōnspi′ciō, –ere, –spe′xī, –spec′tus, *catch sight of, see*   [*speciō, look*]
con′trā, prep. with acc., *against*
crē′dō, –ere, crē′didī, crē′ditus, *believe, entrust* (with dat.)   (credit)
fal′lō, –ere, fefel′lī, fal′sus, *deceive*   (fallacy)
interfi′ciō, –ere, –fēcī, –fectus, *kill* (cf. "done for")   [*faciō*]
lēgā′tus, –ī, m., *envoy*   [*lēgō, appoint*]
sū′mō, –ere, sūmp′sī, sūmp′tus, *take*   (assumption)
tri′buō, –ere, tri′buī, tribū′tus, *grant*   (contribute)

481.   English Word Studies

In the fourteenth century there began a great revival of interest in the ancient Latin and Greek authors. This revival is known as the **Renaissance** (**re-nāscor**). Beginning in Italy, it spread over western Europe and reached England in the sixteenth century. Ever since then many new words have been added to English from Latin and Greek. As a result, over ninety per cent of the words in Caesar and Cicero have English derivatives. Words of this last period are easily distinguished by their similarity to the Latin originals.

One result of the introduction of new words directly from the Latin was the formation of a number of **doublets,** words derived at different periods from the same Latin word and having different meanings. Note the following (the earlier form precedes): *sample, example* (**exemplum**); *feat, fact* (**factum**); *Mr., master* (**magister**); *loyal, legal* (**lēx**); *mayor, major* (**maior**); *chance, cadence* (**cadō**).

Show how the above doublets got their meanings from the original Latin meaning.

Regulus returns to Carthage. A painting by Maccari

LESSON LXXII

482. REGULUS

Contrā Carthāginiēnsēs arma ā Rōmānīs sūmpta erant.[1]
Rēgulus, dux Rōmānōrum, imperiō acceptō, ad Āfricam nāvigāvit
et hostēs superāvit. Multa mīlia captīvōrum in Italiam mīsit sed
ipse, opere difficilī nōn iam perfectō, in Āfricā remānsit. Contrā
trēs Carthāginiēnsium ducēs pugnāns victor fuit. Victī hostēs 5
pācem ā Rōmānīs petīvērunt. Quam[2] Rēgulus dīxit sē dūrissimīs
condiciōnibus datūrum esse. Itaque Carthāginiēnsēs auxilium ā
Lacedaemoniīs[3] petīvērunt. Xanthippus[4] dux, quī ā Lacedaemoniīs
missus erat, cum quattuor mīlibus mīlitum et centum elephantīs
contrā Rōmānōs prōcessit. Rōmānīs victīs, Rēgulus captus est. 10

Rēgulus in Āfricā mānsit sed quīntō annō Carthāginiēnsēs
superātī eum ad urbem Rōmam mīsērunt. Eum iussērunt pācem ā
Rōmānīs obtinēre et permūtātiōnem captīvōrum facere. Is dīxit,

---

[1] First Punic or Carthaginian War, 264–241 b.c. These wars were for the supremacy
of the world. Carthage was in northern Africa.

[2] In Latin, a relative is often used at the beginning of a sentence to connect with
the preceding sentence. In English, a demonstrative is used instead.

[3] *the Spartans.*   [4] *Xanthippus (Zanthip′pus).*

pāce nōn factā, sē ad eōs reversūrum esse. Illī crēdidērunt eum sē
15 trāditūrum esse.

Itaque Rēgulus in Italiam pervēnit. Ductus in senātum
Rōmānum dīxit sē esse captīvum, nōn iam Rōmānum. Itaque
etiam uxōrem, quae eum cōnspexerat et ad eum cucurrerat, ā sē
remōvit. Dīxit hostēs, frāctōs multīs proeliīs, spem[1] nūllam nisi[2]
20 in pāce habēre; nōn esse ūtile multa mīlia captīvōrum prō sē ūnō,
aetāte cōnfectō, hostibus reddī. "Captīvōs Rōmānōs aurō emere
nōn dēbēmus," explicat; "nam virtūs eōrum āmissa est, nec vēra
virtūs aurō emī potest." Senātus hōc cōnsiliō numquam ante
datō permōtus pācem cum hostibus nōn fēcit. Itaque Rēgulus,
25 opere perfectō, Carthāginiēnsēs nōn fefellit sed in Āfricam
revertit et sē Carthāginiēnsibus trādidit, ā quibus omnibus sup-
pliciīs interfectus est. Posteā Rōmānī eī honōrēs tribuērunt.

Haec prīmō bellō Pūnicō accidērunt. Posteā Rōmānī, pāce
frāctā, duo alia bella cum eīsdem hostibus gessērunt et imperium
30 suum maximē auxērunt.

Thought Questions.—1. How long was Regulus in Africa before he
won his first victory? 2. What caused his later defeat? 3. Why did he urge
the Romans not to make peace?

Read Haaren and Poland, pp. 114–121; Mills, pp. 140–142; Guerber
(*Story*), pp. 124–128.

483.   Declension of *Duo* and *Trēs*

The cardinal numbers from 4 to 100 are indeclinable. You have
learned the declension of ūnus (409). Duo, *two*, and trēs, *three*,
are declined as follows:

	M.	F.	N.	M. AND F.	N.
Nom.	du'o	du'ae	du'o	trēs	tri'a
Gen.	duō'rum	duā'rum	duō'rum	tri'um	tri'um
Dat.	duō'bus	duā'bus	duō'bus	tri'bus	tri'bus
Acc.	du'ōs	du'ās	du'o	trēs	tri'a
Abl.	duō'bus	duā'bus	duō'bus	tri'bus	tri'bus

[1] *hope.*   [2] *except.*

340

The library of Columbia University, New York, in Ionic style with Roman dome. Cf. pages 265, 275, 280.

484.   Declension and Use of *Mille*

Mīlle, when used of one thousand, is usually an indeclinable adjective (like **centum**): **mīlle hominēs**. When used of two or more thousands, it is a neuter plural i-stem noun (cf. **mare, 353**). The word used with the plural forms of **mīlle** must be in the genitive: **duo mīlia hominum** (lit., *two thousands of men*), *two thousand men*.

	SINGULAR	PLURAL
Nom.	mīl′le	mī′lia
Gen.	mīl′le	mī′lium
Dat.	mīl′le	mī′libus
Acc.	mīl′le	mī′lia
Abl.	mīl′le	mī′libus

Practice.—Give in Latin: *two boys, one hundred children, one thousand citizens, two thousand sailors, three thousand soldiers.*

341

(*a*) 1. Nāvī frāctā, omnēs certē interficientur. 2. Duōs optimōs librōs ēmī quōs hāc aestāte legam. 3. Mīlle nautās cum tribus ducibus in maria ultima mīsimus. 4. Post duās pugnās hostēs cōnfectī nōn iam vim nostram sustinēre poterant. 5. Centum mīlia agricolārum, agrīs suīs relīctīs, ad oppida contendērunt.

(*b*) 1. Anna was third in rank, but her brother was fifth. 2. The lower part of this river is between two nations. 3. Three men were killed, and two received wounds. 4. All the boys easily completed the work in three hours.

486.   Vocabulary

cen′tum, indecl. adj., *hundred*   (centennial)
e′mō, –ere, ē′mī, ēmp′tus, *take, buy*   (redemption)
fran′gō, –ere, frē′gī, frāc′tus, *break*   (fraction)
impe′rium, impe′rī, n., *command, power*   (imperial)
o′pus, o′peris, n., *work*   (operate)
perfi′ciō, –ere, –fē′cī, –fec′tus, *finish*   [*faciō*]
trā′dō, –ere, trā′didī, trā′ditus, *give* or *hand over, surrender*   [*dō*]

487.   English Word Studies

Much difficulty is caused in English spelling by silent or weakly sounded letters. This difficulty is often solved by referring to the Latin original: *laboratory, repetition, library, separate, auxiliary, comparative, debt, reign, receipt.* The Latin original often helps in other difficulties: *consensus, annuity, deficit, accelerate.*

Define the above words and give their Latin originals.

Much confusion is caused in English by the combinations *ei* and *ie*. Remember that the derivatives of compounds of **capiō** have *ei*, as *receive.*

Why is a *fraction* so called? Explain *fracture, exemption.* Explain *treason* and *tradition*, which are doublets derived from **trādō**. What is *credit* as used in business? What is a *creed?*

488. Comparison

1. Compare **aptus, celer, levis, iūstus.** Form and compare adverbs from **certus, ācer, humilis.**

2. Decline **ūtilior liber** and **melior aetās** in the singular.

3. Give in Latin in the singular and plural in the case required: *a most beautiful region* (nom.); *a worse time* (acc.); *a rather long journey* (dat.); *the smallest part* (abl.); *a larger ship* (gen.).

489. Reflexive Pronouns and Adjectives

Give in Latin: he deceives him and himself; they praise them and themselves; they will ask their friends and hers; he accuses himself, we praise him; she will see her father.

490. Vocabulary

NOUNS

1. aetās	4. imperium	6. nēmō	8. ōrātiō
2. condiciō	5. lēgātus	7. opus	9. regiō
3. gēns			

ADJECTIVES

10. aptus	14. extrēmus	19. similis
11. centum	15. humilis	20. summus
12. difficilis	16. īnferior	21. ulterior
13. dissimilis	17. proprius	22. ūtilis
	18. proximus	

VERBS

23. accidō	28. explicō	33. iūdicō	38. statuō
24. cadō	29. fallō	34. iungō	39. sūmō
25. cōnspiciō	30. frangō	35. perficiō	40. trādō
26. crēdō	31. īnstruō	36. rapiō	41. tribuō
27. emō	32. interficiō	37. repellō	42. vincō

ADVERB	PREPOSITION	CONJUNCTION
43. bene	44. contrā	45. quam

491. Vocabulary

Nouns

1. *age*
2. *condition*
3. *nation*
4. *command*
5. *envoy*
6. *no one*
7. *work*
8. *speech*
9. *region*

Adjectives

10. *suitable*
11. *hundred*
12. *difficult*
13. *unlike*
14. *farthest, end of*
15. *low, humble*
16. *lower*
17. *one's own*
18. *next*
19. *like*
20. *highest, top of*
21. *farther*
22. *useful*

Verbs

23. *happen*
24. *fall*
25. *catch sight of*
26. *believe*
27. *buy*
28. *unfold*
29. *deceive*
30. *break*
31. *arrange, provide*
32. *kill*
33. *judge*
34. *join*
35. *finish*
36. *carry off*
37. *drive back*
38. *establish, determine*
39. *take*
40. *give over*
41. *grant*
42. *conquer*

Adverb

43. *well*

Preposition

44. *against*

Conjunction

45. *than*

The charming home of Walter H. Mayer at Chiwaukee, Wis., (cf. p. 180) in modified Pompeian style. The paintings represent Neptune and Venus.

A typical example of Roman relief sculpture

492. English Word Studies

(*a*) Give the Latin words suggested by the following English derivatives:

accident, appropriate, conditional, conspicuous, credible, fallacious, instructive, opera, proximity, rapture, regional, redemptive, repulsive, tribute, victor.

(*b*) From the following French numerals obtain the Latin numbers from which they are derived and rearrange in the proper sequence:

trois, sept, un, cinq, quatre, dix, huit, neuf, deux, six

(*c*) Find and use in sentences as many English derivatives as possible from **nāvigō, doceō, vincō, sūmō.**

(*d*) Complete each of the following sentences in accordance with this sample:

Perfectus is to *perfection* as **conceptus** is to *conception.*

1. *Emō* is to *redemption* as ? is to *repulsion.*
2. *Creditor* is to **crēdō** as *instructor* is to ?
3. *Ūtilis* is to *utility* as ? is to *humility.*
4. *Statute* is to **statuō** as *institute* is to ?
5. *Consistency* is to **cōnsistō** as ? is to **currō.**

The triumph of Caesar. A painting by Mantegna

LESSON LXXIII

THE STORY OF LUCIUS (*Cont.*)

493. Caesaris Triumphus

Quondam pater Lūcī ā Forō revertit et dīxit triumphum
Caesaris futūrum esse et posteā magnōs lūdōs. C.[1] Iūlius Caesar
tum erat maximus Rōmānōrum. Galliam, Alexandrīam, Pontum,
Āfricam vīcerat. Decem annōs in Galliā ēgerat atque, multīs
5 mīlibus hostium repulsīs, illam regiōnem in prōvinciam Rōmānam
redēgerat. Pompeius,[2] cum Caesare prō summā potestāte con-
tendēns, in fugam datus erat. Sed nōn satis fuerat: Caesar in
Aegyptum prōcesserat et, Alexandrīnīs[3] pulsīs, Cleopātrae

---

[1] C. = Gāius. [2] *Pompey.* [3] *the people of Alexandria.*

nōmen rēgīnae Aegyptiōrum dederat. Postquam in Asiā rēgem
Pontī celeriter vīcit, ex eius rēgnō nōtās illās litterās mīserat in 10
quibus erant sōla verba, "Vēnī, vīdī, vīcī." Nunc, hōc opere
perfectō, futūrī erant quattuor triumphī, quod Caesar dē bellīs
reverterat, cui summa potestās ā deīs commissa est.

WAITING

Lūcius numquam triumphum vīderat et dē eō multa rogāvit.
Pater eī dīxit triumphum esse similem pompae in Circō habitae et 15
Caesarem per Circum et Sacram Viam ad Capitōlium prōcessūrum
esse. Lūcius permōtus vix exspectāre poterat. Sed omnia ad eum
quī exspectat veniunt; tempus triumphōrum aderat. Prīmus et
clārissimus triumphus Caesaris erat Gallicus. Loca emī nōn
potuērunt sed pater Lūcī familiāris Caesaris erat et optima loca 20
obtinuit. Postquam Caesar in Campō Mārtiō[1] mīlitēs īnstrūxit et
ex praedā eīs praemia tribuit, pompa tardē prōcēdere incipit.

"HERE THEY COME!"

Post longum tempus (ut[2] Lūcius exīstimāvit) pompa aderat.
Prīmī fuērunt cōnsulēs et senātōrēs, post quōs vēnērunt corni-
cinēs,[3] quī Lūciō grātissimī fuērunt. Tum cōnspexit titulōs[4] 25
ducum oppidōrumque captōrum cum fōrmīs exemplīsque[5] oppi-
dōrum. Dē nōminibus nōn nōtīs multa rogāvit: "Quī sunt
Aquītānī? Quī sunt Belgae?" Pater respondit: "Gallia est omnis
dīvīsa[6] in partēs trēs; quārum ūnam incolunt Belgae, aliam
Aquītānī, tertiam eī quī ipsōrum linguā Celtae, nostrā Gallī 30
appellantur. Hōrum omnium fortissimī sunt Belgae." "Quī sunt
Helvētiī?"[7] "Helvētiī statuērunt per prōvinciam nostram iter
facere quod maiōrēs fīnēs habēre cupīvērunt, sed ā Caesare pro-
hibitī sunt." "Quis est Ariovistus?" "Ariovistus erat superbus
rēx Germānōrum, ā Caesare ex Galliā expulsus." "Quī sunt 35
Germānī?" "Maxima pars Germānōrum trāns Rhēnum flūmen

---

[1] *Campus Martius* (*Mar'shius*), a park in Rome.   [2] *as.*   [3] *buglers.*
[4] *placards* (with names of towns, etc.).   [5] *models* (of wood, etc.).
[6] From **dīvidō.** Use derivative.   [7] *Helvetians* (*Helvē'shians*).

incolunt.[1] Etiam trāns Rhēnum Caesar mīlitēs suōs trādūxit et cum Germānīs contendit." "Quid est Britannia?" "Britannia est extrēma īnsula, ā barbarīs culta; etiam eam Caesar attigit. Sed 40 nōn ante centum annōs nostra erit."

Italian stamps with pictures of Caesar and his successor Augustus

HAIL! THE CONQUERING HERO COMES!

Posteā Lūcius cōnspexit arma captōrum prīncipum et prīncipēs ipsōs ligātōs, inter quōs erat Vercingetorīx.[2] Nunc populus maximē clāmat. "Quis est ille?" rogat Lūcius. Pater respondet: "Ille est ultimus dux Gallōrum, quī victōs Gallōs ad bellum 45 permōvit, sed Caesarī trāditus est. Postquam pompa Capitōlium attigit, ille interficiētur." Nunc clāmōrēs audiuntur: "Caesar adest! Caesar adest!" Currus imperātōris, quattuor equīs trāctus, cernitur. Caesar ipse togam pictam[3] gerit et scēptrum tenet. In currū[4] stat servus corōnam super Caesaris caput tenēns. Sed 50 subitō[5] omnēs terrentur: axe frāctō, Caesar paene[6] ē currū iactus est. Hic sōlus nōn commōtus est. Dum cōnstitit ac novum currum exspectat, Lūcium cōnspicit et eum rogat: "Tū, quis es?" Lūcius respondet: "Ego sum Lūcius Iūlius. Patrem meum nōvistī. Mīles erō et multās gentēs vincam." Caesar rīdēns eius 55 caput tetigit et dīxit: "Satis bene incipis. Exīstimō tē imperātōrem

---

[1] In Latin a plural verb may be used when the subject is grammatically singular but refers to more than one.   [2] *Vercingetorix* (*Versinjet'orix*).
[3] *embroidered* (with gold).   [4] Ablative.   [5] *suddenly*.   [6] *almost*.

348

futūrum esse." Pompa intermissa rūrsus[1] prōcēdit, et nunc mīlitēs Caesaris accēdunt, clāmantēs, "Iō triumphe![2] Iō triumphe!"
Etiam carmina canunt. Inter alia Lūcius haec audit:

"Ecce[3] Caesar nunc triumphat quī subēgit Galliās." Itaque
omnēs discēdunt, Lūciō clāmante, "Iō triumphe! Iō triumphe!" 60

Thought Questions.—1. What was a triumph? 2. What two kings did
Caesar defeat? 3. Who came first in the parade and who last?

494.   **Stop! Look! Think!**

The following words, which have already been used, closely
resemble one another in form or sound and must be carefully
distinguished. For difference in meaning, see the Latin-English
Vocabulary.

aetās, aestās	cīvis, cīvitās	ob, ab
accēdō, accidō	gēns, genus	pars, pār
alius, alter, altus	ibi, ubi	pōnō, possum
cadō, cēdō	liber, līber, līberī	vīs, vir

495.   **Vocabulary**

attin'gō, –ere, at'tigī, attāc'tus, *touch, reach*   [*tangō*]
exīs'timō, –ā're, –ā'vī, –ā'tus, *think*   [*aestimō, estimate*]
in'colō, –ere, inco'luī, incul'tus, *live, inhabit*   [*colō*]
post'quam, conj., *after*   [*post+quam*]
potes'tās, potestā'tis, f., *power*   [*possum*]
sa'tis, adv. and indecl. adj., *enough*   (satisfaction)

---

[1] *again.*   [2] Exclamation: *Triumph!*   [3] *look.*

(*a*) Most of the names of our states are Indian, but several of them are of Latin origin or form. Vermont means *green mountain* (**viridis mōns**), Pennsylvania is *Penn's woods* (**silva**), Virginia is the *maiden's* land (named after Queen Elizabeth, the virgin queen), Florida is the *flowery* land (**flōs, flōris**), Colorado is the land of the *colored* or *red* river, Montana is *mountainous* (**mōns**), Nevada is the land of snow (**nix, nivis**), and Rhode Island is said to be named after the Greek island of Rhodes, meaning *rose*. New Jersey means "New Caesarea," named after the island of Jersey, one of many places named in honor of one of the Caesars. The titles *Kaiser* and *Czar* also come from Caesar.

The beautiful Capitol of Havana, Cuba, in Roman-American style, like our Capitol at Washington and many state Capitols

Names whose endings only are Latin are Carolina (Charles II), Georgia (George II), Louisiana (Louis XIV), and Indiana.

(*b*) Explain *conjunction*, *adjunct*, *infallible*, *repellent*, *distraction*.

(*c*) Our word *Capitol*, used of a statehouse and of the seat of the United States Congress, is derived from **Capitōlium**. The word *Capitol* occurs as the name of a business one hundred and fifty-two times in the New York telephone directory, seventy-two in Chicago, fourteen in Baltimore, etc. Do you know of any such firms in your community?

Roman ruins at Sabratha in Libya, northern Africa

LESSON LXXIV

497.   **MARIUS**

C. Marius, vir humilis generis, ob ēgregiam virtūtem cōnsul
ā Rōmānīs factus est. Plūrimī cīvēs exīstimāvērunt eum esse
maximum imperātōrem aetātis suae.

Iugurthā,[1] rēge Numidiae, quae terra in Āfricā est, victō,
Marius bellum contrā Cimbrōs et Teutonēs[2] suscēpit. Hī, quī 5
extrēmōs fīnēs Germāniae incoluerant, Cimbrīs sē iūnxerant.
Multōs mēnsēs hae duae gentēs novās terrās petīverant et prōvinciam Rōmānam attigerant. Tribus ducibus Rōmānīs ā barbarīs
repulsīs, Marius mīlitēs trēs annōs exercuit. Posteā Teutonēs sub
Alpibus proeliō superāvit ac super centum mīlia interfēcit. 10

Cimbrī autem nihil dē victōriā Rōmānōrum audīverant et per
lēgātōs praemissōs sibi et Teutonibus agrōs petīvērunt. Marius
rīdēns, "Illī tenent," inquit, "semperque tenēbunt terram ā[3]
nōbīs acceptam." Proximō annō is cum mīlitibus bene exercitīs

---

[1] *Jugur'tha.*   [2] *Cimbri (Sim'brī), Teu'tons.*   [3] *from.*

351

15 contrā eōs pugnāvit. Nec minor erat pugna cum uxōribus eōrum
quam cum virīs. Illae quae supererant sē līberōsque suōs interfēcērunt.

Multōs annōs Rōmānī hōs barbarōs īnstantēs timuerant sed
post hanc victōriam Alpēs Rōmam ā perīculō prohibēbant.
20 Postquam Rōmānī intellēxērunt necesse[1] esse bellum cum
Mithridāte[2] gerere, hoc negōtium Sullae commīsērunt. Sed
postquam Sulla ex urbe discessit, Marius, quī ipse cupīvit hoc
negōtium super omnia suscipere, summam potestātem obtinuit.
Posteā Sulla cum mīlitibus quōs circum sē habuit Marium in
25 fugam dedit. Cōpiīs praemissīs, paucōs mēnsēs Rōmae[3] mānsit.
Postquam autem Sulla ad bellum discessit, Marius Rōmam
vāstāvit.

Quattuor annōs Sulla cum Mithridāte bellum gessit. Post
mortem Marī in Italiam revertit. Omnēs hostēs prae sē agēns,
30 circum multa oppida cōpiās suās dūxit. Dictātor factus, multa
mīlia cīvium interficī iussit. Amī-
cus eum monuit: "Nōnne intelle-
gis hoc satis esse? Sī omnēs in-
terficiēs, et nēmō supererit, quōrum cīvium dictātor eris?"

Marius—an ancient statue

Thought Questions.—1. What
was the cause of the war with the
Cimbri and Teutons? 2. Which did
Marius defeat first? Where? 3. What
was the cause of the quarrel between
Marius and Sulla? 4. Give some
examples of men in modern times
who, like Marius, rose to high positions from humble beginnings.

Read Haaren and Poland, pp. 148–
155; 162–170; Guerber (*Story*), pp.
155–164; Mills, pp. 215–221; 223–
231; Harding, pp. 170–172.

---

[1] *necessary* (indeclinable).
[2] *Mithridā'tēs.*   [3] *at Rome.*

Duōs annōs remānsit, *He remained two years.*
Flūmen decem pedēs altum est, *The river is ten feet deep.*

Observe that

(*a*) **duōs annōs** answers the question, *How long?*
(*b*) **decem pedēs** answers the question, *How much?*
(*c*) both express *extent* by the accusative;
(*d*) the English and Latin constructions are identical and are not to be confused with the direct object.

499.   *Post, Posteā,* and *Postquam*

The conjunction **postquam**, meaning *after*, must be distinguished carefully from the adverb **posteā**, meaning *afterwards*, and the preposition **post**, meaning *after* (with acc.). Examine the following:

1. **Post hunc mēnsem plūrēs librōs legam,** *After this month I shall read more books.*
2. **Posteā multōs librōs lēgī,** *Afterwards I read many books.*
3. **Postquam opus perfēcī, multōs librōs lēgī,** *After I finished the work, I read many books.*

Observe that

(*a*) the addition of **quam** to **post** makes **postquam** a conjunction, which is followed by a verb, usually in the perfect indicative;
(*b*) **posteā**[1] means literally *after that,* hence *afterwards;*
(*c*) the real difficulty is in the English use of *after,* as both a conjunction and a preposition.

500.   Exercises

(*a*) 1. Exīstimō hunc montem esse mīlle pedēs altum, illud flūmen duōs pedēs altum. 2. Illī hominēs multōs mēnsēs sē exercuērunt. 3. Super tria mīlia Germānōrum, pāce factā, Rōmānīs sēsē iūnxērunt. 4. Ego exīstimō nōs in illō locō duōs annōs

---

[1] Sometimes **post** is used as an adverb like **posteā**.

remānsisse, sed frāter meus dīcit nōs ibi trēs annōs remānsisse. 5. Quis cōnspexit nautās nāvigantēs "plānīs" (in locō nāvium) super caput? 6. Postquam mīlitēs servōs cōnspexērunt, eōs circum viās prae sē ēgērunt. 7. Postquam hostēs ā mīlitibus praemissīs victī sunt, paucī superfuērunt.

(*b*) 1. My brother will arrive next year and remain with me[1] the whole summer. 2. The greater part of the winter we remain in town, but in summer we hasten to the fields. 3. We understand that you have been training yourselves for many months. 4. After the boy fell into the river, his sister ran shouting to her mother.

501. Vocabulary

au'tem, conj. (never first word), *however*
cir'cum, prep. with acc., *around*
exer'ceō, –ē're, exer'cuī, exer'citus, *keep busy, train*   (exercise)
intel'legō, –ere, –lē'xī, –lēc'tus, *understand*   (intellect)
negō'tium, negō'tī, n., *business*   [*ōtium*]
prae, prep. with abl., *before, in front of*
praemit'tō, –ere, –mī'sī, –mis'sus, *send ahead*   [*mittō*]
su'per, prep. with acc., *over, above*   [*superō*]
super'sum, –es'se, super'fuī, superfutū'rus, *be left (over), survive*   [*sum*]

502. Latin and English Word Formation

Ne– is sometimes used as a negative prefix in Latin: nēmō (ne–homō), negōtium (ne–ōtium), neuter (ne–uter), nūllus (ne–ūllus).

Circum, contrā, prae, and super have their usual meanings when used as prefixes in Latin and English. In English prae becomes *pre–*, as *pre–pare, pre–fix;* contrā sometimes retains its form, sometimes becomes *counter–*, as *contra–dict, counter–act.* Super sometimes becomes *sur–* in English, in which case it must be distinguished from assimilated sub: *surplus, surmount.*

Find ten English words with these prefixes, compounded with Latin words which you have studied. Explain *intelligence, supervisor, surplus, precedent.*

---

[1] See 235, footnote.

Haec sunt mea ornamenta.

LESSON LXXV

503. ## GRACCHĪ

Ti. et C. Gracchī Scīpiōnis Āfricānī nepōtēs[1] erant. Dīligentiā
Cornēliae mātris puerī doctī sunt. Cornēlia crēdidit eōs certē
summam potestātem obtentūrōs esse. Quondam hospita, domō
Cornēliae petītā, ōrnāmenta sua pulcherrima manū prae sē
tenēns ostendēbat. Tum Cornēlia līberōs suōs, quī cāsū aderant, 5
manū tetigit atque hospitae dēmōnstrāns dīxit: "Haec sunt mea
ōrnāmenta!"

Tiberius iam vir plēbī amīcus erat. Tribūnus plēbis factus[2]
populō agrōs dare cupiēbat. Hī agrī pūblicī erant sed multōs
annōs ā nōbilibus occupātī erant, quī dīxērunt sē eōs nōn red- 10
ditūros esse. Tamen Tiberius populō eōs reddidit. Tum senātus
convocātus dē Tiberiō cōnsuluit. Multī eum dēspexērunt et eum

---

[1] *grandsons.*   [2] 133 B.C.

interficere cupīvērunt. Tiberiō accēdente, Scīpiō Nāsīca,[1] senātor, clāmāvit: "Venīte mēcum sī reī[2] pūblicae salūtem cupitis." Tum
15 ille et aliī quī circum eum stābant in Tiberium impetum fēcērunt et eum interfēcērunt.

Posteā in somnō Gāius vīdit frātrem suum, quī dīxit: "Cūr dubitās, Gāī? Tū, quī superes, hoc negōtium perficere et vītam tuam populō dare dēbēs." Itaque Gāius opus Tiberī sē perfec-
20 tūrum esse statuit neque eius cōnsilia dēsertūrum. Tribūnus factus plēbī frūmentum dabat et cīvitātem omnibus quī Italiam incolēbant. Mīlitēs autem exercēre nōn potuit et intellēxit sē sine exercitū nihil efficere posse; fugere coāctus interfectus est.

Itaque senātus mortem Gracchōrum effēcit. Sed cōnsilia
25 hōrum mānsērunt, et Rōmānī eōs multōs annōs memoriā tenuērunt.

Thought Questions.—1. Who was the grandfather of Gaius Gracchus? 2. Who was the teacher of Tiberius Gracchus? 3. What was the political policy of Gaius?

Read Mills, pp. 199–208; Harding, pp. 158–165; Haaren and Poland, pp. 142–147; Guerber (*Story*), pp. 146–152.

504. Fourth Declension

We have seen that nouns of the first three declensions are distinguished by the ending in the genitive singular: first declension, –ae, second declension, –ī, third declension, –is. The majority of Latin nouns belong to these three declensions. A few nouns, however, have –ūs in the genitive singular and belong to the **fourth declension.** Many are derived from verbs.

	CASE ENDINGS		cāsus, *chance* (base, cās–)	
Nom.	–us	–ūs	cā'sus	cā'sūs
Gen.	–ūs	–uum	cā'sūs	cā'suum
Dat.	–uī	–ibus	cā'suī	cā'sibus
Acc.	–um	–ūs	cā'sum	cā'sūs
Abl.	–ū	–ibus	cā'sū	cā'sibus

[1] *Nasī'ca.*   [2] Genitive of **rēs.**

Gender.—Nouns of the fourth declension in –us are mostly masculine; the only exceptions in this book are **manus** and **domus,** both of which are feminine.

Practice.—(*a*) Decline **exercitus noster, hic impetus fortis.**

(*b*) Name the case of each of the following words:

senātū, impetum, manibus, ōrātiōne, domuī, exercituum, cāsūs, condiciōnibus.

505.   Exercises

(*a*) 1. Quid manū tuā tenēs? 2. Omnēs cīvēs in suīs propriīs domibus ā barbarīs interfectī sunt. 3. Maiōrēs gentēs iūra minōrum populōrum dēspicere nōn dēbent. 4. Postquam cāsus ducī nūntiātus est, ille mortem suā manū petīvit. 5. Exercitus noster impetum in (*on*) ōrdinēs Gallōrum fēcit. 6. Paucī cūrās cāsūsque vītae leviter dēspicere possunt.

Looking through the atrium of a Roman house at Pompeii. The artist did not need to use much imagination, for much of the house still stands.

(*b*) 1. Soldiers, make an attack upon the enemy. 2. He has said that he will make an attack upon the enemy at the third hour. 3. The house was deserted; I could see nothing. 4. I touched a body with my hand and shouted.

506. Vocabulary

cā′sus, –ūs, m., *fall, chance, accident*	[*cadō*]
dēmōns′trō, –ā′re, –ā′vī, –ā′tus, *show*	[*mōnstrō*]
dē′serō, –ere, dēse′ruī, dēser′tus, *desert*	(desertion)
dēspi′ciō, –ere, dēspe′xī, dēspec′tus, *look down on, despise*	[*speciō*]
do′mus, –ūs[1], f., *house, home*	(domestic)
exer′citus, –ūs, m., (*trained*) *army*	[*exerceō*]
im′petus, –ūs, m., *attack*	[*petō*]
ma′nus, –ūs, f., *hand*	(manual)
red′dō, –ere, red′didī, red′ditus, *give back*	[*dō*]
senā′tus, –ūs, m., *senate*	(senatorial)

507. English Word Studies

In two earlier lessons (**147, 152**) we saw how many English words are simply the base of a Latin noun, adjective, or verb, or the base plus silent –**e**. A great many such words are derived from the Latin words in this book. A few are *par, facile, prime, just, cede, part.* In the case of verbs, the base of the present indicative, present participle, or perfect participle, or of all three, may furnish an English word: *convene, convenient, convent; remove, remote; refer, relate.*

As previously noted, there are sometimes changes in the base, *e.g.* the dropping of one of two final consonants, as in *remit, expel,* and particularly the addition of a vowel to the main vowel of the word, as in the following (the added vowel is underlined): *peace, mount, reign, remain. Contain, retain,* etc., are from the compounds of **teneō.**

Find ten more words illustrating these principles. Explain *domestic, manual labor, manicure, despicable, impetuous.*

---

[1] Usually has abl. sing. **domō** and acc. plur. **domōs** (**572**).

508.   Roman Social and Economic Conditions

It is interesting to us to learn that the Romans, like ourselves, had periods of business panics and depressions. We can comfort ourselves with the thought that such depressions will disappear as they did in the past.

From time to time the common people of Rome, who were very poor, suffered from lack of food when the wheat crop failed. At one such time the senate, which was the ruling body, obtained a large amount of wheat and was planning to give it away to the poor. We have already read (437) that the plebeians were angry at Coriolanus. The reason was that he advised the senate not to give the wheat free and criticized the plebeians sharply. This happened in the fifth century B.C.—over twenty-five hundred years ago.

In the time of the Gracchi (second century B.C.) economic conditions became especially bad. The rich nobles had acquired large farms by taking over public lands and by forcing out the poor small farmers. These wandered over Italy with their families and many settled in Rome, where they had a hard time. They could not obtain work on the large farms because these were worked by slave labor. Slave labor had the same effect as tractors and other farm machinery today. Tiberius Gracchus planned to force the large landowners to sell all but 500 acres of their lands at a reasonable price. He then intended to cut this land up into small farms to be rented at a low cost to the poor. He felt that the men who fought for their country had as much right to a home as the wild beasts in the forests.

After Tiberius' death his brother Gaius tried to carry out his brother's policies. In addition, he used the unemployed to build roads, stored large amounts of wheat to avoid shortage, gave relief to the poor by selling wheat well below cost, and established colonies. But he, too, met death in a riot.

The problem of dividing up the big estates into small farms and of furnishing relief by cheap or free wheat continued to bother Roman leaders for another century. Julius Caesar, a popular leader who favored such measures, made himself a dictator and established government by emperors. Under his successor, Augustus, a great peace was established which brought prosperity and better living conditions for two hundred years. But the people paid for these advantages by a loss of their liberties and privileges: free speech, political rights, individual liberties of various sorts were gradually reduced.

Questions for Discussion.—1. Discuss the policy of the Gracchi in giving public lands and wheat to the poor and using the unemployed in building roads. Give some modern parallels. 2. In what countries has a program of social and economic reform such as that of the Gracchi led to dictatorship? 3. How can we get a maximum of social reform without abandoning important liberties?

Ancient Rome as imagined by the great English artist Turner

Scipio crowns an African king. From the film "Scipio Africanus"

LESSON LXXVI

509. SCĪPIŌ

P. Cornēlius Scīpiō patrem, quī impetū hostium graviter vulnerātus erat, servāvit.[1] Post pugnam Cannēnsem,[2] in quā Rōmānī interclūsī et gravissimē victī sunt, omnibus probantibus, Scīpiōnī, puerō vīgintī annōrum, summum imperium datum est. Ille lūcem et spem salūtis Rōmānīs reddidit. Postquam sex 5 annōs in Italiā exercituī praefuit, Rōmānī eum cōpiīs Hispānīs praefēcērunt. Ille urbem Carthāginem Novam diē quō vēnit expugnāvit; ita celer erat. Quīnque annīs exercitūs hostium ex Hispāniā expulit. Dēmōnstrāverat cīvibus suīs Carthāginiēnsēs vincī posse. Neque aurum rapuerat neque miserīs nocuerat. 10

Hispāniā victā, hic prīnceps in Āfricam prōcēdere mātūrāvit et ibi Carthāginiēnsēs victōriīs terruit. Tum senātus Carthāginiēnsium Hannibalem ad patriam vocāvit. Sed Scīpiō eum

---

[1] In the Second Punic War, the greatest of the three wars against Carthage, 218–201 B.C.

[2] *of Cannae* (*Căn'ē*). The Carthaginian plan of encirclement used in this battle was imitated by the Germans in their conquest of Poland in 1939 and in Belgium and France in 1940

Zamae[1] vīcit, et ille, clārissimus et maximus omnium ducum quī contrā Rōmānōs pugnāvērunt, patriam suam dēseruit. Scīpiō ob hanc victōriam Āfricānus appellātus est. Nōn iam Hannibal, cuius nōmen līberōs Rōmānōrum terruerat, īnstābat.

Multae rēs dē Scīpiōne Āfricānō trāduntur. Ōlim, dum exercituī praeest, ille ad oppidum mūnītum in quō erant multī mīlitēs interclūsī cōpiās addūxit. Scīpiō exīstimābat oppidum capī posse, sed paucī eandem spem habuērunt. Cāsū ūnus ē mīlitibus hominem ligātum, quī alterī mīlitī nocuerat, ad eum trāxit et rogāvit: "Quō diē locōque iubēs hunc hominem ad tē ad

Ancient statue, supposed to represent Scipio

supplicium venīre?" Tum Scīpiō manum ad oppidum ipsum tetendit et iussit eum hominem in illō oppidō tertiō diē esse. Ita rēs facta est; tertiō diē, impetū factō, oppidum expugnātum est eōdemque diē ibi ille suppliciō hominem affēcit.

Saepe ante prīmam lūcem hic prīnceps populī Rōmānī domum relinquēbat et in Capitōlium veniēbat et ibi sōlus multās hōrās sedēbat. Aliī putāvērunt Scīpiōnem, deīs dēspectīs, hanc rem ad speciem facere; aliī autem crēdidērunt eum dē salūte cīvitātis deum cōnsulere.

Thought Questions.—1. How old was Scipio when he went to Spain? 2. Why was Scipio called Africanus? 3. What explanations were given of Scipio's visits to the temple?

Read Haaren and Poland, pp. 122–134; Harding, pp. 135–146.

---

[1] *at Zama* (202 B.C.).

The last of the noun declensions includes comparatively few words. **Rēs** and **diēs**, however, occur constantly and should be memorized. Other nouns of the **fifth declension**, as a rule, have no plural; all are feminine except **diēs**, which is usually masculine.

	Case Endings		diēs, *day* (base, di–)		rēs, *thing* (base, r–)	
	Sing.	Plur.				
Nom.	–ēs	–ēs	di'ēs	di'ēs	rēs	rēs
Gen.	–ĕī	–ērum	diē'ī	diē'rum	re'ī	rē'rum
Dat.	–ĕī	–ēbus	diē'ī	diē'bus	re'ī	rē'bus
Acc.	–em	–ēs	di'em	di'ēs	rem	rēs
Abl.	–ē	–ēbus	di'ē	diē'bus	rē	rē'bus

Observe that –e– appears in every ending and that in **diēs** it is long in the genitive and dative singular, though preceding a vowel (535).

Practice.—(*a*) Decline **rēs similis** and **ūna spēs**.

(*b*) Give each of the following in the form indicated:

     diēs proximus, abl. plur., **prīnceps noster**, acc. sing.;
     speciēs nova, dat. sing.; **impetus maior**, acc. plur.;
     manus pulchra, gen. plur.; **melior lux**, abl. sing.

511.   **Exercises**

(*a*) 1. Amīcus certus in rē incertā cernitur. 2. Memoria diēī bene āctī est per sē satis magnum praemium. 3. Virum quī huic operī praefuit illī urbī praeficiam. 4. Lēgātus Rōmānus dīxit exercitum suum agrīs domibusque agricolārum nōn nocitūrum esse. 5. Dēmōnstrāvī illum prīncipem nocuisse senātuī populōque Rōmānō. 6. Quid significant (*mean*) hae litterae, in signīs Rōmānīs vīsae, "S P Q R"? Rogā magistrum tuum sī nōn nōvistī. 7. Speciēs illōrum barbarōrum mē puerum terrēbat.

(*b*) 1. Show him your new books; he will not do harm to them. 2. We shall put this general in charge of affairs; he will send grain to the city. 3. By chance I heard our leader say that there was no hope of peace. 4. Most (men) are deceived by the appearance of things; a few, however, see things clearly.

512.   Vocabulary

di'ēs, diē'ī, m., *day*   (diary)
interclū'dō, –ere, –clū'sī, –clū'sus, *cut off*   [*claudō*]
lūx, lū'cis, f., *light*   (translucent)
no'ceō, –ē're, no'cuī, nocitū'rus, *do harm (to)*
  (with dat.)   (innocent)
praefi'ciō, –ere, –fē'cī, –fec'tus, *put in charge of*
  (with acc. and dat.)   [*faciō*]
prae'sum, –es'se, prae'fuī, praefutū'rus, *be in charge of*
  (with dat.)   [*sum*]
prīn'ceps, prīn'cipis, m., *leader*   [*prīmus+capiō*]
rēs, re'ī, f., *thing, matter, affair*   (real)
spe'ciēs, speciē'ī, f., *appearance*   [*speciō*]
spēs, spe'ī, f., *hope*   [*spērō*]

A shop in Pompeii. Those who had no running water at home went to the corner fountain. Maybe the shopkeeper used it too for his wine.

513. English Word Studies

(*a*) English words which preserve the forms of the Latin fourth declension are: **census, consensus, impetus, prospectus, status, apparatus** (plural **apparatuses** or **apparatus**; the latter preserves the Latin plural). Note that **consensus** (from **sentiō**) is spelled with an –s– but **census** (from **cēnseō**) with a –c–. An ablative form is seen in **impromptu**.

What is the girl with the curls and the hairnet going to write with her stylus on the tablet—a poem, a letter, or what?

The fifth declension is represented by **rabies, series, species**. The last two are used in the plural with no change of form (as in Latin).

The accusative singular is represented by **requiem**, the ablative by **specie**, and the ablative plural by **rebus**.

A.M., ante merīdiem, *before midday;* **P.M.**, post merīdiem, *after midday;* **M.**, merīdiēs, *midday.*

(*b*)   **Latin Phrases in English**

bona fide, *in good faith.*

casus belli, *an occasion for war.*

in statu quo, *in the situation in which* (*it was before*); **status quo,** *the situation in which* (*it was before*).

prima facie, *on the first face* (*of it*); e.g. *prima facie* evidence.

sine die, *without a day* (*being set*); used of adjournment by a parliamentary body.

Explain **per diem, post mortem, sui generis.**

The Roman senate house (with the three windows), from the temple of Castor

LESSON LXXVII

514. CATŌ ET SCĪPIŌ

M. Catō, vir humilī genere, ad summōs honōrēs per sē ascenderat. Hic Scīpiōnī, virō nōbilissimā familiā, inimīcus erat et eum dēspexit. Itaque iussit familiārem suum Petīlium in senātū petere et explōrāre ratiōnēs pecūniae praedaeque captae in bellō 5 cum Antiochō[1] ā Scīpiōne gestō. Hōc modō senātum in duās partēs dīvīsit, ūnam quae Scīpiōnī nocēre cupiēbat, alteram quae eum prīncipem maximae virtūtis esse crēdēbat. Tum Scīpiō, cuius īra ex speciē gravī frontis clārē cernī poterat, librum prae sē tenuit et dīxit:

10 "In hōc librō ratiōnēs scrīptae sunt omnis pecūniae omniumque rērum quās accēpī. Hic est diēs quō mihi in animō erat[2]

---

[1] *Antī'ochus*, a Syrian king.   [2] mihi ... erat, *I intended.*

ratiōnēs apud vōs legere atque explicāre. Nunc autem, quod Petīlius eās explōrāre et mihi imperāre cupit, apud vōs eās nōn explicābō."

Hōc dictō, librum suīs propriīs manibus dīscidit.[1]

Thought Questions.—1. In what respect were Cato and Scipio unlike? 2. Why did Scipio tear the book in pieces? 3. According to this story, what is the wrong way to get a person to do something? 4. What other Romans besides Cato rose to high positions from humble origins?

515.   Genitive and Ablative of Description

1. **virī magnae virtūtis,** *men of great courage.*
2. **spatium decem pedum,** *a space of ten feet.*
3. **hominēs inimīcō animō,** *men with* (or *of*) *an unfriendly spirit.*

Observe that in English we may say *men of* or *with an unfriendly spirit.* Both are descriptive. Note also that description is similarly expressed in Latin, *i.e.* either by the genitive or the ablative, but only when modified by an adjective.

While the **genitive** and the **ablative of description** are translated alike, Latin confines the genitive largely to expressions of *measure and number* (see 2) and the ablative to *physical qualities.*

516.   Exercises

(*a*) 1. Mārcus erat puer magnā grātiā apud familiārēs suōs. 2. Lēgātus Gallōrum fuit vir clārissimō genere. 3. Hāc aestāte ascendam montem decem mīlium pedum. 4. Frontem huius montis ascendere nōn poterō, quod ea est praeceps et difficillima. 5. Eum montem sōlī virī maximae virtūtis explōrāvērunt. 6. "Dīvide et imperā" erat cōnsilium Rōmānōrum.

(*b*) 1. After a journey of two days, we arrived at (**ad**) a very beautiful city. 2. We all know that Italy has been divided from Gaul by very high mountains. 3. The general whom Caesar put-in-charge-of the army was a man of great influence. 4. Do you desire to climb a mountain which has never been explored?

---

[1] *tore in pieces.*

a'pud, prep. with acc., *among*

ascen'dō, –ere, ascen'dī, ascēn'sus, *climb (up)*,
ascend   [*scandō, climb*]

dī'vidō, –ere, dīvī'sī, dīvī'sus, *divide*   (division)

explō'rō, –ā're, –ā'vī, –ā'tus, *investigate, explore*   [*plōrō, call out*]

*frōns, fron'tis, fron'tium, f., *forehead, front*   (frontal)

im'perō, –ā're, –ā'vī, –ā'tus, *command* (with dat. of
person)   [*imperium*]

ra'tiō, ratiō'nis, f., *account, reason*   (rational)

518. Latin and English Word Formation

The suffixes –ilis and –bilis are added to verb stems to form adjectives. They indicate what *can be done:* **facilis** is "doable," *easy.* The suffix –ilis usually becomes –ile in English: *facile, fertile.* The more common suffix –bilis becomes –ble, –able, –ible in English: *noble, credible, terrible, amiable, visible, comparable.*

The leopard earns his living in this wall painting from Pompeii while the man takes life easy.

Several suffixes meaning *pertaining to* are added to nouns and adjectives to form adjectives: –āris (English –ar), –ārius (–ary), –ānus (–an, –ane), –icus (–ic). Examples of their use in Latin and English are: **familiāris, frūmentārius, Rōmānus, pūblicus;** *singular, ordinary, human, humane, generic.*

The suffix –tūdō (English –tude) is added to adjective stems to form nouns and means *state of being;* **magnitūdō,** *magnitude.*

Find fifteen other examples of these suffixes in English words derived from Latin words already studied.

Wearers of the toga represented in this beautiful relief from the Altar of Peace erected in Rome during the reign of Augustus

LESSON LXXVIII

THE STORY OF LUCIUS

519. Cīvis Novus Iter Facit

Iam Lūcius aetātem quīndecim annōrum attigerat. Nunc pater eius dīxit eum dēbēre proximīs Līberālibus[1] togam praetextam dēpōnere et virīlem togam sūmere. Hōc tempore plūrimī puerī Rōmānī togās praetextās dēpōnēbant. (Puerī Rōmānī togās praetextās gerēbant, sed virī tōtās albās gerēbant. Brācae,[2] quae 5 ā virīs nunc geruntur, ā barbarīs, nōn ā Rōmānīs, illīs diēbus gerēbantur.)

THE NEW CITIZEN

Līberālia aderant. Multī amīcī convēnērunt. Lūcius, postquam mōrem antīquum servāns togam praetextam ante Larēs posuit,

---

[1] The Liberalia, a festival held March 17.   [2] *trousers.*

369

novam virīlem togam sūmpsit. Omnēs familiārēs cum eō ad Forum pedibus prōcessērunt, et posteā ad Capitōlium, ubi nōmen eius in numerō cīvium scrīptum est. Nunc poterat dīcere, "Cīvis Rōmānus sum!" Tum omnēs cum Lūciō domum[1] revertērunt, ubi optima cēna parāta erat. Multī cibī dē ultimīs terrīs portātī erant, aliī dē Graeciā, aliī dē Asiā, aliī dē Āfricā. Amīcī cēnam variō sermōne in noctem prōdūxērunt et cum Lūciō dē officiīs cīvium, dē bellō et pāce, dē negōtiīs, dē multīs aliīs rēbus ēgērunt. Lūcius nunc intellēxit mūnera et officia cīvis Rōmānī.

THE JOURNEY

Paulō[2] post Lūcius, iam vir, cum patre iter fēcit. Itaque per portam Capēnam[3] ex urbe discessērunt. Raedā ibi inventā, in Appiā Viā prōcessērunt. Sepulchrīs ad viam cōnspectīs, Lūcius dīxit: "Pater, cūr sepulchra ad viās pōnuntur? Hoc numquam intellegere potuī." Pater respondit: "Hōc modō omnēs ea vidēre possunt." Lūcius dīxit sē nocte inter sepulchra iter facere nōn cupere.

GOOD ROADS AND GREAT MEN

Quod iter facile et commodum erat, Lūcius dīxit: "Nōnne exīstimās Appiam Viam optimam omnium esse?" Pater respondit: "Omnēs nostrae viae optimae sunt. Ob eam causam hostēs vīcimus, fīnēs lātiōrēs parāvimus, potestātem patriae nostrae auximus, et nunc gentēs regimus. Aliī pictūrās pulchriōrēs pingunt,[4] aliī ōrant[5] causās melius, sed nōs regimus populōs." "Etiam apud nōs causae optimē ōrantur," respondit Lūcius. "Quis melior ōrātor fuit aut est aut erit quam Cicerō? Hic ōrātor etiam cōnsul fuit et populum Rōmānum rēxit. Ego eum ōrātiōnem habentem in Forō audīvī et eius ōrātiōnēs in lūdō lēgī." "Lēgistīne ōrātiōnēs in Catilīnam, illum quī cīvitātem vī opprimere statuit?" "Illās et aliās lēgī. In prīmā dīxit dē Catilīnā: 'Ō tempora! Ō mōrēs! Senātus haec intellegit, cōnsul

---

[1] "Place to which" is expressed without a preposition with **domum**: *home.*
[2] *shortly.*   [3] A gate in the wall of Rome.   [4] *paint.*   [5] *plead.*

videt; hic tamen vīvit.' " "Optimē!" dīxit pater. "In secundā, sī 40
memoria mē nōn fallit, dīxit, postquam Catilīna ex urbe discessit:
'Abiit,[1] excessit, ēvāsit,[2] ērūpit!'[3] Ex Cicerōnis linguā fluēbat
ōrātiō dulcior quam mel."

SCENES BY THE WAY

Tum altōs et pulchrōs arcūs[4] aquaeductūs[5] cernunt, quī
optimam aquam dē montibus in urbem dūcit. Pater Lūciō 45
dīxit prīmum aquaeductum ab Appiō factum esse. Appius fuit
ille quī Appiam Viam mūnīvit. Ita prōcēdunt, nunc agrōs et
vīllās, montēs silvāsque spectantēs, nunc hominēs in viā ipsā,
quōrum aliī pedibus prōcēdēbant, aliī aut equō aut raedā aut
lectīcā[6] ferēbantur.[7]
50

EPILOGUE

Nōn iam vīvunt Lūcius et eius amīcī, nōn iam vīvunt Caesar et
Cicerō, prīncipēs summae auctōritātis, sed lingua eōrum vīvit,
vīvunt eōrum dicta et facta, lēgēs et mōrēs, glōria et fāma. Haec
omnia in eōrum librīs inveniuntur. Eīs quī itinera parva per illōs
librōs faciunt Rōmānī ipsī vīvere videntur.
55

Thought Questions.—1. What do you think of the idea of having a
ceremony when a boy or girl becomes a citizen? 2. Is it done in your
community? 3. Why were the Roman cemeteries along the main highways?

520.   Vocabulary

dēpō'nō, –ere, dēpo'suī, dēpo'situs, *put* or *lay aside*	[*pōnō*]
mōs, mō'ris, m., *custom*	(moral)
*nox, noc'tis, noc'tium, f., *night*	(nocturnal)
vī'vō, –ere, vī'xī, vīc'tus, *live*	(vivid)

521.   Synonyms

We rarely find a word in any language which has exactly the
same meaning as another word. Words which have almost the

---

[1] *he has gone away.*   [2] Ēvādō, ēvāsus—derivative?   [3] Ērumpō, ēruptus—
derivative?   [4] Accusative plural.   [5] Genitive singular.   [6] *litter.*   [7] *were carried.*

same meaning are called **synonyms**. The diagram may help you to remember the margin of difference between the synonyms **homō** and **vir**, which are often confused.

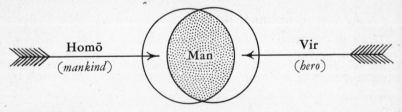

The following synonyms have occurred in previous lessons:

1. **ante,** *before* (of time and place), adverb or preposition (with accusative).
prae, *before* (of place only), preposition (with ablative).

2. **terra,** *land* (as opposed to water), then some particular *land* or *country.*
fīnēs, *borders,* hence a *land* or *country* with reference to its boundaries.
patria, *fatherland,* the *land* of one's birth.

3. **dux [dūcō],** *a leader* in any field, but often in a military sense.
prīnceps [prīmus+capiō], the *first* or *chief* man in a group—usually nonmilitary.

4. **videō,** *see,* the most general word.
cernō, *see clearly.*
cōnspiciō, *catch sight of.*

5. **labor,** *hard work, toil, suffering.*
opus, usually *a piece of work.*
negōtium, *lack of leisure* [ōtium], *business.*

6. **potestās,** *power* in general.
auctōritās, *influence.*
rēgnum, *royal power.*
imperium, *military power, command.*

522. English Word Studies

As Latin synonyms differ, so do their English derivatives (though not always in the same way). Distinguish *antecedent* and *precedent; duke* and *prince; vision* and *discernment; visible* and *conspicuous; laborer* and *operator; labor, opera,* and *negotiation; power* and *authority; royal* and *imperial.*

523.   **The Roman Citizen**

According to tradition, Rome was founded in 753 B.C. April 21 is still celebrated in Italy as the birthday of Rome. The first rulers were kings but the last king was driven out in 509 B.C. because he was a tyrant. The new government was headed by two consuls of equal power, one to be a check on the other. They held office for only a year. The Roman historian Livy sees the origin of Roman liberty in this restriction. But this government was not democratic, for it was in the control of a small group of noble families called patricians. For two hundred years the common people, or plebeians, struggled for equality and justice and gradually won most of the rights of their more fortunate fellow citizens. At first they could not hold office and did not even have fair trials in court. Their struggle for democracy and liberty is of great interest to us in this country. First they secured the right to elect special officials, called tribunes, who could veto the acts of the patrician officials. Then they obtained a set of written laws, called the Twelve Tables, which served as a kind of constitution or bill of rights. In 326 B.C. imprisonment and slavery for debt were abolished. This step Livy calls a second beginning of liberty for the plebeians. In 287 B.C. the plebeians succeeded in establishing the principle that a vote of the plebs should have the authority of law. Such a vote was called a "plebiscitum," from which we get our word *plebiscite*. In these ways a fairly democratic form of government was assured for some time.

While these struggles were going on inside the country, wars

United States Supreme Court, Washington, D. C.

were being fought and the Roman empire was being formed. The heroic deeds of Horatius, Cincinnatus, Fabricius, Regulus, Scipio, and many others accounted for Roman success and molded the Roman virtues of courage, honesty, organizing power, patriotism, devotion to family, strict justice, plain living, and the determination to see things through and never to give up. From all this grew the great system of Roman law and government, one of the greatest of our inheritances from Rome. For the Romans organized law and government on a large scale. Their success in this may be compared to the organization of industry during the last hundred years.

No wonder then that the possession of Roman citizenship was highly prized and that the people said with pride "Civis Romanus sum." This citizenship, bestowed on boys in a solemn ceremony, brought the protection of Roman law everywhere in the world. It also brought the responsibility of protecting the Roman state against its enemies. So today citizenship in any country brings both advantages and duties.

"It is clear that the spirit of '76 had a most diversified origin. . . . In listing the 'founding fathers,' it is not enough to include merely American patriots of the caliber of Jefferson, Franklin, and the Adamses. . . . Demosthenes and Aristotle, Brutus, Cicero, and Tacitus belong there, as do many others of similar stamp and influence. . . . Not less than the Washingtons and the Lees, these ancient heroes helped to found the independent American commonwealth."[1]

Questions for Discussion.—1. The Romans had two consuls as a check on each other. What system of "checks and balances" do we have in our government? 2. The restriction of the consulship to one year was regarded as the origin of liberty. Have we any similar restriction for our highest officials? 3. What is the "Bill of Rights"? 4. Are persons sometimes imprisoned for debt today? Have there been changes in our laws on the subject in the last one hundred years? 5. What are some of the privileges and duties of citizenship today?

[1] Charles F. Mullett in the *Classical Journal*, xxxv (1939), 104.

524. Forms

(*a*) Decline **senātus noster, diēs longior.**

(*b*) Give the genitive and accusative singular and the genitive plural of **id negōtium, haec potestās, illa nox, impetus fortis, īdem prīnceps, quae ratiō, rēs ipsa, cāsus peior, domus ūlla.**

(*c*) Give a synopsis of **noceō,** 3d sing. act.; **dēpōnō,** 3d plur. pass.; **imperō,** 1st plur. act.; **dēspiciō,** 3d plur. pass.; **audiō,** 2d sing. act.

(*d*) **Rapid-Fire Drill on Verb Forms:** *Identify by giving voice, tense and when possible, mood, person, and number:* praemīsit, exīstimābō, incoluisse, exercērī, interclūdēns, dēserunt, redde, dēmōnstrāte, explōrārī, dīvidī, imperāns, superestis, praeerimus, praeficiēmus, ascendam, vīvite, dīvīsus, interclūdentur, intellēctum est, vīsūrus.

525. Vocabulary

NOUNS

1. cāsus	6. impetus	10. negōtium	14. ratiō
2. diēs	7. lūx	11. nox	15. rēs
3. domus	8. manus	12. potestās	16. senātus
4. exercitus	9. mōs	13. prīnceps	17. speciēs
5. frōns			18. spēs

VERBS

19. ascendō	24. dēspiciō	30. incolō	35. praemittō
20. attingō	25. dīvidō	31. intellegō	36. praesum
21. dēmōnstrō	26. exerceō	32. interclūdō	37. reddō
22. dēpōnō	27. exīstimō	33. noceō	38. supersum
23. dēserō	28. explōrō	34. praeficiō	39. vīvō
	29. imperō		

CONJUNCTIONS	ADVERB	PREPOSITIONS	
40. autem	42. satis	43. apud	45. prae
41. postquam		44. circum	46. super

Model of Roman shops. The lady is looking at jewelry instead of buying vegetables. The bar at the right is busy too.

526. Vocabulary

Nouns

1. *chance, accident*	6. *attack*	10. *business*	14. *account*
2. *day*	7. *light*	11. *night*	15. *thing*
3. *home*	8. *hand*	12. *power*	16. *senate*
4. *army*	9. *custom*	13. *first man*	17. *appearance*
5. *front*			18. *hope*

Verbs

19. *ascend*	24. *look down on*	30. *inhabit*	35. *send ahead*
20. *reach*	25. *divide*	31. *understand*	36. *be in charge of*
21. *show*	26. *train*	32. *cut off*	37. *give back*
22. *lay aside*	27. *think*	33. *do harm to*	38. *be left over*
23. *desert*	28. *explore*	34. *put in charge of*	39. *live*
	29. *command*		

Conjunctions	Adverb	Prepositions	
40. *however*	42. *enough*	43. *among*	45. *in front of*
41. *after*		44. *around*	46. *above*

527. English Word Studies

(*a*) Give the Latin words and prefixes suggested by the following English derivatives: *ascendancy, casualty, circumnavigate, demonstration, familiarity, indivisible, innocuous, intellectual, lucid, opponent, preview, subjunctive, superscription, transcend, virtue.*

(*b*) Find and use in sentences as many English derivatives as possible from **pōnō, veniō,** and **pellō.**

528. Accusative with *Ad* or *In*

When *to* implies literally *motion toward* a place or person, we have seen that the accusative with **ad** or **in** is used. This is true after the following "motion" verbs, previously studied:

376

accēdō, cēdō, contendō, dūcō, fugiō, mātūrō, mittō, moveō, nāvigō, portō, prōcēdō, prōdūcō, properō, redigō, redūcō, trāns-portō, veniō

529. Dative of Indirect Object

When *to* does not imply literal motion but indicates the person *to whom* something is given, told, shown, etc., the dative is used. The following verbs, already studied, are transitive and may take an accusative of the *direct object* and a dative of the *indirect object:*

committō, dīcō, dō, dōnō, iungō, mandō, mōnstrō, nūntiō, ostendō, permittō, prōpōnō, reddō, relinquō, respondeō, submittō, trādō, tribuō

Some of these verbs have as the direct object either a neuter pronoun or an infinitive: **dīcō, respondeō, nūntiō.**

Other verbs rarely take any case but the dative: **noceō.**

The beautiful Elks Memorial in Chicago, with Doric columns and Roman dome

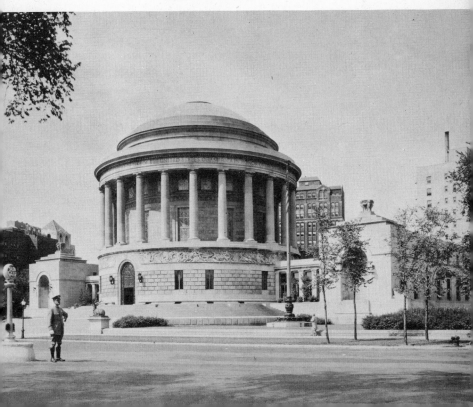

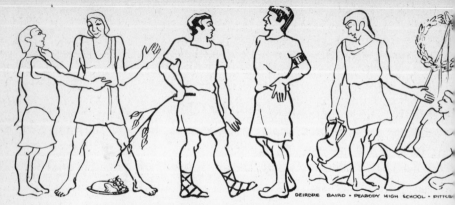

The quarrel of the slaves, drawn by a high school pupil

A LATIN PLAY

530. **SĀTURNĀLIA**[1]

Persōnae

Geta, *pessimus servōrum*   Hector, *maximus servōrum*
Bellus, *pulcherrimus servōrum*   Boadīx, *coquus*
L. Calpurnius, *dominus*   Aliī servī

TEMPUS: Decembrī. LOCUS: in aedibus[2] L. Calpurnī. (*Servī accēdunt.*)

Servī. Iō Sāturnālia! Iō Sāturnālia! Iō Sāturnālia!
          (*Boadīx ā sinistrā parte accēdit, currēns*)

Boadīx. Quid est? Quem clāmōrem audiō? Quid accidit? Quis interfectus est?

5 **Servī.** Ho, ho, ho! Coquus est.

Bellus. Nōnne pulcher est? Gravissimus est. Eō currente, audīre vidēmur—montem cadentem!

Servī. Ha, ha!

Boadīx. Quid? Montem cadentem? Ubi?

10 **Hector.** Mōns nōn cadit; stupidus es.

Geta. Sāturnālia adsunt. Nōnne Sāturnālia in Galliā erant?

Boadīx. Quae sunt? Nūlla in Galliā, patriā meā, coxī.

Servī. Ha, ha! "Coxī!"

Geta. Sāturnālia!—Sunt septem diēs quibus deō Sāturnō honō-
15 rēs dōnantur—

---

[1] *Saturnā'lia*, a festival similar to our Christmas.   [2] *house.*

378

Boadīx. Septem diēs! Deī Superī! Cūr rīdētis? Abīte,[1] aut vōs omnēs interficiam.

Hector. Quid? Properāre nōn dēbēs.

Boadīx. Diēbus quibus deīs honōrēs dōnantur, tum labor coquī maximus est. Cūr clāmōrem fēcistis? Fortasse dominus noster ex memoriā hōs diēs dēpōnet. 20

Geta. Sed hīs diēbus servī līberī sunt. Rēgem habent, ē numerō servōrum dēlēctum. Rēx domum regit. Nūllus labor est.

Boadīx. Coquīs labor semper est. Abīte![1]

Hector. Nunc nōn est tempus labōris. Tē teneō. Sī nōbīscum 25 Sāturnālia nōn clāmābis, — in viam tē ēiciēmus.

Bellus. Eat[2] stupidus ad labōrem.

Boadīx. Poenam dabitis, — pessimī. (*Exit*)

Geta (*Hectorī*). Eat, — nam dē graviōribus rēbus agere dēbēmus.

Hector. Dē graviōribus quam dē Boadīce agere nōn possumus. 30 Ha, ha!

Geta (*Hectorī*). Nōnne tū crēdis tē rēgem futūrum esse?

Servī. Iō Sāturnālia!

Hector. Rēgem?

Geta. Rēgem familiae, — servum quī reliquōs servōs Sāturnā- 35 libus regit.

Hector. Mē?

Geta. Tē. Maximus servōrum es. Dominus tē amat. — Mihi dīxit tē sibi cārissimum servōrum esse.

Hector. Dīxitne? 40

Geta. Dīxit. Sed Bellus putat sē rēgem futūrum esse.

Hector. Bellus? Puer est. Rēx nōn erit.

Geta. Tū rēx eris. Iō Sāturnālia!

Hector et reliquī servī. Iō Sāturnālia!

Geta (*Bellō*). Nōnne tū crēdis tē rēgem familiae futūrum esse? 45

Bellus. Mē?

Geta. Tē. Pulcherrimus servōrum es. Dominus dīxit tē sibi cāris- simum servōrum esse. Sed Hector putat sē rēgem futūrum esse.

---

[1] *go away.* [2] *let him go.*

Bellus. Hector? Nōn pulcher est.

50 **Hector.** Servī! Nōnne mē audītis?

Servī. Audīmus.

Hector. Rēx familiae erō.

Bellus. Quid? Ego rēx erō.

Hector. Puer es.

55 **Bellus.** Tē nōn timeō. Tē interficiam.

Hector. Tē in viam ēiciam.

Bellus. Em!

Hector. Em tibi! (*Pugnant*)

Servī. Bellus vincit. Bene, Hector! Bellus eum interficiet. Iō!

60   (*Calpurnius ā dextrā parte, Boadīx ā sinistrā parte accēdunt*)

Calpurnius et Boadīx. Quid hoc?

Servī. Dominus adest. Illī tamen pugnant.

Calpurnius. Quid hoc? Librum meum legere nōn possum.

Geta (*Calpurniō*). Pugnant. Ego eōs fīnem facere iussī, sed mihi
65   nōn pāruērunt. Sī mē rēgem familiae faciēs, mihi pārēbunt.
Rēx bonus erō. —

Calpurnius. Oho! Rēx familiae!

Hector et Bellus. Mēne vocās? Ōh! Dominus est.

Calpurnius. Ha, ha! Rēgem familiae dēligere dēbeō. In memoriā
70   nōn habēbam. Dēligō—

Hector et Bellus et Geta. Mē.

Calpurnius. Dēligō servum mihi cārissimum,——coquum.

Servī. Coquum!

Calpurnius. Boadīx, rēx es. Em, vidēsne? Haec pecūnia tua est.
75   Sī servī tibi pārēbunt, eīs partem dā. Sed in memoriā tenē tē
rēgem esse. Bene rege. Iō Sāturnālia! (*Exit*)

Boadīx. Rēx nunc sum. Vōs omnēs nunc mihi auxilium dabitis.
Meus labor vester est. Iō Sāturnālia!——Cūr nōn iam Sāturnālia clāmātis?

80 **Servī.** Ōh! Ōh! Sāturnālia dūra.

(*Exeunt*)

380

APPENDIX

The Roman amphitheater at El Djem, Tunisia, serves as a background for the Arab market.

APPENDIX

PRONUNCIATION[1]

531. Vowels

In English and Latin, the **vowels** are *a, e, i, o, u*.[2]

At one time the English vowels were pronounced like the Latin, but the pronunciation of English has changed greatly. In French, Spanish, Italian, German, etc., which also have adopted the Latin alphabet, the vowels are still pronounced substantially as in Latin.

Each of the Latin vowels may be pronounced long or short, the difference being one of *time*. This is called **quantity**. In addition, all the long vowels except a have a different *sound* from the short vowels. This is called **quality**. The pronunciation is as follows:

(*a*) LONG	SHORT	LONG AND SHORT AS IN
ā as in *father*	a as first *a* in *aha*	*Martha* (ā, ă)
ē as in *they*	e as in *let*	*lateness* (ē, ĕ)
ī as in *police*	i as in *bit*	*seasick* (ī, ĭ)
ō as in *rope*	o as in *for*	*phonograph* (ō, ŏ)
ū as in *rule*	u as in *full*	*two-footed* (ū, ŭ)

In this book long vowels are regularly marked –; short vowels are usually unmarked, but ˘ is sometimes used.

(*b*) **Caution.**—It is very important to distinguish the *sounds* of the long and short vowels. For a person to say, *I heard the din in the hall*, when he meant the "dean," or *I forgot the debt*, when he meant the "date," is no worse than to confuse ī and ĭ, ē and ĕ in Latin.

The English equivalents of e and o are only approximate. Avoid pronouncing ŏ like *o* in *not* or in *note*.

532. Diphthongs

The first three of the following **diphthongs** (two vowels making one sound) are the ones most commonly used:

---

[1] The best way to learn correct pronunciation is by careful imitation of the teacher; the rules are given for reference.

[2] In English sometimes also *y*, as in *by*, but not in *you*.

ae like *ai* in *aisle*   eu like *eh–oo* (pronounced quickly)
au like *ou* in *out*   ui like *oo–ee* (pronounced quickly); only in
oe like *oi* in *oil*   **cui** and **huic**
ei like *ei* in *freight*

533.   Consonants

All letters other than vowels and diphthongs are **consonants.**
The Latin consonants have, generally speaking, the same sounds as
in English. The following differences, however, should be noted:

b before **s** or **t** has the sound of **p.**
c is always hard as in *cat*, never soft as in *city*.
g is always hard as in *go*, never soft as in *gem*.
i (consonant) has the sound of *y* in *year*. (**i** is a consonant between
    vowels and before a vowel at the beginning of a word.)
s always has the sound of *s* in *sin;* never of *s* in *these*.
t always has the sound of *t* in *ten;* never of *t* in *motion*.
v has the sound of *w* in *will*.
x has the sound of *x* in *extra*.
    (ch=k; ph=p; th=t)

Doubled consonants are pronounced separately: **an'–nus.**

In both English and Latin the combination **qu** forms a single consonant
and the **u** is not a vowel.

534.   English Pronunciation of Latin

The above method of pronunciation is the ancient Roman method.
It should be remembered, however, that Latin words which have become
thoroughly English should be pronounced as English words; *e.g.* in *terra
firma*, the *i* is pronounced as in *firm*, not as in *miracle;* in *alumni*, the *i* is
pronounced as in *mile*.

535.   Quantity of Vowels

The quantity (and quality) of vowels must be learned as part of the
word. There are, however, a few general rules:

1. A vowel is short before another vowel or **h** (because **h** is weakly
sounded).
2. A vowel is short before **nt, nd,** and final **m** and **t.**

536.   Syllables

Every Latin word has as many syllables as it has vowels or diphthongs:
vir-tū'-tĕ, proe'-li-um.

384

A single consonant between two vowels or diphthongs is pronounced with the second: **fī'–li–us, a'–git.** Compound words are divided into their component parts and are exceptions to this rule: **ad'–es.**

When two or more consonants occur between vowels or diphthongs, the division is made before the last consonant: **por'–tus, vīnc'–tī, an'–nus.** An exception to this rule occurs whenever a mute (**p, b, t, d, c, g**) is followed by a liquid (**l, r**), in which case the mute combines with the liquid and both are pronounced with the second vowel: **pū'–bli-cus, cas'–tra.**

The next to the last syllable of a word is called the **penult;** the one before the penult (*i.e.* the third from the end) is called the **antepenult.**

537. Quantity of Syllables

Some syllables of course take longer to pronounce than others, just as some vowels are longer than others.

1. A syllable is *naturally* long if it contains a long vowel or a diphthong.

2. A syllable is long *by position* if it contains a short vowel followed by two or more consonants or the double consonant **x** (= **cs**).

Note.—Exception is made in the case of a mute followed by a liquid (see 536). H is so weakly sounded that it does not help make a syllable long.

Caution.—Distinguish carefully between long syllable and long vowel; in **ĕxĕm'plum** the first two syllables are long, though the vowels are short.

538. Accent

The accented syllable of a word is the one that is pronounced with more stress or emphasis than the others; so in the word *an'swer*, the accent is on the first syllable. In Latin the accent is easily learned according to fixed rules:

1. Words of two syllables are accented on the first: **frā'ter.**

2. Words of three or more syllables are accented on the penult if it is long, otherwise on the antepenult: **lēgā'tus, exem'plum; dī'cĕre, si'milis.**

The material here given may be reviewed in connection with the Lessons. For the use of those who prefer to review Basic Grammar before taking up the Lessons, a number of explanations are given here which will also be found in the body of the book. Teachers can easily devise English exercises for drill with classes which need it. The sentences on these pages may be used for that purpose.

539. The Sentence. Subject and Predicate

A **sentence** is a group of words which completely express a thought. Every sentence consists of two parts—the **subject** about which something is said and the **predicate** which says something about the subject: *The sailor* (subject) *saved the girl* (predicate), **Nauta puellam servāvit.**

A subject or predicate is said to be **modified** by those words which are closely associated with it.

540. Parts of Speech

The words of a language are divided, according to their use, into eight classes called **parts of speech.** These are:

Nouns	Verbs	Prepositions
Pronouns	Adverbs	Conjunctions
Adjectives		Interjections

541. Nouns

A **noun** (from Latin **nōmen**, *name*) is a word that names a person, place, or thing: *Anna,* **Anna;** *island,* **īnsula;** *letter,* **littera.**

Nouns may be classified as:

a. **Common** (applied to any one of a class): *city,* **urbs;** *girl,* **puella.**

b. **Proper** (applied to a particular one of a class): *Rome,* **Rōma;** *Julia,* **Iūlia.**

Note.—Proper nouns always begin with a capital letter.

542. Pronouns

A **pronoun** (Latin **prō**, *for;* **nōmen**, *name*) is a word used instead of a noun. The noun whose place is taken by a pronoun is called an **antecedent** (Latin **ante**, *before;* **cēdō**, *go*).

a. **Personal** pronouns distinguish the three persons: the person speaking (*I,* **ego;** *we,* **nōs**—first person), the person spoken to (*you,* **tū, vōs**—second person), the person or thing spoken of (*he,* **is;** *she,* **ea;** *it,* **id;** *they,* **eī**—third person).

b. **Interrogative** pronouns are used to ask questions: *who*, **quis**; *which*, *what*, **quid.**

c. **Relative** pronouns relate to a preceding (antecedent) word and join to it a dependent clause: *who*, **quī**; *which*, *what*, *that*, **quod.**

d. **Demonstrative** pronouns point out persons or objects definitely—often accompanied with a gesture: *this*, **hic**; *that*, **ille**; *these*, **hī**; *those*, **illī.**

543. Adjectives

An **adjective** is a word used to describe or limit the meaning of a noun or pronoun:

a. **Descriptive** adjectives are either **common** or **proper**: *good*, **bonus**; *Roman*, **Rōmānus** (see **541** *a*, *b*, and **Note**).

b. **Limiting:**

1. **Article**—definite (*the*), **indefinite** (*a*, *an*). There is no word in Latin for "the" or "a."
2. **Numerals**—**cardinals** (*one*, *two*, *three*, etc., **ūnus, duo, trēs,** etc.), **ordinals** (*first*, *second*, *third*, etc., **prīmus, secundus, tertius,** etc.)
3. **Possessive** adjectives (formed from personal pronouns): *my*, *mine*, **meus**; *our*, *ours*, **noster**; *your*, *yours*, **tuus, vester**; *his*, *her*, *its*, **eius**; *their*, *theirs*, **eōrum.**

When interrogative, relative, and demonstrative pronouns (**542**) are used as adjectives, they are called respectively:

4. **Interrogative** adjectives: *what street? quae via?*
5. **Relative** adjectives: *He spent a year in Italy, in which country he saw many beautiful things*, **Annum in Italiā ēgit, in quā terrā multa pulchra vīdit.**
6. **Demonstrative** adjectives: *that road, illa via.*

In English, the demonstrative adjectives are the only ones that have different forms in the singular and plural: *this*, *these*; *that*, *those.*

544. Verbs

A **verb** is a word used to tell something about a subject; it expresses either action or situation: *He fought*, **Pugnābat**; *He is good*, **Bonus est.**

a. According to use, verbs are either **transitive** or **intransitive.**

1. A **transitive** verb (Latin **trāns**, *over*; **eō**, *go*, *pass*) is one in which the action expressed by the verb passes over to a receiver: *Anna is carrying water*, **Anna aquam portat.**
2. An **intransitive** verb is one whose action does not pass over to a receiver: *Anna is working*, **Anna labōrat.**

Contrast "set" (transitive) with "sit" (intransitive), and "lay" (transitive) with "lie" (intransitive).

b. Intransitive verbs are either **complete** or **linking** (copulative).

1. A **complete** verb is one which is complete in meaning without an object or other word: *He sails, Nāvigat.*
2. A **linking** verb is one which links a noun or adjective to the subject: *They are good,* **Bonī** *sunt.*

The chief linking verbs in English are *be, appear, seem, become, feel, look, taste, smell.*

c. An **auxiliary** verb (Latin **auxilium,** *help*) is one used in the conjugation of other verbs: *I am learning;* **Did** *you see? They* **have** *given.*

545. Adverbs

An **adverb** is a word used to modify the meaning of a verb, adjective, or other adverb: *He is working now,* **Nunc** labōrat.

546. Prepositions

A **preposition** is a word used to show the relation of a noun or pronoun, called its **object,** to some word in the sentence: *He sails* **to the island, Ad īnsulam** nāvigat. The preposition is said to **govern** its object.

547. Conjunctions

A **conjunction** is a word used to join words, phrases (564), and clauses (565). Conjunctions may be classified according to their use as:

a. **Coördinate,** connecting words or sentences of equal rank (*and,* **et;** *but,* **sed;** *or,* **aut;** *nor,* **neque**).

b. **Subordinate,** connecting a subordinate clause of a sentence with the principal clause (*if,* **sī;** *while,* **dum;** *because,* **quod,** etc.).

c. **Correlative,** used in pairs (*both . . . and,* **et . . . et;** *neither . . . nor,* **neque . . . neque,** etc.).

548. Interjections

An **interjection** is a word used to show emotion. It has no direct relation to any other word in the sentence: *O! Alas! Ah! Oh!*

549. Inflection

The change of form which words undergo to indicate differences in use is called **inflection:** *boy—boys,* **puer—puerī;** *see, saw, seen,* **videō, vīdī, vīsus.** The inflection of nouns, pronouns, and adjectives is called **declension.** They are declined to indicate change in number and case, and sometimes gender. Some pronouns indicate person (542, *a*).

388

550. Number

A noun or pronoun is **singular** when it refers to one person or thing: *girl*, **puella**; *house*, **aedificium**; *mouse*, **mūs**; *tooth*, **dēns**. It is **plural** when it refers to more than one: *girls*, **puellae**; *houses*, **aedificia**; *mice*, **mūrēs**; *teeth*, **dentēs**.

551. Gender

Gender is a distinction in the form of words corresponding to a distinction of sex. It is shown by change of word, by change of ending, or by use of a prefix: *father*, **pater**—*mother*, **māter**; *master*, **dominus**—*mistress*, **domina**; *he-goat*—*she-goat*. The first words given are **masculine**, the second are **feminine**. Most nouns in English have no gender and are therefore **neuter** ("neither" masculine nor feminine).

552. Case

Case is a change in the form of a noun, pronoun, or adjective to show its use in the sentence: *She* (subject) *is here*, **Ea adest**; *I saw her* (object), **Eam vīdī**.

553. Subject and Object

a. The **subject** of a verb is that about which a thing is said (**539**).

b. The **direct object** is that which is directly affected by the action indicated in the transitive active verb: *Anna carries **water***, **Anna *aquam* portat**. The term object is also applied to a word dependent upon a preposition (**546**).

554. Names and Uses of the Cases

a. **Nominative.**—A noun or pronoun used as the subject of a verb is in the **nominative** case: *The farmer calls*, **Agricola vocat**.

b. **Accusative** (Objective).—A noun or pronoun used as the object of a verb or preposition is in the **accusative** case: *I sent a **book** to him*, **Ad eum *librum* mīsī**.

c. **Dative.**—The noun or pronoun that shows for whom or what the direct object is intended is called the **indirect object** and is put in the **dative** case: *I gave **him** a book*, **Eī librum dedī**.

d. **Genitive** (Possessive).—Possession is expressed by the **genitive** case: *the boy's book*, **puerī liber**.

555. Conjugation

The inflection of verbs is called **conjugation**. Verbs are conjugated to indicate *person, number, tense, voice*, and *mood*.

556. Person and Number

A verb must agree with its subject in person and number: *The girl is good*, **Puella** *est* **bona;** *The girls are good*, **Puellae** *sunt* **bonae.**

557. Tense

Tense is time. There are six tenses:

a. The **present** represents an act as taking place now: *He goes.*

b. The **past** represents an act as having already taken place: *He went yesterday.*

c. The **future** represents an act that will occur at some future date: *He will go tomorrow.*

d. The **present perfect** represents an act as completed, but from the point of view of the present: *He has just gone.*

e. The **past perfect** represents an act as completed at some definite time in the past: *He had gone* (before something else occurred).

f. The **future perfect** represents an act as completed at or before some definite time in the future: *He will have gone* (before something else will occur).

558. Progressive and Emphatic Verb Forms

a. **Progressive** (time or action continuous; used with the auxiliary "be"): *They are studying, they were studying, they will be studying, they have been studying, they had been studying, they will have been studying.*

b. **Emphatic** (with the auxiliary "do," used only in the present and past):

    1. Used in questions: *Do (did) you know this?*

    2. Negative: *I do (did) not know it.*

    3. Emphatic: *I do (did) believe it.*

559. Voice

A transitive verb is in the **active voice** when it represents the subject as the doer or agent: *Anna accuses the sailor*, **Anna nautam** *accūsat.*

A transitive verb is in the **passive voice** when it represents the subject as the receiver of the action: *The sailor is accused,* **Nauta** *accūsātur.*

Note.—Intransitive verbs are used only in the active voice in English.

560. Mood

The **indicative mood** is used to state a fact or to ask a question: *Rome is a great city*, **Rōma** *est* **magna urbs;** *Where is Anna?* **Ubi** *est* **Anna?**

561. Infinitive

The **infinitive** is a form of the verb to which *to* is usually prefixed in English: *to go*, *to sing*. It has tense and voice, but not person, number, or mood.

562. Participle

The **participle** is a verbal adjective. As an adjective it modifies a noun or pronoun: *a losing fight*. As a verb it may have an object or adverbial modifiers: *losing his balance, he fell off*. The participles which are used in English are:

ACTIVE		PASSIVE
Present	*seeing*	*being seen*
Past	*having seen*	*seen, having been seen*

563. Synopsis

A **synopsis** is an outline, showing the given verb in a certain person and number in all moods and tenses (and in both voices if the verb is transitive).

564. Phrases

A **phrase** is a group of words without subject and predicate.

One important kind of phrase is the **prepositional phrase**, that is, a preposition together with the word or words which it governs: *in great danger*, **in magnō perīculō**.

565. Clauses

A **clause**, like a phrase, is a part of a sentence but differs from it in having a subject and a predicate.

Clauses are classified as:

a. **Principal**, when used as the leading or independent statement in a sentence: *The girl whom you saw on the street* **is my sister**, **Puella** quam in viā vīdistī *soror mea est.*

b. **Subordinate**, when used as a dependent statement to modify some word in the principal clause: *The girl whom you saw on the street is my sister*, **Puella** *quam in viā vīdistī* soror mea est.

Subordinate clauses are used as single parts of speech:

1. **Substantive** (or **noun**) **clause**: *It pleases me that you came* (your coming), **Mihi grātum est** *quod vēnistī.*

2. **Adjective clause**: *This boy, who is good, will receive a reward* (this good boy), **Hic puer,** *quī bonus est,* **praemium accipiet.**

391

3. **Adverbial clause:** *I gave him the money because he earned it*, Eī pecūniam dedī *quod eam meruit.*

566.   Sentences

a. A **simple sentence** contains one principal clause: *My friend, the farmer, has many horses*, **Amīcus meus, agricola, multōs equōs habet.**

b. A **compound sentence** contains two or more principal clauses connected by the coördinate conjunctions "and," "but," etc.: *My friend, the farmer, has many horses, but I have not seen them*, **Amīcus meus, agricola, multōs equōs habet, sed eōs nōn vīdī.**

c. A **complex sentence** contains one principal clause to which one or more subordinate clauses are joined by subordinate conjunctions or by relative or interrogative pronouns: *My friend, the farmer, has many horses which I have not seen*, **Amīcus meus, agricola, multōs equōs habet quōs nōn vīdī.**

Boy putting a monkey through his tricks. From a Pompeian wall painting

BASIC FORMS

NOUNS

567.

	FIRST DECLENSION (70)		SECOND DECLENSION (95)	
	SINGULAR	PLURAL	SINGULAR	PLURAL
Nom.	via	viae	servus	servī
Gen.	viae	viārum	servī	servōrum
Dat.	viae	viīs	servō	servīs
Acc.	viam	viās	servum	servōs
Abl.	viā	viīs	servō	servīs
(*Voc.*)			(serve)	

568. SECOND DECLENSION (109, 120)

	SING.	PLUR.	SING.	PLUR.	SING.	PLUR.
Nom.	ager	agrī	puer	puerī	signum	signa
Gen.	agrī	agrōrum	puerī	puerōrum	signī	signōrum
Dat.	agrō	agrīs	puerō	puerīs	signō	signīs
Acc.	agrum	agrōs	puerum	puerōs	signum	signa
Abl.	agrō	agrīs	puerō	puerīs	signō	signīs

569. THIRD DECLENSION (332, 348)

	SINGULAR	PLURAL	SINGULAR	PLURAL	SINGULAR	PLURAL
Nom.	mīles	mīlitēs	lēx	lēgēs	corpus	corpora
Gen.	mīlitis	mīlitum	lēgis	lēgum	corporis	corporum
Dat.	mīlitī	mīlitibus	lēgī	lēgibus	corporī	corporibus
Acc.	mīlitem	mīlitēs	lēgem	lēgēs	corpus	corpora
Abl.	mīlite	mīlitibus	lēge	lēgibus	corpore	corporibus

I-STEMS (353)

	SINGULAR	PLURAL	SINGULAR	PLURAL
Nom.	cīvis	cīvēs	mare	maria
Gen.	cīvis	cīvium	maris	marium
Dat.	cīvī	cīvibus	marī	maribus
Acc.	cīvem	cīvēs (–īs)	mare	maria
Abl.	cīve	cīvibus	marī	maribus

393

	SINGULAR	PLURAL	SINGULAR	PLURAL
Nom.	cāsus	cāsūs	cornū	cornua
Gen.	cāsūs	cāsuum	cornūs	cornuum
Dat.	cāsuī	cāsibus	cornū	cornibus
Acc.	cāsum	cāsūs	cornū	cornua
Abl.	cāsū	cāsibus	cornū	cornibus

571. FIFTH DECLENSION (510)

	SINGULAR	PLURAL	SINGULAR	PLURAL
Nom.	diēs	diēs	rēs	rēs
Gen.	diēī	diērum	reī	rērum
Dat.	diēī	diēbus	reī	rēbus
Acc.	diem	diēs	rem	rēs
Abl.	diē	diēbus	rē	rēbus

572. IRREGULAR NOUNS (427, 461, 506)

	SING.	PLUR.	SING.	SING.	PLUR.
Nom.	vīs	vīrēs	nēmō	domus	domūs
Gen.	——	vīrium	(nūllīus)	domūs (–ī)	domuum (–ōrum)
Dat.	——	vīribus	nēminī	domuī (–ō)	domibus
Acc.	vim	vīrēs (–īs)	nēminem	domum	domōs (–ūs)
Abl.	vī	vīribus	(nūllō)	domō (–ū)	domibus
(Loc.)				(domī)	

ADJECTIVES

573. FIRST AND SECOND DECLENSIONS (70, 95, 109, 120)

	SINGULAR			PLURAL		
	M.	F.	N.	M.	F.	N.
Nom.	magnus	magna	magnum	magnī	magnae	magna
Gen.	magnī	magnae	magnī	magnōrum	magnārum	magnōrum
Dat.	magnō	magnae	magnō	magnīs	magnīs	magnīs
Acc.	magnum	magnam	magnum	magnōs	magnās	magna
Abl.	magnō	magnā	magnō	magnīs	magnīs	magnīs
(Voc.)	(magne)					

Nom.	līber	lībera	līberum	noster	nostra	nostrum
Gen.	līberī	līberae	līberī	nostrī	nostrae	nostrī
Dat.	līberō	līberae	līberō	nostrō	nostrae	nostrō
Acc.	līberum	līberam	līberum	nostrum	nostram	nostrum
Abl.	līberō	līberā	līberō	nostrō	nostrā	nostrō

Plural, līberī, līberae, lībera, etc.   Plural, nostrī, –ae, –a, etc.

a. THREE ENDINGS

| | SINGULAR | | | PLURAL | | |
	M.	F.	N.	M.	F.	N.
Nom.	ācer	ācris	ācre	ācrēs	ācrēs	ācria
Gen.	ācris	ācris	ācris	ācrium	ācrium	ācrium
Dat.	ācrī	ācrī	ācrī	ācribus	ācribus	ācribus
Acc.	ācrem	ācrem	ācre	ācrēs (–īs)	ācrēs (–īs)	ācria
Abl.	ācrī	ācrī	ācrī	ācribus	ācribus	ācribus

b. TWO ENDINGS

| | SINGULAR | | PLURAL | |
	M.F.	N.	M.F.	N.
Nom.	fortis	forte	fortēs	fortia
Gen.	fortis	fortis	fortium	fortium
Dat.	fortī	fortī	fortibus	fortibus
Acc.	fortem	forte	fortēs (–īs)	fortia
Abl.	fortī	fortī	fortibus	fortibus

c. ONE ENDING

| | SINGULAR | | PLURAL | |
	M.F.	N.	M.F.	N.
Nom.	pār	pār	parēs	paria
Gen.	paris	paris	parium	parium
Dat.	parī	parī	paribus	paribus
Acc.	parem	pār	parēs (–īs)	paria
Abl.	parī	parī	paribus	paribus

575. PRESENT PARTICIPLE (419)

| | SINGULAR | | PLURAL | |
	M.F.	N.	M.F.	N.
Nom.	portāns	portāns	portantēs	portantia
Gen.	portantis	portantis	portantium	portantium
Dat.	portantī	portantī	portantibus	portantibus
Acc.	portantem	portāns	portantēs (–īs)	portantia
Abl.	portante (–ī)	portante (–ī)	portantibus	portantibus

576. NUMERALS (409, 483, 484)

	M.	F.	N.	M.F.	N.
Nom.	ūnus	ūna	ūnum	trēs	tria
Gen.	ūnīus	ūnīus	ūnīus	trium	trium
Dat.	ūnī	ūnī	ūnī	tribus	tribus
Acc.	ūnum	ūnam	ūnum	trēs	tria
Abl.	ūnō	ūnā	ūnō	tribus	tribus

	M.	F.	N.	M.F.	N.
Nom.	duo	duae	duo	mīlle	mīlia
Gen.	duōrum	duārum	duōrum	mīlle	mīlium
Dat.	duōbus	duābus	duōbus	mīlle	mīlibus
Acc.	duōs	duās	duo	mīlle	mīlia
Abl.	duōbus	duābus	duōbus	mīlle	mīlibus

Alius has **aliud** in the nom. and acc. sing. neuter; plural regular

577. COMPARISON OF ADJECTIVES AND ADVERBS

a. REGULAR ADJECTIVES (453, 464, 465)

POSITIVE	COMPARATIVE	SUPERLATIVE
altus, –a, –um	altior, altius	altissimus, –a, –um
fortis, forte	fortior, –ius	fortissimus, –a, –um
līber, –era, –erum	līberior, –ius	līberrimus, –a, –um
ācer, ācris, ācre	ācrior, –ius	ācerrimus, –a, –um
facilis, facile	facilior, –ius	facillimus, –a, –um

b. IRREGULAR ADJECTIVES (471)

POSITIVE	COMPARATIVE	SUPERLATIVE
bonus, –a, –um	melior, –ius	optimus, –a, –um
malus, –a, –um	peior, –ius	pessimus, –a, –um
magnus, –a, –um	maior, –ius	maximus, –a, –um
parvus, –a, –um	minor, –us	minimus, –a, –um
multus, –a, –um	——, plūs	plūrimus, –a, –um

c. ADVERBS (459, 464, 465)

POSITIVE	COMPARATIVE	SUPERLATIVE
altē	altius	altissimē
līberē	līberius	līberrimē
fortiter	fortius	fortissimē
facile	facilius	facillimē

578. DECLENSION OF COMPARATIVES (454, 471)

	SINGULAR		PLURAL	
	M.F.	N.	M.F.	N.
Nom.	altior	altius	altiōrēs	altiōra
Gen.	altiōris	altiōris	altiōrum	altiōrum
Dat.	altiōrī	altiōrī	altiōribus	altiōribus
Acc.	altiōrem	altius	altiōrēs	altiōra
Abl.	altiōre	altiōre	altiōribus	altiōribus

ACTIVE VOICE		PASSIVE VOICE	

ACTIVE VOICE

PERFECT (219)
I taught, I have taught, etc.

docuī	docuimus
docuistī	docuistis
docuit	docuērunt (–ēre)

PASSIVE VOICE

PERFECT (251)
I was taught, I have been taught, etc.

doctus (–a, –um) { sum / es / est }   doctī (–ae, –a) { sumus / estis / sunt }

PAST PERFECT (230)
I had taught, etc.

docueram	docuerāmus
docuerās	docuerātis
docuerat	docuerant

PAST PERFECT (252)
I had been taught, etc.

doctus (–a, –um) { eram / erās / erat }   doctī (–ae, –a) { erāmus / erātis / erant }

FUTURE PERFECT (230)
I shall have taught, etc.

docuerō	docuerimus
docueris	docueritis
docuerit	docuerint

FUTURE PERFECT (252)
I shall have been taught, etc.

doctus (–a, –um) { erō / eris / erit }   doctī (–ae, –a) { erimus / eritis / erunt }

INFINITIVE (258, 425, 431)

Present docēre, *to teach*
Perfect docuisse, *to have taught*

Future doctūrus esse, *to be going to teach*

docērī, *to be taught*
doctus esse, *to have been taught*

PARTICIPLE (249, 419, 420)

Present docēns, *Gen.* –entis, *teaching*
Perfect

Future doctūrus, –a, –um, *going to teach*

doctus, –a, –um, *(having been) taught*

PRESENT IMPERATIVE (71)

2d sing. docē, *teach*
2d plur. docēte, *teach*

Principal Parts: **pōnō, pōněre, posuī, positus**
(Stems: **pōně–, posu–, posit–**)

ACTIVE VOICE	PASSIVE VOICE

INDICATIVE

PRESENT (144)
I place, etc.

		PRESENT (201)	
pōnō	pōnimus	*I am placed*, etc.	
pōnis	pōnitis	pōnor	pōnimur
pōnit	pōnunt	pōneris (–re)	pōniminī
		pōnitur	pōnuntur

IMPERFECT (144)
I was placing, etc.

		IMPERFECT (201)	
		I was (being) placed, etc.	
pōnēbam	pōnēbāmus	pōnēbar	pōnēbāmur
pōnēbās	pōnēbātis	pōnēbāris (–re)	pōnēbāminī
pōnēbat	pōnēbant	pōnēbātur	pōnēbantur

FUTURE (171)
I shall place, etc.

		FUTURE (201)	
		I shall be placed, etc.	
pōnam	pōnēmus	pōnar	pōnēmur
pōnēs	pōnētis	pōnēris (–re)	pōnēminī
pōnet	pōnent	pōnētur	pōnentur

PERFECT (219)
I placed, I have placed, etc.

posuī	posuimus	
posuistī	posuistis	
posuit	posuērunt (–ēre)	

PERFECT (251)
I was placed, I have been placed, etc.

positus (–a, –um) { sum / es / est } positī (–ae, –a) { sumus / estis / sunt }

PAST PERFECT (230)
I had placed, etc.

posueram	posuerāmus
posuerās	posuerātis
posuerat	posuerant

PAST PERFECT (252)
I had been placed, etc.

positus (–a, –um) { eram / erās / erat } positī (–ae, –a) { erāmus / erātis / erant }

FUTURE PERFECT (230)
I shall have placed, etc.

posuerō	posuerimus
posueris	posueritis
posuerit	posuerint

FUTURE PERFECT (252)
I shall have been placed, etc.

positus (–a, –um) { erō / eris / erit } positī (–ae, –a) { erimus / eritis / erunt }

ACTIVE VOICE	PASSIVE VOICE

INFINITIVE (144, 258, 425, 431)

Present pōnere, *to place*
Perfect posuisse, *to have placed*

pōnī, *to be placed*
positus esse, *to have been placed*

Future positūrus esse, *to be going to place*

PARTICIPLE (249, 419, 420)

Present pōnēns, *Gen.* –entis, *placing*
Perfect

positus, –a, –um, *(having been) placed*

Future positūrus, –a, –um, *going to place*

PRESENT IMPERATIVE (144)

2d sing. pōne, *place*
2d plur. pōnite, *place*

587.   FOURTH CONJUGATION

Principal Parts: mūniō, mūnīre, mūnīvī, mūnītus
(Stems: mūnī–, mūnīv–, mūnīt–)

INDICATIVE

PRESENT (155)
I fortify, etc.

mūniō	mūnīmus
mūnīs	mūnītis
mūnit	mūniunt

PRESENT (201)
I am fortified, etc.

mūnior	mūnīmur
mūnīris (–re)	mūnīminī
mūnītur	mūniuntur

IMPERFECT (155)
I was fortifying, etc.

mūniēbam	mūniēbāmus
mūniēbās	mūniēbātis
mūniēbat	mūniēbant

IMPERFECT (201)
I was (being) fortified, etc.

mūniēbar	mūniēbāmur
mūniēbāris (–re)	mūniēbāminī
mūniēbātur	mūniēbantur

FUTURE (182)
I shall fortify, etc.

mūniam	mūniēmus
mūniēs	mūniētis
mūniet	mūnient

FUTURE (201)
I shall be fortified, etc.

mūniar	mūniēmur
mūniēris (–re)	mūniēminī
mūniētur	mūnientur

403

<table>
<tr><td colspan="2" align="center">ACTIVE VOICE</td><td colspan="2" align="center">PASSIVE VOICE</td></tr>
</table>

	PERFECT (219)		PERFECT (251)
	I fortified, I have fortified, etc.		*I was fortified, I have been fortified*, etc.

mūnīvī	mūnīvimus
mūnīvistī	mūnīvistis
mūnīvit	mūnīvērunt (–ēre)

mūnītus (–a, –um) { sum / es / est } mūnītī (–ae, –a) { sumus / estis / sunt }

	PAST PERFECT (230)		PAST PERFECT (252)
	I had fortified, etc.		*I had been fortified*, etc.

mūnīveram	mūnīverāmus
mūnīverās	mūnīverātis
mūnīverat	mūnīverant

mūnītus (–a, –um) { eram / erās / erat } mūnītī (–ae, –a) { erāmus / erātis / erant }

	FUTURE PERFECT (230)		FUTURE PERFECT (252)
	I shall have fortified, etc.		*I shall have been fortified*, etc.

mūnīverō	mūnīverimus
mūnīveris	mūnīveritis
mūnīverit	mūnīverint

mūnītus (–a, –um) { erō / eris / erit } mūnītī (–ae, –a) { erimus / eritis / erunt }

INFINITIVE (258, 425, 431)

Present mūnīre, *to fortify* mūnīrī, *to be fortified*
Perfect mūnīvisse, *to have fortified* mūnītus esse, *to have been fortified*

Future mūnītūrus esse, *to be going to fortify*

PARTICIPLE (249, 419, 420)

Present mūniēns, *Gen.* mūnientis, *fortifying*

Perfect mūnītus, –a, –um, (*having been*) *fortified*

Future mūnītūrus, –a, –um, *going to fortify*

PRESENT IMPERATIVE (155)

2d sing. mūnī, *fortify*
2d plur. mūnīte, *fortify*

Third Conjugation –iō Verbs

Principal Parts: **capiō, capĕre, cēpī, captus**
(Stems: **capĕ–, cēp–, capt–**)

ACTIVE VOICE   PASSIVE VOICE

INDICATIVE

PRESENT (154)   PRESENT (201)

capiō	capimus	capior	capimur
capis	capitis	caperis (–re)	capiminī
capit	capiunt	capitur	capiuntur.

IMPERFECT (154)   IMPERFECT (201)

capiēbam, etc.   capiēbar, etc.

FUTURE (182)   FUTURE (201)

capiam	capiēmus	capiar	capiēmur
capiēs	capiētis	capiēris (–re)	capiēminī
capiet	capient	capiētur	capientur

PERFECT (219)   PERFECT (251)

cēpī, etc.   captus sum, etc.

PAST PERFECT (230)   PAST PERFECT (252)

cēperam, etc.   captus eram, etc.

FUTURE PERFECT (230)   FUTURE PERFECT (252)

cēperō, etc.   captus erō, etc.

INFINITIVE (258, 425, 431)

Present	capere	capī
Perfect	cēpisse	captus esse
Future	captūrus esse	

PARTICIPLE (249, 419, 420)

Present	capiēns, *Gen.* capientis	
Perfect		captus, –a, –um
Future	captūrus, –a, –um	

PRESENT IMPERATIVE (154)

2d sing. cape
2d plur. capite

Principal Parts: **sum, esse, fuī, futūrus**

INDICATIVE

PRESENT (114)

sum, *I am*	sumus, *we are*
es, *you are*	estis, *you are*
est, *he is*	sunt, *they are*

IMPERFECT (132)

eram, *I was*, etc.	erāmus
erās	erātis
erat	erant

FUTURE (132)

erō, *I shall be*, etc.	erimus
eris	eritis
erit	erunt

PERFECT (224)

fuī, *I was*, etc.	fuimus
fuistī	fuistis
fuit	fuērunt (-ēre)

PAST PERFECT (243)

fueram, *I had been*, etc.	fuerāmus
fuerās	fuerātis
fuerat	fuerant

FUTURE PERFECT (243)

fuerō, *I shall have been*, etc.	fuerimus
fueris	fueritis
fuerit	fuerint

INFINITIVE (114, 425, 431)

Pres. esse, *to be*
Perf. fuisse, *to have been*
Fut. futūrus esse, *to be going to be*

PARTICIPLE (420)

———

futūrus, -a, -um, *going to be*

IMPERATIVE   2*d sing.* es, *be*   2*d plur.* este, *be*

---

590.   Principal Parts: **possum, posse, potuī, ——**

INDICATIVE (312)

Pres.	possum, *I am able, I can*, etc.	possumus
	potes	potestis
	potest	possunt
Impf.	poteram, etc., *I was able, I could*, etc.	
Fut.	poterō, etc., *I shall be able*, etc.	
Perf.	potuī, etc., *I was able, I could*, etc.	
Past P.	potueram, etc., *I had been able*, etc.	
Fut. P.	potuerō, etc., *I shall have been able*, etc.	

INFINITIVE (314, 425)

Pres. posse, *to be able*
Perf. potuisse, *to have been able*

PARTICIPLE (419)

potēns, *Gen.* -entis (adj.), *powerful*

BASIC SYNTAX

AGREEMENT

1. **Adjectives.**—Adjectives and participles agree in number, gender, and case with the nouns which they modify (15, 249).

2. **Adjectives as Substantives.**—Sometimes adjectives are used substantively (193).

3. **Verbs.**—Verbs agree in person and number with their subjects (31).
 Note.—When two singular subjects are connected by **aut, aut . . . aut, neque . . . neque,** the verb is singular (207).

4. **Relative Pronoun.**—The relative pronoun agrees in gender and number with its antecedent but its case depends upon its use in its own clause (283).

5. **Appositives.**—Appositives agree in case (149).

NOUN SYNTAX

592. Nominative

1. **Subject.**—The subject of a verb is in the nominative (10, *a*).

2. **Predicate.**—A noun or adjective used in the predicate after a linking verb (*is*, *are*, *seem*, etc.) to complete its meaning is in the nominative (10, *b*).

593. Genitive

1. **Possession.**—Possession is expressed by the genitive (48).

2. **Description.**—The genitive, if modified by an adjective, may be used to describe a person or thing (515).

594. Dative

1. **Indirect Object.**—The indirect object of a verb is in the dative. It is used with verbs of *giving*, *reporting*, *telling*, etc. (58).

2. **With Special Verbs.**—The dative is used with a few intransitive verbs, such as **noceō** (529).

3. **With Adjectives.**—Certain adjectives, as **amīcus, pār, similis,** and their opposites, govern the dative (466).

595. Accusative

1. **Direct Object.**—The direct object of a transitive verb is in the accusative (29).

2. **Extent.**—Extent of time or space is expressed by the accusative (498).

3. **Place to Which.**—The accusative with **ad** (*to*) or **in** (*into*) expresses place to which (117).

4. **Subject of Infinitive.**—The subject of an infinitive is in the accusative (244).

5. **With Prepositions.**—The prepositions **ad, ante, apud, circum, contrā, inter, ob, per, post, super,** and **trāns** take the accusative; also **in** and **sub** when they show the direction toward which a thing moves.

596.   Ablative
(For summary of ablative uses see 375)

1. **From Which.**—The ablative with **ab, dē,** or **ex** expresses place from which (105).

2. **Agent.**—The ablative with **ā** or **ab** is used with a passive verb to show the person by whom anything is done (206).

3. **Accompaniment.**—The ablative with **cum** expresses accompaniment (177).

4. **Manner.**—The ablative of manner with **cum** describes how something is done. **Cum** may be omitted, as a rule, only if an adjective is used with the noun (289).

5. **Means.**—The means by which a thing is done is expressed by the ablative without a preposition (65).

6. **Description.**—The ablative without a preposition is used (like the genitive) to describe a person or thing (515).

7. **Place Where.**—The ablative with **in** expresses place where (88).

8. **Time When.**—Time when is expressed by the ablative without a preposition (389).

9. **Respect.**—The ablative without a preposition is used to tell in what respect the statement applies (368).

10. **Absolute.**—A noun in the ablative used with a participle, adjective, or other noun in the same case and having no grammatical connection with the subject or predicate is called an ablative absolute (337).

11. **With Prepositions.**—The ablative is used with the prepositions **ab, cum, dē, ex, prae, prō, sine;** also with **in** and **sub** when they indicate place where.

597.   Vocative

The **vocative** is used in addressing a person (102).

VERB SYNTAX

598.   Tenses

1. **Imperfect.**—*Repeated, customary,* or *continuous* action in the past is expressed by the imperfect (225).

2. **Perfect.**—The perfect describes an act as performed once. It is translated by the English past, occasionally by *has* or *have* (**217, 225**).

599. Participles

1. The tenses of the participle (present, perfect, future) indicate time *present, past,* or *future* from the standpoint of the main verb (**249, 419, 420**).

2. Perfect participles are often used as simple adjectives and, like adjectives, may be used substantively (**311**).

3. The Latin participle is often a *one-word substitute* for a subordinate clause in English introduced by *who* or *which, when* or *after, since* or *because, although,* and *if* (**323**).

600. Infinitive

1. The infinitive is a verbal indeclinable neuter noun, and as such it may be used as the subject of a verb (**133,** *a*).

2. With many verbs the infinitive may be used as a direct object, like other nouns (sometimes called the **complementary infinitive**) (**134**).

3. Certain verbs such as **iubeō** and **doceō** take an infinitive as object, often with a noun or pronoun subject in the accusative (**244**).

4. Statements that convey indirectly the thoughts or words of another, used as the objects of verbs of *saying, thinking, knowing, hearing, perceiving,* and the like, require subjects in the accusative and verbs in the infinitive (**432**).

601. Imperative

Commands are expressed by the imperative (**71**).

602.   The Romance Languages

The Romance (**Rōmānus,** *Roman*) languages—French, Spanish, Italian, Portuguese, and Rumanian—are modern forms of Latin. Fully ninety per cent of the words in them are derived from Latin. The Latin student, therefore, who is familiar with the principles that govern vowel and consonant changes, as well as other peculiarities of word transfer, can recognize at a glance a large proportion of words in these languages derived from classical (as opposed to late) Latin.

The following pages are intended primarily for older students who have elected Latin after having begun the study of French or Spanish. These rules will, moreover, be found invaluable for reference by the Latin student who may later elect French, Spanish, or Italian (see 1).

603.   Pronunciation

The distinctions in sound between long and short **e** and **o** (531, *a*) are preserved in Romance, though not in all derived words.

Spanish and Italian have no silent letters, except **h,** thus resembling Latin (**h** was weakly sounded in Latin).

604.   Syllable Division

Syllable division in Romance is generally according to the Latin rule (536).

605.   Gender

Nouns which are masculine or feminine in Latin retain their gender in Romance:

Lat.	poēta, *m.*	liber, *m.*	mōns, *m.*	lībertās, *f.*	manus, *f.*
Fr.	poète	livre	mont	liberté	main
Sp.	poeta	libro	monte	libertad	mano
Ital.	poeta	libro	monte	libertà	mano

Exception: Most Latin masculines in –or become feminine in French: **error,** *erreur.*

Nouns which are neuter in Latin become masculine in Romance:

Lat.	*n.*	verbum	tempus
Fr.	*m.*	verbe	temps
Sp.	*m.*	verbo	tiempo
Ital.	*m.*	verbo	tempo

Exception: Many Latin neuters, especially those which were commonly used in the plural (which ends in –a, like the feminine singular), become feminine singular in Romance:

Lat.	n. plur.	arma	data	pecora
Fr.	f. sing.	arme	date	pécore
Sp.	f. sing.	arma	data	pécora
Ital.	f. sing.	arme	data	pecora

FRENCH THROUGH LATIN

606. Accent

The French stress often preserves the Latin accent. The syllables after the accented syllable in Latin were dropped or became silent in French, which fact explains why the French stress is usually on the last syllable.

607. Vocabulary

Many Latin words remain unchanged in French, as in English: *agenda, alibi, errata, humus, omnibus, ultimatum,* etc.

608. Loss of Letters

1. The final syllable or letters of many Latin words are lost in French or changed to silent **e**: *ami* (**amīcum**[1]), *mont* (**montem**), *terre* (**terram**).
2. An unaccented short vowel within a word is often lost: *homme* (**hom*i*nem**), *livrer* (**līberāre**), *peuple* (**pop*u*lus**).
3. A consonant between two vowels is often lost: *cruel* (**crūd*e*lem**), *dire* (**dīcere**).
4. The first of two consonants is often lost: *frère* (**frātrem**).

609. Vowels

The Latin vowels often remain unchanged in French, but the following changes are to be noted:

(A) Change to a single vowel
1. a sometimes becomes e: *père* (**patrem**), *aimer* (**amāre**), *gré* (**grātum**), *mer* (**mare**).
2. e sometimes becomes i: *six* (**sex**), *lire* (**legere**).
3. i sometimes becomes e: *ferme* (**f*i*rmum**), *lettre* (**l*i*tteram**).
4. u sometimes becomes o: *nombre* (**n*u*merum**), *onde* (**u*ndam**).
5. au sometimes becomes o: *chose* (**ca*u*sam**).
6. ae and oe are treated as e.

---

[1] The accusative of all Latin nouns and adjectives is given because the Romance forms are generally derived from it, not from the nominative.

(B) Change to two vowels

This was very common in accented syllables (cf. 407, 507).

1. ai is from a: *aimer* (a**mā**re), *main* (m**a**num).
2. ei is from e or i: *plein* (pl**ē**num), *seing* (s**i**gnum).
3. oi is from e, i, o, or u: *roi* (r**ē**gem), *voie* (v**i**am), *gloire* (gl**ō**riam), *croix* (cr**u**x).
4. ui is from o or u: *puis* (p**o**st), *suis* (s**u**m).
5. au is from al, and eau from el: *haut* (**al**tum), *vaut* (v**al**et), *beau* (be**l**lum).
6. eu, oeu, is from o: *seul* (s**ō**lum), *cœur* (c**o**r).
7. ou is from o or u: *nous* (n**ō**s), *prouver* (prob**ā**re), *jour* (di**u**rnum).
8. ie is from e: *bien* (b**e**ne), *pied* (ped**e**m).

610.   Consonants

1. b and p sometimes become v: *livre* (li**b**rum), *avril* (a**p**rīlem).
2. p and v sometimes become b or f: *double* (du**p**licem), *chef* (ca**p**ut), *neuf* (no**v**um).
3. ct sometimes becomes it: *fait* (fa**ct**um), *huit* (o**ct**ō).
4. t followed by i and a vowel in certain cases becomes s: *raison* (ra**tī**ōnem).
5. s before a consonant is dropped and the preceding vowel receives a circumflex accent: *maître* (ma**g**istrum), *êtes* (e**s**tis).
6. c before a, especially at the beginning of words, becomes ch: *char* (**c**arrum), *chef* (**c**aput), *chose* (**c**ausam).
7. Initial sc, sp, and st become esc, esp, and est: *espace* (**sp**atium), *espèce* (**sp**eciem).

In some words the s is dropped and the e has an acute accent: *étude* (**s**tudium).

611.   Word Formation

The Latin prefixes used in French have undergone the same changes that have been noted for English in this book (cf. especially com-, con-, en-, em-, sur-, tra-). In addition, attention is called to the change from dis- to de-, dés- (déshonneur), inter- to entre- (entrevoir), per- to par- (parfait), pro- to pour- (poursuivre), sub- to sou-, sous- (souvenir), ultra- to outre- (outremer).

Latin suffixes in French show much the same form as in English. Note, however, the change of –ātum to é (am**ā**tum, aimé), –ōrem to –eur (auct**ō**rem, auteur), –ōsum to –eux (ōti**ō**sum, oiseux), –tātem to –té (līber**tā**tem, liberté).

412

612. Inflection

1. Nouns and adjectives of the Latin first declension in –a end in silent –e in French: *chose neuve* (**causa nova**).

2. The French definite article, *le, la,* is derived from the last syllable of **ille, illa.**

3. The comparative forms of Latin irregular adjectives are to some extent preserved in French: *meilleur* (**melior**), *moins* (**minus**), *pire* (**peior**).

4. The same forms constitute the principal parts of verbs in French as in Latin, with the addition of the present participle.

5. Most French verbs belong to the first conjugation, with infinitive in –er. This corresponds to the Latin first conjugation, with infinitive in –āre, but includes a number of verbs of the Latin second and third conjugations; the second, with infinitive in –ir, corresponds to the Latin fourth conjugation (–īre); the third, with infinitive in –re, corresponds to the Latin third conjugation (–ĕre).

6. The Latin personal endings have undergone considerable change in French. The endings of the French past definite can easily be traced to those of the Latin perfect. Many of the irregular verbs in French preserve forms derived from the Latin:

suis	(**sum**)	*sommes*	(**sumus**)
es	(**es**)	*êtes*	(**estis**)
est	(**est**)	*sont*	(**sunt**)

SPANISH THROUGH LATIN

613.   Accent

Accent is greatly simplified in Spanish if the student understands Latin accent. The so-called irregular accent of nouns and adjectives in Spanish preserves the Latin accent of the accusative case:

Lat.	a'mant	venī're	a'nimum	diffi'cilem	prōpo'situm
Sp.	aman	venir	ánimo	difícil	propósito

614.   Vocabulary

Hundreds of words in Spanish are either identical with the original Latin form or resemble it so closely that one who knows Latin can understand their meaning at a glance, without knowing the principles that govern word transfer:

Lat.	aqua	arma	causa	hōra	patria	trēs	victōria	dare	ūtilis
Sp.	agua	arma	causa	hora	patria	tres	victoria	dar	útil

Loss of Letters

1. Final letters and syllables are often lost in Spanish, but not to the same extent as in French: *amigo* (**amīcum**), *monte* (**montem**), *útil* (**ūtilem**).

2. An unaccented short vowel within a word is sometimes lost: *hombre* (**hom*i*nem**), *librar* (**līberāre**), *pueblo* (**pop*u*lum**).

3. A consonant (especially **b, d, g, h**) between vowels is sometimes lost: *leer* (**le*g*ere**), *creer* (**crē*d*ere**), *traer* (**tra*h*ere**).

4. The first of two consonants is sometimes lost, especially **n** before **s**: *escrito* (**scr*ī*ptum**), *autor* (**auc*t*ōrem**), *isla* (**ī*n*sulam**).

5. Double consonants become single: *oficio* (**officium**), *nulo* (**nū*ll*um**), *permitir* (**permit*t*ere**). Double **n** becomes **ñ**: *año* (**an*n*um**); **ñ** is also for **ni**, etc.: *señor* (**sen*i*or**).

616. **Vowels**

The Latin vowels often remain unchanged in Spanish, but the following changes are to be noted:

(*A*) *Change to another vowel*
1. Short **i** sometimes becomes **e**: *lengua* (**l*i*nguam**), *letra* (**l*i*tteram**), *menos* (**m*i*nus**).
2. Short **u** sometimes becomes **o**: *onda* (***u*ndam**), *romper* (**r*u*mpere**).
3. **au** sometimes becomes **o**: *oído* (***au*dītum**), *cosa* (**c*au*sam**).
4. **ae** and **oe** are treated as **e**.

(*B*) *Change to two vowels*
1. Accented short **e** becomes **ie**: *bien* (**bene**), *cielo* (**c*ae*lum**), *cierto* (**certum**).
2. Accented short **o** becomes **ue**: *bueno* (**bonum**), *cuerpo* (**corpus**), *nuevo* (**novem**).

617. **Consonants**

1. **c** sometimes becomes **g**: *amigo* (**amīcum**).
2. **p** sometimes becomes **b**: *pueblo* (**populum**).
3. **t** sometimes becomes **d**: *maduro* (**mātūrum**), *padre* (**patrem**).
4. **ct** becomes **ch**: *dicho* (**dictum**), *hecho* (**factum**), *ocho* (**octō**).
5. **li** becomes **j**: *consejo* (**cōnsil*i*um**), *hijo* (**fīl*i*um**), *mejor* (**mel*i*or**).
6. Initial **f** sometimes becomes **h**: *hacer* (*f*acere), *hijo* (*f*īlium).
7. Initial **cl** and **pl** sometimes become **ll**: *llamar* (*cl*āmāre), *llano* (*pl*ānum).
8. Initial **sc, sp,** and **st** become **esc, esp, est**: *escribir* (**scrībere**), *esperar* (**spērāre**), *estar* (**stāre**).

The Latin prefixes used in Spanish are easily recognizable. Note the following changes which sometimes occur: **ex–** to **ej–** (*ejercer*), **dis–** to **des–** (*descrédito*), **super–** to **sobre–** (*sobrehumano*).

The Latin suffixes are also used in Spanish. Note the following changes: **–ātum** to **–ado** (*amado*), **–tātem, –tūtem,** to **–tad, –tud** (*libertad, virtud*), **–tiōnem** to **–cion** (*oración*), **–tiam** to **–cia** (*gracia*).

619.   Inflection

1. Nouns and adjectives of the Latin first declension ending in **–a** retain the **–a** in Spanish: *tierra nueva* (**terr***a* **nov***a*).

2. Nouns of the Latin second declension in **–us** and **–um** end in **–o** in Spanish: *carro* (**carr***us*), *reino* (**rēgn***um*).

3. The comparative and superlative forms of Latin irregular adjectives are to some extent preserved in Spanish: *peor* (**peior**), *mayor* (**maior**), *óptimo* (**optimus**), *libérrimo* (**līberrimus**).

4. The Spanish first conjugation, with infinitive in **–ar,** corresponds to the Latin first conjugation (**–āre**); the second, with infinitive in **–er,** corresponds to the Latin second and third conjugations (**–ēre, –ĕre**); the third, with infinitive in **–ir,** corresponds to the Latin fourth conjugation (**–īre**) but also includes many verbs of the third conjugation.

5. Many of the tenses of the Spanish verb are very much like the Latin. Cf. the imperfect:

Lat.	amābam	amābās	amābat	amābāmus	amābātis	amābant
Sp.	amaba	amabas	amaba	amábamos	amabais	amaban

Observe that final **–m** and **–t** of the personal endings of Latin verbs disappear in Spanish.

The Spanish past definite is very similar to the Latin perfect.

6. The Latin perfect participle will suggest at once the past participle of the Spanish verb, if it is irregular: **impressus,** Sp. *impreso;* **scrīptus,** Sp. *escrito.*

ITALIAN THROUGH LATIN

620.   Vocabulary

Hundreds of Italian words are either identical with the original Latin form or resemble it so closely that one who knows Latin can understand them at a glance, without knowing the principles that govern word transfer. Even the accent is preserved:

Lat.	altus	aqua	causa	dare	littera	ūtilis	victōria	vīta
Ital.	alto	acqua	causa	dare	lettera	utile	vittoria	vita

621. Loss of Letters

1. Final consonants are usually lost in Italian so that most words end in a vowel: *amico* (**amīcum**), *fece* (**fēcit**), *utile* (**ūtilem**). Syllables are lost less often: *libertà* (**lībertātem**), *fu* (**fuit**), *può* (**potest**).

2. An unaccented short vowel within a word is sometimes lost: *donna* (**dom*i*nam**), *posto* (**pos*i*tum**), *altro* (**alterum**), *conte* (**com*i*tem**).

3. h is generally lost: *onore* (**h*onōrem**), *ora* (**h*ōram**).

4. g is sometimes lost: *intero* (**integrum**), *maestro* (**magistrum**).

5. n is lost before s: *mese* (**mēnsem**).

622. Vowels

Many Latin vowels remain unchanged in Italian except as follows:

(A) *In accented syllables*

1. Short e usually becomes ie before a single consonant or another vowel: *dieci* (**decem**), *tiene* (**tenet**), *miei* (**meī**).

2. Short i often becomes e: *lettera* (**litteram**), *meno* (**m*i*nus**), *detto* (**d*i*ctum**).

3. Short o usually becomes uo before a single consonant or a vowel: *buono* (**bonum**), *nuovo* (**novum**), *luogo* (**locum**), *muove* (**movet**).

4. Short u often becomes o: *molto* (**m*u*ltum**), *secondo* (**secundum**), *correre* (**c*u*rrere**).

5. au sometimes becomes o: *cosa* (**c*au*sam**), *oro* (**a*u*rum**), *o* (**a*u*t**).

6. ae and oe are treated as e.

(B) *In unaccented syllables*

1. e (long or short) sometimes becomes i: *sicuro* (**sēcurum**), *rimanere* (**remanēre**), *migliore* (**meliōrem**).

2. u (long or short) sometimes becomes o: *popolo* (**pop*u*l*u*m**), *sottrarre* (**s*u*btrahere**).

3. au becomes u or a: *udire* (**a*u*dīre**), *agosto* (**A*u*gustum**).

623. Consonants

1. Italian very carefully prolongs double consonants in pronunciation. Sometimes it doubles a Latin single consonant: *tutto* (**tōtum**), *legge* (**legit**).

2. b and p sometimes become v: *avere* (**habēre**), *scrivere* (**scrībere**), *provare* (**probāre**), *lavoro* (**labōrem**).

3. c sometimes becomes g: *lagrima* (**lacrima**), *luogo* (**locum**).

4. t sometimes becomes d: *madre* (**mātrem**), *podestà* (**potestātem**).

5. ph becomes f: *filosofia* (**philosophiam**).

6. x becomes s or ss: *prossimo* (pro*x*imum), *sasso* (sa*x*um), *destro* (de*x*trum).

7. ct and pt become tt: *otto* (o*ct*ō), *scritto* (scrī*pt*um), *detto* (di*ct*um).

8. di, ti, and ci before a vowel become z or zz: *grazia* (grā*ti*am), *mezzo* (me*di*um), *prezzo* (pre*ti*um), *uffizio* (offi*ci*um), *terzo* (ter*ti*um).

9. l after a consonant becomes i: *fiume* (f*l*ūmen), *piano* (p*l*ānum), *più* (p*l*ūs), *tempio* (temp*l*um). cl becomes chi: *chiamare* (*cl*āmāre), *chiaro* (*cl*ārum), *chiudere* (*cl*audere), *occhio* (o*cul*um).

10. li becomes gli: *consiglio* (cōnsi*li*um), *moglie* (mu*li*erem), *figlio* (fī*li*um).

11. Initial consonant i often becomes gi: *già* (*i*am), *giusto* (*i*ūstum). In the interior of a word it sometimes becomes gg: *peggio* (pe*i*us), *maggiore* (ma*i*ōrem).

624. Word Formation

The Latin prefixes used in Italian are easily recognizable. Besides the usual changes note that ex– changes to es– or s– (*spedire*).

Latin suffixes which have changed most are –tia to –zia (*amicizia*), –antia, –entia to –anza, –enza (*sapienza*), –tātem to –tà (*bontà*).

625. Inflection

1. Nouns and adjectives of the Latin first declension ending in –a retain the –a in Italian: *lingua*. The plural in –ae becomes –e: *lingue*.

2. Masculine and neuter nouns and adjectives of the Latin second and fourth declensions in –us and –um end in –o in Italian: *amico, prezzo*. The plural ends in –i: *amici, prezzi*.

3. Nouns and adjectives of the Latin third declension end in –e in the singular, –i in the plural in Italian: *gente, genti; grave, gravi.*

4. The comparative and superlative forms of Latin irregular adjectives are to some extent preserved in Italian: *meglio* (melius), *ottimo* (optimus), *minore* (minor), *minimo* (minimus).

5. The Italian regular conjugations correspond to the four Latin conjugations, though there has been some shifting of words from one to another.

6. Many of the tenses of the Italian verb are like the Latin. Cf. the imperfect:

Lat. portābam portābās portābat portābāmus portābātis portābant
Ital. portava portavi portava portavamo portavate portavano

The Italian perfect is similar to the Latin perfect. This is especially true of Latin sum:

| *Lat.* | fuī | fuistī | fuit | fuimus | fuistis | fuērunt |
| *Ital.* | fui | fosti | fu | fummo | foste | furono |

I. BOOKS FOR SPECIAL ASSIGNMENTS (referred to in the lessons)

Baker, Emilie Kip, *Stories of Old Greece and Rome*. The Macmillan Company, New York, 1913.

Bulfinch, Thomas, *The Age of Fable* (Everyman's Library). E. P. Dutton and Company, New York, 1910.

Colum, Padraic, *The Adventures of Odysseus and the Tale of Troy*. The Macmillan Company, New York, 1927.

Davis, William Stearns, *A Day in Old Rome*. Allyn and Bacon, Boston, 1925.

Gayley, Charles Mills, *Classic Myths in English Literature and Art*. Ginn and Company, Boston, 1911.

Guerber, H. A., *Myths of Greece and Rome*. American Book Company, New York, 1921.

Guerber, H. A., *The Story of the Romans*. American Book Company, New York, 1924.

Haaren, John H., and Poland, A. B., *Famous Men of Rome*. American Book Company, New York, 1921.

Harding, C. H. and S. B., *The City of the Seven Hills*. Scott, Foresman and Company, Chicago, 1902.

Harding, C. H. and S. B., *Stories of Greek Gods, Heroes, and Men*. Scott, Foresman and Company, Chicago, 1897.

Johnston, Harold W., *The Private Life of the Romans*. Scott, Foresman and Company, Chicago, 1932.

McDaniel, Walton Brooks, *Roman Private Life and Its Survivals*. Longmans, Green and Company, New York, 1924.

Mills, Dorothy, *The Book of the Ancient Romans*. G. P. Putnam's Sons, New York, 1927.

Sabin, Frances E., *Classical Myths That Live Today*. Silver Burdett Company, New York, 1940.

Showerman, Grant, *Rome and the Romans*. The Macmillan Company, New York, 1931.

Tappan, Eva March, *The Story of the Roman People*. Houghton Mifflin Company, Boston, 1910.

II. NOVELS AND OTHER BOOKS FOR HISTORICAL BACKGROUND

Cowles, J. D., *Our Little Roman Cousin of Long Ago*. L. C. Page and Company, Boston, 1913.

Hall, Jennie, *Buried Cities*. The Macmillan Company, New York, 1922.

Macgregor, Mary, *The Story of Rome*. Frederick A. Stokes Company, New York, 1913.

White, Edward Lucas, *The Unwilling Vestal*. E. P. Dutton and Company, New York, 1918.

III. SUPPLEMENTARY BOOKS FOR THE TEACHER

Burriss, Eli E., and Casson, Lionel, *Latin and Greek in Current Use*. Prentice-Hall, Inc., New York, 1939.

Carcopino, J., *Daily Life in Ancient Rome*. Yale University Press, New Haven, 1940.

Haskell, H. J., *The New Deal in Old Rome*. Alfred A. Knopf, New York, 1939.

Johnson, Edwin Lee, *Latin Words of Common English*. D. C. Heath and Company, Boston, 1931.

Kent, Roland G., *Language and Philology*. Longmans, Green and Company, New York, 1923.

Lawler, Lillian B., *The Latin Club*. American Classical League Service, New York University, New York, 1929.

Picturesque Word Origins. G. and C. Merriam Company, Springfield, Mass., 1933.

Scott, H. F., Carr, W. L., and Wilkinson, G. T., *Language and Its Growth*. Scott, Foresman and Company, Chicago, 1935.

Tanzer, Helen H., *The Common People of Pompeii*. The Johns Hopkins Press, Baltimore, 1939.

Caught by death. Pompeii was buried by a shower of fine ashes, which suffocated many people. The ashes hardened, and, when the modern archeologist came upon hollow places in them, he poured in plaster, making a cast such as this.

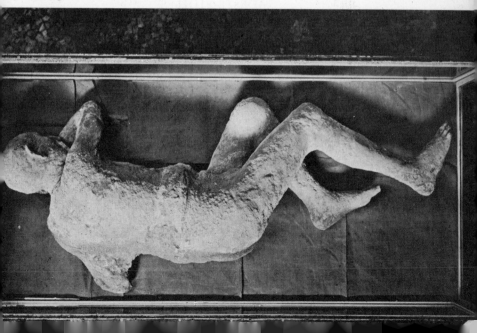

LATIN SONGS

THE STAR-SPANGLED BANNER
Tr. F. A. Geyser

Ōh, potestne cernī, praefulgente diē,
  Salūtātum signum circā noctis adventum?
Lātī clāv(ī) et stellae, dēcertant(e) aciē,
  Glōriōsē cingunt oppidī mūnīmentum!
Iaculumque rubēns, globus sūrsum rumpēns
Per noctem mōnstrant vexillum fulgēns.
  Stellātumne vexillum volāns tegit nōs,
  Patriam līberam fortiumque domōs?

(For "America" see page 7)

GOD BLESS AMERICA

Irving Berlin. Tr. by the Virgil class of Central High School, St. Paul
(Florence E. Baber, teacher).

Dum nimbi cogunt
  Trans maria,
Iuremus fidem
  Liberae terrae;
Gratiam habeamus
  Patriae pulchrae,
Dum nos cantamus
  Solemni prece.

Deus Americam
  Benedicat,
Illam servet et ducat
  Per noctem cum luce alta;
De montibus ad campos,
  Ad maria undis albis,
Deus Americam
  Benedicat.

ADESTE FIDĒLĒS[1]

Adeste, fidēlēs,
  Laetī triumphantēs;
Venīte, venīte in Bethlehem;
  Nātum vidēte
  Rēgem angelōrum;
Venīte adōrēmus, venīte adōrēmus,
Venīte adōrēmus Dominum.

Cantet nunc "Iō!"
  Chorus angelōrum;
Cantet nunc aula caelestium:
  "Glōria, glōria
  In excelsīs Deō!"
Venīte, etc.

Ergō quī nātus
  Diē hodiernā,
Iēsū, tibi sit glōria;
  Patris aeternī
  Verbum carō factum!
Venīte, etc.

---

[1] Sung to the tune of the Portuguese Hymn, "O Come, All Ye Faithful."

GAUDEAMUS IGITUR

Student Song

INTEGER VITAE

HORACE, Odes I. 22
(ca. 25 B.C.)

Dr. F. F. FLEMMING, ca. 1811

1. In - te - ger vi - tae sce - le - ris - que
2. Si - ve per Syr - tes i - ter aes - tu -
3. Nam - que me sil - va lu - pus in Sa

pu - rus Non e - get Mau - ris ia - cu - lis ne -
o - sas, Si - ve fac - tu - rus per in - hos - pi -
bi - na, Dum me - am can - to La - la - gen et

qu(e) ar - cu Nec ve - ne - na - tis gra - vi - da sa -
ta - lem Cau - ca - sum vel quae lo - ca fa - bu -
ul - tra Ter - mi - num cu - ris va - gor ex - pe -

git - tis, Fus - ce, pha - re - tra,
lo - sus Lam - bit Hy - das - pes.
di - tis, Fu - git in - er - mem.

LATIN-ENGLISH VOCABULARY

Proper names are not included unless they are spelled differently in English or are difficult to pronounce in English. Their English pronunciation is indicated by a simple system. The vowels are as follows: ā as in *hate*, ă as in *hat*, ē as in *feed*, ĕ as in *fed*, ī as in *bite*, ĭ as in *bit*, ō as in *hope*, ŏ as in *hop*, ū as in *cute*, ŭ as in *cut*. In the ending *ēs* the *s* is soft as in *rose*. When the accented syllable ends in a consonant, the vowel is short; otherwise it is long.

A

ā, ab, *prep. w. abl.*, from, away from, by.

absum, abesse, āfuī, āfutūrus, be away, be absent.

ac, *see* atque.

accēdō, –ere, accessī, accessūrus, approach.

accidō, –ere, accidī, —, fall to, befall, happen (*w. dat.*).

accipiō, –ere, accēpī, acceptus, receive.

accūsō, –āre, –āvī, –ātus, blame, accuse.

ācer, ācris, ācre, sharp, keen.

ad, *prep. w. acc.*, to, toward, for, near.

addūcō, –ere, addūxī, adductus, lead to, influence.

adsum, –esse, adfuī, adfutūrus, be near, be present.

Aegyptiī, –ōrum, *m. pl.*, the Egyptians.

Aegyptus, –ī, *f.*, Egypt.

Aenēās, –ae, *m.*, Aeneas (Ēnē'as).

Aeolus, –ī, *m.*, Aeolus (Ē'olus).

aequē, *adv.*, justly.

aequus, –a, –um, even, just, calm.

aestās, aestātis, *f.*, summer.

aetās, aetātis, *f.*, age.

Aetna, –ae, *f.*, (Mt.) Etna.

afficiō, –ere, affēcī, affectus, affect, afflict with.

Āfricānus, –ī, *m.*, Africā'nus.

ager, agrī, *m.*, field, farm, country.

agō, –ere, ēgī, āctus, drive, do, treat, discuss, live *or* spend (*of time*); grātiās agō, thank.

agricola, –ae, *m.*, farmer.

āla, –ae, *f.*, wing.

albus, –a, –um, white.

aliēnus, –a, –um, another's, unfavorable.

alius, alia, aliud, other, another; alius . . . alius, one . . . another; aliī . . . aliī, some . . . others.

Alpēs, –ium, *f. pl.*, the Alps.

altē, *adv.*, high, far.

alter, altera, alterum, the other (*of two*); alter . . . alter, the one . . . the other.

altus, –a, –um, high, deep, tall.

Americānus, –a, –um, American; Americānus, –ī, *m.*, an American.

amīcitia, –ae, *f.*, friendship.

amīcus, –a, –um, friendly; amīcus, –ī, *m.*, amīca, –ae, *f.*, friend.

āmittō, –ere, āmīsī, āmissus, let go, lose.

amō, –āre, –āvī, –ātus, love, like.

amor, –ōris, *m.*, love.

amphitheātrum, –ī, *n.*, amphitheater.

Anglicus, –a, –um, English.

animus, –ī, *m.*, mind, courage.

annus, –ī, *m.*, year.

ante, *adv. and prep. w. acc.*, before (*of time or space*).

antecēdō, –ere, –cessī, –cessūrus, go before, take the lead.

antīquus, –a, –um, ancient.

appellō, –āre, –āvī, –ātus, call.

Appius, –a, –um, *adj.*, of Appius, Appian.

aptus, –a, –um, fit, suitable (*w. dat.*).

apud, *prep. w. acc.*, among, with.

aqua, –ae, *f.*, water.

aquaeductus, –ūs, *m.*, aqueduct.

Aquītānī, –ōrum, *m. pl.*, the Aquitā'nians, *a people in Gaul.*

arcus, –ūs, *m.*, arch, bow.

arēna, –ae, *f.*, sand, arena.

argentum, –ī, *n.*, silver.

arma, –ōrum, *n. pl.*, arms, weapons.

ascendō, –ere, ascendī, ascēnsus, climb (up), ascend.

atque (ac), *conj.*, and.

attingō, –ere, attigī, attāctus, touch, reach.

auctor, –ōris, *m.*, maker, author.

auctōritās, –tātis, *f.*, authority, influence.

audācia, –ae, *f.*, boldness.

audiō, -īre, -īvī, -ītus, hear.
augeō, -ēre, auxī, auctus, increase.
aureus, -a, -um, golden.
aurīga, -ae, m., charioteer.
aurōra, -ae, f., dawn.
aurum, -ī, n., gold.
aut, or; aut . . . aut, either . . . or.
autem, conj. (never first word), however.
auxilium, -lī, n., aid; pl., reinforcements.
āvertō, -ere, āvertī, āversus, turn from.
avus, -ī, m., grandfather.
axis, -is, m., axle.

B

barbarus, -a, -um, foreign, barbarous;
  barbarus, -ī, m., foreigner, barbarian.
Belgae, -ārum, m. pl., the Belgians.
bellum, -ī, n., war.
bene, adv., well, well done; comp.
  melius, better; superl. optimē, best,
  very good.
beneficium, -cī, n., kindness, benefit.
bonus, -a, -um, good; comp. melior,
  melius, better; superl. optimus, -a,
  -um, best.
Britannia, -ae, f., Britain.

C

C., abbreviation for Gāius.
cadō, -ere, cecidī, cāsūrus, fall.
caelum, -ī, n., sky.
Caesar, -aris, m., Caesar.
canis, -is, m., dog.
canō, -ere, cecinī, cantus, sing.
capiō, -ere, cēpī, captus, take, seize,
  capture; cōnsilium capiō, adopt a
  plan.
Capitōlium, -lī, n., the Capitol, temple
  of Jupiter at Rome; the Capitoline Hill.
captīvus, -ī, m., prisoner.
caput, capitis, n., head.
carmen, -minis, n., song.
carrus, -ī, m., cart, wagon.
Carthāginiēnsēs, -ium, m. pl., the
  Carthaginians (Carthajin'ians).
Carthāgō, -ginis, f., Carthage, a city in
  Africa.
cārus, -a, -um, dear.
castra, -ōrum, n. pl., camp.
cāsus, -ūs, m., fall, chance, accident.
Catilīna, -ae, m., Catiline.
causa, -ae, f., cause, reason.

cēdō, -ere, cessī, cessūrus, move, retreat, yield.
celer, celeris, celere, swift.
celeritās, -tātis, f., swiftness.
celeriter, adv., quickly.
Celtae, -ārum, m. pl., Celts, a people of
  Gaul.
cēna, -ae, f., dinner.
centum, hundred.
cēra, -ae, f., wax.
Cerēs, -eris, f., Ceres (Sē'rēs), goddess of
  agriculture.
cernō, -ere, crēvī, crētus, separate, discern, see.
certē, adv., certainly.
certus, -a, -um, fixed, sure.
cibus, -ī, m., food.
Cicerō, -ōnis, m., Cicero (Sis'ero).
Circē, -ae, f., Circe (Sir'sē), a sorceress.
circum, prep. w. acc., around.
circus, -ī, m., circle, circus, esp. the
  Circus Maximus at Rome.
cīvis, cīvis, m., citizen.
cīvitās, -tātis, f., citizenship, state.
clāmō, -āre, -āvī, -ātus, shout, cry out.
clāmor, -ōris, m., shout.
clārē, adv., clearly.
clārus, -a, -um, clear, famous.
claudō, -ere, clausī, clausus, close.
cognōmen, -minis, n., cognomen,
  surname.
cognōscō, -ere, -nōvī, -nitus, learn,
  recognize; perf., know, understand.
cōgō, -ere, coēgī, coāctus, drive together, collect, compel.
colō, -ere, coluī, cultus, till, inhabit,
  worship.
colōnus, -ī, m., settler.
Colossēum, -ī, n., the Colossē'um, an
  amphitheater at Rome.
committō, -ere, -mīsī, -missus, join
  together, commit, entrust; proelium
  committō, begin battle.
commodē, adv., suitably.
commodus, -a, -um, suitable, convenient.
commoveō, -ēre, -mōvī, -mōtus,
  disturb.
commūnis, -e, common.
concordia, -ae, f., harmony.
condiciō, -ōnis, f., condition, terms.
cōnficiō, -ere, -fēcī, -fectus, do up,
  complete, exhaust.

cōnfirmō, -āre, -āvī, -ātus, make firm, encourage, establish.

cōnservō, -āre, -āvī, -ātus, save, preserve.

cōnsilium, -lī, n., plan, advice.

cōnsistō, -ere, cōnstitī, cōnstitūrus, stand still, stop.

cōnspiciō, -ere, -spexī, -spectus, catch sight of, see.

cōnsul, -ulis, m., consul, *the highest Roman official.*

cōnsulō, -ere, -suluī, -sultus, consult.

contendō, -ere, -tendī, -tentūrus, struggle, hasten.

contineō, -ēre, -uī, -tentus, hold (together), contain.

contrā, *prep. w. acc.,* against.

conveniō, -īre, -vēnī, -ventūrus, come together.

convocō, -āre, -āvī, -ātus, call together.

cōpia, -ae, *f.,* supply, abundance; *pl.,* forces, troops.

coquō, -ere, coxī, coctus, cook.

coquus, -ī, m., cook.

cor, cordis, n., heart.

corōna, -ae, *f.,* crown.

corpus, -poris, n., body.

crēdō, -ere, -didī, -ditus, believe, entrust (*w. dat.*).

Crēta, -ae, *f.,* Crete.

cum, *prep. w. abl.,* with.

cupiditās, -tātis, *f.,* desire.

cupiō, -ere, cupīvī, cupītus, desire.

cūr, *adv.,* why.

cūra, -ae, *f.,* care, concern; (cum) magnā cūrā, very carefully.

currō, -ere, cucurrī, cursūrus, run.

currus, -ūs, m., chariot.

D

dē, *prep. w. abl.,* from, down from, about.

dea, -ae, *f.,* goddess.

dēbeō, -ēre, dēbuī, dēbitus, owe, ought.

decem, ten.

December, -bris, m., December.

dēfendō, -ere, dēfendī, dēfēnsus, defend.

dēligō, -ere, dēlēgī, dēlēctus, select.

dēmōnstrō, -āre, -āvī, -ātus, show.

dēpōnō, -ere, dēposuī, dēpositus, put *or* lay aside.

dēscendō, -ere, dēscendī, dēscēnsus, descend.

dēserō, -ere, dēseruī, dēsertus, desert.

dēsiliō, -īre, dēsiluī, dēsultūrus, jump down.

dēspiciō, -ere, dēspexī, dēspectus, look down on, despise.

deus, -ī, m., god.

dēvorō, -āre, -āvī, -ātus, swallow.

dexter, -tra, -trum, right (hand).

dīcō, -ere, dīxī, dictus, say, tell.

dictātor, -ōris, m., dictator.

dictātūra, -ae, *f.,* dictatorship.

dictum, -ī, n., word.

diēs, diēī, m., day.

difficilis, -e, difficult.

digitus, -ī, m., finger.

dīligentia, -ae, *f.,* diligence.

dīmittō, -ere, dīmīsī, dīmissus, let go, send away.

discēdō, -ere, -cessī, -cessūrus, go away, depart.

disciplīna, -ae, *f.,* training, instruction.

discipulus, -ī, m., discipula, -ae, *f.,* learner, pupil.

dissimilis, -e, unlike.

dīvidō, -ere, dīvīsī, dīvīsus, divide.

dō, dare, dedī, datus, give, put; poenam dō, pay the penalty.

doceō, -ēre, docuī, doctus, teach.

dominus, -ī, m., master.

domus, -ūs, *f.,* house, home.

dōnō, -āre, -āvī, -ātus, give, present.

dōnum, -ī, n., gift.

dubitō, -āre, -āvī, -ātus, hesitate, doubt.

dūcō, -ere, dūxī, ductus, lead, draw.

dulcis, -e, sweet.

dum, *conj.,* while.

duo, -ae, -o, two.

duodecim, twelve.

dūrus, -a, -um, hard, harsh.

dux, ducis, m., leader, general.

E

ē, ex, *prep. w. abl.,* from, out from, out of.

edō, -ere, ēdī, ēsus, eat.

ēdūcō, -ere, ēdūxī, ēductus, lead out.

efficiō, -ere, effēcī, effectus, make (out), bring about, complete.

ego, meī, I.

ēgregius, –a, –um, distinguished, excellent.
ēiciō, –ere, ēiēcī, ēiectus, throw out.
elephantus, –ī, m., elephant.
em! *interj.*, take that!
emō, –ere, ēmī, ēmptus, take, buy.
Ēpīrus, –ī, f., Ēpī'rus, *a province in Greece.*
epistula, –ae, f., letter.
equus, –ī, m., horse.
ērumpō, –ere, ērūpī, ēruptus, burst forth.
et, *conj.*, and, even; et . . . et, both . . . and.
etiam, *adv.*, also, even, too.
Etrūscī, –ōrum, m. *pl.*, the Etruscans.
Eumaeus, –ī, m., Eumaeus (Ūmē'us).
Eurōpa, –ae, f., Europe.
Eurylochus, –ī, m., Eurylochus (Ūrīl'okus), *a companion of Ulysses.*
ēvādō, –ere, ēvāsī, ēvāsūrus, go out, escape.
ēvocō, –āre, –āvī, –ātus, summon.
excēdō, –ere, excessī, excessūrus, depart.
exemplum, –ī, n., example.
exerceō, –ēre, exercuī, exercitus, keep busy, train.
exercitus, –ūs, m., (trained) army.
exīstimō, –āre, –āvī, –ātus, think.
exit, exeunt, he goes out, they go out.
expediō, –īre, –īvī, –ītus, set free.
expellō, –ere, expulī, expulsus, drive out.
explicō, –āre, –āvī, –ātus, unfold, explain.
explōrō, –āre, –āvī, –ātus, investigate, explore.
expugnō, –āre, –āvī, –ātus, capture by assault.
exspectō, –āre, –āvī, –ātus, look out for, await, wait.
exstinguō, –ere, exstīnxī, exstīnctus, extinguish.
extrēmus, –a, –um, farthest, last, end of.

F

fābula, –ae, f., story.
facile, *adv.*, easily.
facilis, –e, easy.
faciō, –ere, fēcī, factus, do, make; verba faciō, speak, make a speech.

factum, –ī, n., deed.
fallō, –ere, fefellī, falsus, deceive.
fāma, –ae, f., report, fame.
familia, –ae, f., family.
familiāris, –e, of the family, friendly; *as noun,* friend.
fātum, –ī, n., fate; *often personified,* the Fates.
ferrum, –ī, n., iron.
fīlia, –ae, f., daughter.
fīlius, –lī, m., son.
fīnis, fīnis, m., end; *pl.*, borders, territory.
fīnitimus, –a, –um, neighboring, near; *as noun,* neighbor.
firmus, –a, –um, strong, firm.
fleō, flēre, flēvī, flētus, weep.
flūmen, flūminis, n., river.
fluō, –ere, flūxī, flūxus, flow.
focus, –ī, m., hearth.
fōrma, –ae, f., shape, image, form.
fortasse, *adv.*, perhaps.
fortis, –e, strong, brave.
fortiter, *adv.*, bravely.
fortūna, –ae, f., fortune.
forum, –ī, n., market place; Forum (*at Rome*).
frangō, –ere, frēgī, frāctus, break.
frāter, frātris, m., brother.
frōns, frontis, f., forehead, front.
frūmentum, –ī, n., grain.
fuga, –ae, f., flight.
fugiō, –ere, fūgī, fugitūrus, flee.
fulmen, –minis, n., lightning.
futūrus, *see* sum.

G

Gāius, –ī, m., Gā'ius.
Gallia, –ae, f., Gaul, *ancient France.*
Gallicus, –a, –um, Gallic.
Gallus, –ī, m., a Gaul.
gēns, gentis, f., people, nation.
genus, generis, n., birth, kind.
Germānia, –ae, f., Germany.
Germānus, –ī, m., a German.
gerō, –ere, gessī, gestus, carry on, wear.
gladiātor, –ōris, m., gladiator.
gladius, –dī, m., sword.
glōria, –ae, f., glory.
Graecia, –ae, f., Greece.
Graecus, –a, –um, Greek; Graecus, –ī, m., a Greek.

grātē, *adv.*, gratefully.
grātia, –ae, *f.*, gratitude, influence; grātiam habeō, feel grateful; grātiās agō, thank.
grātus, –a, –um, pleasing, grateful.
gravis, –e, heavy, severe.
graviter, *adv.*, heavily, seriously.

H

habeō, –ēre, habuī, habitus, have, hold, consider; grātiam habeō, feel grateful (*w. dat.*); ōrātiōnem habeō, deliver an oration.
habitō, –āre, –āvī, –ātus, live.
haereō, –ēre, haesī, haesus, stick.
Hannibal, –alis, *m.*, Hannibal, *a Carthaginian general.*
herba, –ae, *f.*, grass, plant.
Hibernia, –ae, *f.*, Ireland.
hic, haec, hoc, this; *as pron.*, he, she, it.
hiems, hiemis, *f.*, winter.
Hispānia, –ae, *f.*, Spain.
Hispānus, –a, –um, Spanish.
homō, hominis, *m.*, man, human being.
honestās, –tātis, *f.*, honor.
honor, –ōris, *m.*, honor.
hōra, –ae, *f.*, hour.
hospita, –ae, *f.*, guest.
hostis, hostis, *m.*, enemy (*usually pl.*).
humilis, –e, low, humble.

I

iaciō, –ere, iēcī, iactus, throw.
iam, *adv.*, already; nōn iam, no longer.
ibi, *adv.*, there.
idem, eadem, idem, same.
ignis, –is, *m.*, fire.
ille, illa, illud, *demonst. adj.*, that; *as pron.*, he, she, it.
impedīmentum, –ī, *n.*, hindrance; *pl.*, baggage.
impediō, –īre, –īvī, –ītus, hinder.
imperātor, –ōris, *m.*, commander, general.
imperium, –rī, *n.*, command, power.
imperō, –āre, –āvī, –ātus, command (*w. dat.*).
impetus, –ūs, *m.*, attack.
in, *prep. w. acc.*, into, to, against; *w. abl.*, in, on.

incertus, –a, –um, uncertain.
incipiō, –ere, incēpī, inceptus, take to, begin.
incitō, –āre, –āvī, –ātus, urge on, arouse.
incolō, –ere, incoluī, incultus, live, inhabit.
īnferior, īnferius, lower.
inimīcus, –a, –um, unfriendly; *as noun*, enemy.
iniūria, –ae, *f.*, wrong, injustice, injury.
inquit, said (he).
īnstō, –āre, īnstitī, —, threaten.
īnstruō, –ere, īnstrūxī, īnstrūctus, arrange, provide, draw up.
īnsula, –ae, *f.*, island.
integer, –gra, –grum, untouched, fresh.
intellegō, –ere, –lēxī, –lēctus, understand.
inter, *prep. w. acc.*, between, among.
intercipiō, –ere, –cēpī, –ceptus, intercept.
interclūdō, –ere, –clūsī, –clūsus, cut off.
interficiō, –ere, –fēcī, –fectus, kill.
interim, *adv.*, meanwhile.
intermittō, –ere, –mīsī, –missus, let go, stop, interrupt.
inveniō, –īre, invēnī, inventus, come upon, find.
iō, *interj.*, hurrah!
ipse, ipsa, ipsum, self, very.
īra, –ae, *f.*, anger.
is, ea, id, this, that; *as pron.*, he, she, it.
ita, *adv.*, so.
Italia, –ae, *f.*, Italy.
itaque, *adv.*, and so, therefore.
iter, itineris, *n.*, journey, road, march.
iterum, *adv.*, again.
iubeō, –ēre, iussī, iussus, order.
iūdicō, –āre, –āvī, –ātus, judge.
Iūlia, –ae, *f.*, Julia.
Iūlius, –lī, *m.*, Julius.
iungō, –ere, iūnxī, iūnctus, join (to).
Iūnō, –ōnis, *f.*, Juno, *a goddess, wife of Jupiter.*
Iuppiter, Iovis, *m.*, Jupiter, *king of the gods.*
iūs, iūris, *n.*, right.
iūstē, *adv.*, justly.
iūstus, –a, –um, just.

L

L., *abbreviation for* Lūcius.
labor, –ōris, *m.*, work, hardship.
labōrō, –āre, –āvī, –ātus, work.
lacrima, –ae, *f.*, tear.
lanterna, –ae, *f.*, lantern.
Lār, Laris, *m.*, Lar, *a household god.*
lassitūdō, –tūdinis, *f.*, weariness.
lātē, *adv.*, widely.
Latīnus, –a, –um, *adj.*, Latin, belonging to Latium; Latīnī, –ōrum, *m.*, the Latins.
Latīnus, –ī, *m.*, Latī'nus.
lātus, –a, –um, wide.
laudō, –āre, –āvī, –ātus, praise.
lavō, –āre, lāvī, lautus, wash.
lēgātus, –ī, *m.*, envoy.
legō, –ere, lēgī, lēctus, gather, choose, read.
levis, –e, light (*in weight*).
leviter, *adv.*, lightly.
lēx, lēgis, *f.*, law.
liber, librī, *m.*, book.
līber, –era, –erum, free.
līberē, *adv.*, freely.
līberī, –ōrum, *m.*, children.
līberō, –āre, –āvī, –ātus, free.
lībertās, –tātis, *f.*, freedom.
ligō, –āre, –āvī, –ātus, bind.
lingua, –ae, *f.*, tongue, language.
littera, –ae, *f.*, a letter (*of the alphabet*); *pl.*, a letter (*epistle*), literature.
locus, –ī, *m.* (*pl.* loca, locōrum, *n.*), place.
longus, –a, –um, long.
lūdō, –ere, lūsī, lūsus, play.
lūdus, –ī, *m.*, game, school (*as a place for exercise*).
Lūsitānia, –ae, *f.*, Portugal.
lūx, lūcis, *f.*, light.

M

M., *abbreviation for* Mārcus.
magister, –trī, *m.*, teacher.
magnus, –a, –um, large, great; *comp.* maior, maius, greater; *superl.* maximus, –a, –um, greatest, very great.
maior, *see* magnus.
malus, –a, –um, bad; *comp.* peior, peius, worse; *superl.* pessimus, –a, –um, very bad, worst; malum, –ī, *n.*, trouble.
mandō, –āre, –āvī, –ātus, entrust.
maneō, –ēre, mānsī, mānsūrus, remain.
manus, –ūs, *f.*, hand.
Mārcius, –cī, *m.*, Marcius (Mar'shius).
mare, maris, *n.*, sea.
marītus, –ī, *m.*, husband.
Mārs, Mārtis, *m.*, Mars, *god of war.*
māter, mātris, *f.*, mother.
māteria, –ae, *f.*, matter, timber.
mātrimōnium, –nī, *n.*, marriage.
mātūrō, –āre, –āvī, –ātūrus, hasten.
maximē, *adv.*, very greatly, especially.
maximus, –a, –um, *see* magnus.
medicus, –ī, *m.*, doctor.
Mediterrāneum (Mare), Mediterranean Sea.
medius, –a, –um, middle (of).
mel, mellis, *n.*, honey.
melior, *see* bonus.
memoria, –ae, *f.*, memory; memoriā teneō, remember.
mēnsa, –ae, *f.*, table.
mēnsis, –is, *m.*, month.
Mercurius, –rī, *m.*, Mercury.
mereō, –ēre, meruī, meritus, deserve, earn.
mēta, –ae, *f.*, goal, turning post, *in the Circus.*
meus, –a, –um, my, mine.
migrō, –āre, –āvī, –ātūrus, depart.
mīles, mīlitis, *m.*, soldier.
mīlle, *pl.* mīlia, thousand.
minimus, –a, –um, *see* parvus.
minor, *see* parvus.
miser, –era, –erum, unhappy, poor.
mittō, –ere, mīsī, missus, let go, send.
modus, –ī, *m.*, manner.
moneō, –ēre, monuī, monitus, remind, warn.
mōns, montis, *m.*, mountain.
mōnstrō, –āre, –āvī, –ātus, point out, show.
mors, mortis, *f.*, death.
mōs, mōris, *m.*, custom.
moveō, –ēre, mōvī, mōtus, move.
mox, *adv.*, soon.
mulier, mulieris, *f.*, woman.
multus, –a, –um, much; *pl.*, many; *comp.* plūrēs, plūra, more; *superl.* plūrimus, –a, –um, most.
mūniō, –īre, –īvī, –ītus, fortify; viam mūniō, build a road.

mūnus, mūneris, *n.*, duty, service, gift.
mūtō, -āre, -āvī, -ātus, change.

N

nam, *conj.*, for.
nātūra, -ae, *f.*, nature.
nauta, -ae, *m.*, sailor.
nāvigō, -āre, -āvī, -ātus, sail.
nāvis, nāvis, *f.*, ship.
-ne (*enclitic*), *introduces questions.*
nec, *see* neque.
neglegentia, -ae, *f.*, negligence.
negōtium, -tī, *n.*, business.
nēmō, *dat.* nēminī, *acc.* nēminem (*no other forms*), no one.
Neptūnus, -ī, *m.*, Neptune, *god of the sea.*
neque (*or* nec), and not, nor; neque ... neque, neither ... nor.
neuter, -tra, -trum, neither (*of two*).
nihil, nothing.
nōbilis, -e, noble.
nōbīscum = cum nōbīs.
noceō, -ēre, nocuī, nocitūrus, do harm to (*w. dat.*).
nōmen, nōminis, *n.*, name.
nōn, *adv.*, not; nōn iam, no longer.
nōs, nostrum, we, *pl. of* ego.
nōscō, -ere, nōvī, nōtus, learn; *perf.*, have learned, know.
noster, -tra, -trum, our.
nōtus, -a, -um, known, familiar.
novem, nine.
novus, -a, -um, new, strange.
nox, noctis, *f.*, night.
nūllus, -a, -um, no, none.
numerus, -ī, *m.*, number.
Numitor, -ōris, *m.*, Nu'mitor.
numquam, *adv.*, never.
nunc, *adv.*, now
nūntiō, -āre, -āvī, -ātus, report, announce.
nūntius, -tī, *m.*, messenger.

O

ob, *prep. w. acc.*, toward, on account of, for.
obtineō, -ēre, obtinuī, obtentus, hold, obtain.
occīdō, -ere, occīdī, occīsus, kill.
occupō, -āre, -āvī, -ātus, seize.
Ōceanus, -ī, *m.*, ocean.
octō, eight.

oculus, -ī, *m.*, eye.
officium, -cī, *n.*, duty.
ōlim, *adv.*, once (upon a time).
omnis, omne, all, every.
oppidum, -ī, *n.*, town.
opprimō, -ere, oppressī, oppressus, overcome, surprise.
optimē, *see* bene.
optimus, *see* bonus.
opus, operis, *n.*, work.
ōrātiō, -ōnis, *f.*, speech.
ōrātor, -ōris, *m.*, orator.
ōrdō, ōrdinis, *m.*, order, rank.
ōrnāmentum, -ī, *n.*, jewel.
ostendō, -ere, ostendī, ostentus, (stretch out), show.
ōtium, ōtī, *n.*, leisure, peace.

P

P., *abbreviation for* Pūblius.
pār, *gen.* paris, equal (*w. dat.*).
parātus, -a, -um, prepared, ready.
pāreō, -ēre, pāruī, pāritūrus, (appear), be obedient to, obey (*w. dat.*).
parō, -āre, -āvī, -ātus, get, get ready, prepare.
pars, partis, *f.*, part, side.
parvus, -a, -um, small; *comp* minor, minus, less; *superl.* minimus, -a, -um, least
pāstor, -ōris, *m.*, shepherd.
pater, patris, *m.*, father.
patria, -ae, *f.*, fatherland, country.
paucī, -ae, -a, few.
Paulus, -ī, *m.*, Paul.
paupertās, -tātis, *f.*, poverty.
pāx, pācis, *f.*, peace.
pecūnia, -ae, *f.*, money.
peior, peius, *see* malus.
pellō, -ere, pepulī, pulsus, drive, defeat.
Penātēs, -ium, *m.*, the Penā'tēs, *household gods.*
Pēnelopē, -ae, *f.*, Penĕl'ope, *wife of Ulysses.*
per, *prep. w. acc.*, through, by.
perficiō, -ere, -fēcī, -fectus, finish.
perīculum, -ī, *n.*, danger.
permittō, -ere, -mīsī, -missus, let go through, allow, entrust (*w. dat.*).
permoveō, -ēre, -mōvī, -mōtus, move (deeply).

permūtātiō, –ōnis, f., exchange.

perpetuus, –a, –um, constant.

pertineō, –ēre, –tinuī, –tentūrus (w. ad), pertain to.

perveniō, –īre, –vēnī, –ventūrus, come through, arrive.

pēs, pedis, m., foot; pedibus, on foot.

pessimus, –a, –um, see malus.

petō, –ere, petīvī, petītus, seek, ask (for).

Phrygia, –ae, f., Phrygia (Frij'ia), a country of Asia Minor.

pictūra, –ae, f., picture.

pila, –ae, f., ball.

plācō, –āre, –āvī, –ātus, calm.

plānus, –a, –um, level.

plēbs, plēbis, f., the common people.

plicō, –āre, –āvī, –ātus, fold.

plūrēs, plūra, more, see multus.

plūrimus, see multus.

plūs, see multus.

Plūtō, –ōnis, m., Plu'tō.

poena, –ae, f., penalty, punishment.

poēta, –ae, m., poet.

Polyphēmus, –ī, m., Polyphe'mus, a man-eating giant.

pompa, –ae, f., parade.

pōnō, –ere, posuī, positus, put, place; castra pōnō, pitch camp.

pōns, pontis, m., bridge.

pontifex, –ficis, m., priest.

populus, –ī, m., people; pl., peoples, nations.

porta, –ae, f., gate.

portō, –āre, –āvī, –ātus, carry.

portus, –ūs, m., harbor.

possum, posse, potuī, —, can, be able.

post, adv. and prep. w. acc., behind (of place); after (of time).

posteā, adv., afterwards.

postquam, conj., after.

potestās, –tātis, f., power.

prae, prep. w. abl., before, in front of.

praeceps, gen. praecipitis, adj., headlong, steep.

praeda, –ae, f., loot.

praeficiō, –ere, –fēcī, –fectus, put in charge of.

praemittō, –ere, –mīsī, –missus, send ahead.

praemium, –mī, n., reward.

praesidium, –dī, n., guard, protection.

praesum, –esse, –fuī, –futūrus, be in charge of.

praetextus, –a, –um, (woven in front), bordered; toga praetexta, crimson-bordered toga.

premō, –ere, pressī, pressus, press, press hard.

pretium, –tī, n., price.

prīmō, adv., at first.

prīmum, adv., for the first time.

prīmus, –a, –um, first.

prīnceps, –cipis, m., leader.

prō, prep. w. abl., in front of, before, for.

probō, –āre, –āvī, –ātus, test, prove, approve.

prōcēdō, –ere, –cessī, –cessūrus, go forth, advance.

prōdūcō, –ere, –dūxī, –ductus, lead forth or out, prolong.

proelium, –lī, n., battle.

prohibeō, –ēre, –hibuī, –hibitus, prevent, keep from.

properō, –āre, –āvī, –ātūrus, hasten.

prōpōnō, –ere, –posuī, –positus, put forth, offer.

proprius, –a, –um, (one's) own.

prōvideō, –ēre, –vīdī, –vīsus, foresee.

prōvincia, –ae, f., province.

proximus, –a, –um, nearest, next.

pūblicē, adv., publicly.

pūblicus, –a, –um, public.

Pūblius, –lī, m., Pub'lius.

puella, –ae, f., girl.

puer, puerī, m., boy.

pugna, –ae, f., battle.

pugnō, –āre, –āvī, –ātus, fight.

pulcher, –chra, –chrum, beautiful.

Pūnicus, –a, –um, Punic, Carthaginian.

putō, –āre, –āvī, –ātus, think.

Pyrrhus, –ī, m., Pўr'rhus, king of Epirus.

Q

quadrīgae, –ārum, f. pl., a four-horse team, a chariot.

quam, conj., than.

quārtus, –a, –um, fourth.

quattuor, four.

–que (joined to second word), and.

quī, quae, quod, relat. pron., who, which, what, that.

quī, quae, quod, interrog. adj., what.

quīndecim, fifteen.

quīnque, five.

quīntus, -a, -um, fifth.
quis, quid, *interrog. pron.*, who, what.
quod, *conj.*, because.
quondam, *adv.*, once (upon a time).

R

raeda, -ae, *f.*, carriage, omnibus.
rapiō, -ere, rapuī, raptus, carry off.
ratiō, -ōnis, *f.*, account, reason.
recipiō, -ere, recēpī, receptus, take back, recover, receive.
reddō, -ere, reddidī, redditus, give back.
redigō, -ere, redēgī, redāctus, drive back, reduce.
redūcō, -ere, redūxī, reductus, lead back, bring back.
rēgīna, -ae, *f.*, queen.
regiō, -ōnis, *f.*, region.
rēgnum, -ī, *n.*, royal power, kingdom.
regō, -ere, rēxī, rēctus, rule, guide.
relinquō, -ere, relīquī, relīctus, leave (behind), abandon.
reliquus, -a, -um, remaining, rest (of).
remaneō, -ēre, remānsī, remānsūrus, remain.
remittō, -ere, remīsī, remissus, relax, send back.
removeō, -ēre, remōvī, remōtus, remove.
repellō, -ere, reppulī, repulsus, drive back, repulse.
rēs, reī, *f.*, thing, matter, affair; rēs pūblica, public affairs, government.
respondeō, -ēre, respondī, respōnsus, answer.
restō, -āre, restitī, —, remain.
retineō, -ēre, retinuī, retentus, hold (back), keep.
revertō, -ere, revertī, reversūrus, return.
rēx, rēgis, *m.*, king.
Rhēnus, -ī, *m.*, the Rhine river.
rīdeō, -ēre, rīsī, rīsus, laugh (at).
rogō, -āre, -āvī, -ātus, ask.
Rōma, -ae, *f.*, Rome.
Rōmānus, -a, -um, Roman; *as noun*, a Roman.
ruīna, -ae, *f.*, ruin.

S

saccus, -ī, *m.*, sack.
sacer, -cra, -crum, sacred.

saepe, *adv.*, often.
salūs, salūtis, *f.*, health, safety.
sapientia, -ae, *f.*, wisdom.
satis, *adv. and indecl. adj.*, enough.
Sāturnus, -ī, *m.*, Saturn, *a god*.
saxum, -ī, *n.*, rock.
scēptrum, -ī, *n.*, scepter.
sciō, -īre, scīvī, scītus, know.
Scīpiō, -ōnis, *m.*, Scipio (Sip'io).
scrībō, -ere, scrīpsī, scrīptus, write.
sēcum = cum sē.
secundus, -a, -um, second.
sed, *conj.*, but.
sedeō, -ēre, sēdī, sessūrus, sit.
semper, *adv.*, always.
senātor, -ōris, *m.*, senator.
senātus, -ūs, *m.*, senate.
sententia, -ae, *f.*, feeling, opinion, motto.
sentiō, -īre, sēnsī, sēnsus, feel, realize.
septem, seven.
sepulchrum, -ī, *n.*, tomb.
sermō, -ōnis, *m.*, talk.
servō, -āre, -āvī, -ātus, save, guard, preserve.
servus, -ī, *m.*, slave.
sex, six.
sī, *conj.*, if.
Sicilia, -ae, *f.*, Sicily (Sis'ily).
signum, -ī, *n.*, sign, standard, signal.
silva, -ae, *f.*, forest, woods.
similis, -e, like.
sine, *prep. w. abl.*, without.
singulī, -ae, -a, *pl. only*, one at a time.
sinister, -tra, -trum, left (hand).
socius, -cī, *m.*, comrade, ally.
sōl, sōlis, *m.*, sun.
sōlus, -a, -um, alone, only.
solvō, -ere, solvī, solūtus, loosen, pay.
somnus, -ī, *m.*, sleep.
sordidus, -a, -um, dirty.
soror, -ōris, *f.*, sister.
spatium, -tī, *n.*, space, time, lap (*in a race*).
speciēs, speciēī, *f.*, appearance.
spectō, -āre, -āvī, -ātus, look (at).
spērō, -āre, -āvī, -ātus, hope (for).
spēs, speī, *f.*, hope.
spīrō, -āre, -āvī, -ātus, breathe.
statua, -ae, *f.*, statue.
statuō, -ere, statuī, statūtus, establish, determine.

stō, stāre, stetī, stātūrus, stand.

studium, -dī, n., eagerness, interest; pl., studies.

stupidus, -a, -um, stupid.

sub, prep., under, close to (w. acc. after verbs of motion; w. abl. after verbs of rest or position).

subigō, -ere, -ēgī, -āctus, subdue.

submittō, -ere, -mīsī, -missus, let down, furnish.

suī, reflexive pron., of himself, herself, itself, themselves.

sum, esse, fuī, futūrus, be.

summus, -a, -um, highest, top of.

sūmō, -ere, sūmpsī, sūmptus, take.

super, prep. w. acc., over, above.

superbia, -ae, f., pride.

superbus, -a, -um, haughty.

superō, -āre, -āvī, -ātus, overcome, excel.

supersum, -esse, -fuī, -futūrus, be left over, survive.

superus, -a, -um, above.

supplicium, -cī, n., punishment.

suscipiō, -ere, -cēpī, -ceptus, undertake.

sustineō, -ēre, -tinuī, -tentus, hold up, maintain, endure.

suus, -a, -um, reflexive adj., his, her, its, their; his own, her own, etc.

T

tamen, adv., nevertheless.

tandem, adv., at last.

tangō, -ere, tetigī, tāctus, touch.

tardē, adv., slowly.

tardus, -a, -um, slow, late.

Tarentīnī, -ōrum, m. pl., the people of Tarentum.

Tēlemachus, -ī, m., Telĕm'achus.

tēlum, -ī, n., weapon.

templum, -ī, n., temple.

tempus, temporis, n., time.

tendō, -ere, tetendī, tentus, stretch.

teneō, -ēre, tenuī, tentus, hold, keep; memoriā teneō, remember.

terminus, -ī, m., end, boundary.

terra, -ae, f., land, earth.

terreō, -ēre, terruī, territus, scare, frighten.

tertius, -a, -um, third.

texō, -ere, texuī, textus, weave.

theātrum, -ī, n., theater.

Ti., abbreviation for Tiberius.

Tiberis, -is, m., the Tī'ber, a river of Italy.

Tiberius, -rī, m., Tībē'rius.

timeō, -ēre, timuī, —, fear, be afraid.

timidē, adv., timidly.

timidus, -a, -um, timid.

Tīrō, -ōnis, m., Tī'rō.

toga, -ae, f., toga (cloak).

tōtus, -a, -um, whole.

trādō, -ere, -didī, -ditus, give or hand over, surrender, relate.

trādūcō, -ere, -dūxī, -ductus, lead across.

trahō, -ere, trāxī, trāctus, draw, drag.

trānō, -āre, -āvī, -ātus, swim across.

trāns, prep. w. acc., across.

trānsportō, -āre, -āvī, -ātus, transport.

trēs, tria, three.

tribūnus, -ī, m., tribune, a Roman official.

tribuō, -ere, tribuī, tribūtus, grant.

trīgintā, thirty.

triumphō, -āre, -āvī, -ātus, triumph.

triumphus, -ī, m., triumph.

Troia, -ae, f., Troy.

Troiānus, -a, -um, Trojan; as noun, a Trojan.

tū, tuī, you.

tum, adv., then.

tuus, -a, -um, your, yours (referring to one person).

U

ubi, adv., where; when.

Ulixēs, -is, m., Ūlys'sēs.

ūllus, -a, -um, any.

ulterior, ulterius, farther.

ultimus, -a, -um, last, farthest.

unda, -ae, f., wave.

ūnus, -a, -um, one.

urbs, urbis, f., city.

ūtilis, -e, useful.

uxor, -ōris, f., wife.

V

valeō, -ēre, valuī, valitūrus, be strong, be well; imper. valē, farewell.

vāllum, -ī, n., wall.

variē, adv., variously.

varius, -a, -um, changing, varying, various.

vāstō, -āre, -āvī, -ātus, lay waste.
veniō, -īre, vēnī, ventūrus, come.
ventus, -ī, *m.*, wind.
Venus, -eris, *f.*, Vē'nus, *goddess of love and beauty.*
vēr, vēris, *n.*, spring.
verberō, -āre, -āvī, -ātus, beat.
verbum, -ī, *n.*, word.
vertō, -ere, vertī, versus, turn.
vērus, -a, -um, true.
Vestālis, -e, Vestal, of Vesta.
vester, -tra, -trum, your, yours (*of two or more persons*).
vestis, -is, *f.*, garment, clothes.
via, -ae, *f.*, way, road, street.
victor, -ōris, *m.*, victor.
victōria, -ae, *f.*, victory.
videō, -ēre, vīdī, vīsus, see; *passive,* seem.
vigilia, -ae, *f.*, watchfulness, guard.

vīgintī, twenty.
vīlla, -ae, *f.*, country home.
vincō, -ere, vīcī, victus, conquer.
vīnum, -ī, *n.*, wine.
vir, virī, *m.*, man.
virgō, -ginis, *f.*, virgin, maiden.
virīlis, -e, of a man.
virtūs, -tūtis, *f.*, manliness, courage.
vīs, —, *f.*, force, violence; *pl.* vīrēs, -ium, strength.
vīta, -ae, *f.*, life.
vīvō, -ere, vīxī, vīctus, live.
vīvus, -a, -um, alive.
vix, *adv.*, scarcely.
vocō, -āre, -āvī, -ātus, call.
vōs, vestrum, *pl. of* tū.
vōx, vōcis, *f.*, voice, remark.
Vulcānus, -ī, *m.*, Vulcan, *god of fire.*
vulnerō, -āre, -āvī, -ātus, wound.
vulnus, vulneris, *n.*, wound.

ENGLISH–LATIN VOCABULARY

A

able (be), possum, posse, potuī, —.
about, dē, *w. abl.*
absent (be), absum, abesse, āfuī, āfutūrus.
abundance, cōpia, –ae, *f.*
accuse, accūsō, –āre, –āvī, –ātus.
across, trāns, *w. acc.*
advice, cōnsilium, –lī, *n.*
affect, afflict, afficiō, –ere, affēcī, affectus.
afraid (be), timeō, –ēre, timuī, —.
after, *use abl. abs.;* post (*prep. w. acc.*);
    postquam (*conj.*).
aid, auxilium, –lī, *n.*
all, omnis, –e.
ally, socius, –cī, *m.*
alone, sōlus, –a, –um.
although, *use particip. or abl. abs.*
always, semper.
among, inter, apud, *w. acc.*
and, et, –que.
appearance, speciēs, speciēī, *f.*
approach, accēdō, –ere, accessī, accessū-
    rus (*w.* ad).
approve, probō, –āre, –āvī, –ātus.
arms, arma, –ōrum, *n.*
army, exercitus, –ūs, *m.*
arouse, incitō, –āre, –āvī, –ātus.
arrive, perveniō, –īre, –vēnī, –ventūrus.
as, *use abl. abs.*
ask, rogō, –āre, –āvī, –ātus.
assault, take by, expugnō, –āre, –āvī,
    –ātus.
attack, impetus, –ūs, *m.*
await, exspectō, –āre, –āvī, –ātus.
away (be), absum, –esse, āfuī, āfutūrus.

B

bad, malus, –a, –um.
battle, pugna, –ae, *f.;* proelium, –lī, *n.*
be, sum, esse, fuī, futūrus.
beautiful, pulcher, –chra, –chrum.
because, quod; *use particip. or abl. abs.*
begin, incipiō, –ere, –cēpī, –ceptus.
best, optimus, –a, –um.
better, melior, melius.
between, inter, *w. acc.*
blame, accūsō, –āre, –āvī, –ātus.

body, corpus, corporis, *n.*
book, liber, librī, *m.*
boundary, terminus, –ī,*m.;* fīnis, fīnis, *m.*
boy, puer, puerī, *m.*
brave, fortis, –e; bravely, fortiter.
breathe, spīrō, –āre, –āvī, –ātus.
brother, frāter, frātris, *m.*
but, sed.
by, ā, ab, *w. abl.*

C

call, vocō, –āre, –āvī, –ātus; appellō,
    –āre, –āvī, –ātus; call out, ēvocō; call
    together, convocō.
camp, castra, –ōrum, *n.;* pitch camp,
    castra pōnō, –ere, posuī, positus.
can, possum, posse, potuī, —.
cannot, nōn possum.
care, cūra, –ae, *f.*
carefully, cum cūrā.
carry, portō, –āre, –āvī, –ātus; carry on,
    gerō, –ere, gessī, gestus.
cart, carrus, –ī, *m.*
catch sight of, cōnspiciō, –ere, –spexī,
    –spectus.
cause, causa, –ae, *f.*
certainly, certē.
chance, cāsus, –ūs, *m.*
(put in) charge of, praeficiō, –ere, –fēcī,
    –fectus.
children, līberī, –ōrum, *m.*
citizen, cīvis, cīvis, *m.*
citizenship, cīvitās, –tātis, *f.*
city, urbs, urbis, *f.*
clearly, clārē.
climb, ascendō, –ere, ascendī, ascēnsus.
close, claudō, –ere, clausī, clausus.
colonist, colōnus, –ī, *m.*
come, veniō, –īre, vēnī, ventūrus.
complete, cōnficiō, –ere, –fēcī, –fectus.
comrade, socius, –cī, *m.*
constant, perpetuus, –a, –um.
contain, contineō, –ēre, –uī, –tentus.
country, patria, –ae, *f.;* terra, –ae, *f.*
courage, animus, –ī, *m.;* virtūs, –tūtis, *f.*

D

danger, perīculum, –ī, *n.*
daughter, fīlia, –ae, *f.*

day, diēs, diēī, *m.*
death, mors, mortis, *f.*
deceive, fallō, –ere, fefellī, falsus.
deep, altus, –a, –um.
(deeply) move, permoveō, –ēre, –mōvī, –mōtus.
defend, dēfendō, –ere, dēfendī, dēfēnsus.
depart, excēdō, –ere, excessī, excessūrus; discēdō.
desert, dēserō, –ere, dēseruī, dēsertus.
deserve, mereō, –ēre, meruī, meritus.
desire, cupiō, –ere, cupīvī, cupītus.
determine, statuō, –ere, statuī, statūtus.
dismiss, dīmittō, –ere, dīmīsī, dīmissus.
divide, dīvidō, –ere, dīvīsī, dīvīsus.
do, faciō, –ere, fēcī, factus; agō, –ere, ēgī, āctus; do harm to, noceō, –ēre, nocuī, nocitūrus (*w. dat.*).
drag, draw, trahō, –ere, trāxī, trāctus.
drive, agō, –ere, ēgī, āctus; drive back, repellō, –ere, reppulī, repulsus.
duty, officium, –cī, *n.*

E

eagerness, studium, –dī, *n.*
easy, facilis, –e; easily, facile.
end, fīnis, fīnis, *m.*
endure, sustineō, –ēre, –tinuī, –tentus.
enemy, inimīcus, –ī, *m.* (*personal*); hostis, –is, *m.* (*national*).
entrust, mandō, –āre, –āvī, –ātus; committō, –ere, –mīsī, –missus; crēdō, –ere, crēdidī, crēditus.
equal, pār, *gen.* paris.
establish, cōnfirmō, –āre, –āvī, –ātus.
even, etiam.
every, omnis, –e.
example, exemplum, –ī, *n.*
excel, superō, –āre, –āvī, –ātus.
excellent, ēgregius, –a, –um.
explore, explōrō, –āre, –āvī, –ātus.

F

fall, cadō, –ere, cecidī, cāsūrus.
fame, fāma, –ae, *f.*
familiar, nōtus, –a, –um.
family, familia, –ae, *f.*
famous, clārus, –a, –um.
farmer, agricola, –ae, *m.*
father, pater, patris, *m.*
fear, timeō, –ēre, timuī, —.
few, paucī, –ae, –a.
field, ager, agrī, *m.*

fifth, quīntus, –a, –um.
fight, pugnō, –āre, –āvī, –ātus.
find, inveniō, –īre, invēnī, inventus.
first, prīmus, –a, –um.
fit, aptus, –a, –um.
flee, fugiō, –ere, fūgī, fugitūrus.
fold, plicō, –āre, –āvī, –ātus.
foot, pēs, pedis, *m.;* on foot, pedibus.
for (*conj.*), nam; (*prep.*), prō, *w. abl.;* ob, *w. acc.*
forces (troops), cōpiae, –ārum, *f.*
foreigner, barbarus, –ī, *m.*
foresee, prōvideō, –ēre, –vīdī, –vīsus.
forest, silva, –ae, *f.*
fortify, mūniō, –īre, –īvī, –ītus.
four, quattuor.
free (*adj.*), līber, –era, –erum; (*v.*), līberō, –āre, –āvī, –ātus.
freedom, lībertās, lībertātis, *f.*
fresh, integer, –gra, –grum.
friend, amīcus, –ī, *m.*
friendly, amīcus, –a, –um.
friendship, amīcitia, –ae, *f.*
from, out from, ē, ex, *w. abl.;* away from, ā, ab, *w. abl.*
furnish, submittō, –ere, –mīsī, –missus.

G

gate, porta, –ae, *f.*
Gaul, Gallia, –ae, *f.;* a Gaul, Gallus, –ī, *m.*
general, dux, ducis, *m.*
get, get ready, parō, –āre, –āvī, –ātus.
girl, puella, –ae, *f.*
give, dōnō, –āre, –āvī, –ātus; dō, dare, dedī, datus; give thanks to, grātiās agō, –ere, ēgī, āctus.
go away, discēdō, –ere, –cessī, –cessūrus.
god, deus, –ī, *m.*
good, bonus, –a, –um.
grain, frūmentum, –ī, *n.*
grateful, grātus, –a, –um; be *or* feel grateful, grātiam habeō, –ēre, –uī, –itus.
gratitude, grātia, –ae, *f.*
great, magnus, –a, –um.
guard, vigilia, –ae, *f.;* praesidium, –dī, *n.*

H

hand, manus, –ūs, *f.*
harm, do harm to, noceō, –ēre, nocuī, nocitūrus (*w. dat.*).

harmony, concordia, –ae, f.
harsh, dūrus, –a, –um.
hasten, mātūrō, –āre, –āvī, –ātūrus; properō, –āre, –āvī, –ātūrus.
have, habeō, –ēre, –uī, –itus.
he, is; hic; ille; often not expressed.
head, caput, capitis, n.
hear, audiō, –īre, –īvī, –ītus.
heavy, gravis, –e.
her (poss.), eius; (reflex.), suus, –a, –um.
hesitate, dubitō, –āre, –āvī, –ātus.
high, altus, –a, –um.
himself (intens.), ipse; (reflex.), suī.
hinder, impediō, –īre, –īvī, –ītus.
his (poss.), eius; his own (reflex.), suus, –a, –um.
hope (v.), spērō, –āre, –āvī, –ātus; (noun), spēs, speī, f.
horse, equus, –ī, m.
hour, hōra, –ae, f.
house, domus, –ūs, f.
how (in what manner), quō modō.
however, autem.

I

I, ego, meī; often not expressed.
if, sī; abl. abs.
in, in, w. abl.
increase, augeō, –ēre, auxī, auctus.
influence, addūcō, –ere, addūxī, adductus; (noun), grātia, –ae, f.; auctōritās, –tātis, f.
injury, iniūria, –ae, f.
instruction, disciplīna, –ae, f.
interest, studium, –dī, n.
into, in, w. acc.
island, īnsula, –ae, f.
it, id; hoc; illud; often not expressed.

J

journey, iter, itineris, n.
just, aequus, –a, –um; iūstus, –a, –um.
justly, aequē.

K

keep, teneō, –ēre, –uī, tentus; retineō, –ēre, –uī, –tentus.
kill, interficiō, –ere, –fēcī, –fectus.
king, rēx, rēgis, m.
kingdom, rēgnum, –ī, n.

know, perfect tense of nōscō, –ere, nōvī, nōtus, or of cognōscō, –ere, –nōvī, –nitus; sciō, –īre, scīvī, scītus.

L

land, terra, –ae, f.; native land, patria, –ae, f.
language, lingua, –ae, f.
large, magnus, –a, –um.
late, tardus, –a, –um.
lay waste, vāstō, –āre, –āvī, –ātus.
lead, dūcō, –ere, dūxī, ductus; lead across or over, trādūcō; lead back, redūcō; lead forth or out, prōdūcō.
leader, dux, ducis, m.; prīnceps, prīncipis, m.
learn, nōscō, –ere, nōvī, nōtus; cognōscō, –ere, –nōvī, –nitus.
leisure, ōtium, –ī, n.
letter (of alphabet), littera, –ae, f.; (epistle), litterae, –ārum, f.
level, plānus, –a, –um.
life, vīta, –ae, f.
little, parvus, –a, –um.
live (a life), agō, –ere, ēgī, āctus; dwell, habitō, –āre, –āvī, –ātus.
long, longus, –a, –um; no longer, nōn iam.
look at, spectō, –āre, –āvī, –ātus.
loot, praeda, –ae, f.
lose, āmittō, –ere, āmīsī, āmissus.
love, amō, –āre, –āvī, –ātus.
lower, īnferior, īnferius.

M

maintain, sustineō, –ēre, –uī, –tentus.
make, faciō, –ere, fēcī, factus.
man, vir, virī, m.; homō, hominis, m.
manner, modus, –ī, m.
many, multī, –ae, –a.
memory, memoria, –ae, f.
messenger, nūntius, –tī, m.
middle of, medius, –a, –um.
money, pecūnia, –ae, f.
month, mēnsis, –is, m.
most, plūrimī, –ae, –a.
mother, māter, mātris, f.
motto, sententia, –ae, f.
mountain, mōns, montis, m.
move, moveō, –ēre, mōvī, mōtus; cēdō, –ere, cessī, cessūrus.
much, multus, –a, –um; magnus, –a, –um.
my, meus, –a, –um.

N

name, nōmen, nōminis, *n.*
nation, gēns, gentis, *f.*
native land, patria, –ae, *f.*
nature, nātūra, –ae, *f.*
neighboring, fīnitimus, –a, –um.
neither (*adj.*), neuter, –tra, –trum.
neither . . . nor (*conj.*), neque . . . neque.
never, numquam.
new, novus, –a, –um.
next, proximus, –a, –um.
no (*adj.*), nūllus, –a, –um; **no longer**
(*adv.*), nōn iam; **no one** (*noun*),
nēmō, *dat.* nēminī, *m.*
noble, nōbilis, –e.
nor, neque.
not, nōn.
nothing, nihil, *indecl. n.*
now, nunc.
number, numerus, –ī, *m.*

O

obtain, obtineō, –ēre, obtinuī, obtentus.
offer, prōpōnō, –ere, –posuī, –positus.
on, in, *w. abl.;* **on account of,** ob, *w. acc.*
one at a time, singulī, –ae, –a; **one . . .
the other,** alter . . . alter.
opinion, sententia, –ae, *f.*
order (*v.*), iubeō, –ēre, iussī, iussus;
(*noun*), ōrdō, ōrdinis, *m.*
other, alius, –a, –ud; **the other** (**of two**),
alter, –era, –erum.
ought, dēbeō, –ēre, dēbuī, dēbitus.
our, noster, –tra, –trum.
ourselves (*intens.*), ipsī; (*reflex.*), nōs.
out of, ē, ex, *w. abl.*
owe, dēbeō, –ēre, dēbuī, dēbitus.
(his) own, *see* his (*reflex.*).

P

part, pars, partis, *f.*
peace, pāx, pācis, *f.*
people, populus, –ī, *m.*
pitch camp, castra pōnō, –ere, posuī,
positus.
place, locus, –ī, *m.; pl.* loca, –ōrum, *n.*
plan, cōnsilium, –lī, *n.*
pleasing, grātus, –a, –um.
poor, miser, –era, –erum.
praise, laudō, –āre, –āvī, –ātus.

prepare, parō, –āre, –āvī, –ātus.
present (be), adsum, –esse, adfuī, adfutūrus.
present, dōnō, –āre, –āvī, –ātus; prōpōnō, –ere, –posuī, –positus.
price, pretium, –tī, *n.*
prisoner, captīvus, –ī, *m.*
prove, probō, –āre, –āvī, –ātus.
province, prōvincia, –ae, *f.*
public, pūblicus, –a, –um.
punishment, poena, –ae, *f.;* supplicium,
–cī, *n.*
put, pōnō, –ere, posuī, positus; **put in
charge of,** praeficiō, –ere, –fēcī,
–fectus.

Q

quickly, celeriter.

R

rank, ōrdō, ōrdinis, *m.*
rather, *expressed by comparative.*
read, legō, –ere, lēgī, lēctus.
ready, parātus, –a, –um; **get ready,**
parō, –āre, –āvī, –ātus.
reason, causa, –ae, *f.*
receive, accipiō, –ere, accēpī, acceptus.
region, regiō, –ōnis, *f.*
reinforcements, auxilia, –ōrum, *n.*
remain, maneō, –ēre, mānsī, mānsūrus.
remember, memoriā teneō, –ēre, tenuī,
tentus.
remove, removeō, –ēre, remōvī, remōtus.
report, nūntiō, –āre, –āvī, –ātus.
rest (of), reliquus, –a, –um.
reward, praemium, –mī, *n.*
right, iūs, iūris, *n.*
river, flūmen, flūminis, *n.*
road, via, –ae, *f.;* iter, itineris, *n.*
rule, regō, –ere, rēxī, rēctus.
run, currō, –ere, cucurrī, cursūrus.

S

sacred, sacer, –cra, –crum.
safety, salūs, –ūtis, *f.*
sail, nāvigō, –āre, –āvī, –ātus.
sailor, nauta, –ae, *m.*
same, īdem, eadem, idem.
save, servō, –āre, –āvī, –ātus; cōnservō,
–āre, –āvī, –ātus.
say, dīcō, –ere, dīxī, dictus.

scare, terreō, -ēre, terruī, territus.
sea, mare, maris, *n.*
see, videō, -ēre, vīdī, vīsus.
seek, petō, -ere, petīvī, petītus.
seize, occupō, -āre, -āvī, -ātus; capiō, -ere, cēpī, captus.
send, mittō, -ere, mīsī, missus; send away, dīmitto; send back, remittō.
settler, colōnus, -ī, *m.*
severe, gravis, -e.
sharply, ācriter.
she, ea; haec; illa; *often not expressed.*
ship, nāvis, nāvis, *f.*
shout, clāmō, -āre, -āvī, -ātus.
show, mōnstrō, -āre, -āvī, -ātus; dēmōnstrō.
(catch) sight of, cōnspiciō, -ere, -spexī, -spectus.
since, *use abl. abs.;* quod *(conj.).*
sister, soror, sorōris, *f.*
sit, sedeō, -ēre, sēdī, sessūrus.
slave, servus, -ī, *m.*
small, parvus, -a, -um.
soldier, mīles, mīlitis, *m.*
some . . . others, aliī . . . aliī.
son, fīlius, -lī, *m.*
speech, ōrātiō, -ōnis, *f.*
spend (years), agō, -ere, ēgī, āctus.
stand, stō, -āre, stetī, stātūrus.
standard, signum, -ī, *n.*
state, cīvitās, -tātis, *f.*
strange, novus, -a, -um.
street, via, -ae, *f.*
stretch, tendō, -ere, tetendī, tentus.
studies, studia, -ōrum, *n.*
suitable, commodus, -a, -um.
summer, aestās, -tātis, *f.*
supply, cōpia, -ae, *f.*
swift, celer, celeris, celere.
swiftly, celeriter.
swiftness, celeritās, -tātis, *f.*
sword, gladius, -dī, *m.*

T

take, capiō, -ere, cēpī, captus; sūmō, -ere, sūmpsī, sūmptus; take by assault, expugnō, -āre, -āvī, -ātus.
teach, doceō, -ēre, docuī, doctus.
teacher, magister, -trī, *m.*
terms, condiciō, -ōnis, *f.*
than, quam.
thank, grātiās agō, -ere, ēgī, āctus (*w. dat.*).

that (*demonst.*), ille, illa, illud; is, ea, id.
that (*relat.*), quī, quae, quod.
their (*poss.*), eōrum, eārum, eōrum; (*reflex.*), suus, -a, -um.
themselves (*intens.*), ipsī, -ae, -a; (*reflex.*), suī.
they, eī, eae, ea; illī, illae, illa; *often not expressed.*
thing, rēs, reī, *f.; often not expressed.*
think, putō, -āre, -āvī, -ātus; exīstimō, -āre, -āvī, -ātus.
third, tertius, -a, -um.
this (*demonst.*), hic, haec, hoc; is, ea, id.
thousand, mīlle.
three, trēs, tria.
through, per, *w. acc.*
till, colō, -ere, coluī, cultus.
timber, māteria, -ae, *f.*
time, tempus, -oris, *n.;* one at a time, singulī, -ae, -a.
to, ad, *w. acc.; dat. of indir. obj.*
too, *expressed by comparative.*
touch, tangō, -ere, tetigī, tāctus
town, oppidum, -ī, *n.*
train, exerceō, -ēre, exercuī, exercitus.
transport, trānsportō, -āre, -āvī, -ātus.
troops, cōpiae, -ārum, *f. pl.*
true, vērus, -a, -um.
two, duo, duae, duo.

U

under, sub, *w. acc. or abl.*
understand, intellegō, -ere, -lēxī, -lēctus.
undertake, suscipiō, -ere, -cēpī, -ceptus.
unfold, explicō, -āre, -āvī, -ātus.
upon, in, *w. abl.*
urge on, incitō, -āre, -āvī, -ātus.
useful, ūtilis, -e.

V

varying, varius, -a, -um.
very, *expressed by superlative;* very carefully, magnā cūrā.
victory, victōria, -ae, *f.*

W

wagon, carrus, -ī, *m.*
war, bellum, -ī, *n.*
warn, moneō, -ēre, -uī, -itus.

waste (lay), vāstō, –āre, –āvī, –ātus.

water, aqua, –ae, *f.*

wave, unda, –ae, *f.*

we, nōs; *often not expressed.*

well, bene.

what (*pron.*), quis, quid; (*adj.*), quī, quae, quod.

when, *often expressed by particip. or abl. abs.*

where, ubi.

which, quī, quae, quod.

who (*rel. pron.*), quī, quae, quod; (*interrog. pron.*), quis, quid.

whole, tōtus, –a, –um.

why, cūr.

wide, lātus, –a, –um.

winter, hiems, hiemis, *f.*

with, cum, *w. abl.; sometimes abl. alone.*

without, sine, *w. abl.*

woods, silva, –ae, *f.*

word, verbum, –ī, *n.*

work (*verb*), labōrō, –āre, –āvī, –ātus; (*noun*), opus, operis, *n.*

worst, pessimus, –a, –um.

wound, vulnus, vulneris, *n.*

write, scrībō, –ere, scrīpsī, scrīptus.

Y

year, annus, –ī, *m.*

you, tū (*sing.*); vōs (*pl.*); *often not expressed.*

your, tuus, –a, –um; vester, –tra, –trum; yourselves (*reflex.*), vōs.

INDEX

(The numbers refer to sections unless otherwise stated. The illustrations are separately indexed.)

xxii

INDEX OF ILLUSTRATIONS

xxviii

ACKNOWLEDGMENTS

The authors gratefully acknowledge their indebtedness for illustrations to the following:

Acme Newspictures: pages 43, 102; Robert Aitken: page 161; Alinari: page 164; The Bettmann Archive: page 68; Brown Brothers: pages 94, 322, 341; Cleveland Museum of Art: pages 138, 142; Asahel Curtis: page 242; Charles Phelps Cushing: page 27; DeCou from Galloway: page 89; George A. Douglas from Gendreau: page ii; Edwards & Company: page 169; Esperia Film Distributing Company: pages 331, 361; Ewing Galloway: pages xvi, 26, 28, 93, 211, 244, 255, 303, 349; Philip Gendreau: pages 55, 71, 114, 123, 217, 265, 373, 382; Gramstorff Bros., Inc., Malden, Mass.: pages 228, 311, 355; Harris & Ewing: pages 120 (copyrighted), 274 (copyrighted), 334 (copyrighted); Kaufmann-Fabry Company: page 90; Keystone View Company: page 145; Konstantin J. Kostich: pages 112, 195, 257; Arthur Lang: page 350; The Macmillan Company for the illustration on page 108 from Colum's *Golden Fleece;* Metro-Goldwyn-Mayer Pictures: pages 62, 216, 218; Metropolitan Museum of Art: pages 168, 181, 247, 275, 308, 309; Museum of Fine Arts, Boston, photo by Raymond & Raymond, Inc.: page 170; Copyright 1940, Paramount Pictures, Inc.: pages 102, 269; Raymond & Raymond, Inc.: page 226; William Ridington: pages 72, 73, 328; Roland Riggs from Atlas Photos: pages 5, 37, 65; James Sawders: pages 3, 19, 28, 46, 52, 79, 92, 96, 99, 116, 122, 127, 130, 132, 156, 173, 177, 187, 189, 191, 200, 204, 222, 223, 250, 259, 270, 280, 283, 285, 287, 288, 310, 351, 366, 369, 377; Society of the Cincinnati: page 295; George R. Swain: page 323; Saul Weinberg: page 115; Wide World Photos: page 42; and to Irving Berlin, Inc. for permission to use the Latin translation of "God Bless America" on page 420.